Business Biographies and Memoirs – Titans of Industry

Business Biographies and Memoirs – Titans of Industry

Andrew Carnegie, J.P. Morgan, John D. Rockefeller, Henry Ford, Cornelius Vanderbilt

J.R. MacGregor

Business Biographies and Memoirs – Titans of
Industry

Published by CAC Publishing LLC

ISBN 978-1-950010-37-0 paperback

ISBN 978-1-950010-36-3 eBook

Table of Contents

Andrew Carnegie

Insight and Analysis into the Life of a True Entrepreneur, Industrialist, and Philanthropist

Andrew Carnegie

Insight and Analysis into the Life of a True Entrepreneur, Industrialist, and Philanthropist

JR MacGregor

Introduction

Andrew Carnegie was born November 25, 1835, in the attic of his parents' one-story house, located on the corner of Moodie Street and Priory Lane in Dunfermline, Scotland.

His father, William Carnegie, was a damask weaver, who supported the family by weaving fabric and selling it in the neighborhood.

The Carnegies, from Grandpa Carnegie all the way down to little Andrew, were well known in this little Scottish town that dates back to 1071 when Malcolm III reigned.

It was Malcolm's queen, Margaret, who commissioned the construction of the abbey that Carnegie would spend hours looking at when he was six years old.

Carnegie's mother, Margaret, was a strong woman who believed that it was her place to care for her husband and children. Even when she had to mend shoes for extra income, she would do it after all her chores were done and her boys were fed and put to bed.

Andrew Carnegie deeply admired and cherished his parents and learned from them the value of family and the power of hard work.

His parents did everything they could in an economy that was dwindling and an age that was rapidly changing.

Chapter 1 Dunfermline

Dunfermline was the center of the Scottish linen industry during Andrew Carnegie's childhood. It is located approximately twenty miles northwest of Edinburgh, the capital of Scotland.

It was a small town measuring no more than nine miles from north to south and six miles from east to west. At the time of Carnegie's childhood, the town had about three thousand homes, which were laid out in orderly fashion with the abbey and the castle ruins in the center where the two main roads crossed. The castle ruins are what is left of King Malcolm's court.

From the city's center crossroads, all other streets and lanes branched out to checker the city's cottages and businesses.

It is important to note that before the Industrial Revolution the commercial structure across Britain consisted primarily of agrarian and cottage industries where everyone worked on individual farms and in their cottages.

Being known for its high-quality linen, the city was centered around the marketplace, where merchants would hawk their wares. At its height, the Dunfermline marketplace had more than three thousand high-quality handlooms on sale in a vibrant and prosperous atmosphere. After buying up their supply of woven fabric and fancy damask from various individual weavers in town, merchants would offer them for sale in the marketplace.

The linen was in such high demand that merchants would come from other towns and cities in the fiefdom and surrounding parishes to take stock and then travel south to England or across the channel into France in search of customers.

Andrew's father was one of these high-quality and sought-after weavers. The handlooms that William Carnegie produced were in high demand and popular with merchants. William only had to stay at home and spend his time weaving, and merchants were almost beating down his door for more supply.

Then came a seismic event that shook the world. It was a confluence of agriculture and industry when the British started to take their supply of cotton from India and had it shipped to Manchester.

Manchester was the industrial world's first success story. It was driven by mechanization and the first city to build factories that dominated the textile industry.

Thanks to Richard Arkwright's first textile mill in 1781, the price of woven fabric had started to fall, forcing other textile merchants to keep up with the falling prices and, in turn, demanding a cheaper process from the weavers.

This was the first wave of problems in the handloom industry. The second wave came when factories began springing up outside Dunfermline and were able to produce linen at cheaper prices.

Besides the regular linen looms that were in these mechanized textile mills, they began to outfit some of them with the mechanical addition that could handle damask weaving, which was a specialization and not something the regular mills could handle.

To be able to do damask looms for specialty linen used in table cloths and expensive clothing, they had to attach another invention that came from France—the Jacquard machine.

That came soon after, and by 1847, the demand for William Carnegie's handlooms had almost vanished. Merchants who had beaten down his doors for supply were now taking their linen from the mills that were just outside the town.

It was not just the Carnegie household that came under the heel of industrialization; most of Dunfermline felt the smack of progress.

Chapter 2 Family in Scotland

Carnegie was surrounded by radicals. His father and relatives were all politically involved and quite vocal. His Uncle Bailie Morrison was once arrested for holding a political meeting that had been forbidden as unlawful assembly. That type of law was common in those days to prevent uprisings and revolts. If you couldn't congregate, you couldn't conspire.

The meeting had taken place some distance away from Dunfermline, and Carnegie's uncle was brought into the city after being arrested. The townspeople planned to free him, but that would have caused a riot. The mayor of Dunfermline, however, convinced him to send the would-be protestors away. His word dispersed his fellow radicals, and they returned to their homes in peace.

As a clan, the Carnegies were radical, strong-minded, and clear-eyed, but they were not troublemakers.

Carnegie came from a land where each person worked for their own well-being. There was no talk of slaves in Dunfermline, and so when thrust into the debate of slavery some years later in the United States, he didn't see it as a righteous issue. Given his vocal ancestry, like his uncles and father before him, he was vocal about politics in the U.S. as well. This combination of opinion and loquaciousness fueled his political preference.

Carnegie was a strong supporter of antislavery, and when the Republican party had its first meeting on February 22, 1856, Carnegie supported the abolition of slavery. Although just a few months short of being able to vote, he supported Lincoln with full vigor and principle.

Strong opinions notwithstanding, the matter at hand in old-world Scotland was still about the daily necessities of living.

As the despair among the hand weavers deepened, the Carnegies sunk with it. They had to relocate, move into smaller dwellings, and minimize their expenses. Their circumstances became tight.

The once lucrative career of a damask weaver no longer yielded much. It was made worse by the existence of a middleman—the merchants—who were getting it cheap from the mills and then adding their markup before selling it to the end consumer.

The only way William Carnegie could keep up was to go directly to the customer himself. There was little demand for the higher priced handlooms, so the entire family had to live on little to nothing.

It was a difficult time, as William had to make the fabric and then spend time going from door to door, town to town trying to make a sale. This went on for some time, and to make ends meet, Margaret started selling groceries from the house. She also put up a sign and started mending shoes for neighbors.

For the better part of Carnegie's early childhood, he did not attend formal school. His parents had decided that they would not send him until he asked to go. He never asked.

After some time, however, they began to worry. They convinced a Mr. Martin, the headmaster of a nearby school, to give their son a nudge. Mr. Martin took Carnegie out for a field trip with the other children in the school, and Carnegie soon asked his parents to send him to school.

He loved school so much that he would get upset if he was late or couldn't go. Since he had to fetch water from the neighborhood well, he had to do that first before going to school, which sometimes delayed him.

When Carnegie reached the well in a rush to get back to school, he would meet several older ladies waiting to collect their water. While he waited, he had the tendency to argue with them, which earned him the moniker of "awfu' laddie." Mr. Martin, however, understood the reasons whenever Carnegie showed up late.

Carnegie admired Mr. Martin and was deeply grateful to him. He saw the headmaster as a good person and was glad to attend school. Due to his fondness of Mr. Martin, he was bullied and given the nickname, "Martin's pet," which bullies shouted as he walked the streets. He did not fully understand its meaning, so he didn't respond. A strategy that would serve him in his adult life—when faced with a bully—was never engage.

Carnegie had to stop at the store after school to pick up supplies so that his mother could sell them in her little grocery store. Shopkeepers soon got to know him and liked this personable young man. Once they knew he was fairly good with numbers, they got him to help with their accounts. From such unexpected circumstances, Carnegie was suddenly exposed to the world of business and commerce.

As children, Carnegie and his cousin, George Lauder, whose nickname was "Dod," were taught Scottish history and other world events by their Uncle Lauder.

One of the strategies their uncle used was to tell the boys to imagine the subject of their lesson to be somewhere in the room doing what they were known for.

So, for Carnegie, he imagined King John reciting the *Magna Carta* while sitting on the Carnegie mantelpiece. It made him giggle, but it also made him remember.

Carnegie also learned about King Robert the Bruce and Wallace, a Scottish hero. He and his cousin used to carry out plays and recite dialogue in the play.

Whenever Carnegie or his cousin had to say the word, "hell," they usually omitted it and filled the blank space with a guttural sound, which caused their audience to laugh. They were not accustomed to swearing, and uttering "hell" in the Carnegie household was swearing. Carnegie's uncle let him off the hook, however, and allowed the boys to say the word without fear of punishment. Soon, they were saying it quite often with ease.

Carnegie's favorite place in Dunfermline was the Dunfermline Abbey, which was not very far from his home.

Whenever Carnegie was about to return home from the house of his Uncle Lauder and Dod, he was asked by his uncle which path he was going to take. There were two paths. One was brightly lit and much more welcoming than the second path, which was by the dark abbey in the churchyard. Carnegie was always tempted to take the brightly lit path, but thinking about what Wallace might do, he never once took the comfortable path. He always stuck to the dark abbey.

While he strode through the abbey, he whistled to keep up his courage and hide from his fears. He also thought of what William Wallace would do if he encountered an enemy, be he natural or not.

William Carnegie was striving hard at this time to make enough money to move back into a larger house, and eventually he was able to pull it off. Carnegie's father's looms occupied the ground floor, and the family resided upstairs.

It was not long after this that the family was all gathered in the upstairs area and looking over a map of a country called America. It was Carnegie's earliest memory of hearing about this strange and mythical place.

In the upstairs residence, the adults had spread the map on the dining table and were trying to find a place called Pittsburgh. Soon thereafter, Aunt Aitken set off for this city.

The brief upswing they had in their fortunes didn't last long. William was soon struggling to sell linen, and the family started to struggle too.

This time they didn't see any way out of it that would be lasting. It was clear that handlooms were a thing of the past, and that mechanization of the textile industry had changed things forever.

The only option they had was to try for a new beginning and follow in the footsteps of Aunt Aitken.

This is what they decided to do. As long as they could save enough to make passage, they would throw their destiny to the winds of the North Atlantic. They made contact with a Mrs. Henderson, an old friend of Margaret Carnegie, who had settled in Pittsburgh.

Mrs. Henderson said she would welcome them, and the Carnegie family began accumulating the necessary money to set sail. When the time finally came to leave the house in Dunfermline, the Carnegie family boarded the carriage on the coal line and headed for the port. As the carriage rumbled away, Carnegie watched Dunfermline disappear from the window. The last thing he saw were the towers of his favorite abbey. His young eyes welled up with tears, but he managed to control himself and swore that he would return someday.

This departure from Dunfermline was difficult for young Andrew, but he stood fast. He bit lip so hard that it bled and said to himself, "No matter, keep cool; you must go on."

When the family was about to board the ship to New York, Carnegie found that he could not let go of his Uncle Lauder. His mind commanded that he leave, but his heart clung to his uncle. For his part, Uncle Lauder could not hold back his tears or unlock his arms from around his favorite nephew.

In the end, one of the sailors intervened to help Margaret with her son and hoisted Carnegie up onto the ship. That sailor later remarked that it was the saddest parting he had ever seen—and he had seen quite a few.

Carnegie's heavy heart followed him as the ship weighed anchor and set sail out of the harbor. As the ship slipped over the horizon and the land behind them was no longer in sight, the thrill of new beginnings and the prospect of being in a ship distracted him into laughter and joy.

Carnegie enjoyed the trip aboard the *Wiscasset*. He befriended the crew and explored various parts of the ship. This friendship only deepened over the course of the voyage, and by the time they disembarked in New York, Carnegie was crestfallen to leave his new friends.

After clearing immigration and health inspections, Carnegie had his first taste of New York. He was overwhelmed by the chaos and rush of the city.

To get to Pittsburgh, Carnegie's father was advised to go through Buffalo. To do that, they needed to take the

Erie Canal to Lake Erie and then up to Beaver before reaching their destination.

This journey lasted three weeks, but Carnegie was happy with the trip. The only thing that was rather uncomfortable was the night spent on the ferry at Beaver. They were waiting for the steamer to arrive so that they would be transported on the Ohio River up to Pittsburgh. That night was truly hellish, for the family faced mosquitos for the first time. They were badly bitten, yet Carnegie was still able to sleep soundly. The night had been so severe that his mother and father looked ghastly from the swelling the following morning.

Once the Carnegies arrived in Pittsburgh, Mrs. Henderson opened her house to them, where she provided lodging free of charge. Uncle Lauder's brother, Hogan, was also in Pittsburgh, and he was a weaver as well. He had a small shop in Pittsburgh, which he soon quit, and William was more than happy to take over and get right back to weaving.

The money he earned, however, was not sufficient to provide for the family. By this time, the problem he had faced in Dunfermline was beginning to rear its ugly head across the Atlantic as well. Machines were already doing the sewing, and nobody wanted to employ a weaver to sew their items. Carnegie's father was forced to sew his own fabrics and then go door to door to try to sell what he had made. This was not at all sufficient, and Carnegie's mother again started mending shoes.

Margaret was well versed in mending shoes because she used to do it as a young girl for extra pocket money to buy pins for little girls to wear in their hair. Now she was doing it to protect her family.

The Carnegie family had no servants, and Carnegie's mother was forced to do all the cleaning and cooking. When she finally had a short interval of time, Carnegie's younger brother, Thomas, would sit on her lap and thread needles. While he did so, his mother would recite Scottish poetry. At midnight, she would be seen mending shoes.

Carnegie was thirteen years old when the family began this new life in Pittsburgh. He was aware of the difficulties that his parents were facing and wanted to help.

Just after they moved to Pittsburgh, Uncle Hogan suggested to Margaret that Andrew could make some money selling knickknacks at the wharf. When he suggested this, Margaret was sewing but found the energy to jump up and begin screaming at him. She said, "What! my son a peddler and among rough men upon the wharves! I would rather throw him into the Allegheny River. Leave me!" and pointed to the door.

Margaret wanted more for her sons. That much was clear. She did not want them to become just anyone who sold goods at the wharves. She wanted her children to become something great.

It was apparent to Carnegie's father that his current line of work was not going to be enough. So, he entered the cotton business under one Mr. Blackstock, a fellow Scotsman.

It was an all-hands-on-deck situation. Their financial situation was dire and compounded and complicated because they were in a new land. William continued working at the cotton business, and Margaret continued with her shoe mending. Andrew's younger brother was still too young to get a job, but Andrew was able to find work in the cotton business too.

He was hired as a bobbin boy at a textile mill and paid the sum of $1.20 a week. He hated the job but felt proud that he was helping his family. He loved that he was no longer merely a consumer but part of the solution.

Despite his pride, the job was difficult. He and his father had to rise very early in the morning and reach the factory before daylight to start work. They would only have a very short break for lunch, and then they would get back home long after dark.

After spending some time at this work and not liking it at all, fate dealt him a break when he was able to land a job that paid more.

This next job was under one Mr. John Hay, who manufactured bobbins. Carnegie's job was to manage the boilers at the bobbin factory. It turned out that he despised this job even more than the last one. He was paid $2 a week and spent his time managing the steam gauges. He was in constant fear that the steam might be too low and that there would be not enough power for the workers above. He was also in constant fear that the steam would be too high and that the boiler would explode.

He never mentioned these difficulties to his parents, though, and just did the work and contributed to his family.

All the while he kept his ear out for a better job—one that would be easier to do and pay more. He never complained. He just wanted better,

And he got what he wished for. Carnegie's next job was as a telegram delivery boy. This job had been offered to him by a Mr. Brooks. Carnegie's mother supported the idea, but this time his father opposed it. He thought Carnegie was too young and small in size to be able to protect himself. What if he needed to send a telegram in the dead of night? Could he defend himself?

Soon, however, Carnegie's father relented but said he would follow his son to meet Mr. Brooks. Andrew told his father, however, that he could follow him only to the telegraph office.

So, when Carnegie and his father reached the office, his father waited outside, and Andrew entered to meet Mr. Brooks. His interview was successful, and when Mr. Brooks asked when he could start, he said that he

would start now if he could. So began the life of
Andrew Carnegie as a telegram delivery boy.

Chapter 3 Telegram

After having been hired as a telegram delivery boy, Carnegie had to learn the layout of the city so that he could deliver the telegrams to the right houses. He soon memorized the different places and was able to deliver the messages with ease.

Shortly after he started work, another boy was hired to deliver telegrams in the same area as Carnegie. His name was David McCargo, and he was a fellow Scotsman. Later, Carnegie was asked to find another boy who could be hired to deliver telegrams. Without a second thought, Carnegie recommended Robert Pitcairn, who was also a countryman. The three grew to be good friends and had monikers for each other. Andrew was Andy, David was Davy, and Robert was Bob.

During Carnegie's tenure, the telegram delivery business paid a bonus of ten cents to the delivery boy if he delivered a message to someplace farther away than usual.

These bonuses were highly sought after, and the telegram delivery boys began to argue over who was to deliver the messages. It was sometimes the case that some boys had delivered messages assigned to someone else. It had become a real problem.

Carnegie had an idea and soon decided that the delivery boys would combine their earnings. Since it was his idea, the boys decided that Carnegie would manage the money.

Unlike Carnegie, the other boys did not think about saving their money but spent every penny lavishly at the confectionery shop nearby—and they would do it on credit.
Carnegie had to inform the confectioner that he was not going to pay for what the boys spent if they spent more than their share.

Robert Pitcairn was the worst spender of all. He kept racking up his bill at the confectioners. When Carnegie confronted him about it, he said that monsters lived inside him, and that they chewed on his insides until he fed them.

The pay each month was $11.25. Carnegie was always the first to be paid. All the boys would stand in a line, and the man paying them would walk down that line, paying all the boys, and Carnegie, being first in line, was paid first.

Then came the day when things changed. All the boys had lined up as usual with Carnegie at the front of the line, but when the time came, he was looked over and not paid. Mr. Glass simply paid all the other boys. Carnegie was deeply worried. He felt that he had been dismissed. His greatest worry was the repercussions this would have on his family.

After all the boys had been paid and left the room, Mr. Glass took Carnegie behind the counter and told him that he was worth more than any of the other boys. His salary was raised to $13.50 a month.

Carnegie took the money, and without even saying "Thank you" or anything else for that matter, started walking home. This time, however, he found himself going a little faster than usual. When he reached home, he did not speak of his raise and only gave his mother the usual $11.25. That night, however, when Carnegie and his younger brother, Thomas, were in bed, Carnegie went to his brother and showed him the remaining $2.25. Even Tom, as young as he was, could understand the situation, and Carnegie explained to him how the two of them would go into business together and start the firm of Carnegie Brothers. This money was really very important to Carnegie.

At breakfast the next morning, Carnegie placed the $2.25 on the table. His parents were speechless, and it took them a moment to realize what it really meant. Carnegie's mother was immensely happy, and his father was immensely proud. The extra money meant that Carnegie was good at his job and worthy of being paid more.

Although working as a telegram delivery boy had many benefits, Carnegie did not like that he never had time to read his books. His end time was different every day. He might be let off at 6:00 p.m. one day but at 11:00 p.m. the next. Soon, however, to Carnegie's delight, Colonel James Henderson opened his library of four hundred books to all the working boys. The question then was whether or not a telegram delivery boy would be able to borrow books from the library. Carnegie thus wrote a letter to the press stating that although he and his fellow telegram delivery boys did not work with their hands, some of them had, and they should be allowed to visit the library. Colonel Henderson then widened the scope of classification for those who entered his library.

The boys who visited the library would go in one Saturday, borrow a book, and then exchange that book for another one the following Saturday.

Carnegie was delighted to have a chance to read books. During his short breaks, he would spend his time reading the book he had borrowed from the library and not put it down until it was time to get back to work.

Carnegie's path to being the assistant operator started when he entered the telegram business, but it started directly when he began meddling in the operator's office. One operator, who was all too lazy, was more than happy to let Carnegie do the work. Later, when a telegram operator in Greensburg said that he had to go off for some time, Carnegie was sent to work as acting operator until he returned. One stormy night, Carnegie sat close to the machine at all times, not wanting to turn off the connection. At one point, he got a little too close to the keys of the machine and was thrown off his stool after being electrocuted by lightning that had struck just when Carnegie was near the machine. He was seen as being cautious and able to complete his duties to the satisfaction of those who held higher office. Later, Mr. Reid, who was the superintendent of the line, needed an assistant operator, and Mr. Brooks recommended Carnegie for the position. Mr. Reid was more than willing to accept Carnegie as long as Mr. Brooks considered him up to the task. Carnegie then became an assistant operator and paid the handsome sum of $1 for every day he worked, which amounted to $25 a month.

The Pittsburgh newspapers always sent reporters to take down the letters of the press. After a time, one man was put in charge of this and asked if perhaps the newspapers could be duplicated several times. Carnegie was the one to do it, and for this job he was paid $1 a week, raising his monthly earnings to $30.

After some time, Carnegie wrote all his telegrams by sound and no longer used traditional print. Finding someone who could take down telegrams by sound was not normal. Many people visited the office simply to watch how it was done. Carnegie had attracted so much attention from this work that when a flood destroyed the telegram communication lines between Steubenville and Wheeling, which were twenty-five miles away from each other, Carnegie was sent to Steubenville to take in all that was going on between the East and the West. At hourly intervals, Carnegie was to send dispatches to Wheeling. These were transported in small boats. Wheeling would then send out more dispatches back to Steubenville. In this way, telegraph communication between the East and the West as far as Pittsburgh was concerned continued to work smoothly.

While Carnegie was in Steubenville, he received word that his father was traveling to Cincinnati and then to Wheeling to sell his tablecloths. Carnegie went to wait for the boat to meet his father. The boat did not arrive until late evening, and Carnegie did not like his father riding as a deck passenger. He had not wanted to pay the hefty expense of traveling as a cabin passenger. Carnegie said to him that he and his mother would soon be riding in their carriage. Carnegie's father, being Scotch, rarely praised his son or anyone else for that matter. Now, however, he was not able to hold back and told him, "Andra, I am proud of you." He then said goodnight and told Carnegie to go back to his office. Andrew was deeply pleased by his father's words.

Shortly afterward, Carnegie's father passed away. Carnegie himself has described his father to be the personification of kindness itself. Andrew admired his father, and although he, his brother, and his mother all loved him, they had no time to sit and sob. They had to tend to work to keep the household alive.

A certain David McCandless, however, who was a member of the Swedenborgian Society, offered to assist the Carnegie family with money. Carnegie's mother, however, refused the aid. They didn't need it. Despite not needing his help, he had earned a place in their hearts.

Carnegie soon met a man by the name of Thomas A. Scott, who would bring him back to work for the Pennsylvania Railroad Company, which had only come into existence in 1846, just seven years before he began his job in the company. Carnegie began working at the Pennsylvania Railroad Company as Mr. Scott's secretary. Mr. Scott had actually asked if he could hire Carnegie, but his assistant had replied that he could not for he was already an operator. Carnegie, however, wanted more than just sitting in an office writing telegrams all day. He accepted the job and began work on February 1, 1853. He would eventually work his way up to become a division superintendent of the Pennsylvania Railroad Company.

Chapter 4 Railroad

The railroad industry began in 1812 when Colonel John Stevens invented the first locomotive. It was exactly like a horse carriage but was powered by a steam engine.

Stevens also built the railway for the locomotive to travel on. He was later called the Father of American Railroads. Stevens had planned to build the New Jersey Railroad Company, but his plans never came to life.

In 1827, the Baltimore and Ohio Railroad, which is the oldest railroad company in the United States, created the first common carrier railroad, which carried both freight and passenger trains. Three years after the Baltimore and Ohio Railroad came into existence, the first mechanical train was invented and thus began the modern age of the railroad industry.

Many small railroad companies emerged several years later and created their own railway operations. After a few decades, some nine thousand miles of track was spread across the country.

Other railroad companies soon appeared. The New York Central Railroad Company, for instance, resulted from the merger of twelve small railway lines, while the Illinois Railroad Company's growth was boosted by the rights it had been given by the federal government. As for the Pennsylvania Railroad Company, it did not come into existence until late in 1846. When it did come about and became better known, its division superintendent was none other than Andrew Carnegie.

Carnegie began working at the Pennsylvania Railroad Company in 1853, eight years before the first shots were fired at Fort Sumter.

In the wake of Abraham Lincoln's election to the presidency in 1861, he signed the Railroad Act of 1862, which served as the impetus for the construction of the first transcontinental railroad.

The Union Pacific began building on the East Coast, while the Central Pacific began construction in the West. It took seven years for construction to make its way inland, and on May 10, 1869, the two railroads met at Promontory Point, Utah.
It was there that the Golden Spike, also known as the Last Spike, was thrust into the ground, marking the completion of the first transcontinental railroad.

During the Civil War, expansion of the railroad industry reduced, while use of the railroads increased.

Smaller railroad companies began to disappear after the Civil War, and larger companies came into existence. By 1917, more than 250,000 miles of track was spread across the United States.

Carnegie's Early Time in Rail

At first, Carnegie did not like his job at the railroad company. The problem had nothing to do with the work he did but was more about the people he had to rub shoulders with. Carnegie was not the rough and tumble kind of teenager. He had grown up surrounded by well-mannered people, and he behaved the same way.

His mother, who was his living role model, was well-mannered and cultured. She was a humble, churchgoing lady of polished upbringing. This is what he was used to.

Those who worked in the rail industry, however, such as firemen, engineers, and others, were rather gruff characters. They chewed tobacco and often cursed. It was a mind-wrecking experience for him, and Carnegie's only solace was that after work he could return to the comfort of his home, where all was good and pure.

Sometime early in his career, he was sent by Mr. Scott to Altoona to collect the checks and payrolls that were issued every month. The trip to Altoona was not going to be made over the Allegheny Mountains but rather across the plains. This made the trip rather enjoyable for Carnegie. In Altoona, he met with the general superintendent of the Pennsylvania Railroad Company, a Mr. Lombaert. At the time, Mr. Lombaert's secretary was Robert Pitcairn (Bob with the voracious appetite for confectionary), whom Carnegie had recommended for the post. David McCargo (Davy, who was also one of the delivery boys) was also at the Pennsylvania Railroad Company, and thus the three friends were in the same line of work.

The evening before Carnegie headed back to Pittsburgh with the checks and payrolls Mr. Lombaert asked him to tea much to Carnegie's surprise. Carnegie accepted his invitation with trepidation and anxiously waited for the time. Mrs. Lombaert, his host for the evening, was very kind when he arrived at the Lombaert home. He was introduced to Mrs. Lombaert with the words, "This is Mr. Scott's 'Andy'." Carnegie felt rather proud to be seen as belonging to Mr. Scott.

Carnegie set off to return to Pittsburgh the next morning with the checks and payroll tucked under his waistcoat, which he thought was a safe place. Since Carnegie rather liked trains, on his ride back to Pittsburgh, he spent his time in the engine room. After some time, he discovered that the checks and payroll were gone.

They had fallen onto the tracks somewhere over the last few miles. Thinking quickly and unhesitatingly, he asked the driver to back up the engine until they found it. Thankfully, the driver consented. While the train chugged in reverse, Carnegie scanned the area for his lost package. After some time, he spotted it along the banks of a river. He then held onto it the rest of the way back to Pittsburgh.

The fireman and engineer were the only ones who knew about the mishap, and Carnegie made them promise not to say a word of it to anyone. This "little" mishap really could have cost Carnegie his job.

It was during his time with the railroad that he became interested in politics. It was also a tumultuous time in the history of the nation.

As he became more certain of himself and understood the workings of the railroad business, one could see the metamorphosis that altered his vision and his presence.

As division superintendent, among other duties, Mr. Scott had to attend to wrecks and mishaps on the company's lines. He was the only person with the authority to send telegraphic orders to trains that operated under his jurisdiction.

His other duties as division superintendent took him away the office rather often. Sometimes his absence was caused by a wreck somewhere or perhaps other company business.

One morning Carnegie found that Mr. Scott was not in the office. He was away tending to an accident, which had caused the trains to stop in certain places, but then there was another accident in another part of the line that Mr. Scott didn't know about since he was away from the office. The trains along those lines were being guided by a flagman.

Carnegie then resolved to solve the matter by himself. To do that, he had to break the rules of access to the telegraph. He knew that if his plan failed it would mean the end of his job and perhaps even have criminal consequences. He also knew, however, that he could pull it off. He was confident.

Carnegie then started to look at where all there trains were and what problems they were facing. Keeping in mind the accident that was being handled by Mr. Scott, he made sure not to direct any trains toward that line and sorted the other trains toward their destinations with slight detours.

He then wrote out all the telegraphic orders under the name of Thomas A. Scott. Once all the orders were dispatched, the drivers and engineers as well as the flagmen complied and began to do as Carnegie had instructed.

Within a few hours, all the trains were on their way and moving smoothly. None of the lines had any more delays, and all went well.

After Mr. Scott returned to the office, he inquired about how things were going. Carnegie told him that all was fine. He then told him what had happened while he was away. Mr. Scott began to write on a piece of paper. Carnegie also told him the current locations of all the different trains and mentioned the reports that came from the different stations the trains passed through.

Mr. Scott said nothing but simply stared at the daring young Scotsman. He then left Carnegie's desk and retired to his own. He said nothing of approval or reproach. If the consequences were favorable, then all was well, but if they were disastrous, the responsibility was Carnegie's alone.

Carnegie did not feel very easy about what he had done until that evening. Mr. Scott had talked with the head of the freight agency, who was at the time a Mr. Franciscus. Mr. Scott told him what Carnegie had done, and when Mr. Franciscus asked whether or not everything went well, Mr. Scott replied that Carnegie had done all right. Carnegie was satisfied with this outcome and promised never to give telegraph orders again unless he was given the proper authority to do so. That promise was unnecessary because from then on Carnegie was trusted to manage the fleet and send out orders.

This aspect of Carnegie's character was inherent. He was a well-mannered child, but he had a level of tenacity that allowed him to make bold moves and take unconventional steps. Just this incident alone and the one where he dropped the payroll on the tracks should give an astute observer insight into the mind of this future titan of industry.

The core of Carnegie's ability can be divided into three layers. On the one hand, he had a different way of assessing risk. Not everyone can do this since assessment of risk is a skill that you have to work hard to develop if it is not something that comes naturally to you.

The second layer was his ability to minimize that risk before assuming it. If you are not observant and do not take steps to mitigate much of the risk, then you are taking on the risk at a higher level than you need to. Carnegie instinctively knew what needed to be done because he had been observing the way operations at the office were conducted, and this gave him the added skill set to solve a problem when it presented itself.

The Chinese logogram for "crisis" is interesting. It defines this moment perfectly. It is the combination of two other words—danger and opportunity. In Carnegie's case, that track crisis that he could have easily washed his hands of turned out to be an opportunity.

The third layer requires the active willingness to do something or to take on the crisis and convert it to an opportunity. If you look at this instance, the crisis was not even Carnegie's doing or his responsibility to fix. No one would have said anything to him for not lifting a finger, but he seized the opportunity, and because he had been observant in the past, he was successful.

When John Edgar Thomson, a colleague of Mr. Scott, visited the office, he addressed Carnegie as "Scott's Andy." Carnegie thought that one needs to do something beyond what he is expected to do to be noticed by those above him. That is how one opens doors to higher places.

As an example, when Mr. Scott was once away, Carnegie had been appointed to take care of things while he was gone. At the request of Mr. Scott to Mr. Lombaert, Carnegie had to take care of an accident that had occurred. To resolve the matter, Carnegie held a court-martial. He relieved the one most responsible for the accident, and two more were also suspended. When Mr. Scott returned, several of the workers that Carnegie had dismissed asked for the case to be reopened, but Mr. Scott refused.

Carnegie actually suspected that Mr. Scott thought Carnegie's actions were too severe, and Carnegie felt this way too. After years of experience, he concluded that severe punishments are always the least effective. Minor punishment was all that was necessary, but forgiveness is best.

This is how he conducted his business. It is sort of a Zen way of doing things, but it worked well for Carnegie in his career.

Years after this incident, when Carnegie became the division superintendent, he felt pity for those who were suspended, and they also had a place in his heart.

Mr. McMillan was a strong Calvinist of the old generation, while his wife was a Calvinist of the new generation. Carnegie and his friends enjoyed being at her events and attended her church. There, Tom Miller, one of Carnegie's friends, had listened to a sermon on predestination. He certainly did not really agree with it, for he later remarked to Mr. McMillan, "Mr. McMillan, if your idea were correct, then your God would be a perfect devil." After having uttered those words, he left, leaving Mr. McMillan completely surprised.

Things were already looking up for Carnegie. His hard work, diligence, and eye on the ball had started to pay off. Mr. Scott walked in one day and asked if Carnegie had $500. He only had $5 but said he could raise it.

Mr. Scott told him that he could buy shares of the Adams Express Company. Carnegie told his mother about it that evening, and she consented to put together the necessary money. She left by train for East Liverpool the next morning, where her brother held investments from farmers. She arrived in in the evening and got the necessary funds. They also mortgaged the Carnegie house. She then returned with the money, and Carnegie gave it to Mr. Scott. With the money fully paid, for the first time in his life, Carnegie owned some of a company's shares—ten shares of the Adams Express Company.

As time went by, Carnegie kept up his usual routine. He came into the office one morning and found a letter addressed to "Andrew Carnegie, Esquire." *Esquire* was a title that Carnegie and the other boys at the railroad company liked. Inside the letter was a check for $10 drawn on the Gold Exchange Bank of New York. There was also the signature of J.C. Babcock, a cashier.

This $10 was the dividend he earned from the Adam Express Company after he bought their shares. It was the first return on an investment that Carnegie made.

Carnegie later showed the check to his friends. They were utterly surprised, and from then on they all decided to accumulate their money and look for opportunities to invest their capital, which they did through small investments here and there and shared it with each other.

Carnegie was rather shy about going into other people's houses. Whenever he delivered a telegram to Mr. Franciscus, the freight agent, Mrs. Franciscus always tried to make him come in, but he never did, and it was years later before she succeeded in making him join in a meal in her house. When Mr. Scott took Carnegie out for a meal at a hotel, however, he was more than happy to attend.

On the one hand, you could consider Carnegie's shyness to be a side of his personality, but he was not really shy. He just appreciated and respected decorum.

As an agent of the telegraph company, he was there on a job, and it would be inappropriate to accept an invitation to tea.

When he finally entered Mr. Franciscus' home, he decided that he had never seen a home so wonderful except for the home of another superior, a Mr. Stokes, who had invited Carnegie to his home, although Carnegie could not imagine why. He believed that he had nothing to interest such a learned and intelligent man, who was then the chief counselor of the Pennsylvania Railroad Company. What Andrew liked best about Mr. Stokes' home was a carving on the marble mantel of a bookcase with the words,

"He that cannot reason is a fool,

He that will not a bigot,

He that dare not a slave."

Carnegie then said to himself that he would someday have a library where he would have a mantel with these words on it, and his plans did come to fruition, for both in Skibo and New York are libraries with these same words.

Chapter 5 Life in Altoona

Until this point of his life at the railroad, Mr. Scott was responsible for promoting Carnegie, but both were soon promoted to a higher position at the same time by a higher authority.

Mr. Scott became superintendent of the Pennsylvania Railroad Company in 1856 and took Carnegie with him to Altoona. The move from Pittsburgh to Altoona was not too easy for the Carnegie family, but they were willing to do it, and Carnegie was not going to allow anything to stand in the way of his success.

When Carnegie and Mr. Scott were in Altoona, they first stayed in the railway hotel. Later, however, they would live in a house where Mr. Scott's children would stay. Before Mr. Scott's move to Altoona, his wife had passed away. He now always wanted Carnegie close to him, and he was really the only friend he had in Altoona. The railwaymen in Altoona organized a strike as soon as Mr. Scott took office as superintendent. The men running the trains had stopped their work, causing traffic to pile up. Carnegie was awakened in the middle of the night and informed of the problem. He did not want to wake Mr. Scott because he felt very stressed and was always very nervous. Mr. Scott, however, stirred when Carnegie asked him if he should tend to the problem. Mr. Scott barely managed to give his approval, for he really was only half-awake. Carnegie then slipped out and told the railway men that they could have a hearing the following day at Altoona. The men then continued their work, the trains went on, and the traffic cleared away.

It wasn't just the railwaymen who were ganging up to strike against Mr. Scott, but the shopkeepers were also coming together to strike. Carnegie learned about this while he was walking home one night. A man was following him and soon came up to him and said that Carnegie had once done him a favor, and that he had promised himself to pay it back if he could. The man had earlier called the Pennsylvania Railroad Company in Pittsburgh inquiring about a job as a blacksmith. Carnegie had said that there wasn't any job available in Pittsburgh, but that there might be one in Altoona. Carnegie then asked the man to wait a little while and said that he would check. He checked by telegraph and told the man that the job was available.

The man told Carnegie that he was doing very well, and his family was with him in Altoona as well. He went on to tell Carnegie about the strike. He said that he had learned that several men were signing a paper pledging themselves to strike the next day. Carnegie immediately informed Mr. Scott of the problem, and he at once put up posters in the shop saying that all who had signed the paper were dismissed and were to head to the office to be paid. A list of the names of the people who had signed the paper was received by Mr. Scott and Carnegie, and the fact that they had received the list was announced. Fear and anxiety spread among the workers, and the strike was called off.

Through experience, Carnegie had found that doing favors for people who are disinterested and receiving no reward is better than carrying out a favor and then being repaid for it. It is better to carry out favors for a man who would not be able to repay his "debt" than to do a favor for someone who is capable of returning the favor. The reward for carrying out these favors is simply happiness, which is more important than money or any other sort of payment.

A suit was once brought against the Pennsylvania Railroad Company, and the case was about to be tried by a Major Stokes, who feared that Carnegie might be compelled to attend court by way of a subpoena. He then asked Mr. Scott to send Carnegie out of the state as soon as possible, and Carnegie liked being sent away.

After he had left, he had a rather interesting train ride. He was seated at the back of the carriage in a window seat looking out when a "farmer-looking" man, as he described him, approached him. The man was carrying a small green bag. He said that he had spoken to the brakeman, and the brakeman had told him that Carnegie was with the Pennsylvania Railroad Company. He then said that he wished to show Carnegie an invention. He then pulled out a model of the back of a sleeping car from his small green bag. The sleeping car represented the train carriages meant for night travel. This man was Theodore Tuttle Woodruff, inventor of the sleeping car, a coffee-hulling machine, a steam plow, and a surveyor's compass.

Carnegie was very interested in this invention. He badly wanted to go back and tell Mr. Scott what had happened. When he finally managed to do so, Mr. Scott did not think much of it but was willing to consider it. He told Carnegie that he might call Mr. Woodruff to the office.

After the meeting, they decided that they would try the sleeping cars, and an agreement was made. All that remained was for Mr. Woodruff to begin building the sleepers.

To manufacture them, Mr. Woodruff asked Carnegie for assistance. He needed to get together enough money to pay for the carriage to be built, and he was offering a one-eighth share in the endeavor. He already had the rest of the money he needed to help him build the cars.

The total investment required was to be paid in monthly installments, and Carnegie's share of the payment was one-eighth of the total monthly sum, which amounted to $217.50. Carnegie did not know how he would amass that sort of money on a monthly basis but said that he would do so anyway.

He applied for a loan from a Mr. Lloyd, a banker. Carnegie told him why he needed the loan, and the banker willingly agreed. He told Carnegie, "Why of course I will lend it. You are all right, Andy."

There are two parts of this anecdote that require explanation. The first is that Carnegie had a particular way about him that put those around him at ease, but he was also very conscious of his personal trustworthiness. If he said it, he would do it. It is a quality that too many people do not have today. True titans of industry, from Vanderbilt to Ford, could always be relied on to do what they said, and because of that they were always trusted. That may not seem like much, but when the time comes and opportunity presents itself, the need for others to trust you even if they do not like you is important. Carnegie conducted himself with pride and dignity that caused his reputation to precede him. Not only was he capable and willing to take risks, but he was also trusted by his peers and superiors alike to do what he said he would do.

Once he received the loan, he invested the money that was required to build the sleeping cars. In the end, the sleeping cars were a great success, and Carnegie's investment paid off abundantly. He paid off the bank and saved the profits.

The move to Altoona presented as many opportunities as it did challenges, and Carnegie had fared well in navigating almost all of them, but they were not limited to just professional or work-related issues. His life was changing, and his lifestyle was certainly on the upswing, which was something that he was not yet used to.

One time that this was most apparent was when the family was going to hire a servant for the first time. In the past, they had always been alone, living together with no outsider in their home. Carnegie's mother had always been the one to cook and clean the house as well as wash and mend the clothes for her two sons. She was not ready to allow anyone else to handle that. She was their mother, and no one could do what she did. Carnegie, however, managed to convince her to let a servant take care of all the chores. He wanted his mother to rest and take on hobbies and activities to pass her time. After hiring a maid, however, the family was not happy with a servant in the household. Although sufficient and edible, the food served was not as good as that prepared by their mother.

Someone who is surrounded by his or her family and nurtured and raised only by the family is much more privileged and better off than the rich child who is raised in the arms of a governess or some caretaker.

After a servant was hired to take care of the household chores, Carnegie's mother had for the first time the opportunity to go out with her sons, visit her neighbors, and have some fun. She was always of high class and never, according to Carnegie, met anyone who was of equal class.

After Mr. Scott had moved to a house and his children were there as well, he sometimes went off to Philadelphia or other places. While Carnegie stayed in the house of Mr. Scott, his niece, Rebecca Stewart, made things a little more homelike for Carnegie. She was like an older sister to him, and the two became good friends. They went for drives together in the woods in the afternoons, and their friendship endured. Later, they did part, for Rebecca's daughter married the Earl of Sussex, and she was thus always abroad. One time, however, Carnegie and his wife did meet Rebecca, who was at the time already an old woman in widowhood. Carnegie has said that friendships formed in youth can never be replaced.

Mr. Scott and Carnegie stayed in Altoona for about three years. In 1859, Mr. Scott was promoted to vice president of the Pennsylvania Railroad Company, taking Mr. Lombaert's place. Carnegie was deeply affected, as he did not want to be separated from Mr. Scott much less serve another person who would hold his former position. Carnegie also understood that his job in the railway company depended very much on Mr. Scott. So what would happen to him?

After Mr. Scott returned from his interview in Philadelphia, he called Carnegie into his private room. It was then that he confirmed to Carnegie that he had been promoted to the position of vice president.

That was bad enough, but then he was told that a Mr. Enoch Lewis would take Mr. Scott's position, which would mean that Carnegie would be out of a job because the superintendent would hire his own assistant the way Mr. Scott had hired Carnegie.

But Mr. Scott asked Carnegie, "Now about yourself, do you think you could manage the Pittsburgh Division?"

At the time, Carnegie felt that he could do anything, but never before had anyone thought that someone the age of twenty-four could handle the job, and Mr. Scott seemed the last person to want Carnegie as superintendent of the Pittsburgh Division. Carnegie replied that he thought he could. Mr. Scott then went on to tell Carnegie that a Mr. Potts, who was then superintendent of the Pittsburgh Division, was being sent to the transportation department, and Carnegie would take his place. He then went on to discuss Carnegie's salary. He asked, "What salary do you think you should have?" Carnegie was rather offended by Mr. Scott's question. "Salary?" "What do I care for salary?" He did not care about the money and said that working in the former position of Mr. Scott was good enough for him. He said that the position was more important than the money. He said that he could be paid what he was getting then, which was just $65 a month.

Mr. Scott went on to say that Mr. Potts was being paid $1,800, and he was paid $1,500 when he held the post. He said that Carnegie could start off with $1,500 for his trial, and his salary could be raised to $1,800 if he did well. Carnegie's first job as bobbin boy paid him $5 a month or about $60 a year.

Carnegie then took the job of division superintendent of the Pittsburgh Division, his new position becoming official on December 1, 1859. The Carnegie family then left their home in Altoona and returned to Pittsburgh. The family enjoyed the move, as it meant picking up contacts with old friends. Back in Pittsburgh, Carnegie's younger brother, Tom, would become his secretary, for he had learned telegraphy during his time in Altoona.

The family rented a house on Eighth Street, which then was called Hancock Street.
The city was so dirty with soot in the air that one's hands would be soiled just by touching the balustrade

as one ascended the stairs. If you washed your hands and face, they were dirty within an hour. Furthermore, the soot in the air soaked your hair. It really was a rather miserable time for the Carnegie family after having moved from the clean air of the mountains and the refreshing smells of Altoona.

The first winter during Carnegie's time as division superintendent was rather bad. The tracks were not laid properly, being placed on stone and being held by cast-iron chairs. Carnegie said that sometimes as many as forty-seven of these chairs would break in one night. Being division superintendent meant that by night he sent out orders by telegram, and he was always seeing to some wreck or obstruction. The winter, being a bad time for the trains, caused Carnegie to always see some sort of wreck.

He later considered himself to have been the most unmindful of superintendents concerning the condition of the workers. He did not understand what the limits of the human body were and was not accustomed to fatigue, always running on responsibility as his fuel. He could always sleep, and he usually slept thirty minutes or so in a dirty freight car. That was sufficient for him, and he thought everyone was the same way. They weren't.

It was all in all a tough time. Work was hard, the atmosphere was harsh, and the Carnegies had had better. A freight agent that Carnegie knew, a Mr. D.A. Stewart, told Carnegie about a house in Homewood, the neighborhood where he lived.

The Carnegies immediately moved in. Homewood was a place where the rich lived. The residents there were of a higher class, and the surrounding area was clean, smelled better, and was overall more pleasant. Carnegie's mother had the happiest time of her life here, tending to a large garden of several acres. She developed somewhat of a green thumb, and when Carnegie once pulled a weed from the ground, she scolded him, saying that it was something green.

The residents of Homewood usually hosted parties with music, and Carnegie was always invited to these and enjoyed them. The most important family Carnegie met in Homewood was the Wilkins. They were the leading family of Western Pennsylvania, and the most important member of the family was Judge Wilkins. He was eighty years old but still in tip-top mental condition—sharp as a tack. He was rather like history in the flesh for Carnegie. To young Andy, it seemed as if Wilkins really had experienced everything. He always talked about how President Andrew Jackson had said something to him or how he told the Duke of Wellington something. In fact, Wilkins had actually worked as the minister of Andrew Jackson to Russia, and he recounted his interview with the czar.

As Carnegie always attended the classy house parties of the wealthy residents of Homewood, he always heard of things he did not know, and he made it a rule that he would learn something about them immediately. He was rather pleased with himself to find that he was always learning something new every day.

There was only one thing that the Wilkins family and Carnegie did not agree on, and that was politics. Carnegie was an ardent supporter of equality, and the Wilkins family was rather supportive of the South regarding slavery. One day Carnegie entered the home and saw that the household was talking about something very passionately. Mrs. Wilkins then said to him, "What do you think? Dallas writes me that he has been compelled by the commandment of West Point to sit next to a negro! Did you ever hear the like of that? Is it not disgraceful? Negroes admitted to West Point!" Dallas was the lady's grandson. Carnegie then replied, "Oh! Mrs. Wilkins, there is something even worse than that. I understand that some of them have been admitted to heaven!"

What always stood out about Carnegie's personality is that he was direct and vocal but also quite witty.
This trait seems to have come from his mother, who was charming and witty when she needed to be and fiercely protective of her family and the high moral ground. It was never about money but about what was right.

As for the whole Dallas-West Point affair, the entire family said nothing in response to Carnegie's snide retort. Their silence reverberated throughout the house with a din of disapproval. After a short moment, Mrs. Wilkins responded, "That is a different matter, Mr. Carnegie."

Carnegie was very opposed to slavery and a strong supporter of equality. His statement was basically stating that God treated blacks equally, so why were they upset about a black man at West Point?

Soon afterward, Mrs. Wilkins began knitting an afghan for Carnegie. While she was doing this work, people kept asking who it was for, but she didn't tell. Finally, however, when it was complete, it was nearing the time of Christmas, and she wrapped it up as a gift and told her daughter to send it to Carnegie. He received it in New York and kept it as a most precious and valuable possession. He showed it only to a few close friends, but other than that it was not useful for him.

While Carnegie was in Pittsburgh, he met Leila Addison, the daughter of a Dr. Addison. Carnegie considered Leila to be a close friend, for she took the trouble to polish him up. She improved him by teaching and critiquing him. He began to pay more attention to his English and the English classics and read them with great passion.

She also taught Carnegie how to be a little more refined. He found that it was better to speak nicer and on the whole to be well-behaved. Until Carnegie met Leila, he did not care much for his attire, wearing shirts with loose collars and big boots. His entire appearance regarding his clothes was considered strange, although among his associates it was considered manly. Whenever there was anything seen as dapper delicate regarding dressing, Carnegie and his associates looked down on it. One instance of this was when a man of the railway, a gentleman, wore kid gloves. He became the subject of scorn among Carnegie and his associates, for they were the kind of people who wanted to be manly.

Thanks to Leila Addison, Carnegie became much more refined and better clothed.

Several years later, after Carnegie became superintendent of the Pennsylvania Railroad Company in Pittsburgh, he once again visited the home of Mr. Stokes, who was a prominent figure in the Democratic Party and talked about how the North was using force to hold the Union together. He did not agree with that. Carnegie then blurted out, "Mr. Stokes, we shall be hanging men like you in less than six weeks." Mr. Stokes laughed at Carnegie's statement and called to his wife, "Nancy, listen to this young Scotch devil. He says they'll be hanging men like me in less than six weeks."

Later, when Carnegie was working in the office of the Secretary of War, Mr. Stokes came to Carnegie trying to be ranked as a major as a volunteer. Thus, Mr. Stokes became Major Stokes.

The man who had earlier criticized the North for how it kept the country united was now fighting for the North. All people cared about at the time of the Civil War was the Union—the unification of the United States. Major Ingersoll once said, "There was not enough air on the American continent to float two."

The American people wanted only one American flag. They wanted unity.

Chapter 6 The Civil War

The Civil War began April 12, 1861, and ended May 10, 1865. It was a four-year war that was fought between the Confederacy of the South and the Union forces, commonly known as the North.

The rationale for the war is complicated and not really appropriate to discuss here, but what is important to understand, though, is that the war was one of the defining moments in American history—not just in terms of the moral compass that derived from it but also because it was the defining moment that altered the country from a state-centered power that was fragmented to a federal structure that was stronger in the middle. Carnegie referred to it as a centripetal force versus centrifugal force.

Although this man had little formal education, the nuances of the Civil War were not lost on him, as he realized that a nation that was loosely bound together and concentrated the powers of legislation and control within the limbs of the body versus the power of a central and fortified federal system were like the centrifugal force versus the centripetal force, respectively.

Then there was another aspect of the war that made something else clear to him. Coming from an immigrant background, it was easy for him to see that it was important to be one country united against its external challenges than to be divided within the country fighting for transient differences. It was important that disagreements could be decided at the ballot box. Once the ballots were cast, the decision was made. No need for referendums. After the end of the Civil War, the United States turned every ballot cast for every state and federal office into a referendum on what was being proposed. The country chose what their candidate was advocating as the way to voice their choice on the matter. Carnegie could see that clearly.

In essence, this was what was supposed to have happened with the election of Abraham Lincoln. In setting up the election, the platform they stood on served as the platform the population wanted. If one stands for slavery and one stands for emancipation, then the winning candidate shows that the platform he stood on is what the constituents want, but that wasn't the case with the election that Lincoln won. The Democratic Party had split the vote by fielding two candidates, and Lincoln won the majority with only 40% of the vote.

Lincoln may have been right on the moral spectrum of reality, but it was not what the South wanted. To them slavery was a way of life, and the reason for the Civil War was because any changes in the status quo would have brought about significant repercussions to their competitive advantage on world markets. Slaves were not paid, and if they had to hire people to do their work, they had to pay them a salary, thus putting a strain on their profits.

The South had seceded from the North, and Northerners did not respect this new nation. They did not believe in the legitimacy of secession because they feared that the United States might be broken down into several states that saw each other as enemies. Northerners wanted unity.

The beginning of the Civil War started when the Confederate Army opened fire on Fort Sumter in Charleston, South Carolina. They forced the fort to surrender, and the United States flag was taken down. President Lincoln called for the uprising to be put down, and in response, four more slave states severed all ties with the North and joined the Confederacy.

From 1862 to 1865, the Confederate army under the leadership of General Robert E. Lee repelled the attacks of the Union army that was commanded by a string of incapable commanders. Finally, in 1864, General Ulysses S. Grant became commander of the Union armies and after many battles, such as The Wilderness, Cold Harbor, Petersburg, and Spotsylvania, Grant was able to corner Lee at Appomattox in Virginia.

While this was happening, Union armies were able to win several victories over the Southerners in the Southern states west of the Appalachian Mountain range. Between 1864 and 1865, General William Tecumseh Sherman led his Union soldiers into Confederate hubs, such as Georgia and Virginia. By 1865, practically all Confederate armies had surrendered, and finally on May 10, 1865, the president of the Confederacy, Jefferson Davis, was taken prisoner while trying to escape. All resistance from the South was put down, and the bloody four-year war was at an and.

The Civil War resulted in the deaths of 625,000 American soldiers, which was nearly the same number of U.S. soldiers killed in all the wars the nation had ever fought, combined. The Civil War was the most devastating conflict of the West after the Napoleonic Wars from 1803 to 1815 and the First World War.

Carnegie was very much opposed to slavery and to all war. He was a strong advocate of freedom for all and condemned slavery and racism. We have seen that when he heard his friends, the Wilkins, talking about how it was a disgrace that one of their relatives had to sit next to a Negro, he replied by saying that God treated them equally, and yet they were making a fuss. Carnegie repeatedly made his point about the sense of equality that was important in the building of a young nation. It was also the morally right thing to do.

At the start of the Civil War in 1861, Carnegie received a telegram from his old boss Mr. Scott. He was told to come to Washington, D.C. posthaste. Carnegie was unaware that Mr. Scott had been appointed Assistant Secretary of War in charge of the Department of Transportation. The Secretary of War at that time was Simon Cameron.

To be clear, there was no Department of Defense during the Lincoln Administration. It wasn't until 1947 when that department was created. Until then it was called the War Department.

When Carnegie reached Washington, Mr. Scott told him that his country needed him. Mr. Scott needed an assistant for his new position in the Transportation Department, and he wanted Carnegie to fill that post.

As Mr. Scott's assistant, Carnegie was to be in charge of the railways and government telegrams.
Carnegie was exhilarated. He had not expected to have such a position in government, but he gladly accepted the job and left Pittsburgh.

His first duty was to put together a force of railwaymen and head to Baltimore. Some Union troops that were passing through Baltimore had been attacked, and the railway line that stretched from Baltimore to Annapolis Junction had been severed. This cut off all communication with Washington.

Carnegie's duty was to take his group of assistants to the site and repair the damage. When they arrived, they began to repair the tracks so that heavy trains could use it safely. This job lasted a few days. By the time General Butler and his troops arrived, Carnegie had repaired the tracks, and the general and his men were able to go on to Washington.

On their way to Washington, Carnegie realized that some of the telegraph lines had been staked. He called for the train to come to a stop and then ran down to free the lines. He did not notice, however, that the lines had been pushed to one side before staking, and when he released the wires, they sprang up and struck him in the cheek, causing his face to bleed heavily.

Carnegie said that except for a few other soldiers who were wounded in Baltimore he was among the first to shed blood for his country. He was willing to do anything for the country that had done so much for him, and he worked night and day to try and establish communications with the South.

Shortly afterward, Carnegie established his headquarters in Alexandria, Virginia, and while there the Battle of Bull Run was fought, a battle in which Confederate troops defeated Union soldiers. Carnegie then sent out trains to pick up the retreating soldiers. The closest station was Burke Station, and Carnegie traveled there and began loading trains with wounded soldiers. It became clear that the station had to be closed, and the operator and Carnegie were the last to leave.

Everyone was in a state of panic. Some conductors and engineers were able to obtain boats and cross the Potomac. Some of the railwaymen were missing. All in all, most of the railwaymen did not flee nor did any of the telegraphers.

After this experience, Carnegie established his headquarters in Washington once more with Mr. Scott, who was now Colonel Scott. Being in charge of the telegraph allowed Carnegie to meet President Abraham Lincoln, Secretary Cameron, Mr. Seward, and other important people. Lincoln would usually come to his desk either waiting for a reply to a telegram or just seeking further information.

Carnegie's perspective of Lincoln indicates that he was a homely man when he was relaxed. He has described Lincoln as having so many features that it was impossible to portray him properly in a painting. When he was animated or telling story, he would be bright and energetic. Lincoln was always attentive to what everyone had to say. Carnegie has also mentioned that Lincoln had a unique way of talking.

On November 8, 1861, Confederate diplomats James Slidell and John Murray Mason were taken prisoner by Charles Wilkes, captain of the Union ship the *USS San*

Jacinto while they were aboard the British mail ship, the *HMS Trent*.

Prior to this, on May 13, 1861, Queen Victoria of Great Britain made Britain neutral regarding the American Civil War, although the British press supported the Confederacy, and many British citizens secretly funded the Confederates.

The British were very serious about not letting anyone step onto their ship without permission much less capturing people on their ships. Thus, the arrest of Mr. Slidell and Mr. Mason was going to result in either war between the Union and Britain, or the Americans would have to return the Confederates.

Lincoln's Cabinet convened to discuss the matter. At the time, Secretary Cameron was not able to attend, and Mr. Scott was to take his place at the meeting as Assistant Secretary of War. Before the meeting, Carnegie tried to convince Mr. Scott to argue to return the prisoners, for, as he said, the British would wage war because of what had happened. Furthermore, it was American policy that ships were not to be searched. Mr. Scott, however, was inclined to keep the prisoners, but after the meeting, he told Carnegie that Seward had said that it meant war, concurring with what Carnegie had said. Lincoln was also more inclined to keep the prisoners but soon agreed to

Seward's plan. It was decided, however, that no action was to be taken until those who were absent, including Secretary Cameron, could be consulted on the matter. Thus, Mr. Scott was instructed to discuss the matter with Cameron the next day when he arrived, for it was believed that he was in no mood to relinquish the prisoners.

In the beginning, those who were in charge of handling problems were rather incapable of doing so. They were old, handicapped men, such as General Scott. The question was how to manage situations when these old men were taking days to come up with an answer to a problem that needed quick action. How were they to rely on leaders that did not fully understand what was happening?

Soon, however, much to Carnegie's surprise, matters began to work well. Secretary Cameron gave Colonel Scott the authority to do things as he saw fit. This was a very good position to be in, for Carnegie and Mr. Scott could now do what they saw was best. Soon, Secretary Cameron was dismissed by Lincoln, for the public was calling for his dismissal. Those who worked with Lincoln, however, knew that if the other departments had been run as well as the War

Department under Cameron things would have gone a lot better.

Cameron, who liked to be called Lochiel, when ninety years old, visited Carnegie in Scotland, where the two men rode through the glens, and Cameron told Carnegie how he had secured second terms for two U.S. presidents, James K. Polk and Abraham Lincoln. He had drawn up new resolutions for a certain state and hoped that other states would follow. He used this strategy to secure a second term for both Polk and Lincoln. One day Cameron went to Lincoln's public reception in Washington. Lincoln called out to him and said, "Two more today, Cameron, two more." That meant that two more states had passed the Jackson-Lincoln Resolutions.

What's important here is how one man was called by two presidents from different times to seek advice about the same thing.

The next person that should be mentioned is General Ulysses S. Grant, who was also the eighteenth president of the United States. Grant appeared to be an remarkable man. He had the looks of someone who was a nobody, yet he was very accomplished. Once, when the Secretary of War, Stanton, had Grant and three of his associates enter his car, he looked at them, and once they were all inside, he thought that one of them was Grant, but *this* one wasn't. *This* one *was* Grant.

Carnegie himself was sometimes mistaken as Ulysses S. Grant.

Carnegie found that when Grant was general there was a lot of talk about strategy and how to do things. Grant was very open with Carnegie about these things and did not keep anything hidden. Once he said that he was instructed to go east and said that he would. He said that he was just going to go west to get everything ready. Carnegie replied by saying, "I thought as much." Grant went on to say that he was going to put Sherman in charge. Carnegie responded by saying that it was expected that General Thomas would be the one to succeed. Grant responded by saying he knew this but said the men and Thomas both thought that Sherman should be chosen. He went on to say that they were winning in the West and now had to win in the East.

Once when Grant was in the West, he started to drink a little too much. Finally, after some time, his chief of staff, Rawlins, mentioned his drinking problem. At first, Grant said, "You do not mean that? I was wholly unconscious of it. I am surprised!" Rawlins responded by saying, "Yes, I do mean it. It is even beginning to be a subject of comment among your officers." Grant replied by saying, "Why did you not tell me before? I'll never drink a drop of liquor again."

Grant did not say this in passing. He really did mean it, and he kept his word for as long as he lived. When Carnegie dined with the Grants, he noticed that Grant always turned down wine. He never drank after Rawlins told him that his drinking was a problem. Grant's willingness and strength of mind was what prevented him from breaking his word. Not many people can abstain from alcohol for life. One of Carnegie's associates once abstained from alcohol for three years but then relapsed into drinking again.

When Grant became president, charges were raised that he was accepting money dishonestly. Those who were wiser, however, understood that he was really so poor that he had to cancel his attendance at traditional state dinners, which cost him $800 each time. When his annual salary as president was raised from $25,000 to $50,000, he was able to save a little money, but he did not care for it.

When Grant was at the end of his first term, Carnegie understood that he had virtually no money, yet when he was in Europe, he found that high officials there believed Grant had benefited. In America, people knew how to brush away these accusations, but in other countries they seemed quite real.

The reason democracy does not do too well in such places as Britain is because American politics is thought to be corrupt, and that Republicanism is the main cause of this corruption. Carnegie thought that in such countries as Britain bribery was common in land holdings, but such matters were considered titles rather than bribes.

When Carnegie was summoned to Washington in 1861, people thought that the Civil War would end very quickly, but soon it became clear that it would be a matter of years. After some time, Mr. Scott realized that Carnegie was needed in Pittsburgh to manage the Pittsburgh Division of the Pennsylvania Railroad Company. The railroad company badly needed Carnegie's attention, for the American government was placing a major strain on it during this time. Mr. Scott and Carnegie then left Washington and returned to their former duties, Mr. Scott carrying on his work as vice president of the Pennsylvania Railroad

Company and Carnegie as superintendent of the Pittsburgh Division.

After leaving Washington, Carnegie suffered his first important illness. He experienced what felt like sunstroke. After consulting with his physician, he was told that he could no longer be in the heat, and the summers of America were not suitable for him. Carnegie felt that the air in the Highlands, being clean and cool, would be a universal cure for him.

Later, his leave was approved by the Pennsylvania Railroad Company, and he, his mother, and his friend Tom Miller returned to Scotland, their homeland. They boarded the steamer *Etna* and landed in Liverpool. From there, they headed straight for Dunfermline. As they approached, Carnegie's mother caught sight of a familiar bush and cried out, "Oh! There's the broom! There's the broom!" Carnegie tried to calm her, but in doing so she only felt happier.

Carnegie himself felt that he might be able to kiss the ground.

When they arrived in Dunfermline, Carnegie was quite surprised by how small everything seemed. He felt as if he were walking in a city of the Lilliputians, the tiny people mentioned in Jonathan Swift's *Gulliver's Travels*. He described it as if he could almost touch the roofs that extended over the sides of the houses, and that walking the full length of the beach now felt very short, for it was really only three miles. Furthermore, he felt that the grounds on which he had played as a boy were now very small, and that the houses he previously felt to be grand and magnificent were also very small. In short, everything had shrunk for him.

The feeling must have been very peculiar, but the explanation is perhaps quite simple. He had left Dunfermline and Scotland when he was just a boy, and this was the first time that he was returning to Scotland in more than a decade. When he left, everything towered over him. Now he was twenty-seven years old and felt the size of Dunfermline to be like what any other adult of Dunfermline felt it to be, only it seemed rather small, for his last memories of his hometown were when he was a young lad.

Everything seemed to have shrunk for Carnegie, but what still appeared to be as grand was the abbey. Still on the tower were the words "King Robert the Bruce," whom he had learned so much about as a young boy with his cousin, Dod, from his Uncle Lauder. Everything, even the well at the head of Moodie Street from which he had collected water and argued with old ladies, seemed different.

To Carnegie, though, Dunfermline Abbey was still magnificent, and its bell still rang sweetly in his ear. The area around the abbey seemed small, but all soon came back to normal in his mind after hearing the abbey bell and seeing the magnificent site.

Carnegie's relatives were very kind to him and his mother, the kindest of all being his Aunt Charlotte, who said, "Oh, you will just be coming back here some day and keep a shop in the High Street." To her, to have a shop in the High Street was a success.

Carnegie's Aunt Charlotte had sometimes taken care of Carnegie when he was young and told him stories that he had to be fed with two spoons, for he screamed whenever the spoon left his mouth. Later, when Carnegie was in the steel business, Captain Jones said that he had been "born with two rows of teeth with holes punched for more." Carnegie really was always pushing for better results.

Other stories he was told included one where his father had to carry him back for some distance from the sea. While walking up the steep hills, his father hinted about the heavy load on his back, hoping that Carnegie might offer to walk for a little while. To his surprise, however, Carnegie responded by saying, "Ah, father, never mind. Patience and perseverance make the man, ye ken."

His father laughed and continued to walk up the hill with Andrew on his back. Carnegie felt best when he was once again with his Uncle Lauder, who had taught him so much and had made him like literature when he was just eight years old. Carnegie was called "Naig" by his uncle just as he had been when he was a young lad.

During Carnegie's stay in Dunfermline, he was so excited that he just could not sleep. He soon caught a cold and tried to recover by spending six weeks in his uncle's house. Soon, however, he was not getting any better and was forced to return to the United States. During the journey, he began to recover and felt so good that he could return to his work duties at once.

On his way back to his office, the railwaymen of the Pennsylvania Railroad Company under Carnegie welcomed him warmly, and Carnegie was glad to see that the caring feelings he had for them were returned.

According to him, working men always reciprocate kindness.

Chapter 7 Trains, Tracks, and Opportunity

Once locomotives were introduced to the New World, they went through a period of rapid growth and then some slow periods, as the fragmented industry went through consolidation. Cornelius Vanderbilt had maneuvered the landscape and set the industry on its trajectory with a series of consolidations that made the services more organized and efficient.

Then it was time for growth again, but this time there was a need for a different sort of infrastructure to fuel the growth. America was, and still is, a land of hills, plains, and rivers, and building around them was expensive. It was better to use bridges to conquer ravines, but the technology was not there to develop the proper designs. Bridges had already been built, but many had collapsed, and constant maintenance was often needed. The culprit, it turned out, was the material. Even iron easily eroded under the stress and strain of the repeated passing locomotive. In time, bridges weakened and failed.

Then there was another problem. Aside from the bridges that carried the rails, the rails themselves were not hardy. In the mid-19th century, a passenger in one of the open cars could see slivers of shiny iron particles in the air that come off the rails. Each wheel that rolled on the rail would take off a bit of metal, and the rail would later become deformed and warped and come off.

The weakness of the material was a key issue, and Carnegie was one of the men who figured this out early in the game when he had to keep attending to breakdowns and crashes.

Aside from high replacement, rail lines were being extended. More lines covering more cities and over greater distances were needed across the rapidly growing country. The second half of the 1800s was America's greatest period of growth, and railroads were the driving factor behind it.

Carnegie took advantage of the situation and put together a company that built railway lines, but instead of building them with iron, he adopted the system that was created in Britain by Sir Henry Bessemer.

With his friend Thomas N. Miller, Andrew Carnegie also established a company called Pittsburgh Locomotive Works, which built trains. This company rapidly became popular and was a formidable competitor to other companies that had been in existence for much longer.

It all started when Carnegie saw a bridge in Altoona that had been built by the Pennsylvania Railroad Company with iron rather than wood. It worked flawlessly. He understood that it was the iron that made it work so well.

This was in contrast to other wooden or iron bridges belonging to the Pennsylvania Railroad Company that had burned and caused massive delays in traffic for up to eight days. Seeing the opportunity this presented, Carnegie called a meeting with three men: Mr. H.J. Linville, Mr. Schiffler, and John L. Piper. Piper and Schiffler were in charge of the bridges for Pennsylvania Railroad, while Mr. Linville was responsible for the bridge design. Carnegie invited the three men to put together a company that built bridges, but this time they were going to make cast-iron bridges that could withstand the heat of a fire and the weight of the locomotive. Carnegie was also able to convince Mr. Scott to join the project.

A company that built bridges, as Carnegie proposed to make, had never existed before and had great investment potential. When Carnegie invested in Mr. Woodruff's sleeping-coach company, he reaped substantial profits. Just by investing $217.50, he made more than $5,000 per year on it for many years after.

Carnegie also grew more acute with investing as he grew older. In this case, he saw a specific opportunity in bridges and the way they were constructed.

Scott, Linville, Piper, Schiffler, and Carnegie each paid one-fifth interest of $1,250. Carnegie borrowed the money for his share from the bank.

The Keystone Bridge Works came about in 1862. Carnegie felt intense pride in the name he gave the company, seeing that Pennsylvania was the Keystone State.

At this time, iron bridges were rather popular in the United States, but for Carnegie's company it was cast-iron. Some of the bridges that had been built were later modified to support heavier traffic.

Shortly after the company was established, it was commissioned to build a bridge across the Ohio River.

Steel was not yet popular and wrought-iron had only just come into use. When the president of the Erie Railroad Company came to inspect the progress, he said to Carnegie, "I don't believe these heavy castings can be made to stand up and carry themselves much less carry a train across the Ohio River."

After the bridge was built, it was modified to handle heavier traffic and was in service for some time. The profit Carnegie and his company would have made from building the bridge would have been impressive except for inflation. To compensate for the loss of present value, the president of the Pennsylvania Railroad Company, Edgar Thomson, allowed Carnegie and his company to charge more money. He said that before the bridge had been built no one had considered what might be the state of the economy after the job was completed.

Carnegie has described Piper, Schiffler, and Linville as incredible geniuses. President Thomson once remarked that he would rather have Piper at the scene of a burning bridge than the entire engineering corps. As smart as he was, however, Piper had one weakness that was rather beneficial to Carnegie. Piper would often drop whatever he was doing for horses, which turned out to be a chink in his armor.

Seeing that Piper would do anything for horses, Carnegie and others used horses as an excuse to get him to do things. If they wanted him to take a break, they would send him someplace with horses where he could look after them. Carnegie and his associates would also entrust Piper with choosing horses for them. His love of horses, however, also caused him to get into unfavorable circumstances. Carnegie recounts that Piper once showed up at the office with his shirt torn, his hat missing, his face smeared with dirt, and holding a whip. He said one of the reins had snapped when he was riding fast, and the horse lost its direction or he lost his "steerage way" as he called it.

Piper was often known as "Pipe." When he became friends with someone, he was their friend forever and always loyal. In the beginning, this relationship concerned him and Carnegie, and he transferred his loyalty to Carnegie's young brother, Thomas. Carnegie was still a dear friend of Piper's, but Carnegie's brother was much larger in Piper's eyes. Whatever he said, the colonel believed and accepted.

Piper sometimes argued with managers of steel mills about quality and price as well as other matters. He once went to Carnegie's brother to complain that arrangements he had made for the supply of steel for a year was not taken down correctly. He said there was something about "net," and he didn't understand what this meant. Carnegie's brother said to him, "Well, colonel, it means that nothing more is to be added." Piper replied, "All right, Thomas," and he was happy again. Carnegie has noted that it is important how one says something, for if Thomas had said, "Nothing is to be deducted," it would've caused problems.

It was one of those things about the Carnegies that was different from most other titans in nineteenth century America. Not only did Carnegie have an eye for opportunity and did what was necessary to cultivate and profit from it, but he was also able to communicate effectively.

Another incident that proved the point of the art of conversation happened when Piper was once reading Bradstreet's volume about business concerns. He saw that the rating for the Keystone Bridge Company was "BC," meaning Bad Credit. He was so infuriated that it took some effort to hold him back from going to the company's lawyers and suing the publishers! Thomas Carnegie, however, knew how to placate Piper. He said their company was rated Bad Credit because it had never borrowed anything, and the colonel was happy again.

Another notable character of Carnegie's life during his bridge-building days was a Captain Eads from St. Louis. He had drawn up plans for a bridge that spanned from St. Louis, Missouri, to East St. Louis, Illinois. The bridge was named after its designer, James Buchanan Eads. It was called Eads Bridge. Captain Eads had drawn up the plans and submitted them to the Keystone Bridge Company. Carnegie sent those plans to a Mr. Linville, whom he considered the best expert on bridges in the entire nation. Linville later reported to Carnegie that the plans were flawed, and that the bridge wouldn't be able to hold its weight if built from their original design. Carnegie then told him to meet with Eads and point this out. He told him to help Eads get the bridge into better shape.

Everything went well at first, and construction of the bridge began. Piper, however, was not able to keep up with Eads' demands. He was at first very pleased to have the Keystone Bridge Company been given the largest contract the company had ever received. Thus, in the beginning, Piper was very happy and treated Captain Eads very well. At this time, he greeted him with the cheerful "Colonel Eads, how do you do?

Delighted to see you." He didn't call him Captain Eads in the beginning. After some time, though, Piper became less and less friendly with him, and the greeting degraded to "Good morning, Captain Eads." Soon, Piper was heard referring to him as "Mr. Eads." Later, it became simply "Jim Eads."

After the bridge was complete, Carnegie kept Piper with him in St. Louis to guard the bridge, for threats had been made that the bridge would be torn down. Soon, Piper relieved the guards from protecting the bridge and at the same time began to miss home. He wanted to go back to Pittsburgh and was determined to take the night train back home. Nothing could change his mind—except horses.

When Carnegie tried to think about how to convince Piper to stay with him, he finally hit the jackpot, realizing that he could take advantage of his weakness and use horses to make him stay. Thus, during the day, Carnegie spoke to Piper that he wished to get his sister some horses. He said that St. Louis was a good place for them and asked Piper if he had seen anything nice. Piper immediately began to describe them. He decided to help Carnegie and dropped his plans to return to Pittsburgh that night. Piper chose a wonderful pair of horses, but now the issue was transporting them. He did not want them sent by train, and no boat could take them at the time. This problem would keep Piper in St. Louis until those horses were on their way, and it is no exaggeration to say that he might have gone on the ship with the horses.

The Keystone Bridge Company was the most remarkable iron bridge-building company in the nation. All other companies that had built iron bridges had failed. Some of them collapsed, causing some of the most devastating train accidents in the United States. In contrast, no bridge built by the Keystone Bridge Company ever collapsed. Carnegie's company never built a structure that was not safe or not in sync with the modern world. If they were submitted with an unsafe structure, they would at once reject the job. Some of the Keystone bridges even withstood severe winds, while bridges of other companies collapsed. Carnegie has denied that luck was the reason for his company's success. Rather, it was because they knew what they were doing, and that is why they were successful.

Carnegie observed that the key to success was the way the Keystone Bridge Company was run. When you focus on the quality of your work, you, your business, and everything you do will be successful. According to him, in the beginning, your work will be difficult until you establish your quality. Once that is done, your business can go on easily. For any business, quality is of prime importance. Everything else, even cost, comes second.

Carnegie devoted several years of his life to his bridge-building company. When there were large contracts to be accepted or declined, he would often go himself to meet the customer. Once he traveled to Dubuque, Iowa, in 1868 with the engineer of the Keystone Bridge Works, Walter Katte.

Apparently, a bridge-building company from Chicago was trying to secure the contract. This company had been awarded the contract by the board, but Carnegie did not leave. He stayed and talked with a number of directors, all of whom did not know right from left regarding the benefits of wrought iron over cast iron. They simply didn't understand the danger of using cast iron. The Keystone Bridge Works had always used wrought-iron to build the upper cord of their bridges, and the Chicago bridge-building company used cast iron. Carnegie described what would happen if a steamer were to strike the cast-iron or the wrought-iron cord. In the case of the wrought-iron cord, the cord would simply bend, but no substantial damage would be inflicted. In contrast, if a steamer were to strike a cast-iron cord, the entire bridge would crash down.

Only one of the directors was able to understand Carnegie's explanation, and that man was Perry Smith, who had once had an accident where he crashed his buggy into a cast-iron lamppost, which cracked on impact. Carnegie said that if only a little more money could be paid, they would have a superbly strong bridge that would not collapse if hit by a steamer. Carnegie went on to say that none of his bridges had ever fallen.

Senator Allison, who became a friend of Carnegie's, asked for Carnegie to leave the room for a moment. Shortly afterward, he was called back in and given the contract for the bridge under the condition that they could pay Carnegic's firm the lower price, which was lower by several thousand dollars, and Carnegie agreed. With that, the Keystone Bridge Company was awarded a prestigious contract even if it was a little less profitable.

Furthermore, it also meant the start of a friendship between Senator Allison and Andrew Carnegie.

What you should extract from this anecdote is that if you want a contract awarded to your firm as Carnegie did, always be at present and ready to accept it. Furthermore, always remember that a seemingly unimportant thing, such as the cast-iron lamppost in this case, might just help you get what you want.

Carnegie's advice is that if you want to get the contract, stay in it until you get it. When Carnegie was in Dubuque, he was told that he could go back home, and the contract would be sent to him. Carnegie turned down this offer and stayed until he was given the contract.

After Carnegie's bridge-building company had built the Steubenville bridge, the Baltimore and Ohio Railroad Company, the oldest railroad company in the nation and one of the fiercest competitors of the Pennsylvania Railroad Company, had to build bridges over the Ohio River from Parkersburg to Wheeling. During the time that Carnegie was trying to have his company awarded the contract, he had the pleasure of a meeting a Mr. Garrett, the president of the Baltimore and Ohio Railroad Company.

Carnegie and his associates wanted to be awarded the contract for the Baltimore and Ohio's bridges over the

Ohio River. Mr. Garrett, however, was not too inclined to award the contract to Keystone Bridge Works, believing that they would simply not be able to finish the bridges in the allotted time. He wanted to build the bridges himself. He also asked Carnegie whether or not he could use the designs of the Keystone Bridge Works for his bridges. Carnegie willingly gave Mr. Garrett permission to use the patents of his firm, feeling that approval from the Baltimore and Ohio was important.

Mr. Garrett soon became friends with Carnegie and even invited him to his private room, where they chatted. Garrett told Carnegie about his problems and arguments with the president and vice president of the Pennsylvania Railroad Company, Mr. Thomson and Mr. Scott. This prompted Carnegie to say that when he was on his way to meet Mr. Garrett he had met with Mr. Scott, who asked him where he was going. Carnegie told Mr. Scott that he was going to see Mr. Garrett to be awarded the bridge contracts. Mr. Scott replied by telling Carnegie that he seldom did anything pointless but he was doing so now, for Mr. Garrett would absolutely not award the contract to Carnegie's firm. The reason for this was that Carnegie was once in the service of the Pennsylvania Railroad Company, a major competitor of the Baltimore and Ohio. When Carnegie had finished, Mr. Garrett said that he did not care who used to work for whom but only for the benefits of his company. He did not care if Carnegie once worked for his greatest rival. All he cared about was the good of his company. He was thus quite willing to give Carnegie the contract.

In the beginning, the terms of the Keystone Bridge Works in building the Ohio bridges were not too favorable for Carnegie, for his firm was given all the difficult bits, while Garrett was going to build all the smaller items in his own shops and use the designs of the Keystone Bridge Works. Carnegie's firm was going to build the dangerous parts, while Garrett built the parts that could earn him money. Carnegie later confronted Garrett on the matter, asking him whether or not he was doing it because he wasn't confident that Carnegie's firm could finish the job at the end of the allotted time. Garrett was concerned, but Carnegie responded by telling him that he did not have to fret over the matter.

Carnegie asked Mr. Garrett whether or not a personal bond of his could be accepted as collateral. If the bridges were not finished by the allotted time, Carnegie would pay Mr. Garrett a certain sum. Mr. Garrett agreed, and Carnegie asked how much he wanted if his firm failed to meet the schedule. Mr.

Garrett asked for $100,000. Carnegie promptly accepted the challenge, telling him that his company would not allow him to fork out $100,000, and Mr. Garrett replied by saying that Carnegie's company would indeed not stop working until the bridges were complete to save Carnegie that amount of money.

This, in the end, is why the contract was awarded to Keystone Bridge Works. Carnegie's company was able to build the bridges by the time stated, and Carnegie never had to pay even a penny.

Carnegie and those who worked at the Keystone Bridge Works understood what it meant to build a bridge over the Ohio River more than even Mr. Garrett did. It was not an easy task. Carnegie's company began work on the superstructure of the bridge and left it on the banks of the river. He waited for the completion of the substructure, which was then being built in Mr. Garrett's shops.

Soon, the friendship between Mr. Garrett and Carnegie consolidated, and Mr. Garrett brought Carnegie to his mansion in the countryside. It was supposedly magnificent, with a large area of green grass, and the land was dotted with horses, dogs, sheep, and cows.

Eventually, Mr. Garrett decided that the Baltimore and Ohio Railroad Company should begin to build its own railways. He planned to use the Bessemer process, in which the impure materials of the iron were removed by blowing air through the metal when it was still in its molten state. He had already asked for permission to use this process. Carnegie understood that this was far from beneficial for the Baltimore and Ohio, understanding that the company could buy its rails for the same cost it takes to build only a small number. Carnegie thus traveled to meet Mr. Garrett and went over his plans with him.

Mr. Garrett took Carnegie and several other people who worked for him to the quay where imported goods were arriving by steamship. While the goods were being unloaded from the ships and placed into railway cars, he explained to Carnegie why it was necessary for the Baltimore and Ohio to build its own rails. He said, "Mr. Carnegie, you can now begin to appreciate the magnitude of our vast system and understand why it is necessary that we should make everything for ourselves, even our steel rails. We cannot depend upon private concerns to supply us with any of the principal articles we consume. We shall be a world to ourselves."

Garrett basically meant that the Baltimore and Ohio needed so much that buying them from outsiders would not meet the demands of the company. Carnegie understood that Garrett's idea would not work and replied by saying that his system wasn't really a "vast system." Carnegie went on to say that he saw the last annual report of the Baltimore and Ohio and noticed that the company and received $14 million simply by transporting goods of other people. He went on to say that his own companies had made the items themselves and made even more money. He finished by saying, "You are really a very small concern compared with Carnegie Brothers and Company."

As it turned out, the Baltimore and Ohio did not become a competitor of Carnegie Brothers and Company, as Carnegie's firm built steel rails. The friendship between Carnegie and Mr. Garrett continued, and Mr. Garrett once gave Carnegie a dog that he himself had grown. It was a Scotch collie. Mr. Garrett did not mind in the least that Carnegie was in the service of the Pennsylvania Railroad Company, his company's greatest rival. That fact was surpassed by the friendship between the two men.

Chapter 8 Steel & Oil

Carnegie, Thomas N. Miller, a man by the name of Henry Phipps, and Andrew Kloman started a steel mill. Miller was a dear friend of Carnegie and the backbone of the entire venture of Carnegie, Phipps, and Kloman. In his later years, Tom became more relaxed and sedate, and his views on theology much friendlier and welcoming.

Andrew Kloman was a German mechanic who was very skilled in building excellent pieces of machinery or things needed for structures. Everything he made was expensive, but his products always worked well. Carnegie heard about him when he was a division superintendent for the Pennsylvania Railroad. He found out that Mr. Kloman made a fine axle.

Kloman was really the first person to use the cold saw to cut cold iron. He invented a machine that could make bridge links, called upsetting machines. When Captain Eads was building the St. Louis bridge and could not acquire the right couplings, Kloman stepped up and said that he could make them and explained why the contractors responsible for doing so were not able to follow up.

Carnegie and his partners were deeply confident in the German and gave him the job. He was able to construct the right couplings, and all went well.

At the same time, Carnegie was already a friend of the Phipps family, the elder brother of Henry, John, being Carnegie's closest friend in the family. Henry was many years younger than Carnegie, but he did catch Carnegie's attention as being particularly smart. Henry once asked John to lend him a quarter, and John gave it to him without question. The following morning, an advertisement in the *Pittsburgh Dispatch* read: "A willing boy wishes work."

This was what Henry had done with the quarter. Instead of buying sweets and candy, the young man found employment. Shortly afterward, the company, Dilworth and Bidwell, called Henry and offered him a job. His parents approved, and he became an errand boy. His first job was to sweep the office.

His importance in the company grew, and he worked his way up to eventually being one of the richest men in the United States. Soon, Phipps caught the attention of Thomas Miller and Andrew Kloman, who both invested in him. It wasn't much, but it was something.

This led to the building of an iron mill on Twenty-Ninth Street.

Carnegie's brother, Thomas, had been a close friend of Phipps. They had spent their lives together and worked very closely with each other.

Henry Phipps spent his money on building conservatories and public parks. He once said they were to be open only on Sundays. This caused a tumultuous uproar among the church ministers, who called for his condemnation. The people, however, did not support the church ministers. Instead, they accepted the gift happily. Phipps once told the ministers, "It is all very well for you, gentlemen, who work one day in the week and are masters of your time the other six during which you can view the beauties of Nature—all very well for you—but I think it shameful that you should endeavor to shut out from the toiling masses all that is calculated to entertain and instruct them on the only day which you well know they have at their disposal."

This was a nice way of saying that the church ministers had all the time in the world, and on the one day a week that the people could take a break, the ministers force them to gather in a church to listen to long and boring sermons.

Church ministers also argued about whether or not to have music in their churches, and while they were debating this subject, other people were doing it for the public good. There was and still is a stark contrast between the attitudes and the way ministers spend their time compared with the attendees of the churches. As it turns out, the holy men are the losers.

While Carnegie was in the steel business, Kloman and Phipps pushed Miller out of their business. Carnegie immediately stood up for his friend, and the two of them created Cyclops Mills, which was launched in 1864. After their mill became successful, Carnegie united the mill of Miller and himself with that of Kloman and Phipps, forming the Union Iron Mills in 1867. Unfortunately, Miller did not know how to forgive his two former business partners and was adamant about not joining in the business venture. It was planned that Carnegie, his brother, and Miller would hold the controlling interest. Miller, however, was not going to work with the people who had shunned him. He even asked Carnegie to buy his part of the interest, and Carnegie sadly did so, feeling that there was no changing Miller's mind. Much later,

Miller confessed to Carnegie that he was sorry he did not take Carnegie up on his offer, for if he had he would have shared in the millions of dollars that the business provided.

In the steel mills under Carnegie and his partners, the products were of excellent quality. Nothing was ever faulty. The firm was very productive and often built what other firms were not building but whose demand was increasing. A strict rule in Carnegie's steel business was that he would build whatever other steel businesses would not.

As time went by, Carnegie found that no steel manufacturer ever knew how much money he had made or lost until they closed the books at the end of the year. He found that even the leading steel manufacturers of Pittsburgh were completely unaware of whether they had made a profit or suffered a loss. Carnegie wanted to know whether he was making or losing money before the end of the year.

He developed a system that could account for every penny—one that would weigh the materials they were using and note what they were collecting or spending. This system was slowly introduced, and it allowed Carnegie and his partners to know how much money they were spending, what each worker was doing, who wasted material, who was able to save material, and, most importantly, who was able to make the best product.

This system was all well and good, but not too many mill managers liked it. After some time, however, Carnegie and his partners were able to keep tabs on all the activities of the workers in the steel mills. They were not only able to keep an eye on the activities of the department but also on every individual worker.

Carnegie noted that the key to being successful in whatever business you do is to have a flawless system for accounting so that you can keep track of any surplus, loss, wasted material, or saved material. Some steel manufacturers didn't trust secretaries and assistants with money unless there was some kind of account that allowed the manufacturer to keep track of the money, but they provided unchecked quantities of steel to the workers and did not check if the weight was the same when the men returned the steel in the form of finished products.

This really was a very inefficient method of running a steel business or any business for that matter. To have a successful business, one must keep track of everything.

Carnegie's steel business used the Siemens gas furnace to heat the iron. The cost, however, was great, and older and more conventional steel manufacturers were opposed to the amount of money that Carnegie and his partners were spending on melting metal. The benefit of using these furnaces, however, was that they could reduce the amount of material that was wasted.

It would be several years until other producers started following in the footsteps of Carnegie's steel business and paid dearly to melt their iron.

Because Carnegie and his partners had a well-working system in their firm that allowed them to keep track of everything and also watch how much metal was being wasted when it was melted in large quantities, they met a man by the name of William Borntraeger. He was a distant relative of Andrew Kloman and a simple clerk. He had drawn up a detailed assessment showing what the results of Carnegie's firm would be for a certain period of time. Carnegie and his partners were very impressed with his man's initiative and work, and Mr. Borntraeger was promoted to superintendent of the works. He later became a partner of Carnegie, and he was living like a millionaire by the time he died.

Chapter 9 Oil Interest

Carnegie's interest in oil surfaced in 1862 thanks to the oil wells of Pennsylvania. A friend of Carnegie's, one Mr. William Coleman, was interested in the oil wells there, and Carnegie went with him to see them.

Many others had also gone to the oil wells, hoping to make a fortune. There weren't enough lodging spaces for everyone, but many were able to camp out. Although the area has been portrayed in history as dirty and chaotic, according to Carnegie, it was tranquil. Everyone was happy, laughing, and having a good time.

On the banks of streams, people were drilling for oil, their derricks rising one after the other, and chanting, in Carnegie's opinion rather strange mottoes. One of these was "Hell or China," referring to hitting oil but not stopping even if they hit hell or reached the other side of the world, which they thought was China.

Carnegie noted that Americans worked at a much faster pace than the British. Americans could very quickly establish a civilization, but the British would only be done verifying the legitimacy of a certain man to rise to the position of leader based on the status of his ancestors.

In other words, Carnegie was praising this land where everyone was equal to make his way and find his fortune. In his experience back in Scotland, Britain was a place that divided the gentry from the plebs. This kept a perpetual heel on the rise of any man.

It is from here, where Carnegie visited, that the outskirts of Oil Creek grew, and the city that formed around the oil industry was Titusville, just four miles to the south.

Not too long before crude oil was first harvested by Edwin Drake in Titusville it was already coming out of the ground. It seeped into Oil Creek, mixing with the water. Oil was prevalent in many places in the area and could be found in salt wells and water wells, contaminating the water. You could see it flowing in creeks and streams. In the beginning, it was more of a nuisance than a blessing. It was dirty, toxic, and difficult to clean. Nonetheless, it would be considered black gold.

The Seneca natives had a variety of uses for this oil. They used it to paint themselves when going to war, and they used it as medicine albeit ineffectively as a form of a disinfectant for the skin. The Indians harvested the oil by placing blankets or pieces of fabric in the running water in the creek and let them soak it up. They then took the blankets or pieces of cloth to squeeze out the oil.

Around 1850, one Mr. Samuel Kier collected the oil found in the salt wells that his father owned and bottled it. They were half-pints that Samuel sold as medicine, calling it Kier's Rock Oil. It was supposed to cure bronchitis and liver problems, but, of course, it didn't.

The oil also had other uses. It was used to light lamps, but the primary source of flame at the time was whale oil. Whale blubber was rendered and shipped throughout the country, but the demand was so great that whalers were not able to keep up with it. This made it expensive, and only the wealthy could afford such luxuries and light their homes at night. The rest of the people, such as farmers and villagers and the poor in the city, were forced to go without light until morning.

Although there were other ways of lighting their homes, as with tallow (derived from animals) and coal oil (derived from shale), these were also expensive as was the process of extraction, and the oil supply was limited. Other forms of oil that could be used included cottonseed oil and lard oil, but these were not affordable and also not convenient to use. A replacement was necessary, and those who could solve the problem would be paid handsomely. Electricity and the light bulb were still a long way off.

Along came Mr. George Bissell, who had graduated from Dartmouth College and worked as a school principal, a professor of Greek language, a lawyer, and a journalist. In his spare time, he was also an inventor. Sometime in the 1850s, he had an idea for a new way to fuel the lights in people's homes. He thought that perhaps the oil that had been found in the western regions of Pennsylvania could be a better fuel for lamps.

He founded the Pennsylvania Rock Oil Company and sent a small amount of the oil to a Mr. Benjamin Silliman Jr., a professor of chemistry at Yale University. In 1855, Mr. Silliman concluded that Bissell's suspicions were true and that rock oil could be processed to be fuel for lamps.

Now that it was possible, the Pennsylvania Rock Oil Company faced a different problem. They had to gather large amounts of oil. Practically no infrastructure had been built around oil exploration. All they had were streams and creeks with traces of oil, and this looked like a contaminant rather than an asset. They figured that it came from the ground, so it was logical to look for underground oil deposits. Near the end of 1857, close to three years after Silliman corroborated Bissell's suspicions, explorers were commissioned to look for large deposits of oil. Today, there is a body of science and rational thought in the field of exploration, which is a billion dollar business, but back then it was anybody's guess. At this point, Bissell's company had been renamed Seneca Oil Company in tribute to the Seneca tribe.

It was thanks to a Mr. Townsend, a banker in New Haven who helped finance this exploration mission, that someone was able to search for large deposits of oil. He sent Mr. Edwin Drake, a man in his late thirties who suffered from a constant back problem. Mr. Drake was eventually given the title of colonel and dispatched to Titusville, Pennsylvania, in December 1857.

At this time, Oil Creek Valley, situated in Titusville, was not very sophisticated or modern. It was still densely packed with thick forests of hemlock and pine trees and the usual wildlife. These were harsh conditions to search for oil when you consider the dense forest and the lack of expertise in finding something below ground. Pipes had to be brought in, and hauling all the equipment was not easy. The people of Oil Creek liked Drake but thought he was wasting his time. It was impossible to think that there were any deposits of this toxic material.

He used the same kind of methods to find oil deposits that salt miners used in the salt mines. This was the first use of derricks to explore for oil. Back then the derricks were made of wood and towered ten to thirty feet above the ground where they bore into the earth.

Finally, after a long period of time, Drake succeeded in finding a well that contained this heavy, sludge-like material.

On Saturday, August 27, 1859, almost one and a half years after arriving in Oil Creek, Colonel Drake struck oil. It had now been proven that oil did exist in certain pockets beneath the ground, and his method was viable and effective. He now had a system that could be replicated and be the key to future success.

News of his find spread, and before long there was a rush to settle in Titusville. More derricks were set up, and more holes were bored to tap that well. They only had crude oil, and not much could be done with it, as it needed to be refined.

This led to the refining of the toxic sludge. To process the crude oil, many refineries were set up by independent companies to process the oil that was coming from independent drillers.

In less than a year after Drake struck oil, a large number of refineries had been set up in Oil Creek, but they were unable to extract usable heating oil to any profitable degree. Their methods were crude, and their output was low, but it was better than nothing. A lot of sludge was discarded in streams and the ground after the refining process, but most of it was sill heavy with usable hydrocarbons.

The Titusville Oil Creek area had begun by producing meager quantities of oil but was eventually able to produce enough to grow, expand, and thrive.

In the beginning, though, everything was run poorly, as expected. Barrels of oil were loaded into boats that were not very fit for sea anymore. The people who had begun to sell oil from Oil Creek had placed dams in some places in the creek, and when the time was just right, the dams were opened and the water was used to push the boats all the way down the creek, and they were able to float their way along the Allegheny River and finally reach Pittsburgh.

This method of transportation was inefficient and ineffective. Large quantities of oil were lost, and the waters on which they were transported were polluted with crude oil. Two-thirds of the original quantity of oil was lost, one-third having been lost during the time in which the people of Oil Creek were waiting to open the dams and the other third during transportation.

The oil that reached Pittsburgh was bottled and sold at rather high prices, and it was said to be excellent medicine, curing rheumatic problems. The oil was sold at one dollar per vial. As more oil became available, the price dropped and became very cheap.

The most popular wells at the time were on Storey farm. It was offered for sale at $45,000, and Carnegie and his partners bought it. Mr. William Coleman proposed to store 100,000 barrels of oil in the ground. To make up for the losses that would occur from leaks, oil was to be kept constantly flowing into the pool so that when the supply of oil was gone, Carnegie and his partners could sell their bounty and make a nice profit. This was one of the first instances of stockpiling. This day never came, however, and after having lost a great deal of oil, Carnegie and his partners abandoned the plan and did not continue to pool it.

The money made from the oil well from Storey farm was critical to Carnegie's overall success later in life. It had allowed for the construction of a brand-new steel mill in Pittsburgh, which called for all the money that Carnegie and his partners could raise to leverage their credit. From the start, Carnegie's credit was on solid footing, and he made sure it never faulted. He paid his loans on time and more often than not ahead of time. In this respect, he was much like Rockefeller, who valued his credit standing with the banks.

The next venture into the oil business was again with Mr. William Coleman and one Mr. David Ritchie. This oil field was in Ohio, and the oil there was an excellent lubricant. In 1864, Carnegie, Mr. Coleman, and Mr. Ritchie visited the oil field and purchased it.

The journey to the oil field was fine, but the trip back was rather uncomfortable. During the return journey, torrential rains fell, and the carriage in which they were riding started to rock back and forth as it sunk and climbed out of soft spots in the ground where the road had been soaked.

The two men who rode with him were rather portly, while Carnegie himself at that time was rather thin. He was squeezed between them, and they rocked back and forth as the carriage made its way in and out of potholes. Despite the discomfort of the trip, Carnegie and his companions were elated by the business they had just concluded.

They reached a small town the following night. They had seen the church in town and heard its bell toll. When they eventually arrived, it coincided with the arrival of a minister the town was waiting for. The minister was delayed, however, due to the heavy rains, and the townspeople mistook Carnegie for the minister.

The welcoming party asked Carnegie and his partners when they would be ready to enter the meetinghouse. Carnegie, Mr. Ritchie, and Mr. Coleman were all tempted to accept, finding it amusing, but Carnegie was so exhausted that he just could not do it. As Carnegie later noted, that was the closest he ever got to give a speech at a church podium.

After some time, Carnegie found that his business affairs required much of his time and attention and realized that he needed to quit his job at the Pennsylvania Railroad Company. Shortly before Carnegie resigned, he was invited to meet with the president of the Pennsylvania Railroad, Mr. John Edgar Thomson, who was going to promote Carnegie to the position of assistant general superintendent. If Carnegie took the job, he was going to have his office in Altoona, the city where he had stayed with Mr. Scott several years earlier before becoming superintendent of the Pittsburgh Division.

Carnegie refused the offer, saying that he was planning to leave the company and make a great fortune for himself. He said that he did not see how he could accomplish his goal if he continued to work for a paycheck.

On March 28, 1865, Andrew Carnegie resigned from the Pennsylvania Railroad Company. As a gift, the railwaymen presented him with a gold watch. Earlier, President Thomson had written a letter to Carnegie congratulating him on his resignation from the Pennsylvania Railroad. Carnegie took this letter and really cherished his gold watch.

Leaving was a subject of great consternation for Carnegie. No doubt he wanted to pursue his own path, but it was a path that would have its pitfalls and be harder to traverse. Staying at the railroad at such a high position and with the possibility of taking the top spot one day not being too far out of the question would have been tempting for any man, but he knew he had to move on. There was more to explore, more to conquer, and more to do.

He wrote a heartfelt letter of resignation in which he described his dozen years at Pennsylvania Railroad with deep fondness. He had, after all, started at the lowest rung of the ladder and worked his way up to the second highest-paying job in the company. He had learned so much. It had become the foundation of his eventual steel empire. The knowledge he gained from taking care of problems and how to fix them gave him insight into many opportunities, ranging from sleeper cars to carriages to railway lines and bridges. Now he wanted more.

Carnegie left his job at the Pennsylvania Railroad Company and set out to earn his fortune from simply his businesses. He was not going to earn money by working for a paycheck.

Carnegie has said that one needs to be in a service where they answer to superiors. He notes that even leaders and presidents are bombarded with different advice and suggestions, are forced to do certain things, and have very little independence.

Two years after he retired from the Pennsylvania Railroad Company, Carnegie, his friend Henry Phipps, and a certain J.W. Vandevort toured through Europe, particularly in Scotland, Carnegie's home, and England. Vandevort had become "Vandy" between Carnegie and himself, and the two had become traveling buddies.

One Sunday when Carnegie and Vandevort were spending their time in the grass of a field, Carnegie asked, "If you could make $3,000, would you spend it on a tour through Europe with me?"

Vandevort responded by saying, "Would a duck swim or an Irishman eat potatoes?"

That $3,000 was acquired soon afterward in oil stock. Vandevort had invested in the oil stock with just a few hundred dollars he had in store. After that, Carnegie, Vandy, and Henry Phipps, or Harry, set out on a tour of Europe. They visited different capital cities, climbed spires, and even slept on mountaintops. They carried their luggage in knapsacks.

The end of their holiday was at Vesuvius, where they made the solemn promise to one day go around the world.

Carnegie's trip in Europe was, in his own opinion, very good for him. Before then he had not heard of art, particularly sculpting and painting. After his travels, however, he was able to categorize paintings of the masters. He felt that after visiting Europe and truly experiencing beautiful works of art and many other things that so much in America just seemed tasteless. What seemed magnificent before he had left the U.S. he now rejected.

He had strong beliefs that for one to succeed one needs to have a strong mind. This comes from a diversity of experience and thought. That diversity can only be achieved by travel.

Carnegie was already familiar with music, but he was truly affected during his trip to Europe. He had listened to the music of the Handel anniversary, which was being celebrated in the Crystal Palace in London. He had heard the music in cathedrals and the songs sung by the Pope's choir in Rome. All the music that he had listened to during his trip in Europe was really wonderful, empowering, and grand. It was part of the reason why his later endowments went to Carnegie Hall. It was just one way to get others to experience what he had experienced within his heart and how that experience had touched his soul.

Carnegie also found that after leaving the fast pace of the New World that the U.S. was moving too quickly, while countries in the rest of the world were comparatively much slower in progress.

The United States was zipping along like a fast car. There was good to this and bad. The race for prosperity and the pursuit of happiness had gained momentum, but the race for a more mindful and spiritual experience had been left aside as its cost. This was Carnegie's perspective. There was an enlightened side to Carnegie that permeated much of the thinking and reflection when he was older.

Advancing the Oil Wells

As previously mentioned, George Lauder, "Dod," had taken Mr. William Coleman to Wigan, England. There he showed Coleman how they washed the waste from the coal mines and extracted coke. Coleman had always been pressing Carnegie and his partners about the potential of using this supposed waste that was being discarded from the coal mines. Even disposing of the dross was quite expensive, and there would be another way.

Carnegie had great confidence in his cousin, and when he accepted what Coleman was telling them, he immediately started to get other coal companies to send them their dross. A ten-year contract was made with several prominent coal companies and several railway companies for transportation. Carnegie also put together the money to set up shops along the Pennsylvania Railroad.

Dod came to Pittsburgh to watch over everything, and he oversaw the construction of the first coal-washing device in the nation. His project was a success, as all his projects in the area were. It didn't take long before the money that was spent to set up everything and to build the machines was made back. Lauder's invention proved very useful for Carnegie's business, and Lauder became rather famous.

In time, many more Lauder machines were built until Carnegie had 500 of them washing close to 1,500 tons of coal every day. Carnegie was so impressed with all of this that he noted Lauder's genius

His point was that someone who could turn what was considered worthless junk and thrown away into something useful and meaningful was worth praise and admiration.

Another person who became a partner of Carnegie was the son of Carnegie's other cousin, Robert Morrison of Dunfermline. Robert, or Bob, had a son who had become the superintendent of one of the shops of Carnegie's coal business. He asked Carnegie if he knew of a mechanic who was exceptionally skillful and also one of his relatives. Carnegie said no and asked if he might speak to the superintendent.

When they began to talk, Carnegie asked him what his name was, and he replied, "Morrison, son of Robert." "Well, how did you come here?" Carnegie asked. "I thought we could better ourselves," he replied. "Who have you with you?" asked Carnegie. "My wife," he answered. "Why didn't you come first to see your relative who might have been able to introduce you here?" Carnegie asked. "Well, I didn't feel I needed help if I only got a chance", replied Morrison.

That was a classic trait of a Morrison—always very independent. He had been promoted to the position of superintendent of one of the shops in Duquesne. From there he continued to rise in position. In Carnegie's old days, Morrison, still seemingly young, had become a millionaire but still retained his humility.

Carnegie always suggested that he and his partners should expand the business into making steel and iron. Steel manufacturers were not yet very popular in America, and they were concerned that America was importing too much from other countries. That changed through government intervention after the Civil War. Tariffs were placed on imports, and the fear of steel manufacturers evaporated. The Civil War caused people to want to rely only on their own country and to make everything they vitally needed. In the past, the United States had no choice but to buy steel from other countries, largely Britain, the country that had secretly supported the Confederacy during the war. It became a national strategic imperative that critical resources be allowed to prosper.

American citizens wanted nothing more than for their country to produce their own goods. Congress then presented manufacturers with a tariff of 28 percent on steel rails. Thus, for every ton of steel rails bought from outside, 28 percent of the original price was added to that price.

This policy of making their own materials and goods allowed the manufacturing business in general in the United States to flourish. Before the Civil War, this policy was not firmly pressed, and the South and the North differed on it. Southerners viewed it as a policy convenient only for the North, while they stood for free trade. Since the British government had supported the South during the Civil War, Northerners disliked them. The policy of protection was then agreed to by both Southerners and Northerners, and producing your own goods became a patriotic activity after the war.

Many no longer thought twice about venturing into the business of manufacturing. They were sure they were safe. Long after the Civil War ended, people began to call for the tariff on foreign imports to be reduced. In the beginning, this did not happen, and people suspected that some manufacturers were bribing congressmen to keep the tariff so that they could continue to make and sell their products. In truth, however, manufacturers were raising just enough money every year to run the Iron and Steel Association.

Tariffs on steel were eventually reduced, and thanks to Carnegie sometimes dropped to only $7 per ton.

In 1911, the tariff dropped a further ½%.

When Grover Cleveland was president of the United States, he wanted a tariff that was very impractical. His tariff would be a severe blow to many manufacturers making several different products. When this issue came about, Carnegie was summoned to Washington, where he tried to improve what was called the Wilson Bill. Carnegie, Governor Flower of New York, Senator Gorman, and several other Democrats sided with Carnegie and opposed the Wilson Bill. Several of those who stood with Carnegie believed that the Wilson Bill would inevitably damage the nation's manufacturing industry.

Carnegie was given the responsibility of suggesting a lower tariff by Flower, Gorman, and the other protectionist Democrats. He came up with a certain tariff that all of them agreed on, which was called the Wilson-Gorman Tariff Bill. Later, Gorman told Carnegie that he had to be lenient regarding cotton ties to gain Southern senators as supporters for keeping protection intact.

Carnegie's role in the tariffs on imported foods was, conversely, to try to reduce the tariffs. He did not support those who wanted higher taxes paid for imported goods, and neither did he support those who wanted no taxes on imported goods. He stood in the middle, supporting taxes that were reasonable but high enough to keep manufacturing intact. The point of balance that Carnegie straddled was one where the tariffs would help local manufacturers compete, and the people would have inexpensive access to goods and services. Raising tariffs of external suppliers sometimes had the effect of raising the prices of local goods, which meant that the consumer paid the price. Besides, pure competition of goods would also serve as an incentive to develop better technologies.

By 1907, all tariffs placed on steel and iron were able to be dropped. By this time, manufacturing in the United States had already prospered so much that even if someone bought goods from other countries it wouldn't hurt the firms. In the infancy of manufacturing, however, it was extremely important that everyone bought from the manufacturers in the country instead of fattening the wallets of outside manufacturers.

Europe did not produce much, and thus prices there were very expensive. This was another reason why it was all right for the tariffs to be dropped, for very few people would pay so much for so little, as prices in Europe were quite high.

The only "negative" effect that free trade had on manufacturers was that there couldn't be high prices on their products. Other than that, everything was secure. Carnegie himself said this to an audience at the Tariff Commission in Washington in 1910.

Chapter 10 New York

As the steel and oil business of Carnegie and his partners grew, it became necessary for him to regularly travel to the East and most often to New York, where all large businesses had their headquarters. Carnegie said that New York was the equivalent of London, and that no company could ever hope to do well unless it had a stronghold in New York.

He traveled to New York so often that he eventually moved there.

Carnegie's brother, Thomas, had already married Lucy Coleman, daughter of Mr. William Coleman, who had worked with Carnegie and his partners for some time and was a companion at the beginning of the oil industry. Carnegie's home in Homewood was given to Thomas, and Carnegie left for New York with his mother, who wanted to go with him. Although they were happy as long as they were together, Carnegie's mother still felt sad to leave Pittsburgh again. When the family had moved to Altoona when Mr. Scott became superintendent of the Pittsburgh Division for the Pennsylvania Railroad, friendships were cut and relationships ended. Now they had to leave Pittsburgh again to a place totally alien to them.

When Carnegie and his mother arrived in New York, they lived at the St. Nicholas Hotel, and he took an office on Broad Street.

At the beginning of their stay in New York, they were most happy when friends from Pittsburgh visited them. Carnegie and his mother also traveled to Pittsburgh to maintain the friendships.

After some time, however, New York began to feel like home, and they made friends there too. Later, the Windsor Hotel, which was also owned by the owners of the St. Nicholas, opened, and Carnegie and his mother spent their lives there until 1887. They lived solely in these two hotels for twenty years!

The owner of the hotel, Mr. Hawk, became a close friend of Carnegie as did his son and nephew.

Carnegie has noted that he gained many educational benefits in New York, most important being the Nineteenth Century Club founded by the Palmers. Mr. and Mrs. Courtlandt Palmer's club was meant to bring together people every month to talk about various subjects. It was thanks to a certain Madame Botta that Carnegie became a member. She was the wife of Professor Botta, and he was once invited to dine with them. At the meal, he met several other people of high status, and one of them was a certain Mr. Andrew D. White, who went on to become Carnegie's counselor and friend.

At the time, however, White was president of Cornell University and later became ambassador to both Russia and Germany.

At each gathering of the members of the Nineteenth Century Club, men and women gave speeches about the most talked about topics of the day. Soon, the number of attendees grew so large that the meeting could no longer be held in a private room. They were subsequently held at the American Art Galleries.

Carnegie once spoke on the topic "The Aristocracy of the Dollar."

He thought his speaking was excellent, for in order to speak, he had to learn, and he loved learning things.

While in Pittsburgh, Carnegie had found that only a few businesses and businessmen dealt with the New

York Stock Exchange, and the Oil and Stock Exchange in Pittsburgh did not exist at that time. Pittsburgh was a manufacturing city.

Carnegie found that New York was quite different, and nearly all businessmen there were involved with the New York Stock Exchange. Carnegie was constantly approached with questions regarding his dealings with railway ventures. He was also invited to a party where the hosts were intending to buy certain properties, but Carnegie never attended or paid attention to these men.

One of the most important offers he ever received, however, was from a Mr. Jay Gould, who spoke to Carnegie at the Windsor Hotel. This was the same Jay Gould who had crossed Cornelius Vanderbilt. He told Carnegie that he wanted to buy the controlling interests of the Pennsylvania Railroad Company. He wanted Carnegie to manage the company, and he would receive 50 percent of the profits. Carnegie thanked him but declined the offer, saying that he was a close friend of Mr. Scott.

Shortly afterward, Mr. Scott and Carnegie met, and Mr. Scott told him that he had learned that Carnegie had been chosen by several people in New York to become the next president of the Pennsylvania Railroad after himself. Carnegie did not know how Mr. Scott had known about this, for Carnegie had never even said a word of it to him. Carnegie assured Mr. Scott that he would not be the president of any railroad company other than one he had founded.

About thirty years after Mr. Gould made his offer to Carnegie, Carnegie spoke to Mr. Gould's son and told him about the offer his father had presented to him. He said, "Your father offered me control of the great Pennsylvania system. Now I offer his son in return the control of an international line from ocean to ocean."

Carnegie and Mr. Gould's son decided they would first bring the Wabash line to Pittsburgh. Everything went well, and the contract made with the Wabash was that one-third of the business that Carnegie's steel business received was to be given to the Wabash.

Just before Carnegie and Mr. Gould's son were about to expand in the East from Pittsburgh all the way to the Atlantic, a certain Mr. Schwab talked to Carnegie on behalf of Mr. Morgan. Carnegie was asked whether or not he was actually going to retire from business. Carnegie replied that he was, which would be the end of railway ventures for Carnegie and his partners.

Carnegie really only bought a small number of shares of the Pennsylvania Railroad Company when he was very young, and he had done so for the purpose of investment. Carnegie did not pay for the shares because bankers were willing to carry his shares for him for a small price. Carnegie did, however, buy a few shares of companies he did not really get involved in.

Carnegie had a very strict rule. He was not going to buy what he didn't pay for, and he wasn't going to sell what wasn't his to sell.

When Carnegie owned stocks and shares, he wanted to know what the stocks were quoted at in the newspaper. He went on to sell the shares he owned that were part of other companies, and he turned his entire attention to his own business. Carnegie also made it a point that he would not buy or even own a stock that was sold on a stock exchange.

For the most part, he stood by this principle.

Carnegie believed that this principle should be followed by all businessmen. Carnegie has said that this is especially important for a man in the manufacturing industry. In his opinion, it leaves a man distracted and always thinking about his shares. This would wreck his judgment, something that is needed in the business of manufacturing, which requires you to think about a problem calmly. If he is already anxious about his shares, he would not be able to think right and would end up making a reckless or careless decision.

The most meaningful venture that Carnegie undertook in New York was building a bridge across the Mississippi River at Keokuk. Edgar Thomson, who was then still president of the Pennsylvania Railroad, worked with Carnegie for the bridge. Carnegie and Mr. Edgar Thomson were willing to accept stocks and bonds as payment for their work.

Everything went well except monetarily. Thanks to a crisis that occurred, the company that had contracted for Carnegie to build their bridge went bankrupt and was unable to pay Carnegie his fee. In turn, a rival bridge-building concern took up the job and built a bridge across the Mississippi at Burlington. They also built a railway line that ran along the western bank of the Mississippi all the way to Keokuk.

Thomson and Carnegie were never able to receive their profits, but at least they did not suffer a loss.

The bridge that Carnegie had taken up the contract to build was built in the shops of the Keystone Works in Pittsburgh. The project called for Carnegie to frequently visit Keokuk.

These visits permitted Carnegie to meet General Reid and his wife. The English people, in Carnegie's opinion, considered the people of the Far West in the United States to be barely civilized. These people were friends of Carnegie's and well received by Mr. and Mrs. Reid at an impressive gathering in Britain.

Carnegie became so famous for building the Keokuk bridge that he was approached by several people who were entrusted with building the Mississippi bridge at St. Louis. In 1869, Carnegie was approached by a Mr. Macpherson. He was from Scotland and told Carnegie that he was trying to acquire the necessary funds to build the bridge. He was inquiring if Carnegie would be able to get a few of the Eastern railway companies to build it.

After considering it, Carnegie drew up the contract for constructing the bridge to be done by the Keystone Bridge Works. Carnegie was also able to sell $4 million worth of shares of the Keystone Bridge Company. He then set off for London in March 1869 to negotiate the sale of the bonds.

During Carnegie's trip to London, he drew up a description of what was happening. After arriving in London, Carnegie met with Junius S. Morgan, a prominent banker at the time and the father of J.P. Morgan. Carnegie conducted negotiations with him and furnished him with a copy of the prospectus he had made. He was informed the next day that Morgan was positive about the matter. Carnegie sold a portion of the shares to Morgan and said that the rest of the shares were also available. Morgan's lawyers, however, proposed different terms. When Carnegie heard those terms, he made a counter proposal to which Morgan had to revert to his lawyers for advice.

Morgan tried to get Carnegie to go off to Scotland, as he was planning to go there. He said that everything could be ready by the time he returned in three weeks, but Carnegie had no intention of leaving matters hanging in midair while he was away. He responded by saying that he would have a telegram delivered the following morning that stipulated his agreement to the changes. The Atlantic telegram line had already been open for some time, but it wasn't certain if the line would be able to carry a message that was as long as he was writing. He put in the message all the changes and all the official statements and showed it to Mr. Morgan before he sent it. After seeing it, he said, "Well, young man, if you succeed in that you deserve a red mark."

When Carnegie entered the office the following morning, he had a letter from Mr. Morgan's private office. It was the answer to Carnegie's changes: "Board meeting last night; changes all approved." After seeing the answer, Carnegie said to Mr. Morgan, "Now, Mr. Morgan, we can proceed, assuming that the bond is as your lawyers desire."

Shortly afterward, the matter was settled.

During the time that Carnegie was in the office of Junius Spencer Morgan while he was still in London, he was approached by a man by the name of Mr. Sampson, who was at the time the financial editor for The Times. The two men met in Mr. Sampson's office.

Carnegie understood that speaking to him would mean that the price of the bonds that were on the Stock Exchange would rise.

Carnegie talked about Fisk and Gould and spoke of how the St. Louis Bridge Company was related to the national government. Mr. Sampson said he would be happy to place this information in *The Times*. Mr. Sampson left the office, and Morgan then slapped Carnegie on the shoulder and said, "Thank you, young man; you have raised the price of those bonds 5 percent this morning." Carnegie responded by saying, "All right, Mr. Morgan, now show me how I can raise them 5 percent more for you."

Everything went well, and Carnegie was able to acquire the funds necessary to build the St. Louis bridge. This whole affair was Carnegie's first time engaging with European bankers.

Later, a certain Mr. Pullman met with Carnegie and told him that Mr. Morgan had said at a dinner party, "That young man will be heard from." That "young man" was Andrew Carnegie.

After finishing his business with J.S. Morgan, Carnegie took a trip to Dunfermline, his hometown. There he presented to the city public baths as a gift. It was the first real gift Carnegie had made to his hometown. Many years earlier when Carnegie was in the telegram business, his Uncle Lauder had suggested to Carnegie that he subscribe to the Wallace Monument, which was being built on Stirling Heights.

At the time, Carnegie was earning a mere $30 a month, and paying for the seemingly small expense of the subscription was very expensive for a man earning such a salary. Carnegie's mother was not upset about it and was very happy to see that her son's name was listed as someone who had contributed.

Many years later, Carnegie and his mother visited the Wallace Monument in Stirling, and there she presented to the monument committee a bust of Sir Walter Scott.

By this time, Carnegie and his mother were in a much better financial situation, although Carnegie was not yet giving money. He was at the time in accumulation and saving mode.

While Carnegie was on his trip to Europe with his friends Vandy and Harry, he was not completely relaxed. He was always thinking about business.

Letters were regularly sent to him to keep him informed about matters at home. During Carnegie's excursion in Europe, the construction of a railway line to the Pacific was considered, and the United States Congress passed an act that encouraged construction of the line. While Carnegie was in Rome, he realized that this line could be completed long before it was expected to be. Carnegie then wrote Mr. Scott and told him that they could place sleeping cars on the California railway. Mr. Scott responded, "Well, young man, you do take time by the forelock." This was also his reaction when Carnegie had approached him many years earlier when the sleeping car was first thought of by inventor Theodore Tuttle Woodruff.

Despite Mr. Scott's unsatisfactory reply, Carnegie went on with his plans after returning to the United States.

The demand for sleeping cars was so high that it was hard to produce enough to meet the demand. This led to the founding of the Pullman Company by George Pullman. At the time, the Central Transportation Company was not able to meet the demand for the sleeping car, and Pullman very soon became a competitor.

He chose Chicago as the place to start, which was the largest railway center in the nation at that time.

When the president of the Union Pacific Railway was once in Chicago, Pullman met with him. Pullman waited in the office for the railway president, and while there he saw a telegram addressed to Mr. Scott. It read, "Your proposition for sleeping cars is accepted." Later, when Mr. Durrant, president of the Union Pacific, came into the office, Pullman spoke to him about how he had read the telegram and said, "I trust you not decide this matter until I have made a proposition to you."

The railway president agreed to hear what Pullman had to say.

A board meeting of the Union Pacific Railway was held in New York not long afterward. Both Pullman and Carnegie attended the meeting, both eager to be given the responsibility of building sleeping cars.

Carnegie and Pullman met there, and Carnegie said, "Good evening, Mr. Pullman! Here we are together, and are we not making a nice couple of fools of ourselves?" Mr. Pullman asked, "What do you mean?"

The problem was actually quite simple. Carnegie explained that because of their competing for the job at hand they were losing. Pullman responded, "Well, what do you propose to do about it?" Carnegie replied, "Unite. Make a joint proposition to the Union Pacific, your party and mine, and organize a company." Pullman then asked, "What would you call it?"

Carnegie responded, "The Pullman Palace Car Company." This name gelled well with both of them, and Pullman invited Carnegie to his room to discuss the matter.

Everything went well, and they were given the contract. Carnegie's company was joined with Pullman's, and Carnegie and his partners held shares of Pullman's company.

In 1873, a financial crisis came crashing down, and Carnegie was forced to sell his shares in Pullman's company to save his own steel business. Carnegie believed that he was the biggest shareholder in the company until he had to sell his shares.

George Pullman was at first a carpenter, and his first major venture was when a house in Chicago had to be elevated.
Slowly, he became a well-known contractor in the business of elevating houses.

Pullman was so skilled in this line of work that if a hotel needed to be raised by ten feet he could do it without disrupting the business of the hotel or be an inconvenience to the several hundred people staying in the hotel.

Mr. Pullman was a very fast-paced man and saw, as Carnegie did, the necessity for having sleeping cars on the lines. He began constructing sleeping cars after being awarded contracts by different railway companies.

The Eastern Company and Mr. T.T. Woodruff were the real owners of the patents for the sleeping car, and this issue caused a bit of trouble for Pullman.

Carnegie suggested that Pullman's firm and the Eastern Company should merge. This was exactly the same course of action he himself had taken earlier when his company and Pullman's were trying to get the contract to build sleeping cars.

Carnegie decided to fix everything himself, seeing that the relationship between him, Pullman, and the Eastern Company was on good terms, whereas Pullman's relationship with the Eastern Company was rather awkward.

Everything went well, and the Central Transportation Company was joined with the Pullman Company, allowing Pullman to extend his range of activities into the East. Pullman was given control of the Pennsylvania trunk line to the Atlantic.

Carnegie observed that Pullman was a very determined person. He had problems at times as everyone does and sometimes never performed at his best but was determined to do his best.

Pullman once told Carnegie a story about an old man from the West who had suffered a great many illnesses, and one day when he was being spoken to by his neighbors in a most sympathetic tone, he replied, "Yes, my friends, all that you say is true. I have had a long, long life full of troubles, but there is one curious fact about them—nine-tenths of them never happened."

The moral of that story is that the better part of one's problems are created in your mind and don't exist in the real world. One may feel that it is real, but that is because it is conjured in the mind. These imaginary issues should simply be brushed aside.

Carnegie was doing very well at the time and soon attracted the attention of other firms. In 1871, he was approached by the Union Pacific Railway that needed his help to raise $600,000 to keep the company up and running until the problem they were in was over.

He was also told by his friends who worked for Union Pacific that he would be able to raise the funds necessary, and that he could even give the

Pennsylvania Railroad control of the Western line, an important railway.

Carnegie decided that he would do it. He traveled to Philadelphia to speak with President Edgar Thomson of the Pennsylvania Railroad. Carnegie thought that if the Union Pacific was fine with having a few Pennsylvania Railroad men on their board, the business the Pennsylvania Railroad would receive would be a proper reason to help the Union Pacific.

When Carnegie met with Mr. Thomson, he said that if he were to be given the securities regarding the money of the Pennsylvania Railroad and have the Union Pacific borrow their money up in New York, then the Pennsylvania Railroad would be able to control the Union Pacific and use it to its advantage. Carnegie has described President Thomson as a man who cared more for the company's money than his own. He spent his own money freely but was very particular about the expenditures of the Pennsylvania Railroad.

If the whole job were to come crashing down and if the $600,000 were to disappear, the Pennsylvania Railroad wouldn't really suffer a blow. It had already been agreed upon that if the job failed President Thomson would be given the securities of the Union

Pacific that Carnegie now had for giving the loan to the Union Pacific Railway.

The meeting between Carnegie and President Thomson took place at his home in Philadelphia, and just when they had finished their talk and Carnegie was about to leave, Thomson put his hand on Carnegie's shoulder and said, "Remember, Andy, I look to you in this matter. It is you I trust, and I depend on your holding all the securities you obtain and seeing that the Pennsylvania Railroad is never in a position where it can lose a dollar."

This basically meant that President Thomson trusted Carnegie and placed him in charge of keeping the Pennsylvania Railroad's funds intact. Carnegie went on with his job, and everything turned out well.

When all was practically said and done, the Union Pacific was not too comfortable with having the president of the Pennsylvania Railroad as their president as well. Thomson resolutely put down the proposition, and he went on to appoint Thomas A. Scott vice president of the Union Pacific Railway. As for Carnegie and Pullman, they were elected members of the board and took up the position of director. Mr. Scott, too, became a member of the board, and in 1871 all three men were members of the board of the Union Pacific Railway.

In return for securing the necessary funds for the Union Pacific, Carnegie was given $3 million in shares of the company. This payment was kept in Carnegie's safe. After what had happened between the Pennsylvania Railroad and the Union Pacific, the stock of the Union Pacific became much more valuable. It was at this time that Carnegie went off to London to discuss terms of some bonds for building a bridge across the Missouri River from Omaha.

Carnegie had left instructions with his secretary that Mr. Scott was to be allowed access to the safe, for he was part of the business of the Union Pacific. While Carnegie was away in London, Mr. Scott decided to sell the shares of the Union Pacific that he and Carnegie owned.

Carnegie had granted Mr. Scott access to the safe because aside from the fact that Mr. Scott was a business partner, Carnegie felt that the bonds should be within reach of one of his partners if he were away. Carnegie probably never considered that Mr. Scott might actually sell those bonds.

When Carnegie returned from London, he found that he was being pushed aside by the members of the Union Pacific Railroad. He had previously been treated as a partner, and now he was being treated like an outsider.

It was very rare that anyone could say they had worked with a firm as great as the Union Pacific, and now Mr. Scott had just sold their position away! This was the first issue in the relationship between Mr. Scott and Carnegie that caused a slight difference between them.

Both Carnegie and Pullman were not informed of Mr. Scott's decision, and both were quite upset with Mr. Scott's course of action. Pullman responded in a retaliatory manner and once again invested his profits in the shares of the company. Carnegie was very tempted to follow suit, but he understood that it would mean stooping to that level, and, more importantly, it would be unappreciative on his part to cut such a line between him and friend Mr. Scott.

Soon after the incident, Pullman, Mr. Scott, and Carnegie were kicked off the board. This was very difficult for Carnegie to accept, and it was the first thing that was really a dividing wall between him and Mr. Scott. Later, President Thomson of the

Pennsylvania Railroad apologized for the incident and said that since the matter had been left in the hands of Carnegie and Mr. Scott, he concluded that Carnegie had thought that the best course of action was to sell the bonds.

After this regrettable incident with Union Pacific, Carnegie was anxious that he might lose a friend of his, a Mr. Levi P. Morton of Morton, Bliss, and Co. Mr. Morton was somewhat connected with Union Pacific, but after a time he found that Carnegie had nothing to do with selling the bonds.

The contract for the Omaha Bridge was secured, as the people who ordered the bridge had been in league with Union Pacific before Carnegie had ever joined the company. The talks conducted were with the people who ordered the bridge and not with Union Pacific.

Carnegie was unaware of this even though a director of Union Pacific had spoken with him before he left for London.

The negotiations resulted in the people who ordered the bridge purchasing two and a half million bonds.

What also went wrong when Carnegie returned to New York aside from the issue with Union Pacific was that his profit from the bonds and everyone else's, too, was taken by certain people, and they were used to settle their debts. Carnegie had to go without claiming his rightful profit, which was a rather large sum and made nothing for his efforts. He had been swindled out of his share.

Carnegie realized that he was actually still quite green and needed to learn more. He also learned that although most people are trustworthy and honest, you might want to keep an eye on some of them.

Shortly after the incident with Union Pacific, Carnegie was approached by Colonel William Philips, president of the Allegheny Valley Railway. Philips once went to Carnegie's office in New York and said he needed money, and that he could not get any bank in the nation to buy his five million bonds. The bonds were, however, assured by the Pennsylvania Railroad Company.

The bankers had only agreed to purchase them under their terms. He had priced the bonds at ninety cents each, which was considered ridiculously high by the bankers. At the time, bonds of Western railway companies were sold at eighty cents each. After telling him his problem, he wanted to know if Carnegie could help him.

Colonel Philips desperately needed $250,000, and no one was willing to give him that much money—not the banks and not even President Thomson of the Pennsylvania Railroad (the Pennsylvania). The bonds that Colonel Philips was trying to sell were not able to be paid for in gold—only in American dollars. This made the bonds unfit to be sold to outside banks or investors.

Carnegie knew that the Pennsylvania Railroad owned an impressive quantity of 6 percent gold bonds of the Philadelphia as well as the Erie Railroad Company. Carnegie thought about trading the Philadelphia and Erie bonds for the Allegheny Railway bonds that had an interest payment of 7 percent.

Carnegie contacted President Thomson and asked him if the Pennsylvania Railroad Company could lend $250,000 with interest to the Allegheny Railway.

President Thomson willingly agreed, and Colonel Philips was delighted. Philips offered Carnegie the opportunity of purchasing his five million bonds, each being priced at ninety cents. He gave Carnegie sixty days to give his answer.

Carnegie proposed a trade to President Thomson—a trade of the Allegheny Railway bonds in return for the Philadelphia and Erie Railroad bonds. Carnegie then went to London. After arriving at Queenstown, he contacted the Barings of another financial bank in Britain. Carnegie said that he was selling a security that they would most definitely want to purchase. Later, when Carnegie arrived in London, he found a note asking him to call the Barings.

Carnegie telephoned the Barings the following morning and met them shortly afterward. Carnegie was able to get everything in order, and the Barings were willing to purchase the bonds by the time the meeting was over. After the bank sold the bonds to an investor, a customer of theirs, they would subtract their fee from the amount and furnish the loan with 5 percent interest. Carnegie was bound to earn $500,000 in profit by the time everything was said and done.

The necessary paperwork had to be created, but just before Carnegie left the banking house, a certain Mr. Russell Sturgis stopped him and said that Mr. Baring himself was visiting London the following morning, and that they would wait to sign the papers in front of him. Carnegie was told to call at 2:00 the following afternoon.

Carnegie felt that he should telegraph President Thomson, although he had a nagging feeling that he should not. Something didn't feel right. He thus decided to do nothing at the moment and walked back to the Langham Hotel, where he was staying. When Carnegie arrived, he found a messenger waiting for him. The message was a not from the Barings. It was sealed and unopened.

Certain problems involving Chancellor Bismarck of Germany had caused problems for many people, and the Barings contacted Carnegie. They said they could not carry on with the plans and could not try to advise Mr. Baring into proceeding with them either.

The breaking of the deal had seemed so unlikely just a little while earlier, and now it had actually happened. Carnegie was not too disturbed by the breakup of the plans and was just happy that he did contact President Thomson to update him.

Carnegie did not go back to the Barings for this and instead turned to J.S. Morgan & Co., the bank of Junius S. Morgan. He did not go to Morgan at first, but the bank was dealing with several American issues, and Carnegie went to Morgan to complete his duty. In the end, the Philadelphia and Erie Railway bonds were sold to Morgan's bank for a cheaper price than what the Barings had agreed to.

Carnegie did not go straight to Morgan when he arrived in London because Mr. Philips of the Allegheny Railway had said he had already tried Morgan's banking house in the United States, and they did not take him up on his offer. Carnegie thus thought that the banking house of Morgan in London might also feel the same as their office in the States. Carnegie did, however, make it a point to always go first to Morgan. Whenever Carnegie had some proposition to offer, Morgan would try to take it up, but if he couldn't, he would get another bank that was not a competitor and tell Carnegie to go there.

One day Carnegie said to Mr. Morgan, "Mr. Morgan, I will give you an idea and help you to carry it forward if you will give me one-quarter of all the money you made by acting upon it." Morgan replied, "That seems fair, and as I have the option to act upon it, or not, certainly we ought to be willing to pay you a quarter of the profit."

Carnegie talked about how he had traded the Allegheny Railway bonds for the Philadelphia and Erie Railroad bonds. He also spoke of how the Pennsylvania Railroad was guaranteeing the Philadelphia and Erie Railroad bonds. Carnegie went on to say that if a good enough price was put up for the bonds the Pennsylvania might just sell them. At the time, everyone was buying American bonds, and Carnegie said that he could float the bonds. Morgan agreed to Carnegie's plan.

This would basically mean that the Pennsylvania Railroad would sell its Philadelphia and Erie Railroad bonds and make back the money it had loaned.

President Thomson of the Pennsylvania Railroad was then in Paris, and Carnegie met him there. He told him what he had spoken about with Mr. Morgan of J.S. Morgan & Co. Carnegie understood that the Pennsylvania Railroad always needed money, and that's why he knew this plan would work. Carnegie asked Thomson to name a price that Morgan would then place on the bonds. The price he presented was quite high for the time but still plausible. Morgan bought a portion of the bonds, and the Allegheny bonds were put up for sale, and the Pennsylvania Railroad Company was able to make back its money.

Unfortunately, not too many bonds were sold by the time the financial crisis of 1873 struck. At the time, Carnegie was receiving money from the bonds from the son of Junius S. Morgan, John Pierpont Morgan, also known as J.P. Morgan. One day John Morgan said to Carnegie, "My father has cabled to ask whether you wish to sell out your interest in that idea you gave him." Carnegie responded by saying, "Yes, I do. In these days, I will sell anything for money." Morgan then asked, "Well, what would you take?"

Carnegie thought that he now had $50,000 in his credit, and he said that he would take $60,000. The following morning John Morgan spoke to Carnegie once again and handed him two checks for $75,000. One was a $10,000 check, and the other check was for $60,000. Morgan spoke, saying, "Mr. Carnegie, you were mistaken. You sold out for $10,000 less than the statement showed to your credit. It now shows not fifty but sixty thousand to your credit, and the additional ten makes seventy."

Carnegie then held out the $10,000 check, offering it to Morgan. Carnegie said, "Well, that is something worthy of you. Will you please accept these ten thousand with my best wishes?" Morgan, being an honest man replied, "No, thank you, I cannot do that."

Carnegie has noted that it is this virtue of honor that keeps a business alive. What is more important than abiding by the laws is to be honorable.

From this point onward, Carnegie and the Morgans were dear friends.

In Carnegie's opinion, one must always be fair and honorable in business. He said that a business must be known not just for how it is legally righteous but that the managers, owners, and the people who run the business have a clean and respectable reputation not because they fear the law but because of their own virtue.

In his opinion, men who deal with stocks and wish to run a clean business can't do it.

After the incident with Union Pacific, Mr. Scott took up the project of building the Texas Pacific Railway. He called on Carnegie to meet with him in Philadelphia, which Carnegie did. He met with Mr. Scott and some of his friends, one of them being J.N. McCullough, who was at the time vice president of the Pennsylvania Railroad Company.

A loan had previously been secured for the Texas Pacific Railway but had not materialized and was applied for again by J.S. Morgan & Co. However, the only condition under which the bank would provide the loan was if Carnegie were to formally associate himself with those applying for the loan.

Carnegie did not want to do this and was then asked the hurtful question of whether or not he was willing to ruin his friends by not supporting them. Carnegie used all of his money for his manufacturing business. Furthermore, many people depended on him, such as his brother, his wife and his children, Mr. Henry Phipps, and Mr. Andrew Kloman.

Carnegie had already warned Mr. Scott against building such an important railway until he had a sufficient amount of money. He reminded Mr. Scott of his warning and said that such a long railway line could not be built if they were using temporary loans. Carnegie had previously paid $250,000 to be part of the venture, although he did not look favorably on the matter. He was not going to persuaded, however, to deliberately provide business for a manufacturing company that was not his and his partners' company. Carnegie understood that he would not be able to pay back the loan from Morgan's bank at the end of sixty days or even his share of it. In addition, this was just one loan. For Mr. Scott and his partners to continue building the Texas Pacific Railway, they would have to get more loans, which was another headache.

The biggest difficulty for Carnegie was that this was yet another disagreement between him and Mr. Scott.

Soon after the meeting, Carnegie met with Mr. Scott and his friends in Philadelphia, but the meeting did not go well. Some of the most prestigious and promising men of the country were in great difficulty. Mr. Scott sustained great ridicule and humiliation but could only take so much. Due to his stress and state of mind, Mr. Scott died suddenly.

In Carnegie's opinion, Mr. Scott was easily affected.

As for some of the partners of Mr. Scott in the venture to build the Texas Pacific Railway, such as Mr. Baird and Mr. McManus, they too died prematurely. Both of them were not in the railway business, but like Carnegie, were in the business of manufacturing.

Carnegie said that if one is going to undertake a business venture, they should ask themselves these two questions: (1) would you be able to pay for all that might require your payment?, and (2) would you be willing to spend the money for a friend of yours that you support?

Carnegie said that if you could answer "yes" to both questions, then you could most definitely carry on with the venture. If you only answer "yes" to the first question, then you should think about immediately paying all that is required of you. If you have obtained a loan from a bank, the longer you don't pay off the loan, the longer you stay on their leash!

Once you clear the deck of all your debts and outstanding payments, you are free.

Although Carnegie refused to back the loan, he was called to come the following morning to New York with the people who were in the venture. Carnegie was happy to oblige. One other person had been called to join them, a Mr. Anthony Drexel. As the car drove on, Mr. McCullough said that he realized that all of the people in the car except for Carnegie were fools. He said that Carnegie had paid for all of his shares and did not have any debts whatsoever. He also said that all of them should have been as fortunate as he was.

Anthony Drexel then asked Carnegie to tell them how he had been able to believe that way. Carnegie responded by saying that he did so by not joining in something or attaching himself to something that he knew he could not pay when the time came. That was his principle. That kept him free of debt.

Sticking to this principle kept both Carnegie and his partners safe. They were all very strict about not involving themselves with large amounts of money that they could not pay back when called for. The only scenario in which they did this was when they were doing it for the benefit of their company.

While all this was happening, Carnegie regularly traveled to Europe, where he conducted talks for bonds' financial assets. In total, of all the negotiations Carnegie conducted on the continent, he had sold a total of $30 million. At the time, New York was not known as a financial center to those in London, for the Atlantic cable did not yet exist.

At this time, the bankers of London were also giving their balances to such places as Berlin, Paris, and Vienna instead of the United States. This allowed the banks to get a little more money from the interest rates. America was at the time thought to be not too safe for outside bankers wanting to make a profit by Europeans.

Carnegie was at full liberty to take several weeklong trips, and when he did he found himself not worrying about his business while he was away because Mr. Thomas Carnegie, his brother, and his friend Mr. Henry Phipps were taking care of the business very well indeed. He could trust them to look after the business while he was away.

Due to the financial success in negotiating with banks and getting them to buy securities and bonds, he was often given opportunities to enter the world of finance, although he declined. He preferred manufacturing more than he did dealing with money and stocks.

Carnegie thought more about making things and selling them rather than buying and selling pieces of paper. The money he made from his business, instead of investing it in other people, he invested in his own business, making it grow ever larger.

In the past, the Keystone Bridge Works had established workshops, which were rented out by other people. Furthermore, ten acres of land was acquired by Carnegie and his partners in Lawrenceville. They built several new shops there.

The Union Iron Mills was also perfected and improved, with more and more features being added. In the end, these add-ons and improvements made the Union Iron Mills the most prominent steel manufacturing concern in the United States.

Carnegie's business was prospering, and the profits he earned were reinvested in the business, used to buy new machinery, enlarge the business, build more mills and more land, and all that was necessary to expand the business.

Carnegie and his friends began building some rails for the Pennsylvania Railroad Company. More specifically, they were to build rails for the company in states to the west, but Carnegie soon pulled out of the venture. He followed the motto "Don't put all one's eggs in one basket." He thought that the proper way to go about things was to put everything into what you were doing and then always concentrate on that. He was not saying to confine yourself to just one line of work but to invest all your money in your business. He was also saying that if you are unable to invest your money in a business that will not grow and expand then you should invest your money in first-class bonds and shares so that you may receive a respectable profit. Furthermore, he was saying that to be successful you have to focus on your business and not be distracted by investing in others or running ten different businesses at once.

Carnegie's trip to Britain enabled him to meet authorities in the iron and steel manufacturing business. He was able to meet Bessemer, the creator of the Bessemer process; Sir Bernard Samuelson; Edward Martin; Sir Lothian Bell; Sir Windsor Richards; Evans; Bingley; and several other people.

Carnegie soon became a member of the council of the British Iron and Steel Institute and soon after that the president of the institution. He was the first president of the organization who was not British. This was something really grand indeed, and despite the glamor of being president of the British Iron and Steel Institute, Carnegie turned down the offer at first, fearing that he might not be able to serve the organization well enough because he lived in the United States.

Because Carnegie's bridge-building concern was using wrought iron to build its bridges and other things, Carnegie and his partners decided to get a blast furnace to make pig iron, the metal that is produced after being melted in a furnace. Pig iron is also known as crude iron.

Thus, in 1870, the Lucy Furnace, named after Carnegie's sister-in-law and the wife of his brother, the daughter of William Coleman, came into existence. If Carnegie and his partners understood the implications of getting a blast furnace for their business, they would put the matter off to a later time. Older manufacturers negatively viewed the expansion of Carnegie and his partners' business. Carnegie and his partners, however, did not care for negative mind-sets.

They believed that they would succeed by getting just one blast furnace.

Guesses were made for the cost of the blast furnace but only half of the real cost. Andrew Kloman did not know anything about blast furnaces, but this didn't matter, and no serious mistake or mishap occurred.

The Lucy Furnace was a big success. It performed better than Carnegie and his partners expected it to, and the furnace was melting one hundred tons of steel every day for one week, which had never happened before.

Carnegie and his partners' business was at the top of the list in terms of the number of products made every day, and many people came to watch what was being done.

Just because Carnegie and his partners had a blast furnace didn't mean their business would do well, and sometimes things did not turn out not as well as they hoped.

After the Civil War, the price of iron had decreased from ninety cents per pound to a mere three cents. Despite this drop, Carnegie and his partners' company was able to hold on. The financial manager of the business was always releasing the necessary money to solve pressing problems. Most troubling was the manufacture of pig iron in the workshops. Carnegie and his partners were able to make the acquaintance of one of the brothers who owned the company, Whitwell Brothers of England, a company that sold blast furnaces. Mr. Whitwell was able to advise

Carnegie what to do, and after Carnegie and his partners incorporated his design, their furnace worked flawlessly. Whitwell was one of the visitors who came to see the Lucy Furnace, and Carnegie told him of the problem his business was facing. He replied by saying, "That comes from the angle of the bell being wrong." He went on to tell Carnegie how to fix the problem, but Kloman was unable to fully grasp what to do.

Carnegie said that two glass models of blast furnaces should be made and two bells as well. One of the models was to be a model of the Lucy Furnace, and the other model was to be a model of a blast furnace with the improvements that Mr. Whitwell had suggested. The two models were made, and experiments were conducted with both of them. What Whitwell had said was true. The Lucy Furnace's bell placed the large pieces of metal on the sides, and in the middle was a mass of metal that became extremely dense, which proved the metal was largely unaffected by the blast. As for Whitman's bell, the bell placed the pieces of iron in the center, which left only the surrounding part dense. This was what made the Lucy Furnace much more effective.

Carnegie has described Mr. Whitwell as a man who was cordially open with his knowledge and was not reserved simply because he might be giving away a secret ingredient. He very openly and willingly told Carnegie how to improve the Lucy Furnace, and thanks to him, Carnegie and his partners' steel business improved, with the Lucy Furnace performing much better. The Whitwell brothers became dear friends of Carnegie and remained so. This surviving Whitwell brother became the next president of the British Iron and Steel Institute after Carnegie.

Chapter 11 Carnegie's Steel Business

In 1870, chemistry was not at all related to steel—at least it wasn't thought to be. Unlike his fellow steel manufacturers, Carnegie decided to include the study of chemistry in his business, which resulted in even greater success. He has noted that the manager of the blast furnaces was always very rude and unrefined. He was a person who knew how to dole out punishments to set an example so that no one else would be a problem. He was also supposed to be able to miraculously find water or an oil well as how some people do with hazel rods.

The Lucy Furnace, the first blast furnace of Carnegie's steel company, did not work too well at first because there were several different types of limestone and ore. The furnace was always working with coke, which are the impure elements that are the by-product of heating steel. Finally, after the Lucy Furnace had experienced several problems, Carnegie and his partners decided to remedy the situation. The rough and clueless man who managed the furnace was dismissed, and a new man was put in charge. This gentleman was Henry M.

Curry. He was a shipping clerk, but due to his impressive performance, Carnegie and his partners made him manager of the Lucy Furnace.

Mr. Henry Phipps, a friend of Carnegie, was the ultimate manager of the Lucy Furnace. He came to see the furnace every day and kept it working well. The Lucy Furnace was simply very large compared with other blast furnaces, which made it more prone to faltering.

Instead of attending church on Sunday mornings, Mr. Phipps went to see the furnace, while his sister and father went to Mass. Furthermore, if he were to go with his father and sister to church, his prayers would be about the Lucy Furnace!

After having appointed Mr. Curry to be manager of the Lucy Furnace, a chemist was hired to work with him. This chemist was Dr. Fricke, a German gentleman. Dr. Fricke enlightened Carnegie and his partners about several things. First of all, the iron sold by mines that were thought to be good were actually not. In reality, they had less iron than was believed. In contrast, the mines that were discredited and were not at all popular were really the ones with better ores. Thanks to Dr. Fricke and the use of chemistry, pig-iron manufacturing was able to flow smoothly in Carnegie and his partners' business.

When the Lucy Furnace once needed to produce an exceptional result for the good of the company, the ore that was going to be used was replaced by less impressive ore. This ore produced less than one-third the amount of iron of the superior ore. The error was caused because too much lime was used. In the end, nothing was gained.

Carnegie and his partners were in a far better position than their elder competitors. No steel manufacturer had ever engaged a chemist to work with them. They said they could not pay to have a chemist, but they were really worse off without one.

In the end, the Lucy Furnace was a good investment. It proved very profitable for Carnegie and his partners because they had chemistry on their side.

In 1872, Carnegie and his partners built a second blast furnace, now feeling that they knew how to properly use it. They also had more financial resources to use for the second furnace. In the past, several iron ore mines were not earning much and were not too popular, but they were having their goods purchased by Carnegie's company. On the other hand, the steel mines that were well known and said to produce good-quality ores did not have Carnegie's company as a customer.

One of the mines that Carnegie's company did purchase ore from was a mine called Pilot Knob in Missouri. The ore produced from this mine was very rich in silicon and had a low amount of phosphorus. Only a small amount could be used at a time so as to not damage the furnace. In truth, the ore was very valuable, and Carnegie and his partners bought large quantities of it. The owners of Pilot Knob were quite happy to have a good customer.

For some time, Carnegie and his firm were spending more money on eliminating the phosphoric cinders produced by the blast furnaces than it would have cost to buy pure cinder from other steel manufacturers. Every once in a while, a steel manufacturer had the bright idea to use his blast furnace to smelt flue cinder, but a blast furnace was not suitable for doing this work. Thus, the steel manufacturers of Pittsburgh were always discarding the cinders by throwing them into the river.

A steel-making company that an associate of Carnegie's Mr. Chisholm was working for was throwing their roll scale into the river, finding it utterly valueless. Carnegie then decided to obtain the roll scale. He contacted the son of a man who, among others, had come up with a method to obtain iron through a "direct process" as Carnegie described. The son agreed to do so, and he purchased the roll scale from the company Mr. Chisholm was working in for a mere half a dollar per ton! Carnegie was playing a joke on Mr. Chisholm, waiting for him to find out what was really happening. Unfortunately, Mr. Chisholm died prematurely and never realized Carnegie's joke.

After Mr. Chisholm's passing, those who assumed his position began to follow in the footsteps of Carnegie's steel manufacturing company.

Carnegie's time in the steel industry always showed him improving his business and reinvesting his money into it. Whenever his workers were not happy about something, Carnegie knew how to solve the issue, and they would be pleased.

Chapter 12 The Workers Strike

The workers at Carnegie's steel mill in Homestead led a strike, with the most prominent figure being a Mr. McLuckie, a splendid mechanic who worked at the mill. McLuckie was paid well, was married, and had a rather nice and comfortable life, but he still chose to support the strikers. As he had been given the position of burgomaster, he felt he could arrest the police officers who had come to the mill to keep everything peaceful. Everything was becoming worse and worse. McLuckie had even gone so far as to order that the police officers be murdered!

Carnegie was in the Highlands of Scotland at the time and only knew about the strike two days after it had begun. McLuckie would say several years later after everything was over that he believed that if Carnegie had been there everything would have been fine.
After the strike was put to an end, McLuckie had to flee from the authorities. He was charged with rioting, treason, murder, and several other crimes. He ran and hid and waited until everyone calmed down and forgot about what had happened. Aside from fleeing and

hiding, his wife passed away, leaving him utterly alone. An associate of Carnegie's, the man who edited his autobiography, a John Van Dyke, bumped into McLuckie while he was trying to get a job at a mine that was fifteen miles away from the Mexican town of La Noria Verde. It was decided by all steel manufacturing concerns that they would not hire McLuckie, and thus he had decided to go to Mexico to find a job. Securing a position at the Mexican mine wasn't very easy, though, for the Mexicans wanted an inexperienced and ignorant person who would accept low wages.

After spending some time with McLuckie, Van Dyke wrote to Carnegie and said that he thought McLuckie had been treated unfairly. Carnegie replied and wrote with a pencil in the margin of the letter the following words, "Give McLuckie all the money he wants, but don't mention my name."

Van Dyke then contacted McLuckie and offered him some money, but McLuckie refused to accept, saying that he would make it on his own. Eventually, McLuckie was able to get a job as a well driver, and his life improved. He even remarried, marrying a Mexican lady. Finally, when all was better, Van Dyke told McLuckie the truth about the offer of money he had made sometime earlier. He said that it was Carnegie who had offered the money and not him. Surprised, McLuckie responded by saying, "Well, that was damned white of Andy, wasn't it?"

McLuckie really was appreciative of what Carnegie had done and even wrote a poem for him called "Just by The Way."

Another strike that took place involved the workers of the blast furnaces who worked producing steel rails. The workers had threatened to abandon the furnaces unless their salaries were raised to a higher amount by 4:00 on a Monday. In Carnegie's mind, if you make an agreement with someone and that person breaks or violates the agreement, there is no point in making another agreement with them. Despite his belief, Carnegie traveled from New York down to the striking workers to settle the matter. Once he was there, he called for the meeting of the blast furnace committee, the sole body that was leading the strike. He also called for the converting works and mill committees even though they were not involved in the strike. At the meeting, Carnegie spoke first to the leaders of the mill and converting works committees, asking them both whether or not they had an agreement with the company to work until the end of the year. Both answered in the affirmative. When Carnegie posed the same question to the leader of the blast furnace committee, Kelly, an Irishman, replied that he wasn't certain. A piece of paper was then passed around to all of the men seated, and they were to sign it. When it was Kelly's turn, he didn't go over what was on the paper and simply signed his name, not understanding what signing that piece of paper meant. Captain Jones, the manager, who was present at the meeting, immediately jumped up and censured Kelly for just signing the paper. Carnegie then said that he himself had signed many things that he did not fully read. He said that Kelly had been compelled to do so but went on to say that he should in the future read what he was about to sign for his own good. Carnegie went on to say that perhaps the blast furnace committee could continue their work for another four months and then properly go over the document they should sign if they wanted to renew their agreement. No one said anything to this proposition.

Carnegie then said, "Gentlemen of the Blast Furnace Committee, you have threatened our firm that you will break your agreement and that you will leave these blast furnaces unless you get a favorable answer to your threat by four o'clock today. It is not yet three, but your answer is ready. You may leave the blast furnaces. The grass will grow around them before we yield to your threat. The worst day that labor has ever seen in this world is that day in which it dishonors itself by breaking its agreement. You have your answer."

The members of the blast furnace committee then exited the room, and when Mr. Kelly reached the furnaces where the workers were waiting, he urged them to return to work. Carnegie was able to keep the blast furnace committee working, and all was well. Mr. Kelly even became an admirer of Carnegie from that moment forward.

The second strike involved the workers of the steel rail mills. They had sworn together that they would quit their jobs unless it was agreed they would be given higher salaries. That particular year was not too good for business, and even other steel manufacturers were decreasing the salaries of their workers. Because of this, Carnegie's company could not raise their workers' pay. Despite the low amount of revenue that the company was making, the workers of the steel rail mill in Pittsburgh still wanted higher salaries. If they were not going to be given higher pay, then they would abandon the mills.

Carnegie traveled to Pittsburgh to meet with the workers but was informed when he arrived that they were not there. The mills had been abandoned before the workers had originally planned to. The men had left and had decided to meet with Carnegie the following day. Carnegie said they could not meet him the following day for he would not be in Pittsburgh.

Carnegie then spoke to his partners and informed them that he was returning to New York.

Not long after the steel rail mill workers received Carnegie's message, they asked to meet with him in the afternoon before Carnegie left for New York. Carnegie welcomed their meeting.

When the workers came into his office, he told them that their leader, Mr. Bennett, said that Carnegie would take care of them. He went on to say that Mr. Bennett was correct and pointed out that Mr. Bennett had said that Carnegie was not able to fight. Carnegie corrected that by saying that he could, and that Mr. Bennett had not realized Carnegie was Scotch. Carnegie added that he would not fight his men, and the works would be started if two-thirds of the men voted in favor of starting the mills. The meeting came to an end.

Two weeks later Carnegie received a message at his house. The names of two workers in Carnegie's company and the name of a reverend were listed on the message. Carnegie asked his servant to check whether or not the two workers were among those who had shut down the furnaces before they were meant to do relative to an agreement. He was told that the two men were not among the workers who had violated the agreement with the company. Carnegie then said he would be glad to meet them.

During the meeting, the minister brought up the question of the striking workers. Carnegie then asked whether or not they had already voted and learned that they had not. Carnegie then said that he was not supposed to discuss this until the furnaces were restarted. Carnegie then showed them around New York.

The men soon returned to Pittsburgh, with nothing more said about the situation with the banked blast furnaces and the striking workers. The men had also now voted on the question of restarting or leaving the furnaces cold. The majority of the workers voted for restarting them. Carnegie thus traveled to Pittsburgh, where he presented to them the sliding scale for a second time. The sliding scale basically meant that the amount of money made from the the company's production determined the amount of money the workers received. This, in Carnegie's opinion, closely connected labor and money. When one prospered, the other did, and when one failed, the other shared the hardship.

In the end, the sliding scale was agreed to, and when everything was said and done, Mr. Bennett asked Carnegie for a favor. Carnegie responded by saying that he would agree to a reasonable request. Mr. Bennett then said that he wished for the "officers of the union," as he said it, to sign the agreement. Carnegie immediately agreed and asked for a favor in return. He asked that after the officers had signed the agreement the workers would too. He explained that if only the officers signed it the workers might feel upset with the decision of their superiors. A man standing next to Mr. Bennett then whispered in his ear, "By golly, the jig's up!" The "jig" really was up. Carnegie understood that if he did not grant Mr. Bennett his wish to allow the officers to sign the agreement it would have been used as an excuse for conflict between the men and the company.

That same sliding scale lasted for many years and was extremely successful among the workers.

Carnegie was often able to handle situations with style. He once had to meet with a certain group of men working for his company who had unreasonable requests. Carnegie had been told that a man who secretly ran a pub was dealing with these men.

He met with them and their leader, the owner of the secret bar. At the meeting, Carnegie was seated at one end of the table, while the leader of the workers making the demands was seated at the other. After Carnegie spoke to the other men around the table, suggesting a settlement, their leader prepared to leave and slowly put on his hat. Before he even got up, Carnegie spoke, "Sir, you are in the presence of gentlemen! Please be so good as to take your hat off or leave the room!"

No one said anything. It was clear that the man was in a tight spot. If he left the room, it would be considered rude, and if he stayed and removed his hat, he had been defeated by Carnegie. The man then removed his hat and placed it on the floor. He was completely silent for the rest of the meeting.

This showed that Carnegie knew how to deal with people. He knew how to control people by understanding how they behave and think, and he thus knew the right words to say to get someone to do something. In this case, he was speaking to a bully, as Carnegie called him. He knew how to force him to do something by putting him in a tight spot.

Chapter 13 Books & Marriage

With several friends, Carnegie took a trip around the world and wrote down his experiences, not at all intending for the book to become popular. The book was entitled *Round the World*. After being published, many distinguished people read and loved it. One of them said that he had never read any book but his ledger for several years, and that Carnegie's was the first he had ever read during those years. Another said that he had read the book from cover to cover. One said that he had not been able to sleep, having started the book and finished reading it at 2:00 the next morning. The book was very popular.

Just after 1885, Carnegie fell ill from typhoid fever. Several days before he left New York, he had not been feeling very well, and he became more ill after he returned. Doctors and nurses were called in to nurse him. Shortly after Carnegie fell ill, his mother did as well. At the same time, his brother, Thomas, also fell ill. While Carnegie was recovering, his brother and mother passed away. He was deeply affected when he found out. He felt alone and deeply shaken. It was as if he had been rocked to the core. This was when he got married. A friend of his, Louise Whitfield, would become his wife. She had already known Carnegie but said that she could not be with him for she had to care for her family. When Carnegie lost his family, he was also in need, and that is when Miss Whitfield turned her attention to Carnegie and married him. On April 22, 1887, the couple became husband and wife.

Carnegie has described his wife as a person who cared for all others and was a true "peace-maker," as he called her. He described his wife as the person who filled the gap in his heart after he lost his mother and brother. The pair were really very suitable for each other, with Louise taking care of him, and Mr. Carnegie feeling on top of the world with her by his side. She meant the world to him, and Carnegie said in his autobiography that he could not even begin to imagine a life without her.

Ten years after the couple married, on March 30, 1897, Margaret Carnegie was born. Louise had named their daughter after her husband's mother, and she asked for one thing from Carnegie. She said that now that they had a child they should be in a home where they could stay in peace—a home that was theirs. She meant that they should not always have to move but stay put. She said that their house should be in the Highlands of Scotland. Carnegie wholeheartedly agreed, and Skibo

Castle was bought as the official home of the Carnegie family.

Living in the Highlands was really wonderful for him, as the cool, pure, and fresh air did him good.

Conclusion

After having made so much money from his business, Carnegie decided that it was time to distribute that wealth. When it was confirmed that he was going to retire, John Pierpont Morgan, son of Junius S. Morgan with whom Carnegie had previously dealt, bought Carnegie's steel company in 1901. Now a retired man, Carnegie lived the rest of his days giving to the public. He presented parks, libraries, university institutions, and funds to help thousands of people.

Pittencrief Glen, a wonderful place in Scotland according to Carnegie, was one of his many gifts to the public. His uncle, Bailie Morrison, had wanted to obtain for the town of Dunfermline a portion of the palace land in Dunfermline and the Dunfermline Abbey.

Carnegie's uncles, Morrison and Lauder, would later be the ones to lead a group of men to break down a specified wall. In the end, the Laird of Pittencrieff declared that no Morrison was to be allowed into the Glen, and thus Carnegie was not allowed in.

When he grew up, however, he would be able to buy the Glen and become Laird of Pittencrieff himself. He would then proudly present Pittencrieff Glen to the public, a place where he hoped people would find peace.

One of the funds that Carnegie created was the Hero Fund. He had learned of an incident when the superior of a coal mine had sacrificed his life for the survival of the miners, and this inspired him to start the Hero Fund. The hero who had given his life had wanted to help in any way he could and lost his life in caring for them.

The Hero Fund was meant to provide financial support for the families left behind by heroes who sacrificed their lives to save others. Carnegie did not think that anyone would act as a hero simply for financial rewards. No. Carnegie believed that a true hero carried out heroic deeds not because he yearned for his reward but because he wanted to do good. If you ever do something *for* the reward, you are not a hero no matter how good or kind that act may be.

Carnegie also helped universities that were not doing too well at the time.

His acts of kindness and charity greatly benefited thousands of people in many ways. I will mention three: happiness, education, and money.

J.P. Morgan

The Life and Deals of

America's Banker

J.P. Morgan

The Life and Deals of America's Banker

Insight and Analysis into the Founder of
Modern Finance and the American
Banking System

JR MacGregor

Introduction

John Pierpont Morgan Sr., also known as J.P. Morgan, revolutionized the financial world. He brought America and by extension the entire world into the twenty-first century by infusing the trade and banking industries with his ideas.

He was responsible for creating many structured and organized entities as trusts, one of the largest banks in the world, the largest steel production company in America, and one of the largest railroads in the country.

Along the way, he endured a lot of pain and hardship but overcame it by focusing on his work, which was his elixir.

On a personal level, Morgan was highly complex in his behavior, oscillating from total confidence to retiring within himself to absolute diffidence and self-effacement. His confidence was marked with silence, and his diffidence was marked with bravado.

Add to this his expensive upbringing and it becomes difficult to really peg this towering man of vision and intellect.

Morgan's father was his initial role model and guide in navigating the world of international business. Morgan himself was astute, with a unique understanding of money. It was almost a visceral appreciation of how money worked and how it could be harnessed to leverage other resources. Money to him was like a natural resource that could be harnessed and utilized.

At the turn of the nineteenth century, America had begun to transition from an agrarian society and a colonist's mind-set to an industrialized country with a nation-state mind-set. With that change in social activity and aggregate mind-set came the need to have a higher derivative of monetary and fiscal policy and all the tools commensurate with that elevation. In other words, the world of banking needed to change, which included public as well as private finance.

The once simple and geometric relationship between trade and finance had changed. What was just a simple relationship between saver and lender was now inadequate. What was now required had not yet been contemplated. This new world of high finance was only obvious to such men as George Peabody, Marcus Goldman, and Junius Pierpont Morgan.

New instruments were developed to finance endeavors. New structures were created, and many of these came about by men who blurred the lines between public and private finance.

J.P. Morgan ascended through the business world with great difficulty but with a powerful imagination, constantly combating anti-monopoly politicians and presidents who were opposed to large business.

Among the robber barons and titans of the period, J.P. Morgan stood at the center. If it were not for J.P. Morgan, Andrew Carnegie, as successful as he was, would not have been able to sell Carnegie Steel for $480 million, making him a very wealthy man.

J.P. Morgan was a man of exceptional character. He was determined, aggressive, and ambitious and stopped at nothing to get what he wanted.

As smart and sharp as he was, however, Morgan created his banking empire only during the last thirteen years of his life. His early years were spent trying, making mistakes, and developing his abilities. In his lifetime, he worked with two different presidents to avert market failures. He was able to stop the bleeding in the financial markets when they crashed. Twice.

He was also the man behind the Panama Canal. Just as important as the physical structure that cut its way from the Pacific Ocean to the Atlantic, the financial structure was equally important in being able to pay for the materials, equipment, and labor. It was Morgan who structured it and raised the money for it.

He died with a net worth of less than $30 billion, adjusted for inflation today, but he controlled more than 100 billion. If he saw fit to buy something, he could raise an almost unheard amount of money.

By wielding such vast sums of money, he amassed a tremendous amount of power and influence in the last fifteen years of his life.

But his life was not easy. Even though he could sail the Hudson in his private yacht or buy any piece of art that his heart desired, the degree of personal and public stress he endured was immeasurable. Some attribute this stress to smoking as many as twenty cigars a day.

Even though his life was stressful, he enjoyed collecting art and sailing. He was a man of great accomplishment and commensurate success, which hid the peak insecurities and accompanying anxiety

He was afflicted with many health issues and physical problems, which made him unhappy, insecure, and sensitive. In spite of his anxieties and weaknesses, though, he created one of the largest banking houses in the world only to be broken down by the then trust-busting U.S. government.

Chapter 1 Background

John Pierpont Morgan Senior's great-great-great-great grandfather was Miles Morgan, a man from the seventeenth century. He had traveled from Wales to Massachusetts Bay in 1626. That was the first time a Morgan stepped onto the shores of the New World.

Pierpont's paternal grandfather, Joseph Morgan III, was the man who reorganized the Hartford Fire Insurance Company to form the Aetna (Fire) Insurance Company.

Pierpont's maternal grandfather was John Pierpont, a minister and poet. He was eventually removed from his place because of his radical views, and he was also an abolitionist.

Pierpont's maternal uncle, James Lord Pierpont, was a cofounder of Yale University and a songwriter whose most famous composition is "Jingle Bells." The song had originally been published as "The One-Horse Open Sleigh" in 1857.

Those are impressive accomplishments to be concentrated in two houses—the Morgans and the Pierponts.

J.P. Morgan was born to Junius Spencer Morgan and Juliet Pierpont April 17, 1837, in Hartford, Connecticut.

During his lifetime, J.P. Morgan liked to be addressed as Pierpont, his mother's maiden name, which we will also do in this book.

When Pierpont was a young boy, his grandfather, Joseph Morgan, would take him to the Episcopal Church every Sunday. It was something Pierpont loved to do. While in church, his favorite activity was singing hymns along with the choir. He would sing loud and proud and feel elated at the end of every service.

At school, he had the natural characteristics of a leader and exhibited it among his fellow classmates. While he attended many schools and never stayed in one school for very long unlike most children, he learned how to acclimate quickly to each school. Whether he was in America or Europe, Pierpont was able to pick out his comrades and shun those who were of no use to him.

His father raised him with a very specific vision in mind. He wanted Pierpont to be a captain of commerce and industry.

Unfortunately, serious health problems impeded Pierpont's education and progress. As a child, he suffered from headaches and other illnesses that often confined him to his bed.

When he was forced to stay home and recover, he often played solitaire. It was against his grain to just sit around and do nothing. Even when he experienced a migraine, he would find it unacceptable to lie in bed and wait for it to pass. Solitaire became his ally against the pain and a companion during times of loneliness. In later years, it would also be a panacea for frayed nerves.

When Pierpont's health improved, he passed his time by attending exhibitions of art in some of the finest galleries in New York, London, and Paris.

Art touched his soul and chased the blues away. The prospect of attending a gallery or viewing art would instantly place him in better spirits only to be bested by the actual event. It could bring sunshine to Pierpont's internal demons, which would attack at a moment's notice.

His youthful exposure to art and artists made Pierpont an aficionado, which was further enhanced by his early foray into art collection.

By his death, his art collection was worth more than $45 million. That was in 1913. Not accounting for the appreciation in the intrinsic value of the art and just looking at the purchasing power of the currency today, this would now amount to $1.1 billion.

In 1848, when Pierpont was eleven years old, he entered the Hartford Public School and shortly afterward transferred to the Episcopal Academy in Cheshire, also in Connecticut. A few years later, in 1851, Pierpont entered the English School of Boston. This school trained students for a life in the world of business.

Unfortunately for Pierpont's studies and his own future feelings, he was stricken with rheumatic fever in 1852. He was sent to the Azores to recover and returned to Boston to continue his work about a year later. This illness left him with one leg shorter than the other, causing him to limp for the rest of his life. This was the first source of insecurity that struck him, and he was only fifteen years old.

At this age, how a male interacts with those around him and sees himself in the mirror is critical for how he develops in his late teens. In Pierpont's case that was marred by his ailments and limp. It was compounded by his inability to play sports. In time, this lack of physical activity led to gaining weight and clumsy self-perception.

After Pierpont graduated from high school, his father sent him to a village in Switzerland, which was known as La Tour-de-Peilz in the canton of Vaud. He went there to attend the boarding school of Bellerive. He was a good student. By the time he left Bellerive, he could speak, read, and write French like a native Parisian, and he had exceptional math skills. He was so good in this subject that his professor was disappointed that Pierpont was not planning to pursue academia in math. His professor strongly believed that Pierpont would use his skills in math as a basis for a life of academia and research, but Pierpont and his father had other plans.

Pierpont then went to the German University of Göttingen. Junius wanted his son to see the world and learn from different academic settings rather than just grow limp from the boredom of a single source of knowledge.

After studying for six months at Göttingen, he could speak German very well and graduated with a degree in arts. He could converse in German about current affairs, finance, and art without the person he was speaking to ever realizing that he was not a native speaker, but he could speak even better in French. It may have been because Pierpont was a closet romantic, and the French language suited his poetic heart. Being elected valedictorian of his class at Göttingen, he had prepared a speech that was designed to impress the faculty and his fellow students, but much to his chagrin, he made a linguistic faux pas in his speech. He mixed up his words, *and* instead of wishing his fellow classmates a long life, he wished them a life of misery.

His teenage life was not an accurate reflection of his childhood. As a child, he was bubbly, full of laughter, and infectious joy, but that changed when he became sick in his early teenage years. His sickness altered his physical appearance, which eroded his confidence, causing a negative effect on his social skills. All that compounded his propensity for seclusion.

While the sicknesses that plagued him relentlessly as a teenager led him to withdraw from an active social life, his mind wasn't affected. If anything, the lack of social exposure actually focused his mind.

That childish, happy disposition gave way to a serious demeanor and fiery animation just below the surface that was ready to surface at a moment's notice. The insecurity he endured fueled the embers, while his disappointment nursed his bitterness. In the tug of war between his insecurities, persistent limp, and frequent migraines, his self-confidence was marginal at best. His outward demeanor to those who were in his orbit seemed brusque on a good day and downright fiery on a bad.

Pierpont's father partnered with the infamous George Peabody and worked with him for his bank for thirteen years before Old Man Peabody retired and left the day-to-day business of the bank to Junius. Pierpont was seventeen at this point when Junius became a partner.

By 1857, Junius believed that it was time for Pierpont to begin his career. To start, Pierpont began his banking life in the London office of Peabody, Morgan, and Company. It was an entry-level job that was designed to familiarize him with the ropes and get his feet wet. Pierpont had just turned twenty.

With the introduction to the financial world behind him, Pierpont returned to New York in 1858, where he began working at the firm Duncan, Sherman and Company.

Duncan, Sherman, and Company was the U.S. representative of Peabody, Morgan, and Company. Pierpont was neither a partner nor a director of the company, but that didn't stop him from pulling off a rather ambitious transaction that no one expected or sanctioned.

A large shipment of Brazilian coffee beans had arrived in New Orleans without a buyer. Due to some transactional anomaly, the intended buyer had backed off the deal, and the cargo was stuck at port. Pierpont used funds from Duncan, Sherman, and Company to purchase the entire shipment at a deep discount without anyone's permission. He then sold the shipment to merchants and was able to make a substantial return on the quick investment. It was a high-risk move and could have resulted in a total loss if a buyer was not found in time.

The partners at the firm were not at all pleased by what Pierpont had done. Their displeasure at his unsanctioned actions came back to haunt him a few years later when he was up for promotion. They declined his promotion to partner.

With the coffee bean saga behind him, the surge of adrenalin, despite the reproach of his seniors at the bank, was an exhilarating feeling that propelled this young banker in search of the next deal. He had been bitten by the deal bug—a typical ailment of successful bankers.

Now feeling emboldened and confident by his success, Pierpont struck out on his own and opened his own bank, J.P. Morgan and Company. Not to be confused, this is not the bank that is now JPMorgan Chase. This was a small bank that soon fizzled into oblivion. One deal does not a banker make.

As he was exposed to more deals and more transactions, he saw a very different element of the world of finance. His math skills were a great strength in his aptitude for banking. His ability to put the numbers together in his head made him a legend in his field. As he learned the ropes, the Morgan team of father and son found a new area of business that would eventually put them in the driver's seat in America's rise in the world.

The period between 1820 and the Civil War was one of significant consequence and opportunity for those who knew what to look for and what to go after. In the U.S., a new era of finance had developed. Gone were the days of basic banking where a dollar deposited in a bank was loaned out or invested by the banker. That was Banking 101.

Now things had to advance a little more, and other sources of funds needed to be found. Peabody had started that trend by bringing in money for sovereign bonds. Now the Morgans needed to do more. Junius was up to it but had his limits. Pierpont, on the other hand, was a little more brash and a lot more headstrong. He wanted to forge ahead with ideas that were yet to be tried and methods that were not yet tested. This worried Junius, who was a lot more conservative a banker than his son.

This difference of opinion caused constant rifts between the two, with the frustration coming to a boil in the younger Morgan, while the older Morgan was not as feisty.

Pierpont and his father worked to funnel British capital into the United States. In the 1830s and the 1840s, investors in Europe and Britain were wary about investing money in ventures that were three thousand miles away. Thanks to what Pierpont and his father were doing, however, investors started to become more confident in sending their money across the Atlantic Ocean.

Pierpont knew without a doubt that industry could not be financed by just the seasonal cash flow of deposits that came into banks because farmers would deposit them at harvest. They needed a year-round source of funds and had to attract money from the old country, but the old country and old money were hesitant after the defaults of numerous states. They needed assurances of future creditworthiness. They found that assurance in the structures and promises that Morgan brought to the table.

By this time, Pierpont was a grown man with a mustache and a piercing stare. He spent long hours at work but found time to entertain himself and go to social gatherings. During this time, he began to mingle with the social elite, attending the parties of highly respected families. He was frequently a guest at several prominent New York families' homes.

At one party, Pierpont met Amelia Sturges, who would later become his wife. Pierpont was smitten at once and fell in love with her, or Mimi, as he called her. Amelia's mother was a talented pianist, and her father was a supporter of the Hudson River School of Artists.

The feeling between Mimi and Pierpont was mutual. She liked him, and he proceeded to sweep her off her feet. New York, the about-to-be financial capital of the world, had much to offer a young couple. They visited art galleries, took boat rides on the Hudson, and rode horses in the country.

Chapter 2 Early Life

Pierpont's affection and affability were abundant and obvious until he started to withdraw into himself, but the full extent to which he secluded himself and retired from social company was still some years away.

There was a bond between father and son. Junius adored Pierpont and cherished every success, every attempt at success, and the way Pierpont thought. As for the son, he looked to his father with great admiration and wrote to Junius at every opportunity when they were separated by the Atlantic. Much of the correspondence was work related, but they also shared many personal father/son letters.

Being a sentimental man, Junius saved every single letter and memo in a box in his cabinet. Upon his death in 1890, Pierpont had the solemn duty of clearing his father's office. He had no idea that Junius had saved his letters, but Pierpont was not like his father. He was not sentimental. When he found the letters, he burned almost all of them. Only a few remain today and are preserved in the archives of the Morgan Library and Museum in New York.

As aggressive as he was in investing his funds, he always did so prudently. The fact that he was never sentimental about things was a great source of strength and allowed him to transact in large numbers and with a clear-eyed view of the risks involved. One such instance occurred in 1861, when he financed what came to be known as the Hall Carbine Affair.

Five thousand outdated army rifles were in a government munitions depot. An arms dealer by the name of Arthur M. Eastman purchased the entire lot for $3.50 each, with the total price being $17,500. He then sold them to a Mr. Stevens who borrowed $20,000 from Pierpont and purchased all the rifles for $11 each. That came up $55,000. He had $30,000 of his own money to make the deal.

The rifles were then modified, improving their accuracy and range and shipped to Union Field General John C. Fremont, who was at the time leading troops in Missouri. He purchased the rifles for $22 each. The total price was $110,000. Pierpont walked away with $44,000 on an investment of $20,000—a profit of 110 percent.

At the time of the Civil War, Wall Street was filled with people wanting to make money from it. What Pierpont did regarding the Hall Carbine Affair was not illicit. He was the kind of person who saw the war as an opportunity to make money, but he did so without cheating or fleecing the government or anyone else. He did, however, seek to make a return on his investments, and there is nothing wrong with that.

A few years later after Gettysburg Pierpont was conscripted into the army, but he paid a substitute $300 to take his place. At the time, that was a common practice and perfectly legal to do. Pierpont would refer to his substitute as "the other Pierpont Morgan."

In 1861, Pierpont and Mimi were married.

By this point, they had known each other for three years, but the decision to wed was forced on them by fate. Mimi had been diagnosed with tuberculosis, which few people survived.

When Pierpont found out about her condition, he was greatly disturbed. He immediately proposed to her, and she hesitantly accepted. Pierpont wanted to do the right thing and marry the love of his life. He then set about to find a cure for Mimi.

Mimi was so weak that Pierpont had to carry her downstairs to where the ceremony was taking place and had to hold her up. After that, he carried her to a waiting carriage outside.

The couple spent their honeymoon in Algiers, Tunisia. Pierpont thought the warm, dry air of the North African desert would bring her back to health. He also hired the finest physicians to tend to her and bought birds to keep her company.

Mimi wrote to her mother about how dedicated Pierpont was, but despite his attempts to nurse her back to health, she passed away on February 17, 1862, approximately four months after their wedding.

Pierpont was devastated. Even though he knew she would die, he was extremely heartbroken when he returned to New York, where he continued his work.

Three years later Pierpont married Frances Louisa Tracy, daughter of Charles Tracy, who owned a law firm, on May 31, 1865. At first, Frances, Fanny as she was also called, was not very attracted to him, but after one year of pursuit, she married him.

Within their first year of marriage, the couple had their first child, Louisa Pierpont Morgan. Over the next couple of years, they had two daughters and a son, John Pierpont Morgan Jr., or Jack, as he was also called. Jack grew up to become the next head of the House of Morgan. His two daughters were Anne, who became a philanthropist, and Juliet

It was around this time that Pierpont purchased a Victorian mansion close to the Hudson River. By now, he was earning $75,000 a year, which would be equivalent to almost $1.2 million today. He owned two houses, had a family, and was just thirty-three years old.

It was at this time that Pierpont's health began to deteriorate. His migraines were getting worse, and he also had skin problems. When he eventually recovered, he was left with his trademark nose for the rest of his life.

The acne rosacea that he suffered from made his nose abnormally large. Furthermore, his nose was covered with dimples and bulges and was also purple in color.

All photographs taken of him that he posed for were touched up to make his nose look normal. A few photographs, however, show what his nose really looked like.

Pierpont hated being photographed so much that one picture shows him warding off a photographer with his cane, and he appears to be shouting.

In one photo taken of Pierpont in 1903, the photographer asked Pierpont to turn his head a little to the side. Being conscious of his abnormal nose, however, he did not want to turn his head and simply stared straight into the camera.

It was at this time that he actually thought of retiring, but his father was not going to let that happen and made him work at the New York banking house of the

Drexels. He became a partner of the bank in 1871, and the name was rechristened Drexel, Morgan, and Company. Junius also asked the owner of the bank, Anthony J. Drexel, to be a guide and mentor to Pierpont.

Although he was now at Drexel's firm, Pierpont was still a partner at Dabney, Morgan, and Company, where he had begun working in 1864. The owner of the bank, Charles Dabney, tutored Pierpont, and he was able to understand the way the chaotic banking system worked.

Pierpont actually continued at the firm of Dabney, Morgan, and Company until 1872, the year after he joined Drexel's firm.

As time went by, the relationship between Pierpont and Fanny began to sour. They were very different people, each of them liking different things. Pierpont loved luxurious furniture and clothes, while she just liked normal things. When Pierpont wanted to renovate their home, she told a friend that she hoped he wouldn't make their home too flamboyant.

For Fanny, she just liked pictures on the wall, thinking that it wouldn't be so attractive to thieves.

Pierpont would often go off with friends and would not return for months. He had several extramarital affairs, but only two were important.

Pierpont's son, Jack, would be the one who really spent time with Fanny. The two would bond over their depression, and when Fanny became somewhat deaf, he was there for her.

Jack was the exact opposite of Pierpont. When Pierpont was young and even when he grew old, he was always very ambitious, fearless, and aggressive. In contrast, Jack was a timid, reserved young boy with little self-confidence.

Pierpont was fond of Jack, but because he was not as active and enthusiastic as Pierpont was, Pierpont excluded him from business deals and for the better part of their time together kept him in the dark on transactions. When Pierpont formed United States Steel Corporation, Jack had to read about it in the newspapers. Because Pierpont excluded his son from the business, Jack felt even more insecure, which just dug the hole deeper.

Pierpont had a minor quirk concerning extramarital affairs. He always kept them private but rebuked those who were not discreet. He once called a young partner into his office and censured him for having had an affair. The young man replied, "But sir, you and the other partners do the same thing yourselves behind closed doors." Pierpont stared at him for a moment and then said, "Young man, that is what doors are for."

Despite his affairs, Pierpont always showed a great deal of respect to Fanny. He kept his affairs very quiet but took his mistresses out with him. He surrounded himself with people whom he trusted not to speak about the matter. When biographer Jean Strouse was researching his life, she talked to the children of the people who had kept Pierpont's affairs secret, and they, too, remained silent, as their parents who were friends with Pierpont did.

Pierpont's friends kept his affairs secret, but other associates were not completely secretive. They wrote down things, and some even spoke about the matter. Later in life, Pierpont himself did not completely cover up his affairs out of complacency and thinking they would not be found out. It was not possible, however, to keep them a complete secret forever. The press and the public were constantly hammering Pierpont, and it was impossible for them not to see some of the skeletons in his not completely closed closet.

There was a lot for Morgan to be angry about. His affairs were indicative of that. In fact, although he was affectionate toward Fanny, the true love of his life was

Mimi. He had no intention of marrying after her death, but Junius had insisted that he get over her.

In fact, it was Junius who arranged for and cajoled Pierpont into the meeting with Fanny and the subsequent courtship. Neither Pierpont nor Fanny was interested in the idea.

Pierpont's heart was broken when Mimi died. Many people said that her death haunted him to his final days.

What complicated everything was that the son he loved was the product of a union that didn't matter to him. He treated Fanny with the utmost respect and kept his affairs away from her as a sign of that respect. Once she retreated to her room upstairs and led a silent life, he knew there was not much he could do to win her back, so the need to be discreet was no longer as great as it had been. Even in his indiscretions, though, he was still a gentleman.

Chapter 3 Shortcomings

Pierpont's son-in-law, the husband of Louisa Pierpont Morgan, Herbert L. Satterlee, said that perhaps Pierpont did not fix his nose because he did not want the seizures he used to suffer from when he was young to return. Doctors could actually have shaved away the cauliflower-like part of his nose so that it would be normal, but that didn't happen.

The condition of his nose contributed to his hostile personality, which resulted from deep-seated insecurity. Pierpont had two issues that to him were at odds with each other. His life started out with intense seizures. These were debilitating and scary for him when he was young. It shook him to his core. The seizures became increasingly violent and would last longer as he grew older.

At about the same time the seizures stopped, the rosacea erupted on his face and centered on his nose. Rosacea is an inflammatory condition that typically affects the face but can spread to the upper torso as well. It alters the tint of the skin just as a serious case of acne would. In Pierpont's case, the buildup of fluid and white cells in his nose altered its shape and deformed its appearance. The more enraged Pierpont became, the brighter his nose would glow.

Because the Rosacea developed about the same time his seizures stopped, Pierpont associated one with the other. In his mind, fixing his nose, which the doctors assured him could be done, would cause the seizures to resurface. There was no medical evidence of that, but he believed it.

The more his nose grew, the more it preoccupied him until he hardly looked at the mirror except to groom himself. Just as how one can affirm the strength of their psyche by looking at themselves in the mirror, Pierpont had the opposite effect. Each visit to the mirror in the morning was a painful reminder of what greeted the rest of the world. He wanted no record of it, and he didn't like it when people stared at it. Everyone in his office knew better than to look at his nose.

Pierpont was aggressive in his temperament when he didn't want to be photographed. He didn't just stop at that though. If someone said something about his nose, he would do something to get back at them. He never let it go.

When someone once nicknamed him "Livernose," Pierpont banned that person from joining the New

York Yacht Club, a club in which he was a member. When Pierpont was once visiting the family of an associate, the man's wife told her children not to say anything about his nose. She had warned them since she knew they had never met Pierpont and would be distracted by his nose. Little did she realize that she herself was so preoccupied with it that it caused an inadvertent slip of the tongue. Once Pierpont arrived and she was serving tea, she blurted out, "Do you like a nose in your tea, Mr. Morgan?"

Despite his state of mind about his nose, he held his composure and dignity when meeting people. He was no doubt fully aware that they were staring at his nose, and he didn't like it one bit, but his propensity to do the deal outweighed his discomfort. Some close to him believe that his shroud of cigar smoke was a means to obscure the sight of his bulbous nose. This shroud or aromatic cloud that hovered around him perpetually was a trait that became synonymous with Pierpont's personal brand. He used to smoke almost twenty full-sized cigars a day, with Cubans being his favorite, especially the eight-inch Maduro Meridiana Kohinoor cigars also known as "Hercules' Clubs." He smoked so much that you could sniff him coming around the corner, and his presence was unmistakable once he was gone.

In his private life, Pierpont was a deeply devout Christian, who was loyal to the Episcopal Church. It had been that way since he was a child and shepherded to Episcopal services by his grandfather.

As he matured, the foundation of the church and the teachings of the Bible had a significant bearing on his mind and beliefs. He believed every single thing in the Bible and said he believed the story of Jonah and the whale. Most of us understand that the parables in the Bible are instructional. They have their value and are powerful in their representation, but not many believe the parables to be literal and historically accurate. As intelligent and sharp as Pierpont was, he saw the church as more than what most people view it to be.

He was such a devout Christian that he would frequently go for walks and end up at a church. It would be empty, and he would just stand there and commune with God. He would stand there in obvious prayer and then burst into song, singing his medley of favorite hymns. Pierpont would be absolutely mesmerized by the church, both its edifice and its teachings. He was a very pious man in mind, spirit, and action. He made numerous contributions to the church.

Aside from simply being a pious Christian, Pierpont was also involved in the church. He had been both a member of the Episcopal Church and was one time an important leader of the church. Pierpont was also one of the founders of the Church Club of New York, which was an Episcopal club. He also donated $100,000 to help Bishop Charles Brent's idea to come true.

Bishop Brent wanted churches from all over the world to meet and discuss their differences regarding "faith and order." He wanted a General Convention of the Episcopal Church. Pierpont loved the idea very much, which is why he provided financial support.

Chapter 4 Early Deals

In 1879, Pierpont was approached by William Vanderbilt, the son of Cornelius Vanderbilt, who wanted to sell 250,000 shares of the New York Central Railroad.

Vanderbilt could have gone to any competent broker to find the best price and a buyer in a short amount of time, but he had larger concerns. Vanderbilt wanted to make sure that two things were adhered to: (1) that the sale was done discreetly. It had to be done in such a way that the Vanderbilt name did not enter the papers for selling some of their shares, and (2) the sale had to be done in a way that did not affect the price of the shares and the market in general.

It was a large transaction, yet Pierpont was able to pull it off without causing the stock price to fall or the information to become public The maneuver took skill and facility with the ways of the stock market—both of which Pierpont was very skilled at doing. The consideration for this transaction did not stop at fees as with an ordinary transaction. This was extraordinary in nature and deserved extraordinary compensation. In the world of corporate finance and trading, mobilizing large amounts of cash for the purchase of a single stock was not easy, and doing it without shaking the stock price required seismic force and a general touch, which only Pierpont could do at the time.

In return for his service, Pierpont boldly requested and received a directorship position on the board of the New York Central Railway.

Fortune had smiled on Pierpont, and he had taken full advantage of it. He now had jammed his foot in the door of the railroad industry.

Without wasting any time, Pierpont set off another project, which involved raising $40 million through a bond issuance for the construction of the Northern Pacific Railroad from Minnesota to Oregon. To put that in context, $40 million then is equivalent to $1.2 billion today. At the time, it was the largest bond issuance and placement in the history of the United States. Pierpont was not in it to play small. He was geared to play with big dollar amounts, which showed his prowess, intelligence, and ability.

Pierpont was also involved in other major projects. We all turn on the lights in our houses and never for a moment think what it was like before Edison invented the light bulb. It was not very bright then and had a foul stench. The burning of whale blubber or poorly refined kerosene imparted an odious tinge on everything, from one's clothes to one's furniture. It wasn't until the arrival of the light bulb and wired-in electricity that the flip of a switch illuminated the room. It wasn't just Edison who was behind that. Edison certainly improved the design of the bulb, made it work, and then developed the switches, fuse, wires, and cables as well as the power generation stations behind the whole affair of light at the flick of a switch, but behind Edison stood J.P. Morgan, the man who had financed it. Pierpont was the man behind electricity generation and the bulb becoming widely used across the United States.

After Edison perfected the light bulb and the infrastructure behind it, Pierpont had him install electricity in his home at 219 Madison Avenue. A small generator was installed to supply power to the four hundred light bulbs in the house. This same home became a place where Edison conducted his experiments.

Pierpont's father thought it was a waste of time, but electricity soon became a necessity in the homes of well-to-do people.

Pierpont invested a great deal of money in Edison and financed the forming of the Edison Electricity Company. The first power station ever to exist was then created, and half of Manhattan Island had access to electricity. Although this was a splendid success for Pierpont and Edison, it was a great loss for John D. Rockefeller.

Before the rise of electricity, Rockefeller supplied oil to people who had lamps that used oil for power. With his market for oil now reduced, he resorted to fabricating dangers about electricity. He gave these false stories to the newspapers, letting this information spread among the public.

In 1889, the firm of Drexel, Morgan, and Company bankrolled Edison and helped Edison's companies to merge, forming the Edison General Electric Company on April 24, 1889. The companies included in the merger were the Edison Machine Works, the Edison Lamp Company, and the Edison Electric Light Company. In the same year, the Sprague Electric Railway and Motor Company were brought into the company.

Eleven years after Pierpont dealt with William Vanderbilt, Junius Morgan passed away in Monte Carlo. Pierpont and his family had visited him the year before and spent their last summer with the patriarch of the Morgan clan. At that point, Junius had aged, and not much of his spark as a lifelong banker remained. He had become a grandfather excited to see his progeny. In April 1890, Junius went into a coma after an accident. The injuries from that accident precipitated and hastened his final days.

Three years later Anthony Joseph Drexel, founder of Drexel, Morgan, and Company, passed away, leaving the company to Pierpont, who unceremoniously renamed the firm two years later to J.P. Morgan and Company. This firm would become one of the largest banks in the world as well as what is today known as JPMorgan Chase and Company.

Following this rechristening, Pierpont would keep his firm closely connected with the Drexel firm of Philadelphia and Paris. The Paris part of the firm was called Morgan, Harjes & Company, and the Philadelphia branch was called Drexel and Company. J.P. Morgan & Co. also stayed close to J.S. Morgan and Company, which would be renamed Morgan, Grenfell, and Company in 1910.

Chapter 5 The Peabody Effect

Morgan, Grenfell, and Company started as George Peabody and Company, founded by the banker scrooge and philanthropist George Peabody.

George Peabody was a patriotic American from the state of Massachusetts. He arrived in Britain in 1835 and shortly afterward opened his own merchant's dry goods store and furnished it with a safe and some tables. He formed a merchant bank and named it George Peabody and Company. This little merchant bank functioned as a firm that dealt only with rich people, large companies, and governments. He was very proud of his country, and rather than just going about his business and being part of British society, he stood out as an American, spreading the popularity of American goods and showing how good they were.

His claim to fame and success came about in the wake of one of America's shameful moments. After the issuance of numerous bonds for development and floating those bonds to Europe, a number of states that floated bonds, including Indiana, Michigan, Pennsylvania, Arkansas, and the territory of Florida, defaulted on their interest payments to the Bank of England and other private banking houses in 1841 and

1842. This deepened the recession that had been sparked by other factors and prolonged by the famine that hit Ireland and Scotland.

Several American state governors came together and tried to repudiate the remaining debt, but it did not work. Even today the state of Mississippi is still in debt from the 1840s.

British investors were extremely disgusted by what had happened and considered the United States to be an untrustworthy country, filled with people who did not fulfill their end of a bargain.

Since states were defaulting on their debt, the federal credit rating fell. Thus, in 1842 when President John Tyler sent Treasury representatives to Europe, French banker James Mayer de Rothschild said, "Tell them you have seen the man who is at the head of the finances of Europe, and that he has told you that they cannot borrow a dollar. Not a dollar."

Several other people also looked on with disdain with what had happened in the States. One such person was Sydney Smith, a clergyman. He said he felt an urge to "seize and divide him" when he saw a man of Pennsylvania sitting down at a dinner in London. He went on to say, "How such a man can set himself down at an English table without feeling that he owes two or three pounds to every man in the company, I am at a loss to conceive; he has no more right to eat with honest men than a leper has to eat with clean men."

Author Charles Dickens was also disgusted with the Americans. In one of his stories, one of his characters has British assets that are turned into as he puts it, "a mere United States' security."

Needless to say, the entire affair was a dark stain on Americans and this country. The state of Maryland would later join the long list of defaulters as well. Peabody felt very passionate about this particular issue and said that whenever he met a British investor he would be embarrassed.

The defaulting of Pennsylvania and Maryland was the most upsetting for the British because these states were tied to Anglo-Saxon stock.

The person behind much of the sale of bonds to the European banking houses and investors was none other than George Peabody, Junius Morgan's banking partner.

Peabody had sold approximately half of Maryland's shares to European investors, which caused some trouble for him when they eventually defaulted. He became the face of the defaulters since he was personally in London.

Although the *London Times* described Peabody as an "American gentleman of the most unblemished character," he was rejected by the Reform Club because he was from the United States, which defaulted on its debts. It was a hard time for Peabody because he was proud of his American heritage. When the defaults started and then deepened, he was still in London and was called upon to explain what had happened.

Peabody later wrote to a friend, saying, "You and I will, I trust, see that happy day, when as formerly, we can own ourselves Americans in Europe, without a blush for the character of our Country."

This showed how Peabody had been affected. He was evidently very proud of the United States, and this shameful episode was almost unbearable.

He finally had to take matters into his own hands to get some of the states to pay their dues. He had a novel idea that was similar to public relations. Peabody paid reporters to write favorable stories about Maryland. In 1845, Peabody teamed up with Barings to get Maryland to continue paying its debt. The two of them organized a slush fund that was to be used to promote the idea of continuing to pay its debts.

Peabody even persuaded clergymen to deliver speeches talking about the "holiness" of contracts.

From a secret account that Peabody and Barings maintained, they gave one thousand pounds to Baltimore, nine hundred of which came from Barings, while the remaining one hundred came from Peabody. Barings would later enact this scheme for Pennsylvania. Peabody wasn't the only one paying people to promote creditworthiness. Barings paid a speaker as well as the prominent political figure Daniel Webster to promote the idea of paying debts in his talks.

Just because Peabody and Barings were operating in a questionable way by paying people to promote things in the background did not mean they were all right with it. In fact, they did not like what they were doing even if it was not illegal but did feel a little underhanded.

Joshua Bates, a senior partner of the Barings, said to the American Thomas Ward, "Your payment to Mr. Webster would not appear very well if it should get out." Thomas Ward was the man who collected the money for Peabody and Barings' operation. Bates acted very by the book and was a clean "recorded" man who did not look favorably upon Peabody's exploits. He said, "I have a sort of instinctive horror of doing one thing to affect another, or using any sort of subterfuge or reserve."

Despite the questionability of the operation, it was successful. Whigs who favored states to repay their debts were elected in both Pennsylvania and Maryland. The English bankers in London once again received their regular payments from those two states. The states of Mississippi and Florida, however, did not repay their debts.

To go on, just know that Peabody was the kind of person that if you stung him he would sting you back. Now, Mississippi and Florida obviously did not do anything to hurt Peabody except that they hurt his pride for his country by not paying their debts and causing the Victorian bankers of Britain to look at Americans with contempt and disdain. In his later years when Peabody donated to charity and presented gifts to the country, he refrained from giving anything to Mississippi and Florida because they had brought him such shame.

This was not entirely an altruistic move hoping to raise his country's worth in the eyes of Europeans. He had made heavy bets by buying up the junk bonds that ewe in the market for pennies on the dollar.

Junk bonds are bonds rated below investment grade. It means they have defaulted on one or more of their payments and have been downgraded by a rating agency. In the case of the state bonds, there were no rating agencies at the time, but they did indeed default, and as such those who were holding the bonds needed to sell as many as they could to recover as much capital as they could. Peabody was one of few who bought up those bonds at a deeply discounted price.

Once he had succeeded in getting a number of states to pay and the bonds rose in value, he made a fortune.

In time, thanks to his efforts, American bonds soon became much more secure than those of Europe because of the many revolutions that took place in Europe in 1848 and that America was developing and advancing at a pace that was significantly greater than all of the Old World combined.

As the 1840s drew to a close, the Mexican War and the California Gold Rush brought an end to the tumultuous '40s, and Peabody was once again able to hold his head high as he walked the streets of London. He considered himself to be the bridge that brought American culture to Victorian Britain. He presented the English nation with apples of his country, hominy grit, and crackers of Boston.

Peabody's first Independence Day dinner took place on July 4, 1851. At the celebration, the most important guest was Arthur Wellesley, the Duke of Wellington.

Through his actions, Peabody was trying to stitch together friendship between the British and the Americans, but it didn't all go as well as he had hoped. In 1854, Peabody did something that was considered heretical. In this case, however, it was not heretical for the church but for the American government. Peabody had toasted to Queen Victoria before he did for Franklin Pierce, president of the United States at the time. James Buchanan, who was the American ambassador to London and would be the next U.S. president, was upset and immediately left the room. It was a small matter, and Buchanan was indeed acting impetuously.

Peabody also took up the role of showing Americans around London. He took some eighty Americans to dinner and thirty-five to the opera.

When Cornelius Vanderbilt came to London with his wife and all twelve children in tow in 1853, Peabody showed him around.

Commodore Vanderbilt came to Britain to show how great America was since a poor boy could now be richer than the queen. He arrived in his yacht, the *North Star*, a ship that weighed two thousand tons. On board besides himself and his family were a doctor, a caterer, and a chaplain.

In the 1850s, Peabody earned quite a bit of money supplying the United States with railroad rails and financing the silk trade that was taking place with China. Peabody did help some charities, but mostly he accumulated money to have a reserve if a financial crisis occurred.

The small acts of charity included building a library for a secondary education school.

As Peabody made more money, he became more obsessed that he might lose it. He once told an associate that he had a great deal of money and had seen large sums of money lost in financial panics. He went on to say that he had to be careful with his fortune.

Thomas Perman, Peabody's assistant, really seemed to dislike him and gave an account of his "dark" side. He recounted a story about how Peabody used to eat his lunch at his desk every day. He went on to say how he would send a clerk to buy an apple for him, which cost one and a halfpenny. Peabody would give the young man two pence. The clerk wished to be able to keep the halfpenny as a little bonus for himself, but Peabody would not hear of it. He always wanted his change back.

At the beginning of the 1850s, Peabody's health was not too good. He would soon wish to commit himself to charity, but another problem would delay his plans.

By this time, Peabody earned $300,000 a year but only spent $3,000 of it. He was very rich but spent very little. Peabody never married, but he did have an illegitimate daughter, whose mother would frequently receive two thousand pounds from him.

When the daughter grew up, she would constantly pester the Morgan family for money, for Peabody had left nothing for either her or her mother in his will. No one knows why Peabody was so out of touch regarding family matters, but he had "telescopic philanthropy," a term created by Charles Dickens. Telescopic philanthropy simply means that one is kind and loves humanity as a whole but is very unkind and hurtful to individuals he knows.

The world, or more specifically the English would, considered him a benevolent man, but his employees and illegitimate family felt otherwise.

Problems arose when the time came for Peabody to leave the banking business and shift his focus to philanthropy. Although he was master of his own bank, no one else knew enough of the bank's operations to be able to continue in his absence.

Because he had no other choice, Peabody appointed Charles C. Gooch to be a junior partner, hoping that Gooch would then ascend to a position of control. Before holding this position, Gooch was Peabody's office manager. So the fit was just not there to transition from an inward role to one that oversaw everything.

It was never the practice in nineteenth century banking houses for strangers to take over after the incumbent head passed away or retired. They typically passed to an heir. This time, however, Peabody was in the position of having no son to pass on his business. Thus, he had to fish for someone to take over.

Peabody had certain conditions for the man who would take over George Peabody and Company: be an American with a family and have experience in international trade. Furthermore, that American must be a man that could *talk—be a master communicator*—and mingle with other people.

Peabody knew a James Beebe who owned the firm J.M. Beebe and Morgan. He told Peabody about Junius Spencer Morgan, his junior partner. Junius had been with J.M. Beebe for three years. Beebe praised Junius, who was indeed an astute and intelligent individual. He was a true blue-blooded American.

Peabody wanted to see him, so Junius took his family with him to London to meet Peabody in May 1853. Junius brought along his son, John Pierpont Morgan Sr., who was very excited about his first time in Britain. While his father met with Peabody, Pierpont visited Westminster Abbey and the queen's residence, Buckingham Palace. Pierpont also attended a Sunday morning session at the church of St. Paul's.

Junius Spencer Morgan was a very clean, neat, and by-the-book banker. He gave Pierpont a lot of advice and always stood there telling him what to do and what not to do. In Junius' eyes, Pierpont was rash and undisciplined, which worried him. An example of what his father foresaw includes how Pierpont bought an entire shipment of Brazilian coffee with the money of the firm he was working in, which bothered all the senior bankers at the time.

After talking for a few days and assessing this young banker, Peabody asked him to become his partner. They were two very different men. One was an American but had lived his entire life in the Old World, while the other was a dyed-in-the-wool American, who had spent most of his life in the New World. One was a seasoned banker; the other was a novice. One had no family, and the other was a family man by nature. And, since opposites attract, there was a bond that formed between them across the generational divide. The conversation that ensued was kept alive by the generations of Morgans that recounted the event to their children.

Peabody began, "You know, I shall not want to go on much longer, but if you will come as a partner for ten years, I shall retire at the end of them, and at that time shall be willing to leave my name, and, if you have not accumulated a reasonable amount of capital in the concern, some of my money also, and you can go ahead as the head of it."

Junius replied by saying, "Well, Mr. Peabody, that sounds like a very good offer, but there are many things to be considered, and I could not think of giving an answer until I have looked over the books of the firm and have some idea of the business and of the methods by which it is done."

This was evidence that Junius wasn't overexcited at the prospect of becoming a partner of George Peabody and Company—not that he wasn't interested, but that he wasn't the kind of person to immediately jump into something. Junius first wanted to see how well the firm did before he made up his mind.

When Junius saw that the firm of George Peabody and Company had 450,000 pounds, he was deeply impressed. This placed Peabody's firm just behind the Rothschild and Baring houses.

In October 1854, Junius Spencer Morgan agreed to become the partner of George Peabody and Company and took up his office at 22 Old Broad Street.

When Junius moved in, he didn't make any renovations because it wasn't necessary. It was good as it was, and it made no sense to spend hard-earned money on mere renovations. True bankers are traditionally a miserly lot.

When Junius Spencer Morgan became Peabody's partner and moved to London, it was a bit of a nicer time for a banker from the United States in London than when Peabody started there. The Crimean War was going on at the time, and the price of American grain had risen. Railroad companies with lines in the western part of the country were transporting supplies and making money from there, causing many people to want to own shares of these railroads.

A contract between Peabody and his newly minted partner specified what Peabody's firm would do, which included international trade, purchasing and selling stocks, and buying railroad building materials as well as other items on behalf of others. Peabody also gave Junius a budget of 2,500 pounds to amuse visiting Americans.

Ten years after the two men became partners, Junius confronted him about what he had promised when they became partners. Junius would then be in the same group of people that had been pushed aside in an unfair and contemptuous manner.

During their partnership, Junius once found his partner sitting in a countinghouse looking most sickly. He advised Peabody that he should go home, and Peabody agreed. Later, Junius saw his partner standing in the rain and asked him why he did not go home. Peabody replied by saying that a bus had come, but that it was a two-pence bus, and he was waiting for one that cost one pence.

Although he owned a company with 450,000 pounds as capital and earned 300,000 a year with a total wealth of approximately a million pounds, George Peabody was very stingy with his spending. He once marched a cab driver down to the police station for overcharging him. Most bankers have the same psychology: make lots, spend little.

Peabody's firm was one of the most prominent railroad share dealers in London and thus able to benefit nicely from the frenzy of railroad activity in the United States. Railroad companies in the U.S., while starting off slowly, were now earning so much money that they had gained the interest of many investors. During the Civil War, many investors invested a total of $1 billion in railroads, and Junius was the face of that activity in London.

Between 1854 and 1864, Junius wondered whether or not it was the right decision to move to London and become Peabody's partner. Peabody was not easy to deal with, and their relationship had turned rather cold. Whenever Junius wrote to Peabody, he would begin with "Dear Sir" and end the letter "J.S. Morgan."

Junius' opinion of Peabody was that he was spiteful and revengeful. The two were not really very friendly in later years and only showed each other their due respect and courtesy.

Three years after Junius and Peabody became partners, wheat prices fell when the Crimean War ended. This was a serious problem for both American banking houses as well as the railroad companies, which no longer had such a large customer demanding shipments of grain.

In October 1857, American banks in New York ceased paying in gold, which stopped Peabody from receiving funds in London, and he could not pay his obligations. It was soon suspected that Peabody's firm would collapse much to his competitors' delight. Like Junius, many people did not like old man Peabody.

Some of the larger London banking houses approached Junius and told him that they would help the firm of Peabody, Morgan, and Company pay off its debts under the condition that Peabody closed the bank within a year.

Junius relayed the message to Peabody who strenuously refused. He was adamant in his resolve to not shutter his bank.

In an unexpected turn of events, the firm received an offer of a loan from the Bank of England for 800,000 pounds. The loan was guaranteed by the House of Baring.

Peabody felt entrapped and directed his frustrations toward Baring. The entire issue of the financial crisis was very painful for him.

When Pierpont learned that the bank his father was a partner in was going to renege on its loans, he was quite upset.

This financial juggernaut greatly affected Junius and altered his methods of banking. He became significantly more cautious.

He also started to lecture his son to walk safely in the line of business his son was working in, as he was also starting his banking career.

He once wrote Pierpont, "You are commencing upon your business career at an eventful time. Let what you now witness make an impression not to be eradicated . . . *slow and sure* should be the motto of every young man."

Since 1832 when President Andrew Jackson dissolved the Bank of the United States, the nation had no standard way of banking. Furthermore, there were quite a number of places in which people did not have to pay their debts with the dollar but could use the currencies of other countries.

Soon, another financial issue was brewing. The merchant banks in London began to take equity stakes, one example being when Peabody's firm invested 100,000 pounds in the creation of Cyrus Field's transatlantic communication cable from London to New York. It was proved a success on August 15, 1858, when Queen Victoria sent a telegram to President James Buchanan by the transatlantic cable.

For the next two weeks, everyone in New York was celebrating, and the skies were filled with fireworks.

Peabody then wrote to Field, saying, "Your reflections must be like those of Columbus after the discovery of America." Peabody was evidently happy about this new transatlantic cable. Unfortunately, however, the cable broke, and the company's share prices dropped dramatically. The firm of George Peabody and Company as well as Junius and Peabody themselves lost a lot of money. The cable would only be restored eight years later.

Peabody may have remained at the bank until 1864, but from 1859 until then, he was only a figurehead. Junius had already taken control of the bank in 1859.

During the Civil War, Junius traded Union bonds, the value of which changed whenever Union troops either lost or won a battle.

When the Confederates defeated the Union troops at the Battle of Bull Run, Union bonds reduced dramatically but increased dramatically when the Confederates were brought to a halt at Antietam Creek. Vicksburg, Confederate territory, was taken by the Union in July 1863, and Junius' son, Pierpont, wrote to his father through the telegram cable the Nova Scotia and told him about the Union victory. Junius was informed early enough to make a nice profit from American bonds.

This sort of banking was, as historian Ron Chernow put it, "calamity banking," and in the realm of merchant banks, it was quite prevalent. One of the Rothschild bankers said, "When the streets of Paris are running with blood, I buy." This basically meant that they, too, participated in "calamity banking."

At one point in the Civil War, President Abraham Lincoln needed money to pay for the war debt and approached Jay Cooke, a Philadelphia banker. Cooke sent his people to sell war bonds, and the Jewish bankers of German nationality operating from Wall Street were thrown into a frenzy. Among the London buyers was Peabody's firm.

George Peabody went through a change during the Civil War. Before the war, he was a stingy, unlikeable banker whose only focus was making and hoarding money. After the Civil War, however, he became very generous, although he could not fully wrest himself of the habits he had when he used to hoard his money. He said, "It is not easy to part with the wealth we have accumulated after years of hard work and difficulty."

One distinct difference between Peabody and the Morgans and more specifically Pierpont was that Peabody came from nothing. He had no inherited wealth or family that was wealthy. He started off with nothing and worked his way up to become extremely rich and the father of modern philanthropy. The quality of saving in a person comes from when that person starts off with nothing and goes on to become rich from his or her own hard work.

Pierpont's family was already rich. He grew up surrounded by luxury and had the gift to do anything he wanted right then and there. This rich background did not instill in him the necessity to save, and when Pierpont grew up and amassed his own wealth, he was not miserly or frugal with it one bit. He spent lavishly on cigars, yachts, parties, and his art and gem collections. Pierpont died a fairly wealthy man, but John D. Rockefeller allegedly remarked, "And to think, he wasn't even a rich man." His wealth in today's world is a lot of money, but compared with Rockefeller's $300 billion and Andrew Carnegie's wealth, Pierpont's forty-one is actually very little. That did not matter, though, for his success was still paramount—more than his wealth. His success was also more important than the amount of money he had. It was also said that his power was not based on the millions he had, but with the billions he dealt with.

Coming from a rich background is beneficial. It allows you to have all the resources you need and be able to achieve your success in comfort and not have to worry about monetary issues. For Peabody, he had to struggle just to sustain himself and had to work hard to amass his wealth.

He had been saving his money his entire life, and now he was going to spend lavishly through his philanthropy. In 1857, Peabody funded the Peabody Institute in Baltimore. When Pierpont or the Morgan family later did their philanthropy, they did it for the purpose of giving to charity and doing good for the people. They did their charity work anonymously and very calmly. Peabody, however, wanted to be known for his philanthropy. He wanted his name attached to every single thing he funded or endowed. In 1862, Peabody deposited 150,000 pounds into a trust fund, the purpose of which was to build homes for London's poor. These houses, known as Peabody Estates, were nicely furnished with a water supply and gas lamps. They are still standing today.

As a reward for his outstanding benevolence, he was awarded the Freedom of the City of London, the first American as well as the first person who was not British to ever be given that award. When Peabody was having dinner at a mansion, he said, "From a full and grateful heart, I say that this day has repaid me for the care and anxiety of fifty years of commercial life."

Peabody's philanthropy was very impressive during his final years. He funded Yale University's natural history museum and Harvard University's ethnology museum. He also contributed to an educational fund dedicated to former slaves.

Requests for more homes amounted to a total cost of 500,000 pounds. As he was so generous, people started to take a more godly view of him. Victor Hugo, author of *Lès Miserables,* said, "On this earth, there are men of hate and men of love. Peabody was one of the latter. It is on the face of these men that we see the smile of God."

William E. Gladstone remarked that Peabody was able to impress upon people how to use money, not be controlled by it.

Queen Victoria offered Peabody a noble title. He could choose to become either a knighthood or a baron, but Peabody refused. Seeing that he would not accept either position, she simply wrote a letter to the poor of London, writing "princely munificence" in regards to Peabody. Although Peabody was busy providing for the people, he never did anything for his partner and heir, Junius Spencer Morgan. Perhaps this is a case where telescopic philanthropy applies.

In 1864, the time came for Peabody to retire and for Junius to become head of the bank. He had actually already been its head but would now also become known as its leader. Peabody had promised ten years earlier to leave his name with the bank, and if Junius had not accumulated enough money to run the firm, to leave some of his own. Peabody did neither of those things. Junius was deeply disappointed by Peabody's decision. It was then that the firm of George Peabody and Company was named J.S. Morgan and Company. Junius, however, was not very happy. In 1910, it would be renamed once more and be called Morgan, Grenfell, and Company.

Junius was left as the owner and head of the bank.

He was forced by Peabody to buy the office he had worked in that was on 22 Old Broad Street at the end of the ten-year partnership. Peabody demanded that he buy it and gave him very difficult terms and conditions. The grandson of Junius Morgan, Jack, wrote that Junius said that Peabody used to be difficult regarding the price of the office. Junius had been very angry with Peabody but had calmed down because while he was at George Peabody and Co. the firm had earned 444,000 pounds, which had been divided between him and Peabody. Junius was also happy to have taken ownership of the most prominent

American banking firm in London, home of British banking firms.

Peabody passed away five years after he retired from George Peabody and Company. He was seventy-four years old. A temporary grave at Westminster Abbey was dug by the British government.

A statue of George Peabody was unveiled behind the Royal Exchange by Edward VII, then Prince of Wales. This was a rare gesture considering the cramped space of the city. When Peabody was alive, he had worked to establish peace and friendship between the United States and Britain. At the time of his death, the British completed construction of a new warship, an extremely powerful vessel that stirred anxiety in the United States. In the end, however, the ship would be used for peace. Steel tycoon Andrew Carnegie sent a telegram to John Bright, who was then part of the British Cabinet. He wrote, "First and best service possible for *Monarch*, bringing home body Peabody." Andrew Carnegie wrote the message anonymously. Soon afterward, Queen Victoria called for the *HMS Monarch* to be used as the transport vessel to take George Peabody's remains back to the United States. A makeshift funeral chapel was built on the ship. Peabody's coffin was covered with a black sheet, and candles burned in the room. U.S. Admiral Farragut and his men received the ship in the United States. Pierpont Morgan had been given the responsibility of handling the funeral, and he organized a little something for the old banker. He arranged for British and American soldiers to march behind the coffin.

His life even inspired Queen Victoria to pen a Royal letter for his service. It reads as follows:

"I have always understood that Mr. Peabody, though known as a great philanthropist, was one of the meanest men that ever walked. I do not know if you ever saw the statue of him sitting on a chair behind the Royal Exchange. Old Mr. Burns told me once that when subscriptions were invited in the City to erect a statue there was so little enthusiasm that there was not sufficient money to pay for the chair, and Mr. Peabody had to pay for it himself. When I first came here the head of our office was Mr. Perman, and I remember when he had been here sixty years Teddy [Grenfell] and I gave all the staff a dinner at the Saucy, and we took them to a Music hall afterward, and old Mr. Perman was at his desk at nine o'clock the next morning. He knew George Peabody's form well and used to tell Jack many stories . . . indicative of his meanness. I always understood that when he retired he announced he was leaving his money in the business—and at once proceeded to take it out. I believe he left several illegitimate children totally unprovided for."

This letter is quite strange for a letter meant to *thank* someone. It sounded more as if the queen were faulting or criticizing Peabody. It did, however, show that although Peabody was very generous in his philanthropy and a very successful man, he wasn't at all a nice person. But then again, not many nice people have succeeded in life.

If it hadn't been for Peabody, however, the fate of the Morgan household would be unknown at this point. It was Peabody who brought Junius in, and that allowed Pierpont to be exposed to some of the most interesting, historic, and pivotal events in the world of finance and the development of the United States. The life of George Peabody is deeply entwined with that of the Morgans and by extension the House of Morgan that followed decades later.

Chapter 6 Jack Morgan

In 1898, when Jack Morgan was already thirty-one years old, he was working at J.S. Morgan and Company. He, too, had a big nose, but it was nowhere near the size of his father's. Jack learned about what had happened in New York and wanted a piece of the action. He once said to his mother, ". . . when I think of home the time does seem a bit long," indicating that he missed New York, the hub of chaos and American banking.

Jack wasn't comfortable with sitting in a very calm place watching the fun happen three thousand miles away on the other side of the Atlantic Ocean. What he felt more upset about was that Robert Bacon was being favored by his father over him. Robert Bacon was, for a short period of time, the Secretary of State under Theodore Roosevelt. Bacon was also a prominent political person.

The plan was that Jack would be posted in London for a short time, but he would only return to the United States in 1905. In 1897, Mary Lyman Morgan's husband, Walter Hayes Burns of J.S. Morgan and Company, passed away. She was Pierpont's sister. He was replaced by Walter Spencer Morgan Burns, the son of Mary Lyman Morgan, Jack's cousin.

Following the passing of Walter Hayes Burns, more novices were in the firm of J.S. Morgan and Company than seasoned bankers.

Pierpont's niece, the daughter of Mary Lyman and Walter Hayes Burns and the sister of Walter Spencer Morgan Burns, married the first Viscount of Harcourt, Lewis Harcourt.

This tied the Morgan family with British aristocracy. The descendants of that family would include a chairman of Morgan Grenfell and Company, Lord William Harcourt.

Jack felt rather ashamed that he had so little contact with his father. Whenever Jack was asked whether or not Pierpont was going to attend the crowning of Edward VII, he would respond by saying that his father was a difficult man to keep tabs on, and that he had lost nearly all hope in trying to find him.

When Pierpont was going to a naval pageant in Spithead, Jack wanted to go along, but he said that his father "will probably not think of asking us." Pierpont did not really include Jack in the business, and he was kept in the dark regarding the business deals that were going on in his father's bank. To get information regarding the trusts of US Steel, he had to read the newspapers.

Although Pierpont loved his timid son, his son was not like him, and that bothered Pierpont. When he was young and even in his older days, Pierpont was ambitious, fiery, and aggressive. In contrast, Jack was timid, scared, and calm—too calm for Pierpont's liking. The fact that Pierpont did not include Jack in the business just made Jack feel worse. In 1899, Pierpont had been away from New York and was just departing from London. Jack told his mother by a letter about how things could not function when his father was not there. He went on to say, "I only hope it will never come to that with me. Probably it won't, owing to the fact that things always will move on without me." This perhaps shows that Jack considered himself an unimportant player in the Morgan bank.

Pierpont's business was growing so large and the things he dealt with took up so much of his time and energy that he did not have room to deal with his timid, reserved, and insecure son. Jack was always standing in the shadows, waiting for his father to pick him up. He always waited for the day that his father would include him and have confidence in him.

Jack was much like his grandfather, Junius Spencer Morgan, in the way that he always kept an eye on the workload Pierpont was handling. He once saw Pierpont and his aunt, Mary Lyman, playing dominoes. He recounted the incident, "It is too funny to see Father and Aunt Mary gravely sitting down to play that imbecile game."

Jack also took care to account the regality and pride of his father. He said that after doing one good thing he felt absolutely proud. Aside from just seeing the funny and egotistic side of Pierpont, though, Jack also saw in Pierpont what was behind the cold, brusque facade. He wrote, "He is very well and jolly by bits but sometimes I see he feels as lonely as I do and he looks as glum as if he hadn't a friend in the world."

Jack was taking care of both his parents. For his father, not directly, but was watching over him and giving both his father and mother his kindness. His mother, whose health was now faltering and somewhat deaf, was being cheered up by her son. Jack was not very happy about London but was much happier when his father said that he and his wife, Jessie, as she was known, could stay at Pierpont's 13 Princes Gate home. Pierpont soon took possession of the house next door, 14 Princes Gate, and the two residences joined together. 13 Princes Gate was filled with the artworks of Rembrandt, Rubens, Turner, and Velázquez, works of art that Pierpont had collected and spent a fortune on. Due to export duties, Pierpont never brought his vast art collection to the United States.

Aside from 13 Princes Gate, Jack also stayed in Dover House, the house that Junius had purchased. Jack was extremely happy that his father had been so kind and generous and had been more of a father to him in some time. He wrote to his mother, "He has been dear to us ever since we landed, most thoughtful of everything and immensely interested in Jessie's social career! I know he has much enjoyed our being in his house, for it must have been very lonely for him with no one there and we have not hampered him at all or bothered him with responsibilities."

By the time 1900 rolled around, the firm of J.P. Morgan and Company was one of the largest banks in the world. Pierpont focused on the reorganization and consolidation of companies. This sort of reorganization would come to be known as "morganization." One example of Pierpont's consolidation of companies was when he created the United States Steel Corporation, which included the steel company of steel tycoon Andrew Carnegie.

What was morganization? When several railroads in the United States were facing a financial crisis, the House of Morgan stepped in to save the day. Pierpont reorganized the railroad companies and placed them under his control. Most of the railroads east of the Mississippi River were nearly bankrupt and were morganized and placed under the control of the House of Morgan. The railroads that Pierpont morganized included the Lehigh Valley Railroad, the Chesapeake and Ohio, the Santa Fe, the Great Northern Railway, the Northern Pacific Railway, the New York Central, the Erie Railroad, the Southern Railway, the Philadelphia and Reading Railway Company, and the Jersey Central. Today, the Philadelphia and Reading Railway Company is called the Reading Company.

Although morganization placed the Morgan banking house at the helm of several railroad companies and furnished the Morgan partners with a great amount of money, it was dangerous work.

During the time of morganization, everyone worked late into the night. Everyone worked hard, and although the reward was wealth, the side effect was death. Some of the Morgan partners simply dropped dead. In one case, a certain Mr. Wood, one of the partners, who was waiting for the arrival of a train, dropped dead.

The trade-off was wealth for one's life.

Chapter 7 High Finance & Low Times

In 1879, the United States Congress established the gold standard, which, among other things, allowed holders of dollars to exchange their dollars for the equivalent value in gold. To make it look like more than an empty promise, the U.S. government made it a point to have a minimum of $100 million in gold in reserves.

The gold standard was greatly disliked by American farmers. Due to deflation, they could not sell their produce for high enough prices, but they had to repay their loans with a great deal of money. When inflation arrived, however, they could raise their prices.

The gold standard was a source of great consternation in the United States. Quite a few Western states made bankers illegal, and the state of Texas barred all bankers until 1904. Former Secretary of State and three-time Democratic presidential candidate William Jennings Bryan riled up the Populists by speaking negatively about how the United States was financially dependent on Britain.

In 1893, a financial panic occurred, which resulted in a crisis for the gold standard. The federal gold reserve dipped below the minimum of $100 million. Because of the panic, overseas investors who had their money in American banks became worried and began to withdraw their money in gold, hastening the decrease of the gold reserve in the United States. In 1894, the gold reserve dropped to $68 million, and it seemed that the United States government might go bankrupt. Pierpont wanted to solve the problem and approached President Grover Cleveland. While Pierpont was waiting for an answer, he played solitaire.

Unfortunately, Cleveland did not want to meet Pierpont. He wanted to sell bonds to the public and get money from there. Congress, the branch of government that holds the purse, however, wouldn't allow it.

Pierpont understood that Cleveland's method was not going to work. The American government did not have enough time to sell enough bonds to fix everything it needed to. In the end, Pierpont traveled to Washington with Robert Bacon and Francis Lynde Stetson.

When Pierpont and his associates arrived in Washington, they were met by Daniel Lamont, the Secretary of War. Lamont told them that President Cleveland did not wish to meet them, and Pierpont replied in an authoritative tone saying that he was not going to leave until he met the president. In the end, Cleveland relented and decided to meet Pierpont.

The night before the meeting Pierpont played solitaire and then went to the White House the following morning. During the meeting with the president, he said very little and let the other attendees speak. He was in such distress at what he heard that his discomfort and unsettled state caused him to inadvertently crush his fist, which crushed his lit cigar in his palm. Crushed tobacco and amber fell on his trousers and the Oval Office floor.

In the midst of the conversation, Treasury Secretary John G. Carlisle received word that only $9 million was left in the federal gold reserves on Wall Street. Everyone was visibly restless at this point.

This is when Pierpont came in. He said he knew of a $10 million draft, but if they did not receive it, everything would be over by 3:00 p.m.

Presenting a demand draft against the United States Government and not getting paid for it would shatter the credit markets and plunge the U.S. economy overnight. The ensuing catastrophe would reverberate globally. The financial collapse would not be limited to

North America but drag other economies with it. Everyone in the room was well aware of that fact.

The reticent Cleveland then turned to Pierpont for his opinion. Pierpont's plan was that his firm and that of the Rothschild's would purchase 3.5 million ounces worth of gold, of which at least half would come from Europe. In exchange for this gold, they would give $65 million in 30-year gold bonds.

His plan was financially and legally sound. An old piece of legislation enacted during the Civil War stipulated that the country could purchase gold from foreign countries. Pierpont used this to his advantage.

When Pierpont concluded, Cleveland quietly knew that Pierpont's proposal was the only solution. He presented Pierpont with a cigar from the humidor on his desk to replace the one Pierpont had crushed earlier. That cigar was a token of appreciation and a symbol of a truce between two men, who couldn't stand each other.

In the end, everything worked out well, and the gold reserves began to rise and stabilize. The draw on the reserves also diminished, and the dollar stabilized as well. Pierpont had solved the problem with an ingenious and workable solution.

On February 20, 1895, the bonds of the scheme were all sold in two hours in London and just twenty-two minutes in New York. Pierpont was delighted with the outcome. He remarked, "You cannot appreciate the relief to everybody's mind for the dangers were so great scarcely anyone dared whisper them." Although the scheme was a success, the parties involved in pulling it off were not looked on very favorably by most.

First of all, they had bought the bonds they would sell for the scheme for $104.25 each and made the first selling price of $112.25 for each of them. People were bidding on the price until it reached a sale price of $119. To some people, this was evidence that the people who had pulled off the scheme that for the time being saved the gold standard had practically been swindlers.

An interest rate of 3.75% was charged on the bonds, which was considered quite high. The bonds had been sold in just twenty-two minutes in New York as mentioned earlier, and several bankers were able to pocket up to $7 million, all of which was profit.

At a later date, Pierpont would argue that these amounts were exaggerated and were far from the real profits that were made. Pierpont went on to defend the group and said they had made less than 5 percent.

Regardless of how much they made, the credibility of the United States had been saved, something that the naysayers to the transaction could neither understand nor appreciate.

Since the Rothschild family had been involved in the scheme, the condemnations and reproaches went further than just opposition to what the bankers had done. They were laced with a layer of anti-Semitism, for the Rothschilds were a Jewish banking house.

One man who opposed what the bankers had done to save the gold standard was William Jennings Bryan, who always said no to having any hints of anti-Semitism in his political fight with the banking houses that conducted the scheme.

When Bryan was running for president a year later, he once spoke to a number of Democrats in Chicago who were Jewish and said to them, "Our opponents have sometimes tried to make it appear that we are attacking a race when we denounced the financial policy of the Rothschilds. But we are not, we are as much opposed to the financial policy of J. Pierpont Morgan as we are to the financial policy of the Rothschilds."

Despite what most thought, though, Pierpont saw his little plan as an act that turned out beautifully.

Pierpont's structure was, however, not a permanent fix. After all that hard work and public censure, the gold reserve in the United States Treasury once again began to dwindle.

When the time came for President Cleveland to fix the situation at the beginning of 1896, Pierpont came up with the idea of global collaboration to solve the problem. The group was meant to consist of Morgan, Harjes of Paris, the National City Bank of New York, and the Deutsche Bank of Berlin.

Unfortunately for Pierpont, however, President Cleveland was not interested in causing an uproar among the Populists again and wanted to proceed with a loan. Because of this, Pierpont only made half of the bond issue, which amounted to $67 million.

For his firm and all bankers alike, if governments stayed weak and ran on tight budgets, then Pierpont and his fellow bankers would all gain. President Cleveland was not upset with the popular reaction to Pierpont's scheme and heartily praised Pierpont for what he did, saying that Pierpont was a patriot.

Because of Cleveland's attitude toward Pierpont, he lost several supporters, and during the presidential elections in 1896, William Jennings Bryan was more popular than Cleveland.

William Jennings Bryan opposed large businesses, such as the companies of oil magnate John D. Rockefeller and the steel company of Andrew Carnegie. People like J.P. Morgan would also have trouble with Bryan because he was going after large corporations, which included Pierpont's firm.

William Jennings Bryan was going to tear down these large firms if he became president, and no industrial tycoon or Pierpont wanted that to happen.

At the time, such magnates as Andrew Carnegie and John D. Rockefeller were making substantial profits, but the workers in their steel plants and oil refineries were in poor condition. Workers would die while working in the steel plants, and others survived to feel the pain of hard work. Most were earning less than a dollar a day. They were all poor, and Bryan's message, however misguided, resonated with them. He managed to vilify the titans who were responsible for building America.

During the 1896 election, people wanted better for themselves, and they wanted Bryan to be president. The titans of industry, however, wanted Bryan as far away from the White House as possible, for with him as president, their businesses would face tremendous headwinds. J.P. Morgan also wanted Bryan out of the White House. Pierpont's ever-expanding firm was always growing larger, and its growth and dominance would be broken by a man like Bryan.

To save their businesses and everything they built, Rockefeller, Carnegie, and J.P. Morgan teamed up to defeat William Jennings Bryan by supporting his opponent in the general election.

To do this, they donated heavily to Republican William McKinley's campaign. McKinley supported big businesses and would allow Pierpont and the others to proceed unchecked. Each of them donated more $200,000 to McKinley's campaign (more than $6 million today).

That battle at the ballot box was one of consequence. Pursuant to the structure that Pierpont had envisioned and executed to save the gold standard, the battle between McKinley and Bryan was about exactly that. The departure from the gold standard to one that was bi-metallic. McKinley advocated remaining on the gold standard, but Bryan was going after the popular vote of the everyday worker. He used his oratory skills to rile up the base and cast dispersion at the titans of industry. They fell for it. Even with McKinley's better proposals, his win wasn't as decisive as he had hoped.

In 1896, William McKinley became President of the United States. With a man who supported large corporations now leading the country, Carnegie and Rockefeller could go on advancing their business without any hindrances. Pierpont could also continue to expand his business and advance his bank without any problems.

Train Trouble

In the late 1800s, the railroad industry was suffering from rate wars and problems between different railroad companies. The most important of these problems were between the Pennsylvania Railroad Company and the New York Central Railroad of Cornelius Vanderbilt. The issue at hand was the West Shoreline, a small railway that was being built parallel to the New York Central Railroad on the Hudson River, although it was running on the opposite bank. Railroads such as these were being created by people who simply understood how the railroad business worked. Railroads were very easily put in danger when competition entered the picture.

This was a time when people were building rival railroads just so they could later sell them to the big railroad companies. They were thus able to make a nice profit in the end.

It was believed that the Pennsylvania Railroad Company was the one behind the West Shoreline, and thus the New York Central locked horns with it. It began to build a line parallel to a Pennsylvania railroad. The fight between the two companies was a never-ending war that would have led to the collapse of both companies had it not been for John Pierpont Morgan.

Seeing that things needed to be fixed, he got the presidents of the two companies to meet aboard his yacht, the *Corsair*. At first, the men did nothing, and the *Corsair* simply sailed up and down the Hudson River. It soon became obvious that Pierpont wasn't going to let them off his yacht until they had come to an agreement. In the end, a compromise was reached, which became known as the Corsair Compact. The New York Central would incorporate the West Shoreline into their railway, having a second railroad running along the Hudson River.

Steep Merger

In 1901, Pierpont would consolidate several manufacturing companies to form the United States Steel Corporation, which used to be the largest producer of steel. Pierpont wanted to include Carnegie Steel Company in the corporation, but to so, he needed to purchase it. He began negotiations with the president of Carnegie Steel, Charles M. Schwab.

Eventually, Carnegie would write down on a piece of paper the price at which he was willing to sell his company: $480 million. A moment after Pierpont was shown the price he said yes.

This payment was the largest transaction that has ever been made in the history of the modern world. That $480 million is equivalent to more than $14.2 billion today.

Carnegie was happy, but he later realized that he had actually sold his company too cheap—almost by $100 million, and that is why Pierpont agreed to the price with such speed. When he admitted this fact to Pierpont, Pierpont simply said, "Very likely, Andrew."

As for the relationship between Pierpont and Carnegie, Carnegie liked Pierpont's father, Junius, but not Pierpont. Pierpont, on the other hand, found people like Carnegie too gruff for his standards. The pair mixed like oil and water. They never really could get along.

For his part, Carnegie did not like Pierpont for his extramarital affairs. As the president of Carnegie Steel and later the first president of US Steel and cofounder of Bethlehem Steel, Mr. Charles Schwab said of Carnegie, "Carnegie frowned on anything savoring of the flesh and the devil."

Aside from just including many other companies and that of Carnegie Steel, it also included the companies of William Henry "Judge" Moore and Elbert Gary, the second president of US Steel. William Henry Moore was both a financier and a lawyer. He was a director of a number of steel manufacturing concerns that were part of the amalgamation that was US Steel. His brother, James Hobart Moore, and himself had a role in founding the First National Bank, the American Can Company, the National Biscuit Company, the Diamond Match Company, the Delaware, Lackawanna and Western Railroad, the Lehigh Valley Railroad, the Continental Fire Insurance Company, the American Cotton Oil Company, the Chicago, Rock Island and Pacific Railroad, the Western Union Telegraph Company, and Bankers Trust.

The United States Steel Corporation took up its headquarters in the Empire Building at 71 Broadway on Manhattan Island. They would have their headquarters here for seventy-five years.

With Carnegie Steel now in his possession, Pierpont could go on to form US Steel. Before he bought Carnegie Steel, Pierpont financed a company called Federal Steel Company. He combined Federal Steel, Carnegie Steel Company, American Tin Plate, Shelby Steel Tube, American Steel Hoop, American Sheet

Steel, Wire Company, Consolidated Steel, and National Tube. Wire Company and Consolidated Steel belonged to the philanthropist, businessman, and inventor William Edenborn. Shortly after the formation of US Steel in 1901, two other companies were incorporated into the trust: Lake Superior Consolidated Mines and American Bridge. Lake Superior Consolidated Mines was in the control of Standard Oil founder John D. Rockefeller.

Many other industrial companies would be included in the trust in the years to come.

This new trust that was the US Steel Corporation was seen by some as a company that was acting as a monopoly in several kinds of industries. In reality, the company was trying to do it all. It was attempting to make railroad cars as well as rails, nails, wire, bridges, and even ships, so it's understandable why other people saw it as a monopoly.

US Steel was the first billion dollar company to ever exist, at one time being worth $1.4 billion, which is about $41 billion today. Although $41 billion really isn't much today, a company being worth more than $1 billion in 1901 was both unprecedented and mind-boggling.

Schwab and others believed that because it was so large US Steel would be able to advance and become even better. When US Steel was first created, the company had a lot of business, and it was predicted that it would eventually produce 75 percent of all the steel produced in the United States. In 1902, it came close. That year it produced 67 percent of the steel in the country.

Business contracted for US Steel at the end of 1901, and with the prosperity of US Steel retracing, Charles Schwab struck out on his own to create the largest steel producing company second to US Steel, which was Bethlehem Steel, founded in 1904. He partnered with Joseph Wharton to start Bethlehem Steel, which eventually became America's largest shipbuilding concern at one point in its history.

Railroad Consolidation

The year that Pierpont bought Carnegie Steel he also founded the Northern Securities Company along with James J. Hill and Edward Henry Harriman. The Northern Securities Company was the amalgamation of the Chicago, Burlington and Quincy Railroad, the North Pacific Railway, and the Great Northern Railway, which was founded by James J. Hill in 1889.

James J. Hill was president of the Great Northern Railway and a minority shareholder of the Northern Pacific Railway. Edward Harriman controlled the Union Pacific Railroad, one of the largest railroad companies in the nation. Both the Union Pacific and the Great Northern Railroad wanted dominance over the Chicago, Burlington and Quincy Railroad to join their own railroads to be the focal point of railways in Chicago. In the end, Hill managed to win over the CB&Q Railroad by buying the shares of the company for $200 each.

When the Northern Pacific Railroad owned up to 40 percent of the stock of CB&Q Railroad, Harriman began a stock raid aimed at the Northern Pacific Railroad.

If Harriman controlled the Northern Pacific, he would be able to decide who were the directors of the board of the CB&Q Railroad. This would place the Union Pacific Railroad, which was under Harriman, in a better position. The stock raid Harriman began against the Northern Pacific Railroad caused the first stock market crash affecting the NYSE (New York Stock Exchange.) In the end, it would be resolved by formation of the Northern Securities Company, a trust that wouldn't last for long.

Investors had previously sold shares that were not theirs to sell and were now eager to buy up shares regardless of the price. It is believed that some of the shares were sold for as much as $1,000. In the end, thanks to Pierpont Morgan, Hill was able to assume a majority shareholder's position in the Northern Pacific Railroad in spite of what Harriman had done to prevent it.

The Northern Securities Company served Hill as a way to control the stock of his vast railroad empire. Several directors who worked for Harriman became representatives of some of the holdings that Hill had regarding shares of the Northern Pacific Railroad.

The Northern Securities Company was the combination of the Northern Pacific Railroad, the Great Northern Railroad, and the Union Pacific Railroad. Pierpont believed that merging these companies would bring peace to the railroad business and be a better alternative. Others, however, saw the Northern Securities Company as yet another way that Pierpont was gaining more power.

Chapter 8 Turning Tides

In 1900, William McKinley was reelected and began his second term in the White House in March 1901. It seemed that big business was still safe. It was during this time that Theodore Roosevelt entered the picture.

Roosevelt was from a wealthy family and chose to have a career in politics. The problem, however, was his public appearance. He was a rich kid. He thus set out to change his appearance and took photographs holding hunting rifles and made himself look less aristocratic. He then enlisted in the army and served in the Spanish-American War. After that, Roosevelt no longer appeared as a rich kid but a daring warrior who had served his country. At the end of the war, he entered politics.

Unlike McKinley, he was greatly opposed to big business and multicorporation companies. His views were antithetical to Pierpont and the other tycoons of industry.

Six months into McKinley's second term, an out-of-work factory hand by the name of Leon Czolgosz assassinated him—no doubt riled up by the rhetoric of William Jennings Bryan.

President McKinley was at the Pan-American Exhibition in Buffalo when Leon Czolgosz shot him twice. Czolgosz was tried and found guilty, and sentenced to death. He was executed on October 29, 1901, approximately forty-six days after he shot William McKinley, and approximately thirty-eight days after McKinley passed away on September 14, 1901.

With McKinley gone and the nation in shock, Pierpont and Rockefeller were now facing an enemy they were not expecting. They had engineered that Roosevelt would replace McKinley.

With McKinley gone, Theodore Roosevelt ascended to the presidency, and Pierpont's business was immediately in trouble. Roosevelt set out to tear down Northern Securities Company in the name of competition and monopoly.

Near the end of February 1902, the U.S. Department of Justice declared that it was filing a lawsuit against Northern Securities. It was going after Pierpont's corporation under orders from President Theodore Roosevelt. They were attacking the company on the basis of violating the Sherman Antitrust Act, which was created twelve years earlier in 1890. The case, known as Northern Securities Co. v. United States, was one of the first antitrust cases. It went all the way to the Supreme Court and lost five to four.

Over the next seven years, other trusts would fall victim to antitrust policies. U.S. government cases against trusts would cause their dismantling. One such case was when the railroad empire of Edward Henry Harriman, which included both the Southern Pacific and the Union Pacific Railroad, was broken.

Pierpont was incensed over the breakup of Northern Securities. He did not like politicians or anyone for that matter to tell him how to run *his* business. Unfortunately for Pierpont, however, the government won. In 1904, the Northern Securities Company was dissolved, and the three railroads that had merged to form the company were on their own again.

In 1955, fifty-one years after the dissolution of the Northern Securities Company, the Great Northern Railroad and the Northern Pacific Railroad revisited the issue of uniting. In the end, everything was a success. The United States Supreme Court gave its approval of the merger and on March 2, 1970, the Chicago, Burlington and Quincy Railroad, The Great Northern Railroad, the Spokane, Portland and Seattle Railway, and the Northern Pacific Railroad consolidated to form the Burlington Northern

Railroad. It would later be turned into the Burlington Northern Santa Fe Railway or BSNF Railway.

Although Pierpont had lost to the U.S. government, this did not mean that he stopped increasing his power.

When Panama became independent thanks to Theodore Roosevelt, Pierpont's firm became the country's fiscal agent. Instead of seething at Roosevelt in perpetuity, he helped with building the Panama Canal.

Chapter 9 The Panama Canal

The United States wanted to gain control of the Panama Canal and the shipping traffic that passes through it. The well-to-do inhabitants of Panama understood that they were better off working for the benefit of the Americans than remaining a poor South American country.

The Panama Canal is a forty-eight mile passage through the Isthmus of Panama constructed for ships to pass through from the Atlantic to the Pacific. The Panama Canal is approximately forty feet deep and has a minimum width at the bottom of five hundred feet. Construction began near the end of 1903 and was completed approximately eleven years later in 1914. Seventy-five thousand workers constructed the canal, and 5,609 of them died while it was being built either from sickness or accidents. Of those 5,609, 4,500 were West Indians.

Construction cost $375 million. This figure includes $40 million the United States paid to France and the $10 million paid to Panama. Both payments were handled by J.P. Morgan and Company.

Construction of the Panama Canal was the most expensive building project ever taken on by the United States at the time.

The chief engineers included John Findlay Wallace, John Frank Stevens, and George Washington Goethals.

Fifteen days after Panama gained its independence from Colombia, the United States of America and the newly created Panama signed the Hay-Bunau-Varilla Treaty, which designated the Panama Canal Zone and laid the foundation for construction of the Panama Canal.

It was around this time that Colombia was entangled in what is known as the Thousand Day War. It began in 1899 and ended in 1902. It was a war between the Liberal Party of Colombia, the Conservative Party, and radical groups in the country. Panama was one of the places in which this conflict was fought.

The United States government was going to pay $40 million to the New Panama Canal Company of France, or the Compagnie Nouvelle du Canal de Panamá. This money was meant to gain the rights to use the resources belonging to the company and also gain permission to build the Panama Canal, which would cut through the isthmus.

The $10 million paid to Panama was meant to secure the land for the Panama Canal forever. Furthermore, in accordance with the Hay-Bunau-Varilla Treaty, the United States was to pay $250,000 every year as a rental fee.

Pierpont's firm was chosen by the Treasury Secretary of the United States, Leslie Mortier Shaw, to manage the transaction with the French.

Pierpont headed several American banks into slowly turning the Republic of Panama into a tax haven, which eventually became a money laundering haven.

In the beginning, the Republic of Panama got ships from other countries to transport Standard Oil goods to not have to pay taxes to the United States.

The Panama Canal gave the United States control of both the Atlantic and the Pacific Ocean. Thanks to the Panama Canal, ships did not have to travel down to the southern tip of South America and then come back up. If you were living in San Francisco and wanted to travel by ship to New York, you would have had to travel south to hazardous waters south of South America and turn back up. After the construction of the Panama Canal, you could sail just a little south, cut through Central America by way of the canal, and then go up to New York. It saved most ships traveling from the Pacific to the Atlantic a great deal of time and money. It also reduced the risk of disaster.

Sadly, Pierpont was not able to see the first ship that passed through the Panama Canal on August 15, 1914. He had financed the canal, and it was a great success, yet he wasn't able to see it work.

It was a totally American endeavor, from the electricity generation invented by Thomas Alva Edison, the finance and structure by J.P. Morgan, and the oil of John D. Rockefeller to run the generators and motors to make the canal function properly.

Chapter 10 Humble Pie

Several years after construction was started on the Panama Canal, a financial panic gripped the country in 1907, and Roosevelt was forced to call on the man he had persecuted in the Northern Securities antitrust case. Pierpont had already proved himself, and there was no one Roosevelt could turn to but him.

From 1906 to 1907, everyone knew there was an impending financial crisis. One thing in international finance that you can't have is the rumor of impending doom because that rumor almost always feeds on itself and becomes a self-fulfilling prophecy. Once the rumor was on the street, depositors began withdrawing their savings. Since a bank lives on deposits, there was a run on banks, and the delicate balance of finance started to destabilize.

When depositors withdraw, banks need to find cash to satisfy the withdrawals, and they typically do this in one of two ways. They either call back loans they have made, or they liquidate their investments.

That has a ripple effect. Liquidating investments has an added effect. To liquidate their investments means they would have to dump stocks or bonds that they had invested in, which has a further impact. The stock market would fall. This is what happened in 1907.

Everyone was hastily withdrawing their money from banks, and there was so much selling on the New York Stock Exchange that it soon crashed. As the funds got sucked out of the system, the credit markets came to a halt.

While all this was going on, Pierpont was out of the scene and enjoying church activities. He transported bishops on private railway cars and was busy attending the Episcopal Convention in Richmond, Virginia. Pierpont also had with him a relative of his personal physician, Dr. James Markoe. She was from California, and her name was Mrs. John Markoe. She has sometimes been suspected of having been a mistress of Pierpont.

Back in New York, luminaries in the corporate world, such as William Rockefeller, Edward Henry Harriman, Jacob Schiff, and Henry Clay Frick, came together and held a secret meeting at the Corner.

They came up with a plan, but when Pierpont heard about it he said it was foolish, and the plan was canceled the following day.

During the time when Pierpont was traveling through Europe on his yacht, the partners of the Morgan bank were constantly warning him that something bad was going to happen at the stock exchange.

On the day of the panic, Pierpont was attending the Episcopal Convention in Richmond. Gradually, more and more cables from Pierpont's office on Wall Street began to arrive in the middle of the convention. Each cable was more pressing than the last. Pierpont, knowing that something was wrong, although clueless as to what to do, headed back to his office on Wall Street. In a humbling reversal of demeanor, Teddy Roosevelt had to approach J.P. Morgan to help steer the country out of the Crash of 1907. There was no love lost between the two men, especially since it was Roosevelt's Justice Department that broke up

Northern Securities. What happened next was nothing short of a miracle.

Chapter 11 Crash of 1907

Market crashes are not a trivial matter to be trifled with. Sovereign governments go to great lengths to avoid them, but in this case, they had inadvertently caused it. Now they needed help to fix it. The agency that would be in the driver's seat if a crash occurred today would be the Federal Reserve, but in 1907 it was yet to be legislated into existence.

ECON 101

Modern economies work when a number of factors come together. There must be activated, which is measured by GDP and growth. When a country is producing output, regardless of what that output is, whether industrial, agricultural, or technological, the output creates the basis of the economy. The second factor is the liquidity of the system that allows the movement of funds to be directed where they need to go to reward the factors of output, act as consideration for the infrastructure that supports that output, and allows for the expansion of that system. Liquidity is defined by money supply and demand. The greater the demand with reduced supply results in an illiquid economy and recessionary forces; conversely, the greater the supply of money and reduced demand results in inflationary forces. Either side of the spectrum is not ideal. Governments have numerous tools at their disposal to adjust the balance between recessionary and inflationary forces. Finally, an economy needs external activity. In most cases, that comes in the form of trade with other economies. Without the other economies to consume the output of this country, there will be no injection of new liquidity into the system, and thus there will be diminished growth. The only growth that results from an economy that has no new demand will be inflationary in nature.

Within the context of these three factors, it is easier to define the anatomy of a market crash. There are two sides to every stock market. The stock market acts as a barometer for the overall economy from the perspective of the demand for the stocks as an investment avenue for excess capital on one hand. On the other, it acts as a measure for the future valuation of potential. In other words, it values the growth potential of the output factors.

When there are excess funds in the system, instead of it sitting idly, bankers put it to good use by buying us stock from the stock market. That increased demand nudges the process higher, and those higher prices appear as a lofty stock market—something we have taken, albeit erroneously, to mean a healthy economy.

When there is insufficient liquidity in the money supply of the capital markets in general, then the value of investment-grade assets are disposed of to convert their holdings to cash or liquid assets. That disposal of investment assets sends their prices falling.

The third element in an economy is the confidence of its participants. Consumer confidence is key in determining everything from discretionary spending to savings levels. On one end of that spectrum is how much people tend to save. The more they save, the more banks have an excess supply of funds. They take that excess supply and invest it in a number of avenues. Banks can lend it out to others who are planning expansion in the next economic cycle. They could invest in the stock market, which will see the process rise. But what happens when consumers are so worried about their money that they do not spend it and do not want to leave it in the bank? They withdraw it and put it under their pillow. Then all that liquidity is sucked out of the system, and there is no money to do anything in the economy. It is like the kid who takes his ball home—everyone can't play. In the same way, the consumer and saver become worried about the economy because of a poor outlook, political uncertainty, or just a bad rumor.

In a typical stock market crash, one of the factors fails, and that precipitates a crash. It could be that the output of the country comes to a halt. If there is no output, there is no creation of goods and services, which results in zero rewards and zero value. Without value there is no basis for the value of a stock, and that completely erodes the wealth that is locked in the value of a stock and thus the stock market. Or the liquidity of the capital markets could diminish, and that creates a scenario where there is no capital to move from one sector of the economy (let's say the savings side of the equation) to the investing side of the equation. Capital flows stop, and the economy comes to a halt. Or, the third is that the confidence of what could happen in the future results in a withdrawal from the system, and that deflates the air out of the system, which results in a crashed economy.

Overview of the Crash

In the case of the Crash of 1907, it was a combination of many factors. The first was the overzealousness of Roosevelt's trust-busting. That just set the scene. There were, however, three vitiating events that created the perfect storm.

First, a failed attempt at manipulating the stock price of the United Copper Company by the Heinze brothers resulted in the stock market plunging. That, in turn, caused a rumor that the third-largest banking trust in New York, Knickerbocker Trust, was somehow involved in the scheme to manipulate the stock price, and that they may be in trouble with trust-busting Roosevelt. That unsubstantiated rumor caused a run on Knickerbocker within a week of the failed stock manipulation. Within a span of three hours, on October 22, $8 million (equivalent to $250 million in today's value) was withdrawn by more than 15,000 depositors who lined up around the block. This created a liquidity crisis. Knickerbocker ran out of cash to pay depositors. That is one of the reasons why the Crash of 1907 is called the Knickerbocker Crisis.

Without any liquidity, the third-largest bank had to stop trading on the stock exchange and liquidate many of their other holdings to be able to cover their obligations. That created a further drop in the market.

On October 21, a Monday, copper shares dropped dramatically, which weakened the trusts in New York. That created a further liquidation of shares on the stock exchange to cover losses on the copper market.

Within two days, on October 24, a further two dozen trading houses across the country had been sucked into the downward spiral and had stopped trading.

News of these events and the corresponding price drops and volume of trades were part of the messages Pierpont was receiving with increasing frequency as he attended the Episcopal Convention.

At first, he was not inclined to get involved. His frustrations with Roosevelt were certainly a factor, but after Roosevelt requested his help, it dawned on him that it was more about the country than the frustrations between them.

After returning to New York, Pierpont analyzed the problem and understood the factors and nuances of the predicament. He understood that the key to unwinding the situation was to restore confidence in the system and do what would require the infusion of capital to buoy the credit and stock markets.

As soon as he got back, he convened a meeting with many of the principals involved on both sides of the equation. They were from companies that were not affected as well as from those that were already underwater. His first act was to stop the hemorrhage.

He also contacted such men as Rockefeller to lend their liquidity to hold the markets from descending further. They obliged. The plan began to work. The stock market that had lost 50 percent of its value before Pierpont's involvement had now stopped its descent, and while it didn't get back up to pre-crash levels, it had at least regained the markets' collective confidence. A sigh of relief could be heard from Wall Street to Main Street.

Two weeks after Pierpont began work fixing everything up, he had already provided enough liquidity to the system that allowed it to do a course correction and return to a stable version of itself. Men like Rockefeller and others who had lent their liquidity to the system were able to reap modest profits in a matter of weeks, and companies that would have otherwise failed were rescued from the brink. Pierpont's plan had saved many trust organizations, trading houses, banking houses, and the New York Stock Exchange.

The cause of the 1907 panic had been attributed to several things. One was President Theodore Roosevelt's speech in which he inveighed against the wealthy men of the country. In his zeal to shore up populist support, he had neglected and underestimated the contribution to stability that the same men of society he was targeting were the ones keeping the economy together.

Another area that contributed to all this was a tight money supply that was inadvertently in effect. The money supply tools that the government has today were not available at the turn of the century.

In the post mortem to the crash, another element that Pierpont realized was that banks had made numerous loans based on the collateral of stock. There was also a very liberal policy in doing so. Would-be investors would seek a loan, perhaps one-fifth of the price of the stock. In essence, today we call that buying on margin. What happens when the price of the stock falls in excess of the margin? The bank is required to liquidate the stock if the borrower can't come up with the funds to cover the adverse price movement. This is also what happened widely across the trading houses. It is one of the reasons the ripples started touching the two dozen trading houses across the country.

One of the things that Morgan had to do was instruct the trading houses to not liquidate the stocks and then inject the liquidity so that they could hold onto those counters while the market rebounded and unlocked the margin call. It was a severe case of Catch-22, but the force of Pierpont's personality convinced them to do it and placed the resource of cash to help them do it.

Sometime earlier two bankers by the name of Thomas William Lamont Jr. and Henry Pomeroy Davison had set up a new mechanism known as Bankers Trust, which was a company whose founding was aided by William Henry Moore as mentioned before. Lamont was the man who asked in 1946 for the letter Queen Victoria had written in "honor" of Peabody.

Lamont was from Liberty Bank, and Pomeroy was from the First National Bank.

Bankers Trust was a firm that would own trusts. After all, commercial banks were not allowed to conduct business regarding trusts, but they could own them. Pierpont would hand over people who were in the business of trusts to Bankers Trust, and after the BT was done with them, they would be directed back to Pierpont's firm.

When Pierpont needed to lend liquidity to the system in the wake of the 1907 Crash, he put together a syndicate of bankers. Among this committee were Benjamin Strong from Bankers Trust and Henry Pomeroy Davison from the First National Bank. This group of bankers was told to go in and verify the books at Knickerbocker. Later, when Benjamin Strong was the governor of the Federal Reserve Bank in New York, he would tell of how he once saw the sad and anxious faces of the people who had deposited money at Knickerbocker Trust. He said, "The consternation of the faces of the people in the line, many of them I knew, I shall never forget. I know that Harry left the building with a sense of dejection and deafest, which it is quite impossible for me to describe."

Pierpont deemed that Knickerbocker Trust was bound to fail. On October 22, the day that people were lining up to withdraw their money, Knickerbocker Trust collapsed.

Several weeks later, when the former president of Knickerbocker Trust wanted to meet with Pierpont, he was not allowed to. He then committed suicide by shooting himself. His suicide caused a wave of suicides among people who had placed their money in the trust.

On one Tuesday night, Pierpont held a meeting with several other bankers as well as the Treasury Secretary, George B. Cortelyou, in a hotel in New York. Cortelyou promised that the government and the bankers would work together. The following day Cortelyou gave Pierpont $25 million of government money to fix the situation.

This was under orders from President Roosevelt.

The collapse of Knickerbocker Trust caused runs to take place at other trusts, mainly the Trust Company of America, which was not very far from Pierpont's office. On October 23 Pierpont held a meeting of the presidents of the different trusts and tried to make them join up and become a force that would fix everything.

Unfortunately, however, they were not able to work together very well because they did not know each other. After Benjamin Strong of Bankers Trust revealed that everything was good with the Trust Company of America, Pierpont, in his greatly authoritative tone, said, "This is the place to stop the trouble, then." The Trust Company of America was obviously not doing well at the time due to the panic, but the report given by Strong simply showed that they were a firm worth saving.

George Fisher Baker, cofounder of the First National Bank; James Jewett Stillman, chairman of the National City Bank; and Pierpont put together $3 million to rescue the Trust Company of America.

During the two weeks that Pierpont was fixing the crash, people constantly withdrew their money from banks. People would set up seating areas and bring provisions and wait through the night for their bank to open so that they could rush in and withdraw their money. New York police gave people numbers to hold their places in line. A certain Sidney Weinberg, who would later be part of the largest bank in the world, Goldman Sachs, was being paid $10 a day to hold people's places.

At the time, the technique that was used to prevent banks from closing down and reducing the number of withdrawals was for the tellers of the bank to count the money very slowly. Annoying but effective.

The trusts of New York were now devoid of fiat currency to give to people who were withdrawing their money. So, the margin loans they had loaned were called back. Those shares that people had bought with the margin loans were then sold, and the money made from selling those shares was used by the trusts to give money to the people who were withdrawing their money from them. The bad thing about this, however, was that when the trusts were calling back their margin loans and people were selling their shares, the stock price of those shares dropped even further, worsening the panic. Although the trusts were calling back their margin loans, they continued to not have enough money to give their customers who were frantically withdrawing their deposits.

Even during the crisis, the trusts continued to give margin loans but at an exorbitant interest rate of 150 percent!

George Walbridge Perkins, Pierpont's right-hand man, sent a telegram to Jack, who was at the time in London, describing the chaos at Wall Street. He wrote, "At all times during the day there were frantic men and women in our offices, in every way giving evidence of the tremendous strain they were under."

All day long Pierpont was constantly bombarded by brokers who were about to be financially destroyed and needed aid. The Corner was filled with nervous men.

Pierpont was the only man who was calm and could fix everything. All the worried people on Wall Street flocked to the doors of 23 Wall Street and were looking up at the windows of the building as they approached.

On October 24, all trading of stocks had virtually stopped. Ransom H. Thomas, former president of the New York Stock Exchange, met with Pierpont and told him that fifty brokerage firms had the possibility of collapse if $25 million could not be put together that instant. He also wanted to close the NYSE for the time being. Pierpont then asked him, "At what time do you usually close it?" In truth, the NYSE was only a short walk away from Pierpont's office. What's funny is that he didn't know the schedule of the New York Stock Exchange.

Thomas replied, "Why, at 3:00." Pierpont wagged his finger and said that the New York Stock Exchange was not to close until that time.

At 2:00, Pierpont convened a meeting of several presidents of prominent New York banking firms and told them that unless $25 million was put together within the next dozen minutes, a great many brokerage firms were going to collapse. Approximately sixteen minutes later, it was agreed that the money would be given.

After that was settled, Pierpont sent a group of people to go to the Stock Exchange and tell everyone that margin loans were obtainable, and that their interest rate was a mere 10 percent.

A Mr. Amory Hodges, one of the people who had been charged with the duty of telling everyone about the margin loans, had his waistcoat ripped off while men rushed and bumped him frantically. That was the degree of chaos that reigned on Wall Street during the panic. Men were tearing up and down shouting and bumping into one another.

After the announcement was made, everyone cheered, and Pierpont, who was on the other side of Wall Street, heard the noise. He asked what the noise was about. What was happening was that the traders of the Stock Exchange were cheering for him.

On October 25, interest rates on margin loans skyrocketed once more. That week alone eight trusts and banking firms collapsed. Pierpont went to the New York Clearing House that day, which is where checks were cleared. He told the Clearing House to send out scripts to act as a backup form of money because of the dangerously low amount of green money.

Pierpont was very determined as he walked to the Clearing House. It seemed as if he didn't see the masses at Wall Street. He walked with his hat perched firmly on his head, his half-smoked cigar in his mouth, a piece of paper held firmly in his hand. As he walked, people in his path moved out of his way, but others who continued to stand there were pushed out of the way by Pierpont.

What differentiated him from everyone else, according to Pierpont's son-in-law, Herbert L. Satterlee, was that he was always steady in his walk. The other men around him ran here and there and generally walked in an unsteady fashion. In contrast, Pierpont walked calmly, determinedly, and steadily.

On the evening of the following day, October 26, Pierpont spoke to several religious leaders in New York and told them to talk about being calm in their sermons. On Sunday morning, a certain archbishop by the name of Mr. Farley gave a sermon meant for businessmen.

By this time, Pierpont had been suffering from a violent cold for some time and headed to his Cragston home to spend the weekend. On October 28, a

Monday, the mayor of New York City, George B. McClellan, went to the Morgan Library with a problem. Foreign investors in Europe were withdrawing their money from the United States. According to McClellan, New York needed $30 million to settle everything. In the end, George Baker of the First National Bank, Pierpont, and James Stillman of the National City Bank took up the job of putting together the money.

Pierpont ordered that a group of bankers were to keep on eye on how all the firms in the city were keeping their books.

Pierpont was now seventy years old and suffering from a violent cold at the time, yet he was able to handle the crisis of 1907 well and easily. He did not stop working despite his cold and spent nineteen-hour days working as he sucked on throat lozenges.

During his time fixing up the 1907 panic, Pierpont said that he missed Jack. Although he did not really have much confidence in him, Pierpont still loved his son.

Once in a while Pierpont's personal physician, Dr. James Markoe, gave him all sorts of gargles and sprays to soothe his illness. Dr. Markoe also told Pierpont that he should reduce his smoking to a maximum of twenty cigars a day. That should show you that he actually smoked a lot on a regular basis.

During extremely important meetings, the titan banker and the king of finance would sometimes fall asleep, and no one wanted to disturb him. One of the bankers at the meeting once gently removed the cigar in Pierpont's hands that was damaging the varnish on the table as he slept.

Pierpont would fall asleep at meetings for half an hour, while the other attendees talked about loans.

On November 2, Pierpont came up with a plan to save the Lincoln Trust, the Trust Company of America, and a brokerage firm known as Moore and Schley, which owned a large amount of Tennessee Coal, Iron, and Railroad shares that it was using as collateral for its loans. It also had a lot of debt.

Pierpont then convened a meeting of several bankers of New York and held the meeting at his private library, known today as the Pierpont Morgan Library.

US Steel Benefits from the Crash

Pierpont wanted something in return for his troubles.

He was, after all, the quintessential banker, and he didn't see anything wrong in making money out of this calamity while helping his country stave off ruin.

Pierpont's plan was to purchase the TCI shares of Moore and Schley. This would be helpful to the United States Steel Corporation, for the Tennessee Coal, Iron and Railroad Company was a competitor of US Steel and owned several well-to-do mines. Pierpont understood that with TCI tied to him US Steel would be able to make nice profits from TCI's iron ore and coal sites located in Alabama, Tennessee, and Georgia.

It was difficult to achieve this, however, due to antitrust policies and a president who tore down trusts and went after "monopolies."

What Pierpont did was say that he would purchase the TCI shares from Moore and Schley only if the bankers that had met in his library put together $25 million that would be used to save the weaker trust companies.

When Pierpont left to let the men discuss the issue, he closed the door behind him, locked it, and took the key with him. He then played solitaire that night in a room nearby. Sometimes, his staff would come in and tell him that the trust presidents in the locked room had come up with a proposition, and Pierpont would say it wasn't enough and would continue playing his game.

At 4:45 the following morning, Pierpont entered the room where the exhausted bankers had not reached a decision. He placed a gold pen in Edward King's hand, the man who led the trust presidents who were there. Pierpont then said, "Here's the place, King, and here's the pen." Tired out from their long night, King signed the paper, and the other presidents did so as well. Everyone then agreed to set aside $25 million for the purpose of saving the weaker trusts.

That night Elbert Gary, who was at the time president of US Steel, and Henry Clay Frick traveled to Washington. They were going there to get Roosevelt's green light for Pierpont's plans. They needed his approval before the stock market opened the following morning at 10:00.

They met with Roosevelt while he was still eating breakfast. Roosevelt did not object to their plans and gave them his approval. In essence, what happened was that Roosevelt agreed not to attack US Steel for Sherman Antitrust Act violations if they purchased the TCI shares. He understood the dire situation that existed and did not cause any problems.

From the White House, Elbert Gary telephoned Perkins, who was at Wall Street, at 9:55 and told him they had been given Roosevelt's approval.

The stock market was thrown into a frenzy. People suspected that Pierpont had swindled Roosevelt into not attacking him with issues of antitrust. Senator

Robert La Follette of the state of Wisconsin said that the banking firms of Wall Street instigated the 1907 panic so that they could make a nice profit from it.

In the end, Pierpont purchased the TCI shares from Moore and Schley for $45 million.

Later, Grant B. Schley, partner of John G. Moore and cofounder of Moore and Schley, said that he could have simply borrowed the money to pay off the firm's debt instead of liquidating the firm's shares of TCI. In the end, the entire operation benefited Pierpont and US Steel. US Steel had less of a competitor, which was beneficial to Pierpont. So, Pierpont not only saved the country but also got something for himself and his trust.

The panic of 1907 ended on November 7 thanks in no small part to the genius and character of only one man who could whip all the presidents of the New York banks and trust companies. It took a strong man with the will and character to be able to stop what would have been the most calamitous financial event in the history of the United States.

Crashes have been averted since that time without Pierpont's presence, and many may point to that as evidence of its ease in rescue. What most do not understand, however, is that Pierpont was a private banker. He did not wield the force of government. In the years that followed, the Federal Reserve Bank took on the role that Pierpont had in the days right after the Crash of 1907.

Chapter 12 The Rise of Morgan

Pierpont was an extremely powerful man by now. He had saved the United States from a financial crisis twice, and he was the most powerful banker on Wall Street. He may not have been very rich if compared with the likes of Carnegie and Rockefeller, although his wealth was quite impressive at the time. The year 1907 was, however, the last time that any banker would wield as much power and would be more powerful and more capable than the government for fixing a crisis in the nation.

After the panic, future President Woodrow Wilson, who was at the time the president of Princeton University, said that the United States should have a group of people to advise it and suggested that Pierpont be its chairman.

Following the panic, Senator Nelson Wilmarth Aldrich said that something needed to be done. His exact words were, "Something has got to be done. We may not always have Pierpont Morgan with us to meet a banking crisis."

The panic of 1907 led to the formation of the Federal Reserve System, which was established on December 23, 1913, just under nine months after Pierpont's passing.

The power that Pierpont wielded and his purchase of the TCI shares from Moore and Schley during the panic of 1907 inspired a lot of investigation into him.

He was so powerful that people didn't believe he amassed that power through honest work, but that he must have had some sort of illegal or illicit activities to gain that much power. People also thought that perhaps Pierpont had used the panic of 1907 to his advantage, which is true. That is how success is achieved. You have to make use of every single opportunity to be successful.

He lost $21 million during the panic, but he did a great deal for the country. If he had not intervened or did not have the power to fix the situation, Wall Street might have collapsed and suffered irreparable damage. The country itself might even have been in serious trouble. He saved Wall Street and the country, but people chose to focus on illicit things he *might* have done and that he was "too" powerful.

The United States Steel Corporation employed blacks and criminals. Thanks to the Black Codes and the laws made by the states in the South after the Reconstruction era, US Steel was able to hire blacks and pay them very little. It was much cheaper to hire blacks in those times than it was to hire the typical white American. Criminals were also employed, and many died from extremely poor working conditions, lack of food, and abuse. Some of them were not even paid at all.

This practice of hiring criminals and blacks did not stop until the latter part of the 1920s. Besides US Steel, eight of the states in the South also followed this practice.

The United States Steel Corporation was best known perhaps for its unprecedented size rather than for the way it was run. In 1901, the trust was dominating the better part of the steel market as well as manufacturing other products. US Steel also built the largest number of passenger ships under the Pittsburgh Steamship Company.

Because US Steel had large debts, Carnegie, who was involved in the trust, wanted to be paid in gold bonds for his part of the company. US Steel was wary of antitrust policies and tread very carefully.

In 1911, ten years after US Steel was founded, its market share of the steel industry dropped to half.

That same year a certain James Augustine Farrell Sr. became president of US Steel. Thanks to him, US Steel expanded. He also founded the Isthmian Steamship Company, which helped with exports of the company. It was thanks to him that the company became the first billion dollar corporation. He remained president of US Steel for twenty-one years until 1932.

After having solved the financial panic of 1907, Pierpont was already partially retired, spending more of his time relaxing and enjoying himself. Because of his shrewd ways and great skill in banking, several conservatives extolled him for what he had done, for he had improved the economy and generally contributed to the betterment of the American financial world. Left wing liberals, however, censured and politically attacked Pierpont for how he had handled the gold standard issue back in 1895 and how he had solved the panic of 1907.

In December 1912, Pierpont stood before a subcommittee of the House Banking and Currency Committee (the Pujo Committee) and said something that made the crowd cheer. The man who was posing the questions to Pierpont at the committee, Mr. Samuel Untermyer, asked him, "Is not commercial credit based primarily upon money or property?" Pierpont replied, "No, sir. The first thing is character."

Untermyer then asked, "Before money or property?" Pierpont replied with, "Before money or anything else. Money cannot buy it.... Because a man I do not trust could not get money from me on all the bonds in Christendom." Pierpont was able to win back the favor of the public through his reply.

In the end, the Pujo Committee concluded that J.P. Morgan and Company, as well as the National City Bank and the First National Bank, were controlling $22.245 billion worth of material. After all, Pierpont's bank was controlling the largest steel producer ever in the United States that was dominating the production of all kinds of products, from nails to ships. The $22.245 billion that Pierpont and his associate banks dealt with would later be compared to the wealth of all the states west of the Mississippi River.

During the investigations, it was also found that partners of J.P. Morgan and Company were directors on the boards of 112 different companies, with a total capitalization of more than $22 billion, which was not much less than the capitalization of the New York Stock Exchange at the time, which had more than $26 billion.

Pierpont was now partially retired by the time he had solved the financial panic of 1907, and he spent more of his time relaxing and winding down in his last few years. Sadly, however, he would not have many years left.

The Financial Reserve System was born after the panic of 1907. A financial panic was taking place on average every ten years, and the American government needed a system to cushion the effects of a panic. The Federal Reserve System was meant to act as an organization that would provide money to borrowers in the country for the worst possible cases during a financial panic. The creation of the Federal Reserve Act would lead to the formation of the Federal Reserve System.

After the panic, Roosevelt wanted the government to control the different stock exchanges in the country. Charles Evans Hughes, who was a governor from New York, wished for interest rates on margin loans to be increased to 20 percent. The original interest rate was 10 percent.

In 1908, the Aldrich-Vreeland Currency Act was passed, which led to the creation of the National Monetary Commission to understand the way banks functioned and worked in the United States as well as European countries. After the creation of the National Monetary Commission, Pierpont tried to lead his firm to have a hold on the organization.

Senator Nelson Wilmarth Aldrich was chairman of the National Monetary Commission.

Henry Pomeroy Davison was the only banker who was in Aldrich's sphere. He would be the agent of bankers and stand for their values. George W. Perkins wrote a telegram saying, "It is understood that Davison is to represent our views and will be particularly close to Senator Aldrich."

Mr. Davison had worked alongside Pierpont during the 1907 panic, and before leaving with Aldrich and his associates for Europe to see the central banks of the Continent, he went to meet with Pierpont.

Pierpont was hoping there would be a central bank of the U.S. government that was private and similar to the Bank of England.

Not all politicians liked the idea of a central bank. Such people as the Populists and William Jennings Bryan thought that perhaps a central bank would be run by the bankers of Wall Street, people that both Bryan and the Populists despised. They also saw a central bank as an organization that would bring an end to a group of people known as the Silverites. These people believed that silver should be part of the money system in the United States in the same way as gold.

Pierpont did not mind a central bank as long as it was a private organization and that bankers were its directors. Henry Davison was the "representative" of all bankers and of Pierpont Morgan and was able to advocate the needs of bankers. He, too, thought that a central bank should be run not by politicians but by bankers.

In November 1910, several bankers from Wall Street and Davison met on Jekyll Island, where their meeting was very hush-hush indeed. They formed the Jekyll Island Club.

Jekyll Island was a place Pierpont went when he wanted to separate himself from the whirlwind Republic of America and decompress.

On Jekyll Island, the bankers met and discussed the foundations of a central bank. They talked about how banks in different areas of the country would be established and would be headed by bankers on a board.

Mr. Davison was the man who orchestrated these meetings.

In 1910, Senator N.W. Aldrich approached Congress with a bill for a central bank, but it was blocked by the Democrats. Three years later, in 1913, Carter Glass, a member of the United States Congress and a

Democratic politician from Virginia, created the Federal Reserve Act based on the bill that Aldrich had proposed three years earlier, but he changed quite a lot from what Aldrich had proposed.

After President Woodrow Wilson took office, he wanted a network of a dozen banks established in different areas, with its board of directors filled with people he chose as well as the Treasury Secretary.

At the time, Progressives of the era wished that the central bank of the U.S. government would help curb the immense power of Pierpont's firm. In fact, the exact opposite happened. Pierpont's firm would be able to use the Federal Reserve System to its advantage and grow ever more powerful, although Pierpont would not be the one to do this.

J.P. Morgan and Company was able to benefit from the Federal Reserve System, for it would be approached by several central banks from different countries all over the world.

In 1909, Roosevelt's time in the White House came to an end, and President William Howard Taft took office. Perkins believed that Taft would support Pierpont's expanding business. After receiving a copy of Taft's inaugural address, he wrote to Pierpont, saying that it was "in all respects conciliatory and harmonizing in tone."

Perkins believed that Taft would not be so difficult with antitrust policies and go after Pierpont's trusts and other trust corporations. He was deeply mistaken. While Pierpont was vacationing in Egypt, Perkins sent him coded telegrams with updates on the new president's staff. He made it seem as if he was the one who chose his staff. One of his telegrams to Pierpont informed him that Franklin MacVeagh had become Treasury Secretary, and that he was the one who recommended him. He went on to say that George Woodward Wickersham would be the Attorney General and finished by saying that the remaining positions were filled in favor of Pierpont's firm.

Perkins was deeply mistaken in his judgment that Taft would be more friendly to Pierpont's firm. Through the entire four years that Taft was president, he would work with and against Pierpont. Taft's fight against Pierpont was even more riled up than Roosevelt's. Two years after Taft became president, he attacked International Harvester and the United States Steel Corporation with antitrust lawsuits.

International Harvester was established in 1902 after the merging of the Deering Harvester Company and McCormick Harvesting Machine Company. The merger was conducted by Pierpont's firm. International Harvester was a concern that manufactured construction machinery, cars, trucks, household items, and agricultural machines. This trust was not greatly disliked by people, for it was actually helping them.

Aside from just going after Pierpont, he also attacked John D. Rockefeller, calling for the breaking up of Standard Oil. Taft also broke up the trust of American Tobacco owned by James Buchanan Duke.

Although the American government was going after large businesses and Pierpont's firm, something else was in play. In the United States, Pierpont's firm was being attacked by the government, but outside the country, the government was working with Pierpont's firm to spread its influence and domination over other countries.

In the past, U.S. bankers and the American government never could get along. Now, however, the world of finance was uniting with the world of politics, and the two forces were working together and mutually benefiting.

In time, the firm of J.P. Morgan and Company would become deeply connected with the American government.

The American government wanted to team up with Pierpont because it wanted to have other countries allow U.S. products in their country. The government also saw it as a way to boost the good of the United States and build its reputation.

As for people like Pierpont, it was a good way to be paid back for their loans. They had the power of the army and the police to get them their money back. When Jacob Schiff, the head of Kuhn, Loeb, and Company, was once thinking about giving a loan to the Dominican Republic, he asked his colleague, "If they do not pay, who will collect these customs duties?" In response, his colleague, Sir Ernest Cassel, said, "Your marines and ours."

The Dominican Republic was going to use the import tax they made to pay back the loan.

During Taft's first year as president, he teamed up with Pierpont to spread American financial dominance in Honduras. Taft also wanted to settle the financial issues of British people who had loaned money based on bonds.

Pierpont's firm was to purchase Honduran bonds, which had existed for some time. In London, these bonds were being sold very cheaply. After that was done, Philander C. Knox, the Secretary of State, was supposed to place a lien from the United States on the taxes earned by Honduras. Knox was then supposed to sell recently issued bonds of Honduras with the help of Pierpont's firm.

The U.S. Army was to stand behind the plan, but Pierpont did not willingly support it. His firm had been forced by the government to help the government. It was the kind of house that dealt only with certain governments and not low-level, Third World countries, such as Honduras. So, they were not so keen on doing business with it.

Pierpont's son, Jack, once sent a telegram to J.S. Morgan and Company in London, saying, "Negotiations only undertaken because US Government anxious get Honduras settled." This showed that Pierpont's firm actually had no interest in this but was doing it just to get it over with.

Jack and Henry Pomeroy Davison, the banker who was with Aldrich, were not willing to go on with the plan unless they had a contract that guaranteed the bonds. In the end, the American government decided not to follow through with the plan, and that was the end of it.

The place where the new relationship between banker and government was truly exhibited was in China.

Again, Pierpont's firm was not interested in a country like China. It was not as organized as the places in which Pierpont's firm operated. The Chinese government was said to have been dishonest, cheating their debtors. Because of conditions in China, most bankers did not like doing business with it, and the firms of Wall Street turned to Japan, China's long-time nemesis.

In China, there were the domains of the British, French, and Germans. Now the Americans wanted a slice of the cake. The British, French, and Germans had established themselves in China when the country did not have enough money to construct railways. Under McKinley's administration, in 1899, John Hay, Secretary of State, established the Open Door policy, a policy that allowed all countries to trade and conduct business with China, but that changed when Taft came into office.

He would try to get the United States an equal share of power that the British, Germans, and French were enjoying in China.

In 1909, the U.S. Department of State forced all the banking firms of Wall Street to begin dealing with China. A group of German, British, and French banking houses were just about ready to lend $25 million to China to construct a railway running from

Canton to Shanghai. The railway was called the Hukuang Railway. The Americans then came in and wanted to receive the same percentage of interest that the other banks that loaned money to the Chinese were receiving.

A group of banks comprising the National City Bank, Kuhn, Loeb and Company, and the First National Bank was called the American Bankers Group. It was headed by Pierpont's firm according to the wishes of the Department of State.

Before this, these banks fought each other during the cornering of the Northern Pacific Railroad, and now they were being brought together by the American government, which believed that if these banks worked together American dominance would become stronger in other countries.

This group of bankers held their meetings at Pierpont's office on Wall Street. The bankers were being controlled by the State Department, and the government's conduit was Henry Pomeroy Davison. He once told Teddy Grenfell, a partner of J.S. Morgan and Company, "Think it would be very wise if you would casually but firmly point out to those with whom you come in contact that this is a proposition of the Government and not of the Bankers."

At this time, people believed that the U.S. government had the bankers by the neck, and that they were fleeing. As this notion was percolating in the minds of the public, Mr. Henry Davison was saying, "Continue to be governed entirely by wishes of the State Department." In the past, bankers had stood fast and stayed separate from the government, and they were now extremely furious with Davison.

So far, the United States had been trying to bring down the large trusts of the company and suppress the large banks of the financial world, such as J.P. Morgan and Company. What people didn't know was that the American government and the firm they were trying to "suppress" were secretly working together to increase the power of the United States.

Teddy Grenfell was the envoy between the Americans and the French, German, and British banks. He was and would continue to be a bridge between Pierpont's office at 23 Wall Street and the British government.

At this time, the Morgan firms in London and New York were acting in favor of their own governments, which caused a rift between them. Eventually, J.P. Morgan and Company would be an entirely American bank, and everything else was just connected to it.

During Taft's administration, the group of bankers known as the American Bankers Group was how Pierpont conducted business with China. The man who acted as the American Bankers Group in China was a certain Willard Dickerman Straight.

After graduating from Cornell University, Straight had a job in the Imperial Maritime Customs Service. He worked in Peking and learned to speak Mandarin while he was there. In 1904, during the Russo-Japanese War, he was a reporter for the Associated Press and Reuters to cover the war. During the time Straight was in Seoul when Korea was still one country, he met Edward Henry Harriman, head of the Union Pacific Railroad.

Harriman hired Straight, and his job was to get Harriman a chance to build a much needed Chinese railway.

Roosevelt made Straight general of the U.S. consul in Mukden, a railway hub in Manchuria.

Straight was a very relaxed government official. He played the guitar, sang Kiplingesque, painted in watercolor, and enjoyed life. He said that China was "the storm center of world politics, where everyone more or less is spying on everyone else."

In 1909, Straight met a woman by the name of Dorothy Whitney. She was the daughter of William C. Whitney, who was once a navy secretary. Mr. Whitney had earned lots of money by working in the business of cars, tobacco, and other products. He was also involved with the stock market, buying and selling shares. Both of Dorothy's parents had passed away when she was young, and she was raised by Robert Bacon and his wife, Martha Cowdin.

Dorothy was very much like Straight, and they were engaged two years after they met.

The same year that Straight met Dorothy he became the envy of the American Bankers Group.

In 1910, he worked in Pierpont's headquarters at 23 Wall Street, something he thought was good luck, for the number of the street was the same number as Dorothy's birthday—the date of the month perhaps.

He was quite shocked by how Pierpont's firm controlled the Department of State.

Pierpont once told Pomeroy Davison, "You might as well make it clear that when we want to discuss things with the US Government we want the Secretary of State and not the assistant secretary." Straight once remarked, "It was not difficult to see where the real power lies in this country." These two anecdotes show that Pierpont's firm had more dominance over the American government than the American government had control of *it*.

In the end, whenever the Secretary of State, Philander C. Knox, wanted to meet with the American Bankers Group, he would come to 23 Wall Street.

In 1910, another loan was given to China, which would receive $50 million to reorganize its currency. Straight was very happy about it.

The loan was agreed to the following year by envoys from France, Britain, and Germany as well as by Straight and Chinese government officials. It was at this time that Straight wrote to Dorothy and said, "We've arranged it so that we can practically dictate the terms of China's currency reform. When you think of holding the whip hand in formulating the first real sound financial basis for a country of 400 million, it's quite a proposition."

When everyone found out about the loan, Straight became popular. Aside from the fact that he was connected with Pierpont's behemoth of a firm, he had also been a success regarding the loan to China. Because of this, he gained better favor with Dorothy's parents.

Dorothy's foster father, Robert Bacon, had obviously been acquainted with Pierpont, and Dorothy, being part of his family, was too. She wrote a letter to Straight saying, "Dear Mr. J.P. he's such a sweetie underneath the sternness."

Straight remained at Pierpont's firm for as long as he did perhaps because he liked the benefits he received by simply being connected and being part of the firm.

Straight was overconfident regarding the success of the second loan to China. Both he and other financiers had invested their money in the Manchu government, a corrupt leadership. How was that supposed to work?

The lenders who had loaned their money to the Chinese were going to suffer a loss. Straight wanted to do things in such a way that would prevent the loan from being a failure. What Straight didn't understand was that the Chinese people did not like outside financiers.

In 1912, a conference was held in Paris at which both Russia and Japan wanted to be part of the group that was dealing with China. They were granted their seats.

This was what Straight feared most. He did not at all like the prospect of having China's enemies among the group of bankers that were conducting business with the country.

Straight predicted ". . . the inevitable day when China's finances will be administered like Egypt's—by an international board. Another dream shattered!"

Perhaps this meant that he had been expecting that the Americans would be able to have a dominating effect on China, but his hopes obviously did not materialize.

In 1911, a revolution took place in China. The cause of the revolution was partially because the people did not like overseas bankers meddling with their country. Dorothy, now Straight's wife, supported those who were revolting.

In January 1912, a new China was formed and headed by Sun Yat-sen. He led a group of people to bring China together and push out all outside elements.

During the revolution, Straight kept a loaded revolver next to him. His wife, however, was not at all worried and even thought it would be fun. She wrote, "It would be rather exciting to be attacked by a wild mob in the night."

Willard and Dorothy were once preparing to go out and have dinner with one of their neighbors of British nationality. While they were still in their home, they heard gunshots. Straight described what happened. When the gunshots were heard, he told his wife that perhaps something was wrong. Dorothy wasn't at all bothered and went on preparing herself to meet their neighbor. She was quite undisturbed, and when Straight told her to just wear casual clothing so that if they needed to they could make their way to the Legation, she adamantly refused.

When the gunshots ceased for some time and things were calm for a moment, Straight and his wife headed to the home of their neighbor. Soon, however, soldiers began to rob some shops that were in the vicinity. Straight and his wife then took their housekeeper, some clothes, and headed for the Legation. Unfortunately for them, they ran straight into rioters on a street that was a dead end.

Not very long afterward, a group of American marines freed them. In the end, Straight and his wife were able to make it to the Legation.

After Woodrow Wilson became President of the United States in 1913, America would soon back out of China. William Jennings Bryan, the man who was the greatest threat to Pierpont and all the other titans of industry or finance in America, became Secretary of State under Wilson.

Six days after Wilson took office on March 10, 1913, Straight and Pomeroy Davison came to Washington to meet with Bryan, who was certainly not going to go to

23 Wall Street, the office of one of the people he would have tried to destroy had he become president in 1896. So, 23 Wall Street had to go to him.

At their meeting, Bryan asked what they would want from the American government if the Chinese did not pay their debt. Davison said the American government could "be called upon to utilize both its military and naval forces to protect the interests of the lenders."

What he was basically saying was that if China did not pay its debt he and the American Bankers Group would want military force to get their money back.

Both President Wilson and Bryan were opposed to becoming involved with foreign countries as the previous administration of Taft and bankers of American Bankers Group had been. A week after the meeting Bryan had with Pomeroy and Straight President Wilson said that the loan was "obnoxious to the principles upon which the government of our people rests."

The American Bankers Group was disassembled the next day. It had been a conduit through which the administration was acting, and if the current president did not want it or supported it, it could not exist.

Most bankers were happy that things had happened the way they did, for they were not so sure whether or not China was going to pay its debt. Pierpont's firm was also glad to be done with China.

After everything was over, Teddy Grenfell of J.S. Morgan and Company, who was always working during the China issue, wrote a letter to Jack that read, "I think that all of us will have 'China' written on our hearts when we die, with several uncomplimentary epithets after it."

Although the business with China was a failure and an operation that fell flat on its face, it was a success in another area. It made different banks feel more comfortable about working together in a foreign domain. Such firms as the First National Bank, J.P. Morgan and Company, and the National City Bank all joined in a specific part of the financing, which biographer Ron Chernow has called in his book about the Morgan house "Latin Lending."

The unification of these three firms caused the already immense power of Pierpont's firm to increase substantially. Several times the firm of Kuhn, Loeb, and Company would join the group of J.P. Morgan and Company, First National Bank, and National City Bank. These would be the banks that would be dubbed the "Money Trust." They would be brought to the Pujo Committee, where Pierpont had testified.

What the American people didn't know was that what they called the "Money Trust" had inadvertently created the "trust" while it was seeking to extend its domain.

The world was entering a time when bankers and governments were one and no longer arch enemies. The effect was so great that a man like Jack, who, like his father, greatly despised the government, was able to pull himself back from being so open about it. In 1912, Jack sent a telegram to Teddy Grenfell, saying, "You will understand we do not wish to accuse our own Government too loudly in view of necessary relations with the other foreign matters."

Although Jack was as headstrong as Pierpont regarding his dislike for the American government, he understood that he could not voice this dislike.

After everything was over, Straight continued to work at the 23 Wall Street office, but he never did feel comfortable working in that slow environment.

When former president Theodore Roosevelt ran again against Taft and Wilson in 1912, he was supported by Straight and his wife.

In 1914, Straight financed *The New Republic*, a weekly magazine/newspaper that strongly supported Theodore Roosevelt when it was first created.

Straight was the kind of man who could not take a slow environment for very long and found working in Pierpont's bank to be quite difficult. Straight founded the India House, an institution that dealt in trading with other countries. The India House was located in Hanover Square in New York. Straight would continue to work at the Morgan bank for just two more years.

Although a financial genius and a great banker, Pierpont did sometimes choose the wrong ventures to invest in, and they all backfired on him. One such case involved the London Underground. A man by the name of Charles Tyson Yerkes was able to prevent Pierpont from receiving permission from Parliament to build the Piccadilly, City, and North East London Railway. This underground railroad would have been a competitor of Yerkes' railway, the Tube.

Nikola Tesla

Another one of Pierpont's unfortunate business ventures concerned Thomas Alva Edison's rival inventor, Nikola Tesla.

In 1900, Nikola Tesla gained Pierpont's confidence that he would be capable of constructing a wireless communication system that could span the Atlantic Ocean. Pierpont was confident enough to lend Mr.

Tesla $150,000, which now would be equivalent to $4,517,400. It was planned that Pierpont would receive control of 51 percent of the patents. After everything was settled, Tesla wanted to quickly expand his venture by constructing a wireless power transmission system that would work on the land. In the end, Pierpont did not want to lend him any more money to do this and did not want anything different from what had been originally discussed. All the money invested was now gone. Tesla's transatlantic communication system was thrown into the dustbin, and that was the end of it.

Chapter 13 The Sun Sets

Pierpont was a sad and lonely man in his last few years. He traveled everywhere and spent a lot of time in Europe and the continent. Before going somewhere, Pierpont would tell Jack where he was going. Pierpont was once asked what his favorite places were. Pierpont said, "New York because it is my home; London because it is my second home; Rome, and Khargeh."

More than any other place, Pierpont greatly loved Egypt. Between 1910 and 1913, he would go to Egypt three times, and he financed the dig sites in Egypt that were being conducted by the Metropolitan Museum.

Just four hundred miles away from Cairo, excavations were taking place at the oasis of Khargeh. He was deeply interested in the excavations and asked the ship-building concern of Thomas Cook and Son that a ship meant to sail on the Nile River be called the *Khargeh*.

Pierpont would later stand on the *Khargeh* and throw coins into the Nile. Children would jump into the river and fetch them.

But Pierpont was a lonely man, and one of his biographers wrote, "It is said there are scarcely fifty men in the financial district who have a speaking acquaintance with Morgan." Only a few people were really close to him. His family provided him at least a little happiness.

What would be especially painful for him occurred when his daughter would be ripped away from him after having been convinced that she was being used by her father by a certain Bessie Marbury.

This daughter of Pierpont's was the philanthropist Anne Tracy Morgan. She was a mischievous child and took after her father in several ways. She was a jolly, active young child, who liked to play tennis and golf. She was also very difficult to handle when raising her to be a member of the aristocracy.

Anne was smart, authoritative, always had her view of things, and headstrong like her father. A certain Elizabeth Drexel, who would go on to become the wife of Harry Lehr, said that Anne was "a thin lanky child with an elfin face and penetrating eyes." Miss Drexel also described her as a child with "a personality and a will as strong as Pierpont's own and a disconcerting habit of putting her elders in the wrong."

Anne would sometimes insultingly mock her father. One time when Pierpont was having dinner with some of his colleagues he asked Anne what she wanted to be when she grew older. She said, "Something better than a rich fool, anyway." Although she would mock and insult him, she was also close to him and would go with Pierpont on *Corsair III* when he was going to Europe.

When the Kaiser of Germany was once on board her father's yacht, she was the one who tended to him.

At the beginning of the twentieth century, Anne had become a woman who was much like her father. She possessed Pierpont's chilling stare and absolutely despised the drawings that exaggerated and insulted Pierpont because of his nose. She also despised the people who drew them.

Pierpont was a man that liked high-quality and beautiful clothing. His daughter also liked fine clothing.

In 1903, a lady from Washington by the name of Daisy Harriman got Anne to be a cofounder of the first ladies club in the United States, the Colony Club. It was located on 30th Street and Madison Avenue and was made to look like a British club that was for men. It had several Turkish baths and a swimming pool made of marble.

One of the rules of the club was that all men who visited were not allowed to go above the first floor.

Pierpont did not like the club and said, "A woman's best and safest club is her own home."

During the time in which the Colony Club was coming into existence, Anne met Elsie de Wolfe and Bessie Marbury. Wolfe was once an actress and quite well-known. She furnished the Colony Club.

In 1901, Anne, Wolfe, and Marbury began to live together in Villa Trianon in Versailles.

For several years, Anne and her two colleagues would create many pro-feminine institutions and achieve a great many things. One of these was creating a dance hall for Broadway and bankrolling the first musical of American composer and songwriter Cole Albert Porter.

When some female workers once went on strike, Anne supported them. She also started a temperance restaurant in Brooklyn and founded an organization as a fund to provide for young and employed women to take a holiday.

In 1908, Anne had lunch with President Roosevelt in the White House, and Roosevelt was only too happy to be thinking about the uncomfortable state of Pierpont.

Pierpont did not at all like his daughter's behavior. She really was very different from the rest of society.

Certain people who attended the parties and events of Anne and her colleagues included Maxine Elliott and Bernard Berenson. Elliott was once one of Pierpont's mistresses.

Like her father, Anne was always smoking and also very popular. After all, she was ranked among the wealthiest young women in the world. Aristocratic Europeans constantly approached her.

False information once got out that she was engaged to marry a count from France by the name of Boni de Castellane.

At one point, the relationship between Anne and Pierpont would sour thanks to Bessie Marbury. Bessie told Anne that she was being used by her father to cover up his extramarital affairs, and that was why he taken her on his yacht. This was what made Anne separate from her father. One other possible cause is that when she found out about the affairs themselves she was greatly upset about them.

Anne's siblings did not look favorably upon her attitude toward her father.

The breaking of the relationship between Pierpont and his daughter was very painful for him and unimaginably saddening. A friend of Anne's said, "It broke her father's heart when she elected to part from him."

In the end, Pierpont would get his revenge on Bessie Marbury.

Bessie Marbury deeply wanted to be awarded the French Legion of Honor. During her career, she had spoken on behalf of playwrights from France. She had also volunteered her house in Versailles as a hospital during the First World War. She had also been able to put together money for the country. This was obviously after Pierpont's passing because he died in March 1913.

This is where Pierpont would get his revenge. He would stop her from winning that award. In 1909, Robert Bacon became the American ambassador to France. Pierpont did not want Marbury to get the award, and Bacon honored his wishes.

When the French were informed that Pierpont did not support the idea of Marbury receiving the award, France did not want to give it to her. Although past presidents of the United States, such as William Howard Taft and Theodore Roosevelt, supported Marbury, the French were not going to give it to her at the cost of going against J.P. Morgan.

During the last few years of Pierpont's life, his relationship with Jack strengthened and was quite good. Although Jack provided emotional backing for his father, there were a few things he vowed never to do, such as have extramarital affairs. He remained faithful and loyal to his wife, Jessie. Due to Jack's innate low self-confidence and lack of ambition, he would not be as great as Pierpont while heading the Morgan house. He would run it well but not as powerful and impactful as his father.

In 1910, he fell to the ground from extreme exhaustion. Because of his feelings that he was not good enough and could not handle everything, after the incident, he wanted someone else to generally run things. Jack took a more overall position and led the bank as a whole.

In the end, Jack became the leader of the Morgan house, but two other people wanted to be the leader: George W. Perkins and Henry Pomeroy Davison. There were several problems with having Perkins as the leader of the Morgan bank. On one hand, problems had arisen with him when he worked at the New York Life Insurance Company.

In his mind, he also placed himself at the top and forgot that he *served* the firm.

Perkins owned a home and land around it in Riverdale. His home was furnished with a bowling alley, swimming pool, and ballroom. He also had nine servants. Finally, he owned a custom-made car. It was eleven feet long and furnished with a washstand table as well as a desk.

He was very haughty regarding the Morgan bank. He thought that he was better qualified that Pierpont's son to be the next leader of the House of Morgan.

Sometimes, he would do things without first discussing them with the firm. In 1910, for example, Pomeroy Davison and Pierpont had a conversation in which Pierpont said that Perkins had gone against what he wanted regarding the financing agreement of the Studebaker Company. Pomeroy then told Perkins about what Pierpont said, and Perkins then sent a letter to Pierpont, which read, "I am very deeply disturbed by one remark that Davison made, viz., that you felt I had gone ahead and deliberately disregarded an understanding with you and concluded the business to suit myself."

George W. Perkins would leave the House of Morgan in six months. He was kicked out of the bank. Thomas William Lamont Jr. recounted that Perkins "didn't leave on his own accord. Morgan thought he had been a little second-rate on some deals."

Regarding Henry Pomeroy Davison, he was on the path to becoming the chief operating executive of J.P. Morgan and Company.

Davison was from a not very well-to-do family. His father sold farming equipment, and he and his family were quite poor. When Henry applied to Harvard University with a scholarship application, he was rejected. He did not go to school.

One of his early jobs was working in a bank that was in Bridgeport, Connecticut, the state in which Pierpont Morgan was born. One of the directors of the bank, a certain P.T. Barnum, liked Davison and asked him to come and play whist with him every week.

In 1893, Pomeroy married Miss Kate Trubee. He and his newly wedded wife then moved to New York. There, Davison worked in the Astor Trust Company. During his time there, a robbery occurred, which he handled well.

The robber stood before the window in front of Davison at his desk and pointed a gun at him. The robber then gave a check for $1 million and told him to give him the money that was stated on the check. Davison began to count out the money in small notes.

As Davison was going about his business deliberately slowly, the guard of the bank was able to get the police on the scene, and they arrested the robber when they arrived.

At a later date, Baker would come to him and say, "Davison, I think you'd better move your desk up here with us." Davison became the vice president of the First National Bank. He also assisted in founding Bankers Trust.

During the panic of 1907, Davison was involved in talks and discussions regarding the panic and later acted on behalf of the financial hub that was Wall Street on the National Monetary Commission. He soon caught Pierpont's attention.

Stories about Davison show that he was a man who was joyful, confident, and hardworking.

He also enjoyed hunting and killed such animals as elephants, rhinoceroses, moose, antelope, and hippopotamuses.

He also liked to spend time with others and talk to people. He would hold dinners at his Peacock Point home, where he often had at least twenty guests.

When Davison joined Pierpont's bank, he brought with him several skilled people, including Ben Strong, Thomas Lamont, John Davis, and Dwight Morrow.

Thomas Lamont was the most valuable person that Davison brought to Pierpont's firm.

After Lamont left college, he became a reporter for the *New York Tribune* while studying at Harvard University. He later quit being a reporter and went to work at Cushman Bros., which was a company that advertised different companies in the food industry. It was not doing very well financially, and Lamont was able to save the company, and after doing so their name was rechristened Lamont, Corliss, and Company. He basically became a partner.

Soon, Lamont became known for helping out Wall Street concerns, which attracted Davison's attention.

Lamont was the kind of person who did not have to crawl through the mud and trenches to get what he wanted. He could easily sail through and be successful.

In 1903, Lamont, who was now thirty-three years old, was on a train heading for Englewood. This is when he met Henry Pomeroy Davison. When Lamont got onto the train, Davison was thinking about who would be the treasury secretary at Bankers Trust. Davison would approach Lamont about the position.

Lamont replied, "But I don't know the first thing about banking. All my brief business life I have been borrowing money—not lending it." Davison then said,

"Fine, that's just why we want you. A fearless borrower like you ought to make a prudent lender." Lamont took the job and later became vice president of Bankers Trust. He would eventually become a director.

Six years after taking the job as treasury secretary he would become the vice president of the First National Bank. A year later he would be called to the Morgan bank by Pierpont himself.

When they met, Pierpont told him, "You see that room over there? It's vacant." He went on to say, "Beginning next Monday, I want you to occupy it." Lamont acted completely surprised. He then said, "But what can I do for you that is worthwhile?" His answer was, "Oh, you'll find plenty to keep you busy. Just do whatever you see before you that needs to be done."

Lamont was not entirely "game on" about the proposal though. He once spoke with Pierpont and told him that he wanted to travel for three months at a time on an annual basis. Pierpont was not at all irritated or angered and said, "Why, of course, take off as much time as you like. That is entirely in your hands."

Lamont was actually very skilled and could handle situations very well, but he acted very humble, and that just made him more liked.

In his last few years, Pierpont made it clear what was to happen to J.S Morgan and Co. When Pierpont's father was alive, he said that the firm of J.S. Morgan and Co. should exist for as long as one generation or as long as Pierpont's lifetime. Thus, he made it so that his name could be used. Twenty years had nearly passed since Junius' passing in 1890, and Jack said, "As we approached 1910, father said, 'You will have trouble enough when I die without having to think of a new name for this firm, and I suggest that we should now change it to Morgan, Grenfell & Co. and make J.P. Morgan & Co. partners in it. They do keep one million pounds in capital."

On January 1, 1910, J.S. Morgan and Company was renamed Morgan, Grenfell, and Company. This was the first time ever that the House of Morgan had a British name as part of a name of one its representatives or in the name of any firm of the House of Morgan.

Jack and his father were previously partners of J.S. Morgan and Co. Now, the entire firm of J.P. Morgan and Co. was a partner of Morgan, Grenfell, and Company. The direct firm under Pierpont would take 50 percent of the profits made by the London firm.

The way that Pierpont had structured his banking empire was that his office at 23 Wall Street was the center of it all—the capital of the Morgan Empire.

Atlantic Transport

Bernard Nadal Baker owned the Atlantic Transport Line, which owned both passenger ships and cargo ships. He once attempted to sell the Atlantic Transport Line to a certain John Ellerman, who was the chairman of the board of directors for the Leyland Line, a purely cargo ship company. Talks were held, but Ellerman did not purchase Baker's company.

Ellerman had also attempted to take control of the HAPAG shipping company and the Cunard Line.

It was at this time that Pierpont finished finalizing things with the International Navigation Company's president, Clement Griscom. The International Navigation Company controlled both the American Line and the Red Star Line. After talks that lasted for six months, the International Navigation Company merged with the Atlantic Transport Line in December 1900.

Two more companies would soon join the corporation that would be the IMMC: the White Star Line and the Leyland Line, a company where Ellerman was a director. Finally, the International Mercantile Marine Company was established on October 1, 1902.

Pierpont's last year was stressful and painful for him. On one side, the International Mercantile Marine Company was dealing with fierce competition from the Cunard Line, and a disaster would take place that would drive him into a state of grief.

Titanic

The Cunard Line had by now constructed the RMS Lusitania and the RMS Mauretania.

To contend with their major competitor, the IMMC decided to build two new gargantuan ships—the RMS Olympic and the RMS Titanic, both of which belonged to the White Star Line. To have enough room for these ships, Pierpont's firm tried to get the New York Harbor Board to make one of the piers of the Hudson River longer by one hundred feet so that the Titanic and the Olympic could dock at it.

The RMS Titanic was launched on May 31, 1911. Pierpont was present for the launch. He climbed aboard the ship, where he saw the cabin made for him to travel on during the ship's maiden voyage. It was wonderfully furnished, and the bathroom had a special container for his enormous cigars.

Pierpont was supposed to travel on the first trip of the Titanic but cancelled at the last minute. Just think about it: J.P. Morgan was about to go on the ship that would sink to the bottom of the Atlantic Ocean.

On April 16, 1912, the day after the RMS Titanic sank, Pierpont learned of the catastrophe while he was in France. He sent a telegram to an associate of his in New York saying, "Have just heard a fearful rumor about Titanic with the iceberg." He went on to say, "Without any particulars. Hope for God sake not true."

After everyone knew of the calamity, the press of the continent found Pierpont at a chateau. He looked absolutely saddened and depressed. At one time, he said, "Think of the lives that have been mowed down and of the terrible deaths." The sinking of the Titanic greatly affected him. Not only had his firm invested in the company that built the ship, but a great many people had also died.

Of the more than two thousand people who sailed on the Titanic, more than one thousand five hundred died in the accident. Some went down with the ship, and others jumped into the ocean but tired out from the bitter cold and drowned too.

Those that survived the disaster were rescued by the Carpathia, a ship belonging to the Cunard Line.

The sinking of the Titanic caused a serious financial problem for the IMMC. The situation became so severe that in 1915 the company had to seek protection from bankruptcy, which limited the amount of money it could spend to settle its debts. At the time, the IMMC was doing so poorly that it did not have enough money to pay their interest on bonds. At the end of the First World War, the IMMC became known as the United States Lines, a company that would last until 1986, when it would go bankrupt.

Yachts

The first yacht that Pierpont owned was the *Corsair*. It was actually built for a man by the name of Charles J. Osborn by the William Cramp and Sons company. It was ready by May 26, 1880, and Pierpont purchased it two years later.

Pierpont eventually got a second yacht, the *Corsair II*. Sadly for Pierpont, the U.S. Navy included this yacht in its fight against the Spanish in the Spanish-American War. The navy paid Pierpont $225,000 and in 1898 turned it into the gunboat *USS Gloucester*. It fought at the Battle of Santiago, where it was hit by an enemy shell. A fragment of the mast was kept by Pierpont, who was not even willing to give up the ship in the first place.

Feeling so passionate about the loss of his yacht, Pierpont built another yacht, *Corsair III*. This third yacht was really quite regal.

When Pierpont traveled on passenger ships, upon his return he would stand on the deck and wave his handkerchief. His yacht would pull up to collect him, and he would simply disembark from the cruise ship and board his own. This way he did not have to go through quarantine.

Voyages always seemed to be the best cure for Pierpont regardless of how he felt. When he fell into his usual depressions, nothing but a trip at sea would cheer him up.

Pierpont would spend nights on the *Corsair*, and at the beginning of the weekend, he would take some friends with him to his Cragston home. On Sunday evening, they would travel back on the yacht to Manhattan and spend the night on the yacht. The following morning they would enjoy a splendid breakfast, leave the ship, and go off to their respective businesses.

Sea trips were the only thing that made Pierpont happy. Even his successes and his accomplishments did not make him joyful or proud. In fact, they made him more depressed. Jack, wrote to his mother, saying, "JPM has been so worried and bothered by the number of things on his mind and this annoyance of war rumor that it will be a great thing for him to have this voyage. Then if things calm down ... he will come back for his Aix cure and get two more voyages. Those are the only things which really seem to do him any good."

It's possible that this letter Jack wrote to his mother was because he was trying to protect her from knowing that her husband had been participating in extramarital affairs, but Pierpont was happiest at sea.

In response to Pierpont's failing health, his physicians advised him to relax. He obeyed, which is why he bought his yacht. Aboard his boat, he not only conducted business and settled matters but also enjoyed himself.

Pierpont also created the Metropolitan Club. He had previously been a member of the Union Club but left after a friend of his, a man by the name of John King, who was at the time the president of the Erie Railroad, was rejected from joining the club. After the Metropolitan Club was established, King became part of the club, and Pierpont was president of the club from 1891 to 1900.

Pierpont wasn't too excited about having all kinds of land. He did, however, have truly grand homes. The house at 219 Madison Avenue was constructed in 1853 by the publisher John Jay Phelps. Pierpont bought the house in 1882.

This home was also the home in which his daughter Juliet Pierpont married her husband, William Pierson Hamilton. Their wedding took place on April 12, 1894, and a thousand people attended it. As a gift, they were given Pierpont's favorite clock.

Pierpont also owned a summer house on East Island in Glen Cove in Nassau County. That house has recently been priced at $125 million.

Besides being an art collector, Pierpont also collected jewelry. As for his art collecting, he had a vast store that had either been given or loaned to the Metropolitan Museum of Art. In fact, Pierpont was once president of the Metropolitan Museum of Art. Many art pieces were kept in Pierpont's house in London. More were kept in Pierpont's private library not too far from the Empire State Building.

Eventually, his home could not house his many art pieces, which is why he built the Pierpont Morgan Library. It was a place for him to store his collection.

Following Pierpont's will, Jack opened the Pierpont Morgan Library to the public in 1924. The first director of the library was Bella Da Costa Greene. Bella was the caretaker of the library when Pierpont was alive and when it was still a private library. She was probably a mistress of Pierpont, and Pierpont was so jealous of her that when she was having an affair with another man, she told that man to keep their relationship secret so as to not rile Pierpont.

Jack liked her but in a strictly friendly manner.

Several artists painted pictures of Pierpont, including the South American Carlos Baca-Flor, a Peruvian artist, and Adolfo Müller-Ury, who was Swiss but born in the United States. Ury had painted a picture of Pierpont with the son of Juliet Pierpont, Mabel Satterlee, who was Pierpont's favorite grandchild.

This painting was kept on an easel in the mansion of the Satterlee family but has now disappeared.

Gems

As for gem collecting, Pierpont had more than one thousand in his collection. The company that put together Pierpont's first gem collection was Tiffany and Company. The collection was placed under a gemologist by the name of George Frederick Kunz.

Pierpont's gem collection was displayed in 1889 during the World's Fair in Paris. This display received two golden awards. Mr. Kunz built another collection of gems, which was displayed in Paris in 1900. Both of these collections were given to the American Museum of Natural History and were called the Morgan-Tiffany and the Morgan-Bemment collections. Eleven years after the display of Kunz's second collection a new gem discovered by Kunz was named after Pierpont. It was called Morganite.

Pierpont also helped the photographer Edward S. Curtis. In 1906, Pierpont loaned Curtis $75,000 to create a photographic series of Native Americans. In 1907, Mr. Curtis would publish the book *The North American Indian*. In 1914, Curtis sponsored the film *In the Land of the Head Hunters*. In 1974, it was redone and retitled *In the Land of the War Canoes*. Another film was shown three years later. It was called *The Indian Picture Opera*. It was a slideshow shown by a magic lantern. The film included the photographs of Curtis and music composed by Henry F. Gilbert.

After testifying before the Pujo Committee, Pierpont returned to one of his most ardent passions. He traveled.

Unfortunately, however, during his last few months, he would be afflicted with constant health problems. He suffered from panic attacks, digestive problems, insomnia, and depression. Pierpont was so ill that Jack wanted to come and be with him, but Jack's older sister told him, "Your suggestion coming yourself has touched and pleased him, but he is anxious you should remember how much depends upon your being on the spot in New York—how many interests are in your hands. He is too weak to make a decision; he wishes to leave it you." This was the first time in Jack's entire life that Pierpont had entrusted him with that great a responsibility and given him that powerful and meaningful a position. Pierpont basically made his son acting leader of the House of Morgan while he was ill.

Pierpont was very ill and couldn't sleep. He was in so much pain that even morphine did not make him feel better. He was always uncomfortable and unsettled. When he passed away on March 3, he was disoriented and kept thinking back to when he was a boy. He thought of himself being at school and said that his fellow classmates were "a fine lot of boys."

Pierpont had already been feeling ill before he left for Egypt. In Egypt, his illness was compounded by a fever that he contracted there. When he arrived in Rome, physicians tended to him, but his condition worsened. After some time, he was not able to speak and had to communicate with his family that was with him by writing and later only by sign language. Lesions formed on his brain, and his condition grew so bad that by Easter Sunday he became disoriented and went into a state of constant delirium.

He had been able to eat before, and his food was a liquid substance that was given through a tube. He was doing well when he ate but at one point did not want to eat. He began to lose weight rapidly, and his strength plummeted.

Approximately one hour before Pierpont passed away, the doctors who tended to him asked his family to leave the room so that they would be not there to witness his passing, which might have been made ugly by seizures and exhibitions of pain.

The last words of one of the greatest bankers in the history of the world—"I've got to go up the hill." He had already lost his mind and was delerious.

He died shortly after midnight, just over two weeks before his seventy-sixth birthday. Not long afterward, 3,697 people as well as the pope sent telegrams to the Grand Hotel giving their condolences.

Conclusion

It is not an exaggeration to claim that John Pierpont Morgan Sr. was one of the greatest bankers in the world. During the last eighteen years of his life, he accomplished things that most men, rich or poor, could not even dream of. He created the company that was once the biggest steel producer in the United States. He reorganized several railroads and saved the country from two financial crises.

He had amassed so much power and influence that people of lesser minds and even lesser imagination believed he was not honest in his ways. He saved the country, but he was persecuted in return.

He grew his businesses and banks into vast empires, creating one of the largest banks ever to exist. He was a man that although successful went through a lot of pain and heartache. He had lost the love of his life just after he married her. He loved his children, but he felt that his son was not strong enough. His daughter turned against him, and the two of them had been extremely close. She had turned against him because of mistakes he made while he was in pain and unhappy.

He was not only one of the most successful men in the world but also one of the saddest. He had all that power but no happiness—no source of light. He was extremely stressed during his last several years. The sinking of the Titanic was a great pang to his heart, and the investigations led against him and the presidents he had to fight and the anger he had for the top-hat politicians of Washington caused him a lot of pain and stress.

He was a man who worked hard for his success, and he changed the way the world works. He changed the way the financial world operated, and he created a foundation for new systems of banking among the firms of Wall Street, and he invested in things that still benefit the world today.

Aside from what happened in the external world, he was insecure because of his nose and outward appearance. He was so worried about his appearance that he became bitter.

Before he met Amelia Sturges, even when he had a limp, he was still a happy young man. It was only after her death that he became bitter and unhappy. That unhappiness would last for the rest of his life.

After Pierpont's death, the house that Pierpont built was taken over by Jack.

In today's world, J.P. Morgan Sr. would be worth approximately $41.5 billion. He may not have been as rich as the oil magnate John D. Rockefeller or the steel tycoon Andrew Carnegie, but he was rich in a way that couldn't be accounted for in monetary terms. He made a difference in the world. He changed the way the financial world worked. The difference between someone like J.P. Morgan and a banker that just wants to make money is that Pierpont constantly strived for more glory and success. The banker who just wants money will do anything for it. He will cheat, steal, and be corrupt. Pierpont Morgan gained his power through hard work, but many people thought he must have been corrupt.

For Pierpont, he cared about getting what he wanted to be done. As he said, "I don't know as I want a lawyer to tell me what I cannot do. I hire him to tell how to do what I want to do." Pierpont did not like obstacles and problems. He wanted what he wanted, and nothing was going to stop that. His techniques of structuring and reorganizing companies made his firm the largest bank in the world. This was thanks to his ambition and his unrelenting character that strived for even more success despite his feelings that he wanted to retire. The decisions he made before he started his career in banking when he bought the entire shipment of

Brazilian coffee to when he solved the 1895 gold standard issue or how he settled the 1907 financial panic shows that he did not care for rules or regulations. All he knew was that there was something he wanted to be done, and he was going to do it regardless of the risks. For instance, he did not care for problems involving antitrusts. He took care of them, but that did not stop him from achieving his goal.

Decades after Pierpont's death the bank he built would grow so powerful that the U.S. government would force it to break down. In 1931, Morgan Stanley was formed. In the 1950s, Morgan Guaranty came into existence. Near the end of 2000, Chase Bank merged with J.P. Morgan and Company and paid $36 billion in bonds. These two firms formed JPMorgan Chase. Aside from just consisting of J.P. Morgan and Co. and Chase Bank, it also includes Washington Mutual, Bank One, and Bear Stearns.

Although J.P. Morgan and Company no longer exists on its own, and its successor is not the largest bank in the world, his firm is still very meaningful. It was created through hard work and careful planning based on mistakes that Pierpont had learned from and taken to heart. Everything that Pierpont got he worked for.

In the end, John Pierpont Morgan Sr. left this world different from how it was when he entered it. He changed the world and left his mark on it. We—you and I—live in the world crafted by the will of John Pierpont Morgan.

Chapter 1 Early Years

"If you want to succeed you should strike out on new paths, rather than travel the worn paths of accepted success."

— John D. Rockefeller

John Davison Rockefeller's grandfather was Godfrey Rockefeller, who married an English lady, the descendent of a European king. Her name was Lucy. She was very strong. Rockefeller later said she was stronger than his grandfather. By marrying Godfrey, Lucy was actually marrying a family of lower class. At the time, the Rockefellers were just a bunch of drunken rogues worth nothing.

Godfrey and Lucy had ten children, the third of which was William Avery Rockefeller, the father of John D. Rockefeller. From a very young age, William was a solitary person, sometimes wandering off on his own and not returning home for long stretches of time.

The Rockefeller family eventually settled in Richford, New York, while they were on their way to Michigan. There was an obstacle in their path, a hill to be exact, and they could not go any farther. So, they settled down for a life in Richford.

William grew up to be a con man, scheming and swindling people to make money. He was also a lecherous man who committed several appalling acts in his life.

To pull off his schemes, he would ride into a new town with a sign hanging from his buttonhole that informed people that he was deaf and dumb. This allowed him to get close to strangers and listen to their conversations to learn many of their secrets. He would then use those secrets to manipulate them or find ways to sell things to those people and profit.

He was also obnoxious and arrogant in his deception. One family that William had approached to sell things accepted him into their home, and he and the family became close. One day the mistress of the house saw William talking to someone in the market. When she confronted him, he easily lied and told her that he had miraculously been healed that morning.

Eventually, William fell in love with one Miss Nancy Brown. The two of them planned to marry. They dated for some time, and all the plans were made, but an intervening event altered the course of those plans.

William had heard about another lady, a Ms. Eliza Davison, who was an heiress to a wealthy family. Rumor had it that her father was to give her $500 as a wedding gift. William decided that marrying Ms. Davison would be a better deal than marrying Ms. Brown.

William proposed to Eliza, who was overwhelmed with excitement but said she would marry William only if he was not deaf and dumb. He then miraculously regained use of his voice and hearing.

Eliza's father strictly disapproved of their marriage, but she disobeyed him and the two of them wed. After the wedding, William took her to his home in Richford, a simple, rectangular shack with one awning at the side.

Not wanting to leave the love of his life twisting in the wind, he decided to employ her as their housekeeper. William eventually fathered children with both of them. In two years, he had four children, one of which was John D. Rockefeller, born July 8, 1839, in Richford, New York, to the first Mrs. Rockefeller.

The illegitimate children of William and Nancy were both daughters, one of whom died young, and the other grew up to become a schoolteacher. The one who survived never met John, and it is probable that John did not know of the existence of his two half-sisters at all.

When Rockefeller was very young, the Rockefeller family (and Nancy) moved to Moravia for some time and then later to Owego, where he studied at the Owego Academy. William often deserted his family, leaving for months at a time, and Eliza would be forced to take care of the household without any income. He also did the same to the family he had with Nancy.

In frustration, Nancy began to argue with both Eliza and William. Unsure of how much longer he could keep the cat in the bag, he sent Nancy and their two daughters away to live at a friend's house. He didn't completely abandon them and would sometimes place clothing at their front door. The rest was up to Nancy.

Rockefeller did not remember much about his life in Richford before they moved to Moravia. Rockefeller was close to his father at first, but he despised him as he grew older and came to understand what his father was really like. He would later fear having to rely on him, which pushed him to seek his own independence.

Eliza was also not very happy with her marriage. She now understood that she had made the wrong choice by marrying her husband and not heeding her father's advice. She became suspicious about what William was doing while he was away and was miserable. She remained silent, though, keeping what she thought he might be doing in her heart so as to spare her children the pain and suffering of a dishonest father.

Eliza tended to the farm, and the children were given their own chores to do. Later, however, William would get someone to tend to the farm for Eliza and her children. John and his siblings slept in a room heated only by a small pipe in one section of the room. In the morning, the sounds of the town coming alive with people bustling about would waken the tired children and get them to their feet, and the entire family had their share of work to do.

John's morning chore, among other things, was to milk the cow. For warmth, he would stand on the same spot the cow stood to warm his feet.

After much harassment by his wife about leaving the family unattended for months at a time, William told the local shopkeeper to let Eliza and the family take anything they wanted, and he would settle the debt when he returned from his business trips.

This at least gave Eliza a source of food and groceries for the children, but when the amount owed began to pile up, Eliza, fearing that the credit might come to an end, became very frugal. It was a constant fear that she later pounded into her children, telling them, "Willful waste makes woeful want."

Eliza was very strong in character and personality, like her mother-in-law, Lucy. In the beginning, Eliza had been very uncomfortable around her husband's relatives, and Lucy, being the most respected of them all, became Eliza's sanctuary, and she would often be with her.

Many of the Rockefeller family's relatives admired Eliza, saying that she was an extraordinarily strong woman who was able to put up with the difficulties of her life. Despite her strange marriage, she never deserted her family and never left her husband even when the opportunity presented itself. The Rockefeller family was so poor that their neighbor had to drive them to church and buy textbooks for the children.

When John was young, he already began to show signs of enterprise. By buying small amounts of candy, portioning them, and then selling them to his siblings, he was able to make a profit. Another childhood business venture of his was to steal a turkey if it wandered away from its owner. He would catch it, take it back, and raise it for his family. His mother furnished him with milk curds, which he could use to feed the turkeys.

Rockefeller's mother was sharp and alert. Once when she was suffering from whooping cough, a disease common in those days, she kept herself in her room so as to not pass it to her children. She heard burglars one night, and knowing there was no one to protect her children, she cautiously opened her bedroom window and sang a popular Negro tune, making it appear that others were in the house and everyone was still up. The burglars heard the singing and left empty-handed.

Whenever William returned from his wandering, he would spend lavishly and give his family a good time. John would be happy to be with his father and came to associate money with good times.

Eliza eventually hired Anne Vanderbeak to help take care of the house. Unfortunately, William sexually assaulted Anne, and the family was forced to run from the law, which is when they moved to Owego.

This incident ruined the already shaky relationship between William and his father-in-law, John Davison. When William asked John for money to help with his troubles, Davison declined, which caused William to fly off the handle, and he threatened to leave and never return. John then worried about earlier loans he had made to William that were still outstanding. Fearing that he would not see that money again, John sued his son-in-law for $1,210.75. John then went on to edit his will, stipulating that Eliza would not have full control of her inheritance, and that upon her death the money would not pass to William.

It was after this incident that young John D. Rockefeller would come to despise his father, and psychoanalysts have said that he grew emotionless and calm. It had even reached the point the John had urges to kill his own father because of the humiliation and utter madness his father seemed to display.

After the issue with Miss Vanderbeak, William left the Rockefeller family in Cleveland. He needed to escape the law and get as far away as possible from those who knew him. His crime was known throughout the valley. He left John, his siblings, and his mother to fend for themselves in an unfamiliar environment. The children and their mother settled in Cleveland, which is where Rockefeller attended high school and later met his future wife, Laura Celestia Spelman, also known as Cettie.

John was naturally very mature, having been given many responsibilities at a young age. He had a ledger and kept track of the family's expenses, from charity to groceries. Whenever he and his family attended church, his mother would tell him and his siblings to put some money in the donation container.

Rockefeller was raised on the teachings of the Baptist church. It was a strict and pious upbringing. He was an ardent believer and very strict about working, giving, and staying pure. He never drank and always worried that his father's nature would cause him to be like him.

Rockefeller was able to go to school and then to high school, but when it came time for him to go to college, William forbade any further education. John then tried to find a job, not wanting to have to rely on his father.

For six months, he would rise in the morning and spend the better part of the day walking around town looking for a job. It was summer, and the heat was so bad that he hurt his feet, and anyone in his shoes would have given up after the first two weeks, but John pressed on and kept searching.

Finally, he walked into the firm of Hewitt and Tuttle, a small business that acted as a brokerage firm for food. Since Rockefeller was good with numbers and accounts, he proved his ability during a brief interview. It so happened that the small firm needed someone to manage the books. It was a simple job, and Rockefeller had all the skills they needed to do the work. He could write, he could count, and, more importantly, he understood how to record ledgers. He got the job. He was asked to return after lunch and start right away. Rockefeller calmly walked out of the office after the interview but could not contain himself for long and gleefully skipped down the road. This habit of skipping persisted even in his old age whenever something went his way.

He was first paid $16 a month for three months. He did his job so well that his salary was raised to $31, then to $50, and then to $58 a month. Back then, it was a lot of money for a teenager.

In 1857, Tuttle, one of the partners of the firm, left the business, and Rockefeller was promoted to the position of chief bookkeeper. Tuttle had handled a large part of the accounts, and Rockefeller had been reporting to him and knew his job well. Even though Tuttle was paid $2,000 for his work, Rockefeller was only paid $500. Even at just a quarter of the former's salary, however, Rockefeller didn't complain but instead thought of ways to make his small fortune do more.

He received a raise the following year, and his salary increased to $600 a year.

It's amazing what a little money can do when your mind is clear and racing, and you're ambitious. Instead of splashing his newfound freedom, Rockefeller started investing his money and frugally saving the rest. He traded in the business of ham, flour, and pork and was able to make more money from it. As time passed, the company was not increasing his salary in a way that he expected, and, although he accepted it at first, in time he felt he was not getting his fair share and was being taken advantage of.

Rockefeller later approached Hewitt, the remaining partner, and asked for a raise. He wanted $800. Hewitt said that his maximum salary could only be $700. It turned out that Hewitt was not doing well, and even at $700 the firm was being stretched.

As Rockefeller listened to the plight of the company, he understood that the company was not in good shape and had an uncertain future. He also knew that William had recently invested $1,000 in the company. Rockefeller sought out his father and conveyed the message to him. William marched straight over to Hewitt's office and demanded repayment of his investment.

In his later years, Rockefeller admitted that he would not have left Hewitt's firm had he been given the salary he wanted. Many additional factors caused Rockefeller to leave the firm, but it was driven primarily by his need to stretch his wings, and he seized the opportunity of Hewitt's downfall and that he had set aside a substantial amount of money from his salary and investments.

One thing that distinguished Rockefeller from his peers in Cleveland and beyond was that he was never satisfied with the status quo. He was inherently the sort of person who will always try to do better. In his advice to the younger generation, gleaned from his writings and from stories about him, he was always consistent in his stand that it was his duty to move ahead. It was almost a religious calling to do more.

Although he may have seemed the sensitive sort, he was also pragmatic and did not hesitate to swallow his pride. If he had to ask someone for money, he would, but he always paid it back. He learned this from his father. William once loaned his son some money but demanded interest on it. Rockefeller didn't hesitate to pay interest to his own father but took note of it in his heart.

Rockefeller finally left Hewitt's firm in early 1858. At this time, he was neighbors with Maurice B. Clark, a twenty-eight-year-old Englishman with an honest appreciation for Rockefeller's skills and ability, who once said that Rockefeller had "the reputation of being a young bookkeeper of more than ordinary ability and reliability." Rockefeller's reputation had preceded him. He was known as someone who was diligent, trustworthy, and bright.

Clark was working at the firm of Otis, Brownell at the time, and after Rockefeller left Hewitt, Clark approached him with the idea of the two of them setting up a company that bought and sold food on commission. He said that he and Rockefeller should each put $2,000 into the company. In 1858, this was equivalent to $61,276.34 today.

Unfortunately, Rockefeller had only $800 to spare. He did not know how he was supposed to gather together the necessary funds. He approached William for the loan. William told him that he had made plans to give $1,000 to all his children but at a 10 percent interest rate. Knowing better than to argue with his father to not have an interest rate, Rockefeller accepted the loan.

On April 1, 1858, he and Maurice formed the company and established an office at 32 River Street. Rockefeller was just under eighteen years old and already a partner and cofounder of a firm—a prestigious position for someone his age.

Rockefeller remarked, "It was a great thing to be my own employer. Mentally, I swelled with pride—a partner in a firm with $4,000 capital!"

Rockefeller took this partnership very seriously, and after the first day of work at the newly founded firm, he went back home on Cheshire Street and kneeling down begged God to bless his business.

Rockefeller never looked unfavorably upon his time at the firm of Hewitt and Tuttle. He cherished it as his first leap into business. When Rockefeller was ninety-five years old in 1934, he said to one of his grandsons, "Oh how blessed the young men are who have to struggle for a foundation and a beginning in life. I shall never cease to be grateful for three and a half years of apprenticeship and the difficulties to be overcome, all the way along."

Rockefeller was basically saying that anyone who has to crawl through the mud and dirt to be successful is better off than one who floats right into it. He was also expressing how he felt about his time at the firm, feeling it to be most important indeed.

When Clark and Rockefeller was established, they were well-liked, and the local newspaper, the *Cleveland Leader*, wrote, "As experienced, responsible and prompt businessmen, we recommend their house to the favorable consideration of our readers."

The business actually did well. At the time, there was a large demand for food products, including grain and meat. Companies in the produce industry would come to Clark and Rockefeller and ask them to sell it for them, and they would earn money based on commission.

Two months after its founding, a frost adversely affected Midwestern farms. Clark and Rockefeller had already ordered a shipment of beans, but when they arrived, they were partially spoiled and covered in dirt and gunk. They had to separate the good beans from the bad ones. Rockefeller recalled, "When we were not needed in the office, we used to go out to the warehouse, my partner and I, and sort out those beans."

Although this weather problem caused the firm to not do too well at the time, they still did well in the long run. By the end of that year, their company was worth $4,400.

Despite this success, however, the issue with the beans caused Rockefeller to ask his father for another loan, but William was not agreeable. He always found it amusing to play games with his son regarding money.

He once said, "I trade with the boys and skin 'em, and I just beat 'em every time I can. I want to make 'em sharp."

At this time, Rockefeller was already used to how he and his father dealt with each other. In fact, he even softened his father's antics with positivity, saying, "To my father I owe a great debt in that he himself trained me to practical ways. He was engaged in different enterprises; he used to tell me about these things, explaining their significance; and he taught me the principles and methods of business."

Rockefeller's financial relationship with his father was most frustrating indeed. William would ask for the money he loaned to be returned to him at the worst possible moment when Rockefeller was not in a position to return the money. He said to Rockefeller, "My son, I find I have got to have that money." Rockefeller would reply, "Of course, you shall have it at once."

Rockefeller said that he knew his father was testing him, perhaps seeing whether or not he could repay his debt. He further said that after giving the money back to his father he would not use it for anything and would later have it available for lending. Rockefeller also said, "He would never know how angry I felt beneath the surface." That shows Rockefeller was actually incensed by his father's attitude but simply masked his anger with his expressionless face.

On the first anniversary after Clark and Rockefeller was founded, on April 1, 1859, a certain George W. Gardner, who had previously worked with Clark at Otis, Brownell, entered the picture. He was from a particularly well-to-do family and would go on to become the commodore of the Cleveland Yacht Club and mayor of Cleveland.

When Gardner joined Clark and Rockefeller, Rockefeller's name was scratched off, and the firm was reincorporated as Clark, Gardner and Company. Rockefeller was understandably upset about this but did not voice his anger. He said, "Maurice Clark was very pleasant about it." He went on to say, "And he said, 'Never mind. It won't be very long—before many years you'll be doing better than any of us.' Yes, he was very nice about it. I made no objection."

Much later, Rockefeller admitted that it was indeed a great pain to him, and he said, "I considered this a great injustice to me, as I was an equal partner, and Gardner brought in only his share of the capital, but I thought it best to submit."

Rockefeller was the kind of person who thought it was not nice or right to show his anger or his hurt, which were totally justifiable. Rockefeller did not gel with Clark and Gardner. He worked very hard and was very serious about his work. He would tell himself, "Your future hands on every day that passes." Many years before Rockefeller turned twenty-one years old, he was already being addressed as "Mr. Rockefeller."

Rockefeller was always very diligent about his work and only really happy when he secured a deal that was successful. He absolutely despised the attitude of his partners. They were much more relaxed and much less zealous than he was with their work. Gardner and Clark found Rockefeller to be both favorable and unpleasant. He was both a success and a stony-faced, unsmiling person. Do not take it for granted, though, that he was unhappy.

Rockefeller was afraid that if the business was not treated seriously they might have problems getting loans in the future. Thus, he made it a point to reduce their extravagances, keep their books tidy, and make sure they conducted themselves with dignity and integrity, which paid off in the long run.

Rockefeller learned early, thanks in no small part to his father, that bankability was an important issue. He was certain that one must conduct himself with integrity and honor so that in the event they needed to rely on their reputation they would be able to.

When Gardner and three of his friends bought a yacht for $2,000, Rockefeller showed extreme disapproval. It went against his character to splurge and waste on excesses, especially while the business was still expanding. It was always his style to invest the profits in the expansion of the company and then reap more profits. He was always focused on expansion. Spending money on a yacht was not his cup of tea.

Rockefeller often worked Saturdays (but not Sundays to observe the holy day), and on one Saturday afternoon, while Rockefeller was deep in the books, Gardner approached him with a proposition, saying, "John, a little crowd of us are going to stake a sail over to Put-in-Bay, and I'd like to have you go along. I think it would do you good to get away from the office and get your mind off business for a while."

Rockefeller was particularly upset by this proposition, and Gardner would later say that Rockefeller responded most unkindly. Rockefeller said, "George Gardner, you're the most extravagant young man I ever knew! The idea of a young man like you, just getting a start in life, owning an interest in a yacht! You're injuring your credit at the banks—your credit and mine. . . . No, I won't go on your yacht. I don't even want to see it!"

Not only did the thought of not working on a Saturday offend Rockefeller, but he was also infuriated that money was being spent on extravagance and would damage their reputation with the banks.

He returned to his work, and Gardner said, "I see that there are certain things on which you and I probably will never agree. I think you like money better than anything else in the whole world, and I do not. I like to have a little fun along with business as I go through life."

If you are thinking that Rockefeller had an explosive temper and belted out his statement in anger, you would be wrong. He said what he had to say in the calmest of tones and in the most polite way possible.

Rockefeller continuously trained himself to mask his shaky feelings with a calm facade, but in his early days while still at Clark, Gardner and Company, he was not very good at it. Eventually, his Stoic nature earned him a favorable reputation wherever he went. The combination of his Stoic nature and abhorrence of wasting money worked hand in hand most of the time except for a few occasions. Clark, Gardner and Company once bet all of the firm's money on a rather sizeable shipment of grain to Buffalo. Rockefeller told his partners not to pay for the insurance and to simply keep the $150 that they would pay for the premium. Clark and Gardner agreed to Rockefeller's idea but were not entirely comfortable with it.

Later that night, a violent storm occurred over Lake Erie. Rockefeller was found pacing in the office the next morning. He was extremely worried. When Gardner arrived, Rockefeller said to him, "Let's take out insurance right away." He went on to say, "We still have time—if the boat hasn't been wrecked by now." Gardner then paid the premium.

When Gardner returned to the office, a telegram in Rockefeller's hand informed them that the ship was safe and sound at its destination. That day Rockefeller returned home feeling sick to his stomach. This was caused by having paid $150 for nothing!

Gardner and Rockefeller were not the best of friends, but they spoke when needed and kept their distance at other times. Gardner had, however, developed a sort of liking for Rockefeller's father. Gardner said Rockefeller's father was ". . . one of the most companionable and most likeable old men I ever knew. He would crack jokes and have more to say in one conversation than John would utter in a week."

When Gardner asked Rockefeller about his father, John did not reply. He had no intention to speak ill of his father but also had no intention to lie. He didn't have much good to say and so decided that silence was best. With Clark, Gardner and Company expanding to Philadelphia, Gardner thought about meeting William, who was in Philadelphia. To do so, he spoke to Rockefeller and inquired about his father's address. Rockefeller feigned memory loss.

Gardner did not understand it. He knew Rockefeller had a very good memory but asked if he could get the address from Rockefeller's mother at lunchtime. Lunch came and went, but Rockefeller did not make any effort to talk about the matter. When they were later ready to leave the office for the day, Gardner asked Rockefeller for the address. Rockefeller went red and said he had forgotten to ask what the address was when he got home. Gardner did not pester him anymore, and he was thus never able to find out where William resided.

Gardner also observed how Rockefeller's father would come to the office and take out a large amount of money. Gardner said, "I wondered what business a man could be in that he would have $1,000 to spare one month and need it the next."

One of the reasons why Rockefeller had been unwilling to talk about his father or his whereabouts was mainly because of his father's double life. As William had two families in different locations, Rockefeller wasn't going to talk about it. When Rockefeller began to understand the gravity of William's two marriages, he was, on the inside, extremely taken aback. He did, however, hide his shakiness with a very calm outlook.

Rockefeller was always very serious about his work. While he took care of the accounts and the firm's books, Clark took care of what the firm did—purchasing and selling goods. Rockefeller was always the first to arrive at work and the last to leave. He was always very meticulous and looking for mistakes. Clark recalled that Rockefeller was a nice person, but he was ". . . too exact. He was methodical to an extreme, careful as to details and exacting to a fraction. If there was a cent due us, he wanted it. If there was a cent due a customer, he wanted the customer to have it."

As with most successful men, Rockefeller was often forced to battle his own pride, as when a bank once rejected his loan application he swore to himself that he would one day be the richest man in the world.

Every time he would have those thoughts he would tell himself what his mother had told him when he was young, "Pride goes before a fall." Every night when he lay down he would remind himself with a mantra that guided him "Because you have got a start, you think

419

you are quite a merchant; look out, or you will lose your head—go steady. Are you going to let this money puff you up? Keep your eyes open. Don't lose your balance." He was basically telling himself not to be distracted by money, and by telling himself this every night, it was pounded into his head.

While trying to expand the business, Rockefeller travelled across both Indiana and Ohio. He met with people and proposed that they come to his firm. Although most people believed that Rockefeller was a cold person who plucked clients from other firms and forcefully placed them with his own, he was in fact very gentle and calm in the way he operated. He was driven and focused, which sometimes rubbed others against their grain.

Rockefeller would meet with someone, say that he thought his associates in business were up to par, say he hoped he wasn't an intrusion for him, and then say that he had something to offer that he "believed" would be of benefit to the person he was talking to. He would say that he did not expect an answer right away but gave the person time to think about the offer and that he would come back to talk over the matter once more.

Orders for buying and selling goods began to pile up. Rockefeller said, "I found that old men had confidence in me right away, and after I stayed a few weeks in the country, I returned home and the consignments came in and our business was increased and it opened up a new world for me."

Rockefeller was skilled in handling people well. He was a very determined and persevering person. He would overcome whatever he needed to in order to achieve what he envisioned. When he went on sales trips and business started to flow in, he found that he had another problem—not enough carriages to carry all the goods.

One time a customer of Clark, Gardner and Company wanted to pay the firm for their services before receiving the goods he wanted. This customer was a very lucrative customer, and doing such a thing would go against certain business policies. Rockefeller turned down the offer and tried to keep his customer. Rockefeller recalled, "But he stormed about, and in the end I had the further humiliation of confessing to my partner that I had failed."

Rockefeller would later find out that the reason why the customer was so headstrong about carrying out his proposition was that it was actually a trap laid by a banker in the area. The banker was testing whether or not Rockefeller and his partners would be able to hold back from taking the easy route and adhere to their ethics.

Although Rockefeller did not trust bankers, they were crucial for his success. Rockefeller said, "The hardest problem all through my business career was to obtain enough capital to do all the business I wanted to do and could do, given the necessary amount of money."

Banks that were established on Main Street were not really financially strong, and not many people were confident enough to be customers of the banks. Clark, Gardner and Company kept money in a safe that would be used as backup.

The first time Rockefeller received a loan from someone other than his father he borrowed $2,000 from Truman P. Handy, an old and kind banker. Rockefeller felt a certain sense of happiness. He said to himself as he walked, "Just think of it. A bank had trusted me for $2,000! I felt that I was now a man of importance in the community."

When Handy loaned Rockefeller the money, he made him take an oath that he would not use the money for speculative purposes. Handy became an important guide for Rockefeller, who knew that his character dictated his credit rating. What made banks comfortable with Rockefeller was that he was a cornerstone of the Baptist Mission Church on Erie Street.

When Rockefeller was older, he was against borrowing money but was very willing to do it when he needed it. Maurice B. Clark remarked, "Oh, John was the greatest borrower you ever saw!" Just like William, Rockefeller knew how to manipulate the masses to satisfy his needs. If Rockefeller wished to borrow $5,000, he would spread a rumor among the people that he was going to invest $10,000. This would consolidate the credit of the company he was working in and make banks have a reason to lend him money.

The Civil War was a good time for Rockefeller and his firm. Produce companies were able to make a lot of money by supplying food to the Union troops, and Rockefeller was one of them.

Rockefeller viewed the Civil War as a time to make money and hired people to take his place. He supported the North and was very strong in his views about ending slavery. Even as a young boy in school, he wanted slavery abolished. In one of the essays he wrote about freedom in school, he said that the slave owners, whom he called "cruel masters," made their slaves work "beneath the scorching suns of the South. How under such circumstances can America call herself free?"

Before entering his twenties, Rockefeller was donating money to causes that helped African-Americans. During this time, most of the people in Cleveland were against slavery, and it did not exist there. The Underground Railroad was an institution that transported black slaves who had run from their masters to free states and Canada, where they could be free. In Cleveland, blacks would also discreetly board ships not very far from Rockefeller's office.

When slave hunters came looking for slaves near Cleveland, those who stood for the eradication of slavery would hastily go to the Public Square where the Stone Church stood and ring the bell, which served as a warning to Clevelanders.

In the 1860 presidential elections, Rockefeller voted for Abraham Lincoln. On the day before the Civil War began, Rockefeller went to certain gatherings where all the attendees voiced their strong condemnation of slavery. Evangelicals were particularly opposed to slavery as were Baptists, who treated blacks cordially and allowed them to speak in their churches about ending slavery.

The first battle of the Civil War was a Confederate victory when they captured Fort Sumter. In turn, President Abraham Lincoln called for seventy-five thousand people to enlist in the Union army. Rockefeller, however, did not join. He said, "I wanted to go in the army and do my part . . . But it was simply out of the question. We were in a new business, and if I had not stayed it must have stopped—and with so many dependent on it."

Rockefeller's decision to stay at the firm because he thought it would fail was perhaps because his father had left him and his family. He felt he needed to stay and do his duty in this situation. Rockefeller was a complex person with many opposing forces tugging at him from all sides. On the one hand, he took filial duty seriously, and he afforded his father the respect and deference that was due, but it is hard to find evidence that he showed any love in any way. In his younger days when he had yet to form a mind of his own, Rockefeller loved his father and looked forward to being with him. He also enjoyed those times when his father would return after weeks of being gone with money and gifts for everyone. After managing on a shoestring budget with his mother and siblings, the abundance of money and gifts along with the return of his father softened his heart, and he associated his father's presence with happiness and comfort. That, however, did not last long, as William's unorthodox ways and mean streak soon forced Rockefeller to feel very uncomfortable around him. It was hard for Rockefeller to feel warm and fuzzy when his own father would charge him rent for living in his house, charge interest on money he borrowed, and asked for loans to be repaid at a moment's notice.

Chapter 2 The Civil War

"Don't be afraid to give up the good to acquire the
great."

— **John D. Rockefeller**

During the Civil War, the U.S. government needed all
citizens on deck to help with the war effort by joining
the military. They did, however, allow people who
provided for or supported their family, whether it was
their brothers and sisters, their mother and father, or
their own children, to not enlist. Rockefeller was
among those who were the sole providers of their
family. Although Rockefeller was only twenty-one
years old, he acted as a father for his siblings and took
care of a sizeable family with six members, excluding
him—his mother, sisters—Mary Ann Rockefeller and
Lucy Rockefeller Briggs; and brothers, Frank, William,
and Francis Rockefeller. Frank was the only one who
would eventually join the Union Army.

Rockefeller was an ardent supporter of the North and
not only gave to the cause but also supported the

soldiers. One day a Captain Levi Scofield, one of Rockefeller's friends, entered his firm's office with thirty soldiers who had just joined the army. Rockefeller took money from his safe and handed out $10 to each of them, a total of $300! One of the soldiers said, "God, but he must be rich." Another soldier said, "Yes, they say he is a rich man—that he is worth $10,000!"

By this time, people were beginning to believe that Rockefeller was a wealthy man. The year before the Civil War ended Rockefeller was giving $300 a year to stand-ins in the army and the dependent families that relied on them. Furthermore, he was donating money to funds that helped the war.

After the Civil War began, he and Clark would always keep tabs on the conflict. They studied very detailed maps and tracked the progress of the war. Other people also came to their office to see as well. Rockefeller recalled, "Our office became a great rallying-place. We were all deeply interested. Men used to drop in often, and we followed the war keenly, reading the latest dispatches and studying the maps."

Frank, the only Rockefeller brother to join the army, was very much like his father. He could be friendly one moment and then become easily agitated. Frank was sixteen when he wanted to join, but Rockefeller would not let him. When Frank approached him and asked for $75 to join the army, Rockefeller refused to give him the money. According to George Gardner, Rockefeller actually lectured him, saying, "You would be a wild, foolish boy to go away and waste youthful years that you might utilize in getting a start and making money."

In the end, it was Gardner who loaned Frank the $75. This loan was the first of a great many that Frank would get but not repay. Gardner's going against what Rockefeller wanted and helping Frank join the army would cause their already shaky relationship to fray even more.

Before receiving the money to join the army, Frank had actually tried some deceitful tactics to do so. William scolded him, however, for not being open about his wishes and plans. He said to him, "Young man, when you go to war you will say goodbye to the family and go out the front door in broad daylight." William of all people was condemning secrecy. It was quite ironic that a man who lied so often and had hundreds of skeletons in his closet could speak against secrecy.

To join the army, Frank decided to pose as older than he was, and to not lie, he wrote the number eighteen on the sole of his shoe. So, when the recruiting officer asked him his age, Frank said, "I'm over eighteen, sir."

After some time, Rockefeller simply gave up trying to stop his brother from going to war and funded him by paying for all his necessary equipment, such as his gun and clothes, during the three years that Frank fought in the war.

Frank was a soldier of the Seventh Ohio Volunteer Infantry. During the Civil War, he was injured twice, once at Cedar Mountain and again at Chancellorsville. Frank was deeply upset that his brother was nice and comfortable and making lots of money while he was fighting and being injured.

The North was able to greatly advance its economy during the Civil War. The country developed in such a way so as to meet the demands of war, and the railroads, iron mills, and other industries became more efficient. For instance, more sophisticated technology aided the war, such as reapers and sewing machines. The reapers harvested produce that eventually became food for the soldiers, and the sewing machines were used to make their uniforms.

To make progress, the U.S. government issued land grants, which affected Rockefeller's early life. Because more railroads were being built, Rockefeller was able to pay less to transport his goods by pitting two different railroads against each other to his advantage.

Since industry was booming during the Civil War, many people turned their backs on their simple farms and set their sights on becoming rich. It was a mini agricultural and industrial revolution fueled by the ongoing war.

Although Rockefeller's firm did not get any substantially profitable jobs from the government, they were able to make money from the increased prices of goods. Their company bought and sold things that consumers needed and had large quantities of products in their warehouses. In 1863, an advertisement of Rockefeller's company showed the quantity and quality of their inventory. They stored more than two hundred barrels of pork, more than five hundred bushels of clover seed, thirteen hundred barrels of salt, and eight hundred bushels of timothy seed.

As their business grew partly because of the increasing transportation infrastructure in the form of railroads and because the war was still going on, the profits of the company increased, and the other partners saw fit to spend and live lavishly.

For Rockefeller, aside from his support of the war effort and looking after his family, he was more interested in expanding his business. He had built a reputation of being rich, which led him to think he controlled the banks and could go to them at any time and request a loan for a particular project. By this point in his life, Rockefeller's company owned four warehouses, all of which were on River Street.

As the profits rose and the difference between Gardner and Rockefeller grew more stark, the time eventually came for Rockefeller to get rid of him. Not only did he decide to show Gardner the exit, but he also made it a point to remove him from all accounts of his journal. It was some time in 1862 that Rockefeller severed the relationship.

Chapter 3 Titusville

"When people think of the oil industry, they think of Rockefeller, much like when people think of the software industry, they think of Bill Gates."

— H.W. Brands

The Civil War made Rockefeller quite a rich man. This wealth, however, in retrospect, was incomparable to the wealth he obtained from the oil business.

Even before crude oil was harvested by Edwin Drake in Titusville, it was already coming out of the ground. It seeped into Oil Creek, mixing with the water. Oil was prevalent in many places, including salt wells and water wells, contaminating the water. You could see it flowing in creeks and streams. In the beginning, it was more of a nuisance than a blessing. It was dirty, toxic, and difficult to clean. It would nonetheless soon be considered black gold.

Seneca natives had a variety of uses for the oil. They used it to paint themselves when going to war, and they used it as medicine albeit ineffectively as well as a disinfectant for the skin. The Indians harvested the oil by placing blankets or pieces of fabric in the running water in the creek and let them soak up the oil. The Indians then took the blankets and dried them in the sun to let the water evaporate from the cloth. Once the water was gone and the heavier oil remained, they squeezed out the oil.

Around 1850, one Samuel Kier collected the oil in the salt wells that his father owned and bottled it. They were half-pints, and Samuel sold the oil, calling it Kier's Rock Oil as a medicine. It was supposed to cure bronchitis and liver problems. Of course, it didn't.

Oil was soon used in communities around the country. It was used to light lamps, but whale oil was primarily used for this purpose at the time. Whale blubber was shipped throughout the country, but whalers were not able to keep up with the demand, which made it expensive, and only the wealthy could afford such luxuries and light their homes at night. The rest of the people, such as farmers and villagers and the poor in the city, were forced to go without light until morning.

Although there were other ways of lighting their homes with tallow (derived from animal) and coal oil (derived from shale), these were expensive as well, as the process of extraction and the supply of these oils were limited. Other forms of oil could also be used, which included cottonseed oil and lard oil, but these were not affordable or convenient to use. An alternative was necessary, and those who could solve the problem would be paid handsomely. Electricity and the light bulb were still a long way off.

Then along came George Bissell, who had graduated from Dartmouth College and had worked as a school principal, a professor of Greek language, a lawyer, and a journalist. In his spare time, he was also an inventor. Sometime in the 1850s, he had an idea for a new way to fuel the lights in people's homes. He thought that perhaps the oil struck in the western regions of Pennsylvania could be a better fuel for lamps.

Bissell then founded the Pennsylvania Rock Oil Company and sent a small amount of the oil found in the area to Benjamin Silliman Jr., a professor of chemistry at Yale University. In 1855, Silliman concluded that Bissell's suspicions were true. Rock oil could be processed to be a fuel for lamps.

Now that this was possible, the Pennsylvania Rock Oil Company faced a different problem. They had to gather large amounts of the oil. Practically no infrastructure existed for oil exploration at the time.

All they had were streams and creeks that showed traces of this material, which looked like a contaminant rather than an asset. They decided that since it came from the ground they needed to look for underground deposits. Near the end of 1857, close to three years after Silliman corroborated Bissell's suspicions, explorers were commissioned to look for large deposits of oil. Today, there is a body of science in the field of exploration, which is a billion-dollar business, but back then it was anybody's guess. At this point, Bissell's company had been renamed the Seneca Oil Company in tribute to the Seneca tribe that had been wringing oil from blankets they soaked in the river.

It was thanks to a Mr. Townsend, a banker in New Haven who helped finance this exploration mission, that someone was able to search for large deposits of oil. He sent Edwin Drake, a man in his late thirties who suffered from a constant back problem. Drake was eventually given the title of Colonel and dispatched to Titusville, Pennsylvania, in December 1857.

At this time, Oil Creek Valley, situated in Titusville, was not very sophisticated or modern. It was still densely packed with thick forests of hemlock and pine trees and the usual wildlife. These were harsh conditions to search for oil when you consider the dense forest and the lack of expertise in finding something below ground. Pipe had to be brought in, and hauling all that equipment was not easy. The people of Oil Creek liked Drake but thought he was wasting his time. They couldn't imagine there were any deposits of this toxic material.

He used the same methods to find oil that salt miners used in the salt mines. This was the first use of derricks to explore for oil. Back then the derricks were made of wood and towered ten to thirty feet above the ground, where they bored a hole in the earth.

Finally, after a long period of time, Drake succeeded in finding a well that contained this heavy, sludgelike material.

On Saturday, August 27, 1859, almost one and a half years after arriving in Oil Creek, Colonel Drake struck oil. It had now been conclusively proven that oil did exist in certain pockets below ground. Drake's method was viable and effective, and he now had a system that was replicable in the future, which was the key to future success.

His discovery made news, and before long there was a rush to settle in Titusville. More derricks were set up, and more holes were bored to tap that well. All they had was crude oil, though, and you couldn't do anything with it until it was refined.

The next sector of the oil industry that was developed was refining the toxic sludge. To process the crude oil, numerous refineries were set up by independent companies to process the oil that was coming from independent drillers.

In less than a year after Drake struck oil, a large number of refineries were set up in Oil Creek, but they could not extract usable heating oil to any profitable degree. Their methods were crude, and their output was low, but it was better than nothing. A lot of sludge was discarded in streams and in the ground after the refining process, but most of this discarded sludge still had usable hydrocarbons.

We can't say with any certainty what impression Rockefeller may have had when Edwin Drake began producing oil with his derrick, but we do have some insight into his view of oil itself based on what he wrote at the time. "These vast stores of wealth were the gifts of the great Creator, the bountiful gifts of the great Creator." Rockefeller also said, "Colonel Drake and the Standard Oil Company and all others connected with this industry had the opportunity for useful work in preparing and distributing this valuable product to supply the wants of the world."

Even in the midst of commercial success and potential for profit, Rockefeller continued his pious and holy appreciation for the gifts of the earth that came from the Creator. That was his typical frame of mind. He was evidently very grateful to Colonel Edwin Drake and rightfully so. If it hadn't been for Drake, there might have been no way to harvest the oil, and the young oil industry would have bubbled into nothingness.

Because Rockefeller believed the Almighty had furnished the world with kerosene, it emboldened him and propelled him to do what he did and change the world the way he did. It was not all about money, as Ida Tarbell would come to conclude in her writings.

In the beginning, Rockefeller was not very enthusiastic about the young oil industry, and it took him some time to begin working at it full-time. It's possible that at the beginning of 1860 the firm of Clark and Rockefeller was charged with delivering a shipment of crude oil. Although Rockefeller was already in the business of oil (transporting it), he did not pay too much attention to it. In the end, it would be thanks to Samuel Andrews that Rockefeller would enter the oil industry in any meaningful way.

Chapter 4 Rockefeller Meets Oil

"I believe that thrift is essential to well-ordered living."

— John D. Rockefeller

Clark was friends with Samuel Andrews, being that they were both countrymen from Wiltshire in southwest England. Andrews was an ambitious mechanic, a skilled fixer of all things mechanical, and a self-taught chemist. He was congenial, with a bright red complexion and easily stood out in a crowd.

Andrews came to Cleveland in the 1850s and started working in a business owned by C.A. Dean, the owner of a lard oil refinery. During his time with Dean, he learned how to distill coal oil, tallow, and candles. In 1860, the first form of kerosene made from crude oil was developed. Andrews had refined this kerosene from a shipment of ten barrels of crude oil that came from Pennsylvania. Back then refining oil was done with sulfuric acid. Refining crude oil, however, was not common. Only a few people knew how to do it, but many were interested in it.

Andrews believed that kerosene would be the best lighting fuel to replace tallow or blubber. Unfortunately for him, however, he was not financially well off. He did not earn much money for his work, and his wife would sew for customers to make extra income, but two years after making kerosene from crude oil, Andrews began to think about quitting Dean's company. He began to look for people who would finance him and would often go to Clark and Rockefeller (company) in search of an investor.

Andrews and Rockefeller were not strangers. They had met at the Erie Street Baptist Mission Church and Andrews, his wife, and Rockefeller knew one another. Maurice B. Clark recalled how he responded to Andrews about his talk about refining oil. Clark said, "I told him there was no chance, that John and I together did not have more than $250 we could spare out of our business; we simply hadn't enough working capital, together with our credit at the banks, to enable us to make advances to our suppliers, paying insurance and rent." He was basically telling Andrews that they were very tight and could not spare much for his venture.

Andrews wasn't going to back down though. After having no success with Clark, he went to Rockefeller. By now, Rockefeller had already put his money in stock of a railroad, and he also had extra money. He was easier to approach. He was saving his money and investing his profits, not spending it as was the case with Clark. Rockefeller liked Andrews' plan and was willing to help him. Andrews then went back to Clark. At first, Clark just tried to push him away. Then Andrews said, "Mr. Rockefeller thinks well of it." Clark then said, "Well, if John will go in, I will."

Later, Rockefeller would paint himself as someone who was not very enthusiastic and not as interested as others were regarding the oil industry. He said that he was not very confident about the matter but was actually forced into the business by Andrews, Clark, and his two brothers.

In the end, Clark and Rockefeller invested $4,000 in Andrews' company. This amount was only half of what was needed. Andrews' company was called Andrews, Clark and Company. Rockefeller was now twenty-four years old and involved in the business that would make him the richest man in the world.

Because they initially thought the oil industry would not be as lucrative or successful as it turned out to be, Rockefeller and his partners did not pay much attention to it and kept it as a *second* business, something that was not their main line of work and a smaller part of their career.

Rockefeller was quite far from the oil fields of Pennsylvania. Like others who wanted to start a life in the oil industry but were far from the source, he was forced to go into the business of refining.

The location where Rockefeller chose to build Excelsior Works, his first refinery, was in a peaceful countryside more than a mile away from Cleveland. It was a sloping landscape. Kingsbury Run, a small, flowing body of water, was lined with red brick and cradled in serenity. The land where Rockefeller wanted to build his refinery featured grazing cows and towering trees. These were not seen as hindrances, though, and not long after railroads arrived in the area it turned into a bustling center of activity.

On Friday, November 3, 1863, an Atlantic and Great Western Railroad train arrived at a train station in Cleveland. It was nicely decorated and a harbinger of how Cleveland and New York City would be connected. It also allowed for a straightforward trip to the oil site in Pennsylvania.

Rockefeller was able to transport his goods both by waterway and land, and he was able to persuade the railroads to charge him reduced rates. He used the leverage of competition to knock down the price of transportation. He would pit one railroad operator against the other or the railroad against shipping companies to get a better rate. He was indeed a master negotiator.

Thus, during the rest of his life in the oil industry, he would always think very carefully about where he set up his refineries. The site of his refinery was a strategic location. The other refineries that he would establish would also be strategically placed.

Very soon after Rockefeller set up his refinery near Kingsbury Run, several other refineries followed suit. At the time, Cleveland had a population of 44,000 and was filled with young men who were desperately trying to succeed in life. It was really very easy to get into the business of refining oil. It cost less money to start a refinery and hire workers than to open a store. At the time, you could set up a refinery for $1,000 or less.

By the second half of 1863, twenty oil refineries were located in Cleveland, all of which exported 25 percent of the kerosene they distilled. In the beginning, everyone who ventured into the oil business was making lots of money. During the American Civil War, crude oil had many purposes, one of which was nursing injured Union soldiers, and it was also used as an alternative to turpentine that had originally come from the South.

It wasn't long before Rockefeller began to dislike Andrews. He criticized him, saying that he was deceptive and stubborn, which he attributed to his English roots. Their relationship was not always sour, though, and they were actually friendly to one another in the beginning.

The reporter Ida Tarbell, who would later cause the American government to prosecute Standard Oil, wrote nicely about Andrews, going against Rockefeller's judgment of him, saying that Andrews was "a mechanical genius." Tarbell credited him with bettering the standard of kerosene and increasing the amount of kerosene that was distilled from a barrel of oil.

When Rockefeller first entered the oil business, he was quite personally involved. It was only when he grew older that he would become more physically uninvolved. In the early days of Excelsior, Rockefeller would arrive at Kingsbury Run at 6:30 a.m. He would do what normal workers would do even though he owned the company. He would roll the barrels where they needed to go. He would do small tasks here and there and basically did not care that he was doing the work of a regular worker. He wanted to do what was necessary and didn't care that he was doing it himself.

Whenever oil was refined, a small portion of sulfuric acid would be left behind, and Rockefeller came up with a way to put this to use. He wanted to use it as a fertilizer, which was the first time that a waste product had been made into a useful commodity.

To put this into context, you have to realize that his family faced hard times when he was young, sometimes not knowing where the next meal was coming from. This sort of uncertainty and unstable environment drove him to be independent and self-sufficient to the point that he didn't wait for others to do the work. He would just jump in and get it done.

Whenever there were not enough barrels at the refinery, he resorted to constructing them himself. One time Rockefeller became quite upset with how a mistake was made in money owed to their plumber. He decided to take things into his own hands and told Andrews, "Hire a plumber by the month. Let us buy our own pipes, joints, and all other plumbing material."

In the end, contrary to what Rockefeller and his partners had thought in the beginning, the oil business that they conducted became more lucrative than their produce venture. Although the whole oil industry was prone to unexpected events, Rockefeller's refinery never suffered losses or bad years. It was well managed and well run, with foresight and diligence.

Rockefeller was the kind of person who always did what was needed to the best of his ability and to the fullest measure he could provide. There was no shortcuts and no half-baked efforts.

Rockefeller shared a room with William Rockefeller Jr. and would quite often wake him up in the middle of the night and talk about an idea for something and ask William what he thought of it. His brother would simply talk about it later and go back to sleep.

Rockefeller, Andrews, and Clark would often meet at his Cheshire Street home before the sun rose and discuss oil. Mary Ann Rockefeller, Rockefeller's sister, said that Clark and Andrews would always appeal to him. She said, "They did not seem to want to go without him. They would walk in and visit in the dining room while John was at breakfast. Mary Ann could not stand that they were constantly talking about oil. She just couldn't stand it. She said, "I got sick of it and wished morning after morning that they would talk of something else."

Rockefeller was very passionate about his oil business. He was also very passionate when it came to the church or more specifically the Baptist Church. Clark said that "John had abiding faith in two things—the Baptist creed and oil."

From a rather renowned historian's perspective, he was both "very mature and very young." He could be very serious and firm and also very jolly and merry. Rockefeller found happiness in his work and felt especially happy when he secured a profitable contract. One of the people who knew him during his early days said, "The only time I ever saw John Rockefeller enthusiastic was when a report came in from the creek that his buyer had secured a cargo of oil at a figure much below the market price. He bounded from his chair with a shout of joy, danced up and down, hugged me, threw up his hat, acted so like a madman that I have never forgotten it."

Because Rockefeller sometimes acted extremely merry, it made his usual silence and expressionless face more pronounced. Perhaps it showed that he was actually a happy man or that only very few things made him happy, and that the rest of the time he was not.

Part of the reason why Rockefeller was able to achieve dominance in the oil industry was because it was still an unstable industry in the beginning. He took something that was risky and identified the risk that would bankrupt a producer or a refiner and realized that the only way to beat the odds was to grow large and do it with the assistance of numerous participants. That meant that instead of building everything from scratch Rockefeller used the strategy of acquisitions to grow his company and mitigate the risk of competitive forces.

According to Rockefeller's enemies, he was an evil spirit or something that caused people to be afraid. This first occurred along Oil Creek, which is known as the Oil Regions. The Oil Regions surrounded Oil City, Titusville, and Franklin.

Before Excelsior Works was set up, Rockefeller traveled to Titusville. The journey required him to travel by train and then in a stagecoach through the dense forests that lined Oil Creek. He did not like the journey and often showed his displeasure. Many other people also wanted to go to Oil Creek, and the aisles in between the seats of the train were jammed with people, and many more sat on the roof of the carriages. Anyone who was delicate or nervous would have died in those situations.

One of the difficulties in getting the oil to the train was the terrain that existed between the derricks and the station. For the oil to get from Oil Creek to the trains, it had to be transported over twenty miles of undulating terrain. Some men were hired to move them, and they charged quite a preposterous sum for their services—up to $3 or $4 per barrel.

In 1861, $3 was a lot of money—worth about $85 today. In their defense, though, they did have to do a lot of work, transporting forty-two gallon barrels for more than twenty miles over difficult terrain. Each barrel weighed approximately 134 kilos. In volume, that same barrel carried forty-two gallons of oil. It has since been known as a Pennsylvania barrel, and that measurement is still used today.

During the transportation of oil, some of the barrels would fall to the ground, break, and spill their contents. It wasn't long until the landscape was soaked with this toxic and corrosive sludge.

The workers eventually started to use horses to pull the barrels, and these horses would sometimes get stuck in the mud if it rained, and sludge would line the path from the derricks to the station. Extra horses sometimes had to be used just to pull out the horses that got stuck in the mud.

These horses that were used to pull the barrels of oil encountered much difficulty and were whipped incessantly until many of them just dropped dead.

Their carcasses were left to decompose and be broken down by the extremely corrosive crude oil.

Oil was also transported across the Allegheny River in two ways—either loaded on flatbed steamers or the barrels would be flushed down the river to their destination.

To do this, the barrels were placed on barges, and temporary dams and floodgates were used to hold back the water. When a sufficient amount of water was behind the dam, the gates would be released, and the rush of water would then push the barrels downstream to Pittsburgh.

Rockefeller recounted that "Lots of oil was lost by the capsizing of barges and smashing of barrels in the confusion and crush of the rafts." In 1863, the Allegheny River was filled with so much toxic crude oil that the river caught fire. A bridge in Franklin even burned down.

Rockefeller saw that the once peaceful and serene countryside had been turned into a black landscape where the oil industry now blossomed. The area was filled with shacks, derricks, engine houses, and tanks. It was all messy and filthy. Rockefeller observed that the oil industry was filled with people and groups of people who entered the industry and then quickly left it. He said, "You will remember that the business in its early years was a sort of gold-field rush." He also said, "Great fortunes were made by some of the first adventurers, and everything was carried on in a sort of capitalist development, when the colorful daredevils and pioneering speculators give way, as Max Weber wrote, to the 'men who had grown up in the hard school of life, calculating and daring at the same time, above all temperate and reliable, shrewd and completely devoted to their business, with strictly bourgeois opinions and principles.'"

When Rockefeller visited the Oil Regions, the oil industry no longer seemed that it would soon fade into nothingness. Oil was not a passing fad. It was here to stay, and in late 1861 the Empire Well was built, one of the largest at that time. It was owned by two people from Cleveland and produced three thousand barrels a day.

The Empire Well produced so much oil that it came spewing out at such a rapid rate that the owners of the well could not find a way to harvest all the oil and were not given enough time to even acquire barrels to collect the oil. Normal people would rush over with all sorts of containers, from cups to buckets, to collect the precious oil.

Due to the rapid rise in the production of crude oil, the selling price plummeted. It fell to ten cents per barrel, yet they had to pay workers $3 to $4 per barrel just to transport it to the train station. Producers were suddenly losing money.

During the early stages of the oil industry, there were always violent changes in the dynamic. Either lots of oil would be available and prices would plunge, or there would be so little oil that prices would dramatically increase. When this happened, people would wonder if the supply of oil was running out.

When the oil industry first began, people were always afraid that the oil supply would deplete. An associate of Andrew Carnegie once came up with the idea of pooling oil by digging a large area in the ground and storing barrels of oil inside it so that when the oil supply ran out they could sell that collection of oil and make a nice profit. That started the first known event of oil price manipulation by the restriction of supply. We see it happening today with OPEC producers restricting production.

Many stories have been told about Rockefeller's first trip to the Pennsylvanian oil fields, but one story told by Franklin Breed is rather noteworthy. To get to Breed's oil well, the two men rode on horses, but they walked the last half mile on foot. At one point, they had to cross a small body of water that was about four feet deep and five or six feet wide. In the body of water was sediment that had been removed from the bottom of tanks. It looked like tar, sitting in the water, mixed with the mud. Over the wide body of water was a log measuring six inches in length. Breed always crossed over it, and it was like second nature to him. Rockefeller, however, was not so used to walking over logs and said he wasn't going to, but he tried and fell into the water. After falling, he looked at Breed, a smile on his face, and said, "Well, Breed, you have got me into the oil business head and ears."

Rockefeller probably looked very reserved and aloof to the workers who drilled the wells, but in truth, he said that he actually liked being among them and said they were ". . . pleasant fellows, the same type we meet in the mining regions—jolly, good-natured, the happy-go-lucky sort." Although Rockefeller was not totally cordial when he said this, he did not brush off the workers or anyone for that matter. He would always listen to what they had to say and collect all the information that he could gather. He would then repeat all the important parts to himself until they were etched in his memory. In doing this, he respected even the fool's opinion, which only a very small number of people are able to bring themselves to do.

Too many are filled with too much pride to listen to even the worker, but Rockefeller, in his quest for knowledge, listened to everyone regardless of their position or status.

Rockefeller once said, "It is very important to remember what other people tell you, not so much what you yourself already know." Although the place where oil originated in the United States enabled Rockefeller to amass his unfathomable wealth and power, he did not like the area. It was filled with immoral people, gambling and indulging in pleasures of the flesh. The more that Rockefeller went to Oil Creek and the Oil Regions, the more his character hardened against immorality. Due to his passionate feeling about not drinking, he felt most upset when he was around people who drank. It has been suspected that that was a reason why he very rarely went to Oil Creek and the Regions.

At first, the oil business was not treated as an industry. Everyone was uncertain whether or not the oil frenzy and the entire oil business would just suddenly evaporate or if it would last and continue to do good for people. Most oil miners would quickly remove all the oil in their field. At the time, certain miners would not drill straight but in a diagonal direction so as to harvest another miner's oil.

What differentiated Rockefeller from his fellow adventurers in the oil business, aside from his unrelenting character, is that he eventually came to believe that the oil business would not fizzle out. He believed that it would be a long-lasting affair. It was because of this belief that he was able to succeed as he did.

If you look at this psychologically, you could perhaps say that those who thought the oil business would eventually fizzle away treated it very carelessly. Rockefeller, rightfully thinking that the oil industry would continue, devoted his time and care to the business, which allowed *his* business to thrive.

It was wise for Rockefeller to go into the business of oil refining. An oil miner did not enjoy as much success as a refiner because it was more difficult. To harvest oil, you had to land on a site with oil below the land. Mining oil was much more risky than refining. Being a refiner, you could trust that you would always have business, as some miner or another person would always come to you to process his oil, and you were safe.

Very soon after entering the oil business, Rockefeller understood that he could have more control over the oil industry as a refiner. As it would turn out, his company, Standard Oil, would be the largest oil refining company in the world until its breakup in 1911.

Rockefeller was always able to know who would hinder or help him in his business. He never liked to be treated inferiorly even by those who held a higher position than he did. Whenever he sensed that someone was treating him as less than an equal, he would stop it at once.

Clark's brother had joined the firm, and Rockefeller came to hate him as much as he did Clark and Rockefeller's former partner George W. Gardner. They were too lavish in their ways, and Rockefeller absolutely despised them for it. Rockefeller always minded his own business, did his work, and crunched the numbers, and it was because of this that he was seen by his partners as less of a man than he was. He would spend time thinking about how he could get rid of the Clark brothers, and they would not even see the final blow coming.

Rockefeller was always very meticulous and very careful with all the books, and the elder Clark thought this was all Rockefeller could do . . . that he had no imagination or spirit and was just a cold calculator. Rockefeller said, "He did not think I could do anything but keep accounts and look after the finances."

Rockefeller also said, "You see, it took him a long time to see that I was no longer a boy."

Rockefeller believed that Clark was jealous of him because he was successful, which went against Clark's belief that Rockefeller was dispensable. In the beginning, Rockefeller just kept his anger toward Clark within him and said nothing. While he and Rockefeller were talking about business, Clark would often say, "What in the world would you have done without me?" Rockefeller said that he ". . . bore it in silence. It does no good to dispute with such a man."

One thing that was very clear at least in Rockefeller's mind was that he was the one bringing in the money and for the better part making what should've perhaps been his *own* company successful. As Rockefeller said, "I was the one who made the firm's success. I kept the books, looked out for the money."

Rockefeller was naturally very silent and reserved and thus did not warn his partners about his plan. He thought it best to throw it at them when they had no idea it was coming.

After having entered the oil business, Clark's brother, James Clark, joined the business. Rockefeller would grow to absolutely despise James, who was also a prizefighter. James was a bully who liked to trample on

458

those around him. He attempted to make Rockefeller cower, but he failed. Rockefeller was always strong and fearless and was not affected by James' snobbishness and extreme rudeness. One day James stormed into Rockefeller's office and began to swear, scream, and shout at him. In response, Rockefeller simply sat in his chair, rested his feet on the table, and looked most undisturbed. When James stopped speaking, Rockefeller said calmly, "Now, James, you can knock my head off, but you might as well understand that you can't scare me." It was absolutely impossible to make Rockefeller bend his head or make him cower. After this little event, the relationship between the two men continued to slide downhill, but at least James never behaved that way again or anything near it in Rockefeller's presence. The bully had been put down by the seemingly robotic clerk.

Rockefeller argued with James about how to conduct business. He had also faced the same problem with his first partner, Maurice B. Clark. James would proudly say that he had tricked people and done dishonest things, and Rockefeller began to always keep an eye on the money that James spent. Like his brother, James saw Rockefeller's morality in the light of an unethical person. James nicknamed Rockefeller the "Sunday-school superintendent."

Rockefeller wanted to have around him people whom he could trust and who were honest. He wanted people who would not cause others to lose trust and confidence in them but rather stir trust in people who appealed to their services as well as the bankers.

Rockefeller believed that anyone who was not strong, unethical, and dishonest would live a life of failure. He said, "We were beginning to prosper, and I felt very uneasy at my name being linked up with these speculators." He basically did not want himself or his name to be associated with these rogues that were unfortunately his partners. The benefit of their having been his partners, however, was that perhaps they taught him how to choose people he could trust and bring into his business and those to keep as far away as possible from himself or his career.

Not long afterward the Clark brothers would come to share the same hatred that Rockefeller had for them for him. They would say bad things about Rockefeller and paint a negative picture of him simply because they disliked and hated him—a man who would become much richer and much more successful than they ever would be.

Rockefeller didn't like his first Clark partner not just because of who he was but also because of his perspective regarding the oil industry and how fast the industry should advance and grow.

When the Civil War raged on, the oil fields only stopped producing when the owners tried to protect their mines from the Confederates when General Robert Edward Lee attacked the state.

As the market for kerosene grew in overseas countries and was being exported, Andrew, Clark, and Company was able to make a tremendous amount of money.

Although all who were in the oil industry were greatly competitive, prices always fluctuated and never stabilized. In 1861, a barrel of oil would sometimes cost ten cents and at other times $10. In 1864, a barrel of oil would shift from $4 to $12.

Both Andrews and Rockefeller shared the same view: expand. They did not care for these small hiccups in the oil industry and wanted to grow their oil business. Clark, however, was not of that opinion. He wanted to be a little more cautious and was not so keen on involving himself too much in the oil industry.

What perhaps caused Rockefeller to leave his partners is that they were a majority party when it came to pushing his decisions aside. Andrews did not sympathize with Rockefeller but simply took advantage of the higher position of the three Clark brothers. Rockefeller once recounted an incident where Clark became upset with him because he had borrowed money to expand their oil business.

Rockefeller understood that unlike himself Clark was not one to take risks and would never do things that Rockefeller did. Clark was too scared. Rockefeller said, "Clark was an old grandmother and was scared to death because we owed money at the banks."

You could perhaps side with the Clarks because they were upset that their partner was using their money in an unstable venture that they thought should be done with caution. What the Clarks lacked, however, was foresight and confidence. Rockefeller understood that the oil industry would not wither away and thus did everything he could to dominate it. Perhaps if it hadn't been for Rockefeller the oil industry could've collapsed after a few years or decades, and that would have been the end of it. Perhaps the oil industry survived for as long as it did because Rockefeller believed it would be long-lasting, and his actions secured that fate, for his actions would carry the oil industry into the following centuries.

It 1865, Rockefeller thought it was time to finish the Clark brothers. He was just twenty-five years old at the time. His character prohibited him from continuing to be part of something that did not work well, and now he wanted to remove the hindrances in his life, which happened to be the Clark brothers.

For Rockefeller to fully immerse himself in the oil industry, he needed something to happen that would prove that the oil supply would not dry up. In January 1865, a place in Pithole Creek was sending up sulfuric gas from certain trenches in the land.

Some people were using a certain twig as a divining rod and then dug where the rod pointed. Several days later, oil came spewing from where they dug, and once again people were thrown into a frenzy. Pithole Creek used to be a calm and small area with just some houses made of logs, but just a few months later all kinds of people, from onlookers and oilmen to people representing businessmen, came to see the site. Very quickly, Pithole Creek's population soared to twelve thousand, and fifty hotels and even a theater were set up in the area.

One person who watched the frenzy at Pithole Creek was one Miss Ida Tarbell, who was just eight years old at the time and lived in Roseville, just ten miles from Pithole Creek. She would watch groups of people rush to Pithole. Her father opened a business that sold oil tanks, and he made money very quickly.

The frenzy at Pithole Creek ended after several years, for its oil wells had been burned and were exhausted. After the oil boom ended, people did what they could to survive with what was left of Pithole, which had turned into a bustling city. Tarbell's father purchased the Bonta House, a hotel in Pithole Creek, for just $600. It had cost $60,000 to build. He dismantled the hotel and used the pieces to build a home for his family in Titusville.

In 1874, after all the excitement came to an end, nine years after oil was struck in the area, the population had dwindled to just six people.

When you look back, Pithole's return to simplicity after the oil business in the area had collapsed seemed to indicate that the oil industry was not going to last very long. When the frenzy began, however, it seemed to prove that the oil industry would last a long time, and it also encouraged the break between the Clark brothers and Rockefeller. What miners and oil producers did not know was that there was still plenty of oil in the ground. The miners just didn't know how to get it out. In the past, they had relied on the internal pressure of the well to push the oil to the surface, but once that pressure equalized, the well stopped gushing. Today, we have all kinds of technologies to pump oil and exert pressure on the well as well as stimulation techniques, such as fracking.

What Rockefeller did to rid himself of the three Clark brothers was that he very slowly arranged everything and then quickly hit them with his plan before they had time to react.

Chapter 5 Strategic Mindset

"Next to doing the right thing, the most important thing is to let people know you are doing the right thing."

— John D. Rockefeller

When oil was struck in Pithole in January 1865, Rockefeller asked Clark to sign for another loan. Clark was incensed and didn't stay quiet. He said to Rockefeller, "We have been asking too many loans in order to extend this oil business." Rockefeller replied by saying, "We should borrow whenever we can safely extend the business by doing so."

To check Rockefeller, the three Clark brothers tried to intimidate him by saying they would break up the relationship between the partners by ending the partnership. To do this, all partners needed to agree, which would mean the end of the business. This was not the first or the last time that they tried to intimidate him by threatening dissolution, but

Rockefeller knew their tricks and decided to use it for his benefit.

Rockefeller wanted to end his relationship with the Clark brothers and was done working in his current business of selling and buying on behalf of others. Rockefeller was able to get Andrews to join him in his venture to break from the Clark brothers.

He said to Andrews, "Sam, we are prospering. We have a future before us, a big future, but I don't like Jim Clark and his habits. He is an immoral man in more ways than one. He gambles in oil. I don't want this business to be associated with a gambler. Suppose I take them up the next time they threaten a dissolution. Suppose I succeed in buying them out. Will you come in with me?"

Andrews agreed to join Rockefeller since he, too, could plainly see that his fortunes would fare better with Rockefeller than with the crazy Clark brothers. Several weeks later the trigger for Rockefeller to enact his plan occurred. He had an argument with his first Clark partner, and Clark said that he would break up the partnership of the produce firm. Clark said, "If that's the way you want to do business, we'd better dissolve and let you run your own affairs to suit yourself."

On February 1, 1865, Rockefeller made preparations for the final blow. He called his partners to his home and talked about ways they would expand their business in a manner that he knew the Clark brothers would absolutely dislike. Jim Clark tried to intimidate Rockefeller into backing off by saying, as before, "We'd better split up." Rockefeller then asked everyone to say whether or not they supported breaking up the partnership. They all did, but they were merely using it to threaten him, and when they left his house that night they thought nothing of it and thought they had gotten the better of him.

After the Clarks left his home, Rockefeller quickly rushed to the *Cleveland Leader* newspaper office and demanded an announcement to be printed in the papers that the partnership was breaking up. The newspaper ran the notice in the next morning's edition, and before even getting to the office, the brothers saw it.

When the Clark brothers saw this announcement, they were stunned. Rockefeller's first partner, Maurice B. Clark, asked Rockefeller, "Do you really mean it? You really want to break it up?" Rockefeller replied by saying, "I really want to break it up."

In the end, it was decided that the oil refinery part of Clark and Rockefeller would be auctioned off. It turned out that the bidders for the auction were Clark and Rockefeller themselves. Essentially, the buyout would mean that the company would either go to the Clark brothers or Rockefeller.

By this point, Rockefeller was a man who could handle the most troubling of situations with a clear mind and calm nerves. His character was also such that when the people around him became more upset he became even more poised.

When the Clark brothers went to the auction, they had a lawyer with them, who was the auctioneer himself. Rockefeller, however, did not bring a lawyer of his own. He thought he could handle it himself.

The bidding began at $500. It then increased to several thousand dollars. Then it reached $50,000, $60,000, and $70,000. By this point, Rockefeller was afraid that he would not be able to make the purchase. Then the Clarks put up $72,000, and Rockefeller quickly bid $72,500. Clark let go at that point, and Rockefeller asked, "Shall I give you a check for it now?" Clark demurred and said that Rockefeller could pay when he was ready. It was a gentlemanly gesture, and it came with a shock in his voice, as he had no idea that Rockefeller had amassed that much money to make the purchase.

It turned out that Rockefeller's strategy of being prudent and bankable worked in his favor. When the time came, he had lined up a line of credit from the banks that supported his takeover of the company. It was with their backing that he had the strength and tenacity to bid the price up to that level.

The price of $72,500 in 1865 would be about $1.2 million today. Although the price was expensive for the time, it was an important purchase. Rockefeller was just twenty-five years old and now owner of the largest oil refinery in Cleveland, which was refining five hundred barrels of oil every day. Approximately two weeks after the Clarks met with Rockefeller in his home, the *Cleveland Leader* announced that Rockefeller had purchased the firm of Andrews, Clark and Company. It went on to say that Rockefeller had purchased all the materials of the company, and that they would continue their work under the firm of Rockefeller and Andrews.

Chapter 6 Family

"I do not think that there is any other quality so essential to success of any kind as the quality of perseverance. It overcomes almost everything, even nature."

— John D. Rockefeller

The year before the breakup between the Clarks and Rockefeller, Rockefeller married his wife, Laura Celestia Spelman, who was also known as Cettie. The two had met in high school, and Rockefeller was also acquainted with Laura's sister. Her father was Harvey Buel Spelman. He had been a businessman, whose businesses sometimes fell flat, leaving the family in a state of poverty. The Spelman family was always insecure by not knowing when the next round of money was coming.

After moving to Cleveland, the family was better off, and Harvey's business did well. Unfortunately, it all later collapsed, and Harvey and Laura's mother left

Cleveland. To help, Laura and her sister stayed behind in Cleveland and worked as schoolteachers.

Laura strongly supported not drinking and was a devout Baptist. During her marriage with Rockefeller, she would be the strict and stern one, while Rockefeller was the fun one, but they were a match made in heaven.

The entire Spelman family strongly supported the abolition of slavery and did not just sit by the sidelines and wait for that time to come. The Spelman home was a place along the Underground Railroad where slaves were able to flee from the slave drivers and owners of the South to the free land of the North.

Laura's mother would cook food for the slaves making their way along the Underground Railroad, and the entire family devoted themselves to helping them.

Rockefeller's background was quite different from Laura's. At the time of the marriage, her family was rather well-to-do, and she was living a comfortable life but did not indulge in it. Rockefeller, on the other hand, had a rather rough background and was not very wealthy. Still, the two would make it work.

Before their marriage, Rockefeller would go to her home, and they would go over his ledgers, something they both loved. As time went by, Laura's relationship with Rockefeller became less of a loving one and more of a friendship. When Rockefeller became more wealthy, however, he would try ever harder to win her.

In the end, they were married September 8, 1864, in Cleveland. They would have five children: four daughters and one son: Alice, Edith, Elizabeth, Alta, and John. Alice Rockefeller died just after her first birthday. Rockefeller was very close to his wife and took her very seriously. As he said, "Her judgment was always better than mine. Without her keen advice, I would be a poor man."

All of their children were raised to be very pious, devout, and clean people. They were virtually locked up in the family home and shielded from the outside world and the immense wealth of the Rockefeller family. They were raised as if they were poor. Rockefeller Jr. wore his sisters' hand-me-down dresses and skirts until he was eight years old! All of the children shared their toys among themselves.

When Laura was once speaking to a neighbor, she said she was so glad that her son had told her what he wanted for Christmas because, according to her, they could now say "No" to him.

The Rockefeller children were raised to not indulge in money, and one of the quotes from the Bible that

Rockefeller Jr. committed to memory was "It is easier for a camel to go through the eye of a needle than for a rich man to enter the kingdom of God." When John Jr. was ten years old, he was made to swear that he would never smoke or drink. Unfortunately, he would break part of that oath by smoking a packet of cigarettes.

Although the Rockefeller home was grand and nicely built, the interior was bare of any luxuries, and everyone lived simply.

Laura had a certain practice with the children. Every Sunday all of them would sit down and confess what wrongs they had committed that week and would prepare themselves to do better the coming week. The entire Rockefeller family was very pious and enlightened. Laura and Rockefeller were already that way, and their children were being molded to become that way.

Between the two parents, Rockefeller was by far the much more entertaining one. While Laura would discipline the children, Rockefeller would play with them. He would have bicycle chases with them in the large land area of their family home, and he would teach them how to ice-skate. Whenever Rockefeller won a bicycle race, he would act like a young child and cry in joy. He naturally loved children and greatly loved his own.

Chapter 7 Standard Oil

"I always tried to turn every disaster into an opportunity."

— **John D. Rockefeller**

Five years after the breakup between Rockefeller and the Clarks, Rockefeller established Standard Oil of Ohio. Other cofounders included Rockefeller's brother, William Rockefeller Jr., Henry Huttleston Rogers, and Henry Flagler.

With the founding of Standard Oil of Ohio behind him and the refineries of Rockefeller and Andrews absorbed into Standard Oil of Ohio (Sohio), Rockefeller set out to take control of the other twenty-six oil refineries in Cleveland. His main goal was to be the sole oil refiner in the world, but his first goal was Ohio. Within two months from the time he began acquiring control of the other oil refineries, he had taken over twenty-two of them.

He took control of the oil refineries either through a friendly approach or coercion. He would at first talk cordially with the owners of the refineries and try to get them to sell their company to him on their own volition. If that didn't work, he would proceed to force them to sell their company to him. Rockefeller did not like forcing people to do something and preferred getting them to do it themselves, but he was not going to let that get in the way of his success and did what was needed to get the job done.

To cut costs and be in a more advantageous position, he made a deal with the railroad companies known as the South Improvement Company. He would give the railroads more business by giving them his oil to transport, and in return they would charge him lower prices for their services. Meanwhile, they would continue to charge other customers regular rates, which were quite expensive.

Rockefeller was thus able to achieve a superior position in transporting his oil at lower cost and beat out his competitors. Standard Oil operated on a global scale. It was not just confined to the United States, and any competing oil refinery, if not careful, would become prey of the Standard Oil Trust (which was yet to come).

Global Oil

To deepen this facet of Standard Oil, it has to be seen in the context of the global oil industry. Sir Marcus Samuel was a man who worked in the business of buying seashells from the Middle East and selling them to those who were using them as decorations. He and his brother, Sam, also worked in the business of sending goods to Japan and buying from them such things as silk, rice, and other Eastern commodities. Samuel's interest in the oil business sparked when he traveled to Japan.

At this time, the French banking family the Rothschilds had put their money into building railroads and passages through which oil could be transported. Transporting oil was still difficult to do, and shipping was inefficient, as the barrels took up too much space. Finally, Marcus and his brother had a large number of ships transport the oil in barrels.

Instead, however, of loading cargo ships with barrels, which themselves took up space and weight, they decided to make tankers. Their first tanker, which needed to be approved by the Suez Canal Company to be able to pass through its canal from the Mediterranean to the Red Sea, was approved. The oil tanker *Murex* transported a large quantity of oil to Thailand, and Marcus was successful in changing the way oil was transported. He was able to reduce transportation costs of oil for purchasers.

In 1897, five years after the success of the *Murex*, the Samuel brothers renamed their company The "Shell" Transport and Trading Company Limited. It was originally called The Tank Syndicate.

In the East Indies, it was the Royal Dutch Petroleum Company, which had been established in 1890 by King William III of the Netherlands. Because its competitor The "Shell" Transport and Trading Company was able to transport oil at a lower cost, the Royal Dutch Petroleum Company began to build oil tankers for themselves. To be strong enough to compete against the Standard Oil Trust of John D. Rockefeller, in 1903 the Royal Dutch Petroleum Company and The Shell Transport and Trading Company joined to form the Asiatic Petroleum Company.

The following year the first form of what is today the symbol of Shell, the pecten, became the company's logo. Previously, the logo was the shell of a mussel. In 1907, the Asiatic Petroleum Company would become Royal Dutch Shell, also known as the Shell Oil Company.

Out of mere fear of Standard Oil, this was how Royal Dutch Shell came into existence. Shell is now the fifth largest oil company in the world, just behind ExxonMobil, a company that resulted from the breakup of Standard Oil.

The fact that Shell was created on the basis of fear of Standard Oil shows that Rockefeller's power was more than just domination over the industry. It shows that competitors feared destruction from the oil titan. Rockefeller's Standard Oil Trust was more than just an extremely large oil refining company. It was a formidable competitor.

Standard Oil was built upon clever tactics and strategies. Rockefeller may have bribed a few politicians to his benefit, but you can't consider that to have been wrong on his part. All successful businessmen cannot be by-the-book and neat and tidy. They need to do whatever is necessary to get what they want done.

When Rockefeller had to pay off politicians, he viewed paying them as if they were in a higher position than he was rather than considering them as puny, corrupt politicians that he could control.

Chapter 8 Monopolies, Electricity, and Alcohol

"Good leadership consists of showing average people
how to do the work of superior people."

— John D. Rockefeller

In 1879, Thomas Alva Edison perfected the light bulb, and shortly afterward J.P. Morgan financed Edison and worked with him to make electricity widespread and the dominant fuel for lights in America. This was a serious problem for Rockefeller, for Standard Oil was at the time supplying kerosene to people, and it was being used as an illuminant. If electricity replaced kerosene, Rockefeller was going to lose a large market for his product.

So, he set out to stop the advance of electricity by saying bad things about it and reporting these things to the press, hoping that the American people would become afraid of electricity and not use it.

Unfortunately for Rockefeller, his attempts to stop the advance of electricity did not work, and it came to be the dominant power source in the United States, causing Rockefeller to lose his customers who were buying kerosene for their lights.

Something else would soon open up for Rockefeller, however, which was the automobile industry. The first car of modern times was invented by German inventor Karl Benz in 1885. The cars ran on gasoline, something that Standard Oil was happy to supply.

The problem, though, was that electric cars were also being used in the United States. The first electric car had been created in 1884 and posed a threat to such people as Rockefeller. Electric streetcars bused people from one part of a city to another part and powered personal vehicles.

In the end, General Motors, one of the largest automobile companies in the world, would begin to tear down the streetcars and use that material to build their buses, which ran on gasoline whose supplier was Standard Oil.

It is difficult to believe that Standard Oil ended up being the supplier of gasoline for the company that took down the electric streetcars, benefiting Rockefeller's empire just by coincidence. Perhaps he had a hand in the monopolization of the transportation business by General Motors (GM).

The main cause of the downfall of the electric car industry was that an oil derrick began gushing out one hundred thousand barrels of oil a day, dramatically reducing the price of oil, kerosene, and gasoline. Electric cars were extremely expensive, and now that gasoline was a much cheaper alternative, the American people favored that over electric cars. This led to the decline in popularity of the electric car and the rise of vehicles powered by gasoline.

Thus, Standard Oil was rid of the electric car industry and could continue to supply gasoline to customers. Rockefeller was once again at the top, able to supply his oil to the country. Although he had lost the battle against electricity as an illuminant, he managed to succeed in supplying the fledgling automobile industry with a power source: gasoline.

As for alcohol, at one time the automobile industry used alcohol as a fuel source. Those who opposed titans and such large corporations as Standard Oil from dominating an industry supported the use of alcohol as a fuel.

Again, there was a threat to Rockefeller's oil empire. If alcohol became the dominant fuel for cars, Rockefeller would lose his market, as he had lost his market when electricity became the dominant illuminant.

The problem at the time was that Americans drank a lot of alcohol. They drank much more than the average American does today. The average teenager at least fifteen years old was drinking seven gallons of alcohol per year, and people began protesting against it. Howard Hyde Russell founded the Anti-Saloon League, or ASL, to which Rockefeller donated a lot of money.

The intoxicating effects of alcohol and the high drinking rate of the American people led to Prohibition, which lasted from 1920 to 1933. Those that were selling alcohol as a fuel for cars had to mix petroleum with their alcohol so that it would be poisonous, preventing the purchaser from consuming it. It thus became very expensive to use alcohol as a fuel, and the industry declined, allowing Rockefeller to continue supplying the American public with gasoline for their automobiles.

Rockefeller had capitalized on the American people's opposition to alcohol. He had used that to his benefit so stop alcohol from being used as a fuel source and bring gasoline, which was largely supplied by Standard Oil, back to the market.

Perhaps Rockefeller was behind the fall of electric cars in the nineteenth century and also partially behind the beginning of Prohibition, thus allowing him to eliminate two industries—the electric car and alcohol as fuel. Rockefeller's tactics to place his company at the head of the game was what made it a success, but it was also what made him and his company greatly despised by the American people.

Rockefeller's power was so great that he was able to influence the course of American history. He did what was needed to keep his company at the top and maintain the success of his multinational empire, which, if it hadn't been broken up, would be the largest oil company in the world today.

Chapter 9 Heir to the Throne

"I would rather earn 1% off a 100 people's efforts than 100% of my own efforts."

— John D. Rockefeller

John D. Rockefeller Jr. was quite different from his father. He was a much more easygoing person and danced, against his mother's liking, but was also a much more timid and unsure person.

John Jr. could've gone to Yale University but chose to go to Brown University. After graduation, he worked at Standard Oil. There, he was given all the necessities of working in the company but was not told his particular duties. Rockefeller Sr. had retired from Standard Oil in 1897, and John Jr. was responsible for carrying on the business. It was much too stressful for him, though, and he very quickly quit working at Standard Oil and devoted himself to philanthropy and bettering the family name.

At a dance that John Jr. attended, he met Abigail Greene Aldrich, the daughter of Senator Nelson Wilmarth Aldrich of Rhode Island. Senator Aldrich was the man whose actions led to the formation of the Federal Reserve System. Abigail, or Abby as she was also known, would go on to found the Museum of Modern Art.

On October 9, 1901, the couple were married in Aldrich Mansion at Warwick Neck on Rhode Island. Standard Oil directors attended the ceremony as did directors of several other companies.

Their marriage was seen as a fusion of money and politics—an alliance between the wealthy Rockefellers and the political Aldrich family.

Together, they had six children: Abigail, also known as Abby, John D. Rockefeller III, Nelson, Laurance, Winthrop, and David. Nelson Rockefeller was later vice president of the United States under President Gerald Ford. He ran for president four times and would have won had he not married a woman who was already a mother. His campaign was going well until his marriage, and from then on people started to dislike him.

David Rockefeller was later CEO, chairman, and president of Chase National Bank.

David's grandfather, John D. Rockefeller Sr., had been the largest shareholder of Chase Bank.

Rockefeller had wished to live until he was 100 years old. He didn't, as he died when he was 97, but his grandson, David Rockefeller, lived until he was 101, being born in 1915 and passing in 2017 before his 102nd birthday.

After having left Standard Oil in 1910, John Jr. began repairing the family name, for it had been tarnished by muckraking reporters, such as Ida Tarbell, a reporter for *McClure's* Magazine.

His philanthropy included preserving areas, rebuilding sites, and dedicating lands to the public. Everything he did was to make the Rockefeller name shine and change the way it was being seen by the American public.

When everything was proceeding satisfactorily, something extremely disastrous occurred. Workers at the Colorado Fuel and Iron Company, which was controlled by Rockefeller Sr., went on strike. They demanded higher salaries and safer working conditions.

The CFI Company kicked the workers out of their homes since they were provided by the company, and the workers and their families were forced to camp out in tents. The National Guard was called to take care of the situation, as the Ludlow Massacre took place on April 20, 1914, when the workers were fired on by machine guns, but many workers were able to escape the carnage, for a train came through that day, blocking the National Guard of Colorado and the guards of CFI from the workers.

The brakeman of the train said he saw one of the men walking in the workers camp and setting it on fire. People hid in underground compartments. When everything was over, two women and eleven children were found inside one of them. Twenty-four people died that day. The Ludlow Massacre, as it is known, was attributed to the Rockefellers.

John Jr. tried his best to solve the situation. He travelled to Ludlow to see the people. He spent time with them—eating, dancing, and doing his best to make everything good again. In the end, everything turned out well, and John Sr. gave John Jr. a large number of shares of the Colorado Fuel and Iron Company.

A great many Americans did not like the Rockefellers, and the family received ominous threats. John Sr. was pushed to the point that he began keeping a loaded revolver next to him when he slept. Threats of kidnapping and even bomb threats were also made.

These threats were particularly startling for John Jr. because his mother, who was now in poor health, was living in the family home of Kykuit in Sleepy Hollow, New York.

One time a bomb that was believed meant to arrive at the Rockefeller home exploded before it got there, and four people were killed.

To consider how the Rockefeller name was tarnished and why so many people disliked and despised the Rockefeller family, the reporter Ida Tarbell must be mentioned.

Chapter 10 The Three Titans

"I have ways of making money that you know nothing
of."

— **John D. Rockefeller**

In 1896, William Jennings Bryan was running for president. He opposed big business and large corporations, such as Standard Oil, Carnegie Steel, and J.P. Morgan and Company. Bryan was the ultimate enemy of the titans of America. If he became president, all of them, including John D. Rockefeller, Andrew Carnegie, and J.P. Morgan, and their companies, would be severely threatened by his policies.

To avert disaster, they joined forces to defeat Bryan and install a president in the White House whom they favored. They wanted Republican William McKinley. Unlike Bryan, McKinley supported large corporations and big businesses and would be the perfect president for them.

Bryan appealed to the working class, which felt they had had enough of the wealthy men of America who had millions of dollars while they were earning less than a dollar a day. Workers for Carnegie and Rockefeller worked in extremely intolerable conditions in front of extremely hot furnaces and in oil refineries. They wanted better working conditions. These were the Populists, and William Jennings Bryan appealed to them in the presidential election.

If Bryan became president, everything that Andrew Carnegie, John D. Rockefeller, and J.P. Morgan had spent their lives building would be seriously threatened. They needed William McKinley in the White House, so each of them donated more than $200,000 to his campaign. Even $250,000 back then would be $7,477,172.62 today. If they donated $750,000, that would be about $22 million today.

In the end, William McKinley won the 1896 election and became president of the United States. They were safe—for now.

After having succeeded in getting McKinley elected president, the alliance between Morgan, Carnegie, and Rockefeller was no longer necessary. Rockefeller was the first to break from the group. He wanted to find a way to hurt Andrew Carnegie and looked into the steel industry, something Rockefeller actually did not have any interest in at all. He began mining at a certain iron ore mine that Carnegie had brushed off as unimportant. Rockefeller then began selling the iron ore to Carnegie's competitors and was making a nice profit. Carnegie's competitors were also able to have more business and were making more steel.

Rockefeller wasn't the only one causing trouble for Carnegie. Rockefeller had been selling the components of steel to rival steel manufacturers, who believed that perhaps they could sell their steel for slightly cheaper prices than Carnegie did and would get more customers.

The effects on Carnegie Steel were drastic. Within just a few months, the profits of the company reduced dramatically, and Andrew Carnegie had to do something. The worst was still to come. Rockefeller was planning to build a steel mill to hurt his rival even more. Carnegie could not let him do that. If Rockefeller entered the steel industry on a full-fledged scale, Carnegie's steel empire would be under invasion.

Carnegie set out to try to use fear to stop Rockefeller from entering the steel industry, but that wasn't going to work. The two began talks, which lasted for months, and nothing happened. Finally, Carnegie understood that he had to give in and proposed to buy the iron ore mine from Rockefeller, and Rockefeller was to stop building his steel mill. In the end, Rockefeller was able to get Carnegie to pay him a large sum of money to sell something to him that Rockefeller didn't much care for and not build the steel plant that Rockefeller also did not have any interest in.

Rockefeller displayed both a keen intelligence and ruthlessness in this act of business, but you cannot say that he was cruel. That is how proper business is done and how one becomes successful.

This incident shows that Rockefeller was someone who did not care for being delicate and tidy. He only cared about success and doing what he had to do to win. He did not care for niceties and focused on the goal. After realizing what he wanted to do, he got it done in whatever way he had to regardless of how it was seen by the masses.

One thing they had in common was that they would send each other Christmas gifts, although these gifts were more out of spite than being sincere. Rockefeller once sent Carnegie a brown vest made of paper. It was meant to highlight Carnegie's poor background as a migrant from a foreign country. Carnegie, knowing that Rockefeller was a staunch nondrinker, sent him a bottle of liquor.

As they aged and their thoughts turned to their own mortality, the race became more about legacy than pranks. The two began a new race. This time the race was to see how much they could give to charity.

Chapter 11 Ida Tarbell

"After it is all over, the religion of man is his most
important possession."

— **John D. Rockefeller**

Muckraking journalist Ida Minerva Tarbell wrote a
nineteen-part exposé of Standard Oil and John D.
Rockefeller. In her scathing series, she harshly
criticized Rockefeller and Standard Oil for being cruel
and ruthless. More than just chasing after a good story
and wanting to reveal the "truth" of Standard Oil and
Rockefeller, she actually had a personal score to settle
with both.

Tarbell's father had been in the oil industry at the
beginning along with her brother. They were both
destroyed because of Standard Oil, and Tarbell built up
personal animosity and hatred for John D. Rockefeller
and his oil empire.

She was not the only one who was criticizing and rebuking Standard Oil. The press and many people did not like the company or him.

Rockefeller was characterized as a greedy monster who hoarded all his money and hurt others to make money. He was portrayed as a ruthless serpent—an evil force plaguing the American people and the industry.

Her series about Standard Oil was deeply hurtful to the entire Rockefeller family. She harshly criticized the company and Rockefeller. She made it appear that Standard Oil had been built upon deceit, cruelty, ruthlessness, and evil. She made John D. Rockefeller the personification of evil in people's minds, and it is very probable that she really believed it too.

The last two parts of her Standard Oil series were centered more on Rockefeller himself. She described Rockefeller as extremely ugly and looked like a leper. She had actually seen him once. He was walking, and according to her, he was watching everyone, looking for those who may be his adversaries.

At one point, the family employed members of the Pinkerton Detectives to protect their home. These were mercenary fighters willing to fight if the price suited them.

John Jr. devoted his life to repairing the family name, trying to undo the damage that had been caused by Ida Tarbell and all those who rebuked Standard Oil and his father.

Her actions led to passage of the Sherman Antitrust Act in 1890, legislation that would cause trouble for not just Rockefeller but also for many more businessmen, including J.P. Morgan, whose company would be broken up.

Before the breakup of Standard Oil, investigations had been opened into the company, and Rockefeller was called to appear in court. He did not want to appear, though, and ran.

He kept running and running, and no one knew for sure where he had gone. Finally, what made him return was the birth of his grandchild. He did not want to be an absent grandfather and decided to return and appear in court.

He fought the court for some time until the Supreme Court ruled that the Standard Oil Trust was to be dissolved. Rockefeller was accused of creating a monopoly, and the takeover of the oil industry in Cleveland was dubbed the Cleveland Massacre. In the end, despite Rockefeller's best attempts, Standard Oil was dissolved in 1911.

The company was broken down into thirty-four other companies, including Esso, Sohio, Calso, Kyso, Chevron, Amoco, and Mobil.

Calso, which was Standard Oil of California, later took over Standard Oil of Kentucky, or Kyso. Later on, it took control of Texaco and became ChevronTexaco. In 2005, it took over UNOCAL and is known today as Chevron or Chevron Corporation.

Standard Oil of New York joined with MobilGas in 1931 and was later rechristened Mobil in 1963.

Esso, Standard Oil of New Jersey, joined with Humble Gas in 1959 and was rechristened Exxon in 1973. In 1999, Mobil and Exxon joined to form ExxonMobil, the fourth largest oil company in the world.

Service, or Standard Oil of Indiana, became Amoco in 1925 and in 1998 was taken up by the British Petroleum Company, or BP. Standard Oil of Ohio, or Sohio, was also taken up by BP in 1987. Finally, the Ohio Oil Company became Marathon in 1930 and Marathon Petroleum in 2011.

The breakup of Standard Oil made Rockefeller even richer. He was a major shareholder in all the companies, and a certain percentage of their profits went to him. When the automobile industry progressed with the production of the Model T, where almost everyone had a car, the successors of Standard Oil were providing the fuel, and large amounts of cash kept coming in.

Before and after the Standard Oil breakup in 1911, Rockefeller worked hard to restore his image. He had been portrayed as this savage, brutal, cruel, and ruthless monster who had monopolized the oil industry. His company was depicted in cartoons as an octopus strangling the world. He had dominated the oil refining industry in such a cunning and do-whatever-you-have-to way that people despised both him and his company.

So, he set out to repair his image. He began giving dimes to people in the street. He filmed videos of himself and did his best to seem like a very nice person. One video shows him getting in a plane that goes down the runway but doesn't take off. It was meant to look like John D. Rockefeller's first time in an airplane. After the stunt, the video filmed Rockefeller giving a dime to each of the two people who "took him up" in the plane. Someone out of view of the camera had suggested that he give dimes to them.

All in all, Rockefeller gave about thirty thousand dimes to people. Slowly, he began to be regarded as a nice old man rather than a greedy monster.

John Jr. established many parks, restored many areas, and was more of a people person than his father. He built Rockefeller Center, a towering office building in New York City. He dedicated the better part of his entire life, and by the time he passed in his eighties, he had accomplished his goal. The Rockefeller name had been repaired, and the damage done by such journalists as Ida Tarbell was over. By the time John Jr. passed away, the Rockefeller name was no longer a subject of hate and anger but one of much more cordial essences.

Chapter 12 Pipelines, Railroads, and Corruption

"I know of nothing more despicable and pathetic than
a man who devotes all the hours of the waking day to
the making of money for money's sake."

— John D. Rockefeller

Rockefeller's business was not just limited to refineries. He had also dealt in the storage business and pipelines. He had oil tanks that producers could use to store their crude oil, and the pipelines were used to transport oil.

In the 1870s, a certain geologist predicted that the oil reserves in the world would run dry very quickly, causing fear in the hearts of those who worked in the oil industry and who had thought the oil industry would skyrocket. This prediction was proven wrong, however, when yet more oil was struck in Bradford, Pennsylvania. Fortune seekers and young men raced to capitalize on the discovery. So much was being produced that the price for a single barrel of oil dropped to seventy cents a barrel. It used to be \$4 a barrel!

As more and more oil wells were established in Bradford, Rockefeller connected them to his vast network of pipelines to continue his hold on the pipeline business. His storage tanks began to fill to full capacity until he could no longer store the oil that was being drilled.

In response to the problem, Standard Oil instituted the policy of immediately shipping the oil that producers drilled. Standard Oil's storage space was overfull, and producers were not allowed to store their oil. They had to send it immediately to refineries. Rockefeller wanted this oil to go to the refineries of Standard Oil. He was buying the oil from the producers at a price less than the market value by 20 percent and would not pay them immediately. The producers were naturally upset. Not only were they coerced into shipping their oil immediately, but they were also selling it for very low prices and not being paid at the time.

Rockefeller had taken advantage of the storage crisis and was able to benefit from it. He couldn't store the oil for lack of space, so he took the oil and shipped it to his refineries.

People did not like his behavior though. They dressed in white gowns from head to foot and protested in the streets against Standard Oil. They vandalized the buildings of Standard Oil and drew the signature pirate symbol of a skull and crossbones on the walls of the buildings.

To scare those who were drilling for oil, William McCandless was chosen to investigate and closely analyze the oil industry. He went after Standard Oil, but its pipeline executives simply ignored him. Surprisingly, in October 1878, McCandless submitted a report that vindicated Standard Oil. People believed that he might have been bribed by Rockefeller, which could be true. Rockefeller was capable and completely willing to give money under the table if necessary.

An effigy of McCandless was made and hung in Bradford. In the pocket of the dummy was a large check signed by John D. Rockefeller for $20,000.

After this issue, the Pennsylvania Railroad Company would also cause trouble for Rockefeller. Thomas Alexander Scott wanted to ease the monopoly that Standard Oil enjoyed over oil transportation. The PRR Co. had railroads near Bradford, and Scott was plotting to loosen the Standard Oil monopoly.

Colonel Jacob Potts, a man who wanted to be John D. Rockefeller's biggest competitor, did what he could to achieve that goal. He was deeply religious and treated the oil industry as he did his religion. When Potts crossed the line, Rockefeller wanted to meet with Thomas Scott and A.J. Cassatt. Both men were with the Pennsylvania Railroad Company.

Scott was essentially threatening the Standard Oil monopoly, and Rockefeller fought back. He ceased all production in his refineries in Pittsburgh and ramped up production in his Cleveland refineries. Instead of using the Pennsylvania Railroad Company to transport his oil, Rockefeller used the New York Central and the Erie Railroad. To transport the oil, cofounder of Standard Oil Henry Flagler made a deal with William Vanderbilt, son of Cornelius Vanderbilt, to build six hundred oil tank cars.

The Pennsylvania Railroad Company had to keep reducing rates to remain stable, as Rockefeller was skillfully fighting back against it and Scott.

After some time, the company could not continue the fight, and Scott wanted to make a truce with Rockefeller, but Potts wanted to prolong the duel. Not wanting to damage the Pennsylvania Railroad Company any further, Scott went behind Potts' back and tried to make a deal with Rockefeller to smooth things over and end the feud. Rockefeller responded kindly to make peace with him.

Scott offered Rockefeller all the assets of the Empire Transportation Company through which he had tried to sabotage Standard Oil. These included boats, barges, and all sorts of transportation equipment. Rockefeller spent half a day running around trying to get money. Standard Oil didn't have enough cash to buy everything Scott was offering them.

Despite the problems, Rockefeller was very happy with what he achieved.

After that issue with the Pennsylvania Railroad Company, Rockefeller would face the Tidewater Pipe Company, a company cofounded by Byron Benson, which would set to work building six-inch wide pipelines from Coryville to Williamsport, both in Pennsylvania, for the purpose of transporting oil and breaking the Standard Oil monopoly. Rockefeller could not let this happen, for it would threaten his domination over the pipeline business.

The Tidewater Pipe Company's pipeline from Coryville to Williamsport was 110 miles long. During its construction, Rockefeller's right-hand man would carry out his dirty work to try and prevent the construction of the Coryville-Williamsport pipeline.

Before the pipeline was built, Rockefeller ordered that it be stopped. Despite his best efforts, however, they were unsuccessful.

After the building began, Rockefeller's people worked hard to stop it. They bribed legislators and used unscrupulous methods to try and stop construction. They purchased stretches of land and got railroads to not allow the Tidewater Pipe Company to build pipelines under their land.

Rockefeller even purchased a vast expanse of land hoping to stop construction of the pipeline, but it didn't work. The builders simply built around the bought-up land. Despite Rockefeller's best attempts, construction of the Coryville-Williamsport pipeline was completed in less than ninety days.

Oil was pumped from Coryville, and people watched earnestly as the oil slowly made its way to Williamsport, making the Tidewater Pipe Company successful in having bypassed the Standard Oil Trust. The Tidewater Pipe Company had defeated Standard Oil and succeeded in building a pipeline that transported oil that did not belong to John D. Rockefeller or Standard Oil Trust.

Because of Rockefeller's associates' tactics and strategies to try to defeat the Tidewater Pipe Company, the American government and people wanted them behind bars. Many of the people who worked for Standard Oil were called to testify before court. Rockefeller, however, was not needed to appear in court.

He was very worried about the case, and for the next thirty years of his life, starting in the 1880s, he would keep as far away from the law as he could. During one summer, he spent his time at Forest Hill, where he could be safe.

After suffering from a long period of worry and distress, Standard Oil finally pledged that it would return to the norms of business. It would buy products at market price and play fairly. It was all a facade, though, as was later revealed.

Chapter 13 Philanthropy

"Giving should be entered into in just the same way as investing. Giving is investing."

— John D. Rockefeller

During the 1880s, people were constantly pestering Rockefeller for money. He enjoyed peace, solitude, and being nice and calm. Large throngs of money-hungry people following him robbed him of those things he cherished.

Rockefeller said that they would be there during and after dinner when all he would've liked to do was to chit-chat with his family until it was time to go to bed. They would constantly be badgering him for money, and he really couldn't stand it. They would eat with him, walk to his office that was at 26 Broadway with him, walk back with him to his home, and would basically be real pests.

Rockefeller wanted to fix this problem. He understood that you can't really do philanthropic work unless you help solve a problem. Rockefeller's view of philanthropy was that he only cared about solving the main problem, not doing small, menial things that helped that individual person for a short time but not in the long term. Rockefeller believed in doing philanthropic work for the sake of helping the masses.

He wanted to use his money intelligently, and he was going to do it through charity. He was going to use his money to help people in a substantial way. Perhaps his most noteworthy philanthropic work was establishing the University of Chicago in 1890.

In the late 1880s, Baptist minister Augustus H. Strong, an associate of Rockefeller's, wanted to build a university for Baptists in New York City of which he would be master. He kept pestering Rockefeller to fund his idea, but Rockefeller wasn't very enthusiastic about it. Strong continued to talk to him until Rockefeller banned discussion of the subject.

The relationship between Rockefeller and Strong became more personal as the relationship between the Rockefeller family and that of the Strongs became closer. Whenever Strong came to Cleveland, he and his family were one of the few people who rarely ever came to the Rockefeller home in Forest Hill. Strong's son, Charles, was friends with the Rockefeller children, but in the beginning Rockefeller and Laura were afraid that Charles would damage their religious core. The Rockefeller children and Charles got along perfectly well, though, and their relationship was fine. In the beginning, Charles liked Alta, but later he grew to like Elizabeth, or Bessie, as she was also known. Later on, Bessie and Charles would become husband and wife.

Bessie later went to Vassar, a girls school that had been chosen for her since the elder Strong was a trustee on the school's board of trustees. She had eye problems and thus had trouble reading, so it was arranged that she didn't have to take the entrance exam and that she could share a room with someone who would read the books to her. It was at Vassar that Rockefeller met the first president of the University of Chicago, William Rainey Harper.

Harper was a prodigy when he was at Muskingum College at the age of ten. He graduated when he was fourteen and received his PhD when he was just eighteen years old. Harper was an ardent Baptist whom Rockefeller grew to like. When Rockefeller came to Vassar to see his daughter on the weekends, he would always dine with Harper. They developed a very close relationship and would often cycle together.

Harper taught at Yale University but came to Vassar to teach Bible classes on Sundays.

Rockefeller and Harper talked about building a school for Baptists in a well-to-do urban center, but Harper made the mistake of pressuring Rockefeller. Another person who had done that before was Augustus H. Strong. He had made the fatal mistake of pressuring and pestering Rockefeller for his university. Rockefeller did not like being pressured. If you wanted something from him, you needed to calmly and coolly ask him for it. If you pressured him and pestered him, he'd dislike you at once and wouldn't consider your wishes. Harper had complied with Rockefeller's wishes to not talk about the issue of building a university, but when he brought it up again, he headed down a path that ruined his dreams, and Rockefeller dismissed the idea.

Not wanting to exclude Strong due to their family relations, Rockefeller invited Strong to travel with him to Europe. Strong accepted his invitation, seeing that it was a good way to press his idea on Rockefeller.

The relationship between Charles Strong and Elizabeth Rockefeller became very deep indeed, but a disaster, or actually an awakening, came over Charles, ripping him away from the Baptist Church. His time at Harvard University and his outside influences had led him to leave the Baptist Church, and he realized that none of it was real. This revelation was a great disappointment to his father.

Augustus had trained Charles to live a Baptist life of piety. Now, all his dreams, hopes, and expectations for his son were shattered, but they decided not to speak about it to the Rockefellers.

So, Charles proceeded with his relationship with Bessie, and Augustus continued to pressure Rockefeller to fund his university. In the end, the couple married on March 22, 1889.

William Harper and Baptist priest Frederick Taylor Gates would also convince Rockefeller to build the University of Chicago.

Harper had failed, initially, in trying to convince Rockefeller, but Gates, being a man who knew how to talk to people and convince them without upsetting them, was able to get Rockefeller on board with building the university.

Gates was always there to advise Rockefeller on his philanthropic work and worked closely with him in building of the University of Chicago.

For Rockefeller to build a university really did seem quite strange. He himself had never gone to a university, and he never suggested others to go to college either. He still agreed to build the university, however, thanks to Harper and Gates. He had been told that the only Baptist schools were in backwater areas. In the minds of these Baptists who were trying to establish the university, a Baptist educational institute was needed in an urban center.

Rockefeller kept delaying giving money for the university, but eventually proposed $400,000. Gates said it wasn't enough, and when Rockefeller offered $500,000, Gates said it still wasn't enough. Finally, $600,000 was accepted, and the university was supposed to raise another $400,000.

Unfortunately, William Harper, who later became the first president of the University of Chicago, was not able to raise the necessary funds. In fact, he spent too much money in other ventures. He wanted to upgrade from college level to university standards in a flash. Rockefeller favored a more gradual approach, one where the school started off as a college and slowly evolved to become a university.

The University of Chicago was established in 1890, and William Rainer Harper was its first president, beginning in 1890 and ending in 1906 upon his passing. When it first began, the university had 750 students, of which a portion were women, another extremely small number were Jewish, and some blacks were also in the group.

Harper expanded the university and persuaded other professors to come and teach there. So, the university had a moderate number of students in the beginning as well as high-quality teachers.

After the founding of the University of Chicago, the relationship between Rockefeller and Harper began to deteriorate, for Harper was spending too much money trying to expand the school too quickly. He wanted the school to be a major establishment, and he was doing all he could to achieve his dream. He was spending a lot of money, however, and Rockefeller had to keep providing funds for the university. He was initially reluctant to give more money, but he would eventually give in and hand out the funds.

When Harper once said that no well-run school could be run free of a deficit, Rockefeller and Gates were outraged. Although Rockefeller suffered a lot of stress and had health problems at this time, he still said that it was the "best investment I ever made."

He had to constantly keep spending money, which was very difficult for him to do. Rockefeller was a very thrifty person who did not take money lightly. He did not spend freely and was always very strict about how much he spent. When he was a young boy, he would keep track of the accounts for his family and had a ledger, the famous Ledger A, in which he jotted down all of his expenses no matter how small. He included his donations to the Baptist Church and all of the money he spent in that little book, something that he greatly cherished and kept in his safe. From the time Rockefeller was a young boy, saving and frugality had been pounded into his head by his mother and by the circumstances and necessities of his surroundings. Now, because of Harper, Rockefeller had to keep spending hundreds of thousands dollars.

The matter affected him greatly, and he became unhappy.

Rockefeller grew so ill that he would spend days in bed. He suffered from digestive problems and sometimes ate only crackers and drank milk, something that he actually liked. Rockefeller grew so stressed that he needed to relax, and he took a few months off to recuperate. He worked with other workers near his home, but he was able to relax, had fun, ate his crackers and milk, and his health was restored not very long afterward, but he was not very eager to return to work.

He considered retirement, but could not and continued work until 1897.

When he got back on his feet, he attended a gathering where William Harper spoke. During Harper's speech, he turned to Rockefeller and addressed him on a matter of paying for something the school needed. Rockefeller simply smiled but was actually extremely uncomfortable with that prospect.

During the gathering, Rockefeller stood up and gave a short talk to the other people who had attended. They cheered heartily, and he was seen as a hero.

He had been considered a villain, vilified for how he had established Standard Oil and for his business strategies, but now he was seen as an idol—a hero.

In the end, when Rockefeller had had enough of Harper's overspending and leaving the school with a deficit, he decided to do things without going through him. He had Thomas Wakefield Goodspeed, who was a secretary on the University of Chicago's board, and Henry Rusty hold a meeting with Frederick Gates and Rockefeller Jr. Rockefeller himself did not go to the meeting and let his representative take care of everything.

In the end, the relationship between Rockefeller and Harper was tarnished. Harper was not to talk about money, but one story indicates that since he could not mention money or even bring up the topic of getting more money from Rockefeller, he would resort to asking for money during prayer in front of him.

Chapter 14 The Final Chapter in Greatness

"If your only goal is to become rich, you will never achieve it."

— **John D. Rockefeller**

During the late nineteenth century when Rockefeller was in his fifties, he suffered from a disease that would cause the loss of all or just some hair from one's body. Rockefeller lost all of his and started wearing toupees. He would change this toupee regularly to ones with longer hair to make it look as if his hair were growing. It wasn't just the hair on his face. It was everywhere. He had lost his hair around the time Standard Oil was getting bombarded in the press and in the courts.

After Rockefeller's wife passed away in 1915 from a heart attack, Rockefeller spent the next twenty-two years of his life having fun. He played golf, gave dimes to people, and went for a drive in the countryside every afternoon. He and another person would go, each in one car. Rockefeller always sat in the back of one of the cars with two women, one on each side. In his old days, Rockefeller was a much more relaxed old man who took slight pleasure in the company of younger women. He would invite them to play golf with him and go on drives.

In his later years, Rockefeller was as childish as a boy of nine. He hadn't been able to enjoy childhood when he was young, living as he did under the roof of a messed-up father and in a household always suffering from uncertainty and discomfort. In his eighties and nineties, he enjoyed life and relaxed. He eventually transferred the Rockefeller fortune to his son John D. Rockefeller Jr.

His long and fulfilling life came to an end on May 23, 1937, in the Casements on Ormond Beach in Florida. He was just short of ninety-eight years old.

At the time of his passing, Rockefeller's wealth equaled 2 percent of the American economy. Today, he would have been worth between $250 and $300 billion.

Ida Tarbell, the reporter and author who hounded Rockefeller, had written much about him. None of it was complementary or kind, and she was certain that the motivation behind his success was attributable to his greed for money. It was a simplistic assumption that was incorrect.

What motivated Rockefeller was not money or the luxury it afforded. Money was just a consequence, and real wealth was not measured in how much one could buy or earn. Rather, it was measured by how much one did. Money was just a metric of that. The distinction is rare among the billionaire wannabes of today, but it is nonetheless a window into one of the world's most unique minds.

One should note that Rockefeller was pragmatic about his approach to work, success, and wealth. He was not driven by the reward but by the success of the endeavor. The reward was merely an afterthought. This is a difficult concept to comprehend in a world of stock traders and fast-money con artists who are looking to make a quick buck and then take it easy for the rest of their lives. Such men as Rockefeller, Carnegie, Morgan, and others worldwide were and are not done once they make their money. They reinvent themselves and go on to the next success. If they start something and fail, they get back up and keep going.

You have to ask yourself and contemplate the answer to the simple question of what does it take for someone such as Rockefeller to start from nothing and end up with everything. You have to evaluate your answer and ask yourself whether you want to emulate his own steps or in your particular limited way in your own life.

Conclusion

The story of John D. Rockefeller's life is deep and detailed that shows how a man whose background was most uncomfortable and terrible came to be one of the most successful and accomplished in the world and the world's richest man.

Rockefeller created the Standard Oil empire through hard work, determination, and perseverance. He may not have been completely honest in creating Standard Oil and the way he ran his business, but he did what he had to to make it the most successful oil company in the world.

Rockefeller's life was full of happiness, sadness, stress, and sickness. He despised his father, a rogue con man and bigamist who ruined his mother's life. He was very close to his mother and to his wife and was very serious about his morals. He never drank a single drop of alcohol, and he was an extremely pious and devout Baptist.

By the time he passed, he was just under ninety-eight years old and a happy, accomplished man.

John Davison Rockefeller had worked hard for every single penny he earned and for every single article of luxury he received and deserved. He made his fortune not for money's sake but to help the world and be a success. He changed the way America worked and had a significant role in its development and maybe even in how the world developed. When Rockefeller died, he had left his mark on it.

Indirectly, he caused the founding of one of the largest oil companies in the world: Royal Dutch Shell. It was established because the owners of the companies that merged to form the Shell Oil Company were uniting to be stronger against Standard Oil. So, you could say that it was because of him that the Shell Oil Company came into existence.

The lesson we can learn from Rockefeller's life is that being successful and being rich is never about the wealth or the money but the success and the accomplishment.

If someone is tempted to take his achievements lightly, forgetting his stressful childhood, his disappointments, and his relentless pursuit of objectives amidst seemingly insurmountable challenges, think about the world without him and think about how far we would have come without his contribution to the development of the oil and gas industry. It is not about the hundreds of millions of dollars that he amassed in his lifetime. That is not necessarily what makes him great. Rather, it is the uphill battles he fought and in the process changed the world we came from into the world we now live in

Unlike those who die rich but in actual fact are poor because the money they had was either dishonestly accumulated or inherited, John D. Rockefeller passed away wealthier than his monetary wealth because money earned through hard work and effort means more than money. As Rockefeller said, "If you're only goal is to become rich, you will never achieve it."

Henry Ford

Auto Tycoon

Henry Ford

Auto Tycoon

Insight and Analysis into the Man Behind the
American Auto Industry

JR MacGregor

Introduction

Many men have been responsible for the rise of America—from Columbus to Lewis and Clark to today's titans of industry, including Bill Gates and Warren Buffet. Henry Ford stands atop this pantheon of titans for a number of reasons.

It is not because his wealth was greater than any of them. It is not. Rockefeller takes that title. It is also not because he invented a string of gizmos and machines. He didn't. That honor belongs to Edison. It is also not because he helped form the financial backbone of the United States. That title would easily go to J.P. Morgan.

Ford was none of these and often sorely misunderstood. He was cast with the devil for a few things he did in his life that may not be agreeable with the politics of today. He has been labeled a Nazi sympathizer. He was mentioned favorably in Hitler's *Mein Kampf* and awarded that country's highest honor that could be given to a foreigner—the Grand Cross of the German Eagle.

Ford purchased the *Dearborn Independent,* and in that paper, which had a circulation of almost one million, a series of articles were published that were anti-Semitic in nature. A lawsuit was brought against him and the paper, but in sworn testimony many people familiar with the operation of the paper testified that Ford himself had no idea that the articles were published. It ended in a mistrial, and nothing more came of it, but the specter of anti-Semitism always lingered around him.

The series of articles that were printed in his paper were eventually collated into a book called *The International Jew*. For his views, Ford gained a friend in Hitler, and it cost him a great deal at home, but he wasn't an anti-Semite or a racist.

The problem with the anti-Semitic innuendos was accentuated by many smaller issues and Ford's failure to explain what actually happened and why he did it. What made it worse is that he was memorialized by Hitler. Just because he had opinions that were different from others didn't make him a monster, and just because Hitler wanted to implement his ideas in Germany doesn't make Ford the architect of Nazi Germany.

Mohandas Gandhi, the man who orchestrated India's independence, also drew the ire of the world for a short time when he was sympathetic to Hitler. Gandhi was willing to talk to him when others weren't. Gandhi even wrote to him. Those around Gandhi at the time were quick to jump on this act and condemn him.

By not seeing Ford or Gandhi as the kind of people they really were, you lose sight of what they contributed.

Ford and what he did for Americans and the world can't be thought of in terms of just automobiles. His goal was not just to make cars. It was to make inexpensive cars. Yes, other car manufacturers were also interested in making cheaper cars, but Ford was able to think from both an engineering and a humanitarian perspective. He didn't just want to put a car in every garage. He wanted to make sure that it was durable and lasted for a very long time.

The cars he manufactured that rolled off the assembly line every twenty-four seconds were workhorses and easily affordable. To be successful, Ford studied and devised ways to make parts in different ways and assemble them in ways that were not common at the time.

He also studied how human beings worked and thought they should be paid a living wage. He was the first person to think this way. Not even Carnegie or Rockefeller thought about treating workers the same way.

He insisted to his partners that his workers must be paid $5 per day. This may not seem like much today, but this was back in the early 1900s. A dollar in 1920 had the same purchasing power as $13 does today, which means that the average factory worker was taking home $65 per day. It was unheard of at the time. In fact, when Ford worked for the Edison Illuminating Company in Detroit as Chief Engineer, he made the same amount.

Ford thought people should be paid for the worth they brought to the table. He eventually raised those wages and even gave every employee a share of the company's profits. In return, he was rewarded with an endless supply of labor. Everyone wanted to work at the Ford plant.

He was, however, a strict employer and demanded a lot from his workers. They were rewarded handsomely not just in above-normal wages but also with better working conditions than could be found in most other factories. He wanted them to live in good conditions and be able to look after their families.

The amount of money he gave his workers earned him a reputation, and he demanded that everyone put in an honest day's work. They knew that if they did poorly they would be fired and that a hundred men were outside waiting for a job and could take their place.

Ford was indeed a genius and was always thinking ahead. Since he wanted a flawless and uninterrupted assembly line, he didn't want his workers worrying about what might be going on at home. Most of the time a man worries about money and looking after his family. To keep their minds on their work, he paid them well. He also didn't want them to be upset and go on strike to disrupt operations. He calculated that it was better to always pay the workers a good wage than to deal with disruptions.

To be able to pay above-market wages and produce high-quality products meant higher costs. Most manufacturers thought that the only way high costs could be balanced was by selling expensive cars, yet Ford was able to sell a large number of cars because he kept the price low and made money on the volume sold.

To be able to keep the assembly line constantly humming, he standardized the parts to such a high degree that you could move a line so quickly that a car would take about ninety minutes to go from the start of the line to the end of the line. In a day, he could make over a thousand cars due to his innovation of the moving assembly line.

The moving assembly line is not like what you would find in many car factories back then. In those days, cars were made by specialists, who would mill around the car doing different things. Each person would have many responsibilities, and days or weeks would be needed to complete just one car.

In a moving assembly line, the track that carries the unassembled vehicle would be constantly moving at a crawl. The worker would be installing something on it while walking along the car from a certain point on the line to the next point. He would then come back and get started on another car. The stations were timed carefully, and the workers would not have an opportunity to talk or be distracted. The job was so simple, though, that even a child could do it. Ford made sure to keep each job as simple as possible.

This was Ford's greatest contribution—the moving assembly line. He tied a rope to the front of the car (n tracks), and that motor would pull the car at a certain rate while the workers worked on it. Each event was timed so that the cars would take approximately the same length of time. The design of the car was integrated into the design of the assembly line. Parts were not made just for the car but also on how it would fare on the moving assembly line. If the part was too complex or required too much attention and a longer time to install, it was replaced with something that was easier. In Ford's way of doing things, he didn't just design the car. He also included the process of building it at the same time.

That is one reason why all Ford Model Ts were black in color. At that time, black paint was the fastest to dry and the easiest to apply. It allowed the assembly line to move faster.

He also didn't include any other colors because that would complicate the process and raise the price. He is quoted as saying, "People can have whatever color car they wanted as long as it was black."

He thought of everything right down to the last bolt, nut, and cotter pin. He thought about where each would go and in what order. Then he would stretch the sequence out on a line and test it, which would result in the shortest time on the assembly line.

At first, the Model T took twelve and a half hours to build. With further improvement, it took six hours and then just ninety-three minutes. The basic idea that Ford took as an example of this came from a meat-packing plant in Chicago. The butchers would hang the animal overhead and pass it along a line of workers who would skin, slaughter, process, and pack the meat from one station to the next.

In the same way, it wasn't just the car that was assembled that way. Many parts also needed assembly.

For the car to be priced at less than $900, they had to get this process right.

Instead of having a magneto or a headlamp that involved many parts built by one person, Ford recognized that one person would work faster if they only had to do one task. So they broke up the assembly of even smaller parts. The magneto, for example, was broken up and had an assembly line of twenty-nine stations. Instead of just one man making one magneto, twenty-nine stations would come together to make the magneto as it passed from one man to the next. It stayed for only a few seconds at each station, and that took only five minutes to make each magneto. When they first started, it took one man more than thirty minutes to do it, and the reject rate was high. With twenty-nine men doing one part each and each of them being an expert at that part of it, the reject rate of the final assembly dropped drastically.

Such improvements and across the individual lines of assembly for all the parts allowed for $1,000 per car, which was his original threshold to drop the price to $350. The affordability goal was achieved, but Ford didn't stop there. He kept going until the Model T was able to come out of the plant every twenty-four seconds and the price of the vehicle had dropped below $300 each. It was 1927, and more than 15,000,000 Model Ts had been made, and one out of every two cars in America at the time was a Model T.

That price point altered the face of America. The terms *urban* and *suburban* were introduced into the vernacular from that point on because there was no longer any need for workers to live close to where they worked where it was congested and smoggy. They could now move out of the city and live somewhere that was better to raise their family and then drive to work in the morning. It is almost what we do today in larger cities, and that was created by the revolution that Henry Ford inspired.

Ford's objective resulted in improvements in so many areas. From the rapid assembly of the car and the lower costs to the quality of the car were unheard of at the time.

He looked at every detail, including hiring highly qualified machinists to make better quality parts so that they mated perfectly when assembled. They also made sure that the parts were easily accessible so that the owner could maintain it. It was a level of efficiency and effectiveness that was unheard of at the time.

This level to which Ford aspired in his endeavors is usually lost in the enigma of the story and the casual narrative that follows typical quotes and common anecdotes. But to find the genius of this man, one has to look at the lineage he came from—not just because we are slaves to our ancestors—but because Henry Ford was inspired by his family, including their hardships.

One of the things you can see from this was his friendship with the man who eventually solved the problem of the blithe potato that caused the Potato Famine in Ireland, which caused his family's sufferings and the reason they emigrated.

Many other clues point to Ford's sensitivity to his past. The home that Henry built in Dearborn was named Fairlane. When the Fords first moved to Cork from their farm, they lived on Fair Lane, the street where they sought shelter before leaving for Canada.

The life that Ford lived was influenced by William, his father, but it was done in opposition to what his father had envisioned for him. It would come to pass that whatever disappointed William about his son, Henry would feel the same way about his own son.

The disappointments were not about the failures of the subsequent generation but the decision by the next generation to not do things the way the older generation had prescribed.

William had wanted Henry to build up the farm, but Henry wanted to mechanize everything around him. Henry wanted his son, Edsel, to manage the plant with stricter hands, but Edsel wanted to do it with a gentler touch.

To each man, his son was a bit of a disappointment; to each son, his father was someone they could not live up to. What was common among all of them was that they were all stubborn.

Henry had troubles in his life that took him through periods of uncertainty. The investments he had solicited to build a company around his first vehicle didn't yield anything, and neither did the second.

He was almost forty years old and had not yet made a name for himself, but, more importantly, he had not accomplished what he had set out to do. The words of his father and the direction he had been given as a child kept playing in his head. "Maybe he should have stuck to farming." "Maybe he should have done what his father had wanted." An avalanche of thoughts plagued him, but Clara, his wife, always stood by his side.

It was Clara who pointed him in the right direction while they tried to make ends meet. It was because of her and Thomas Edison that he kept pursuing his dream. Thomas Edison was one of Ford's closest friends. The two of them would take annual vacations together, and President Harding and his team of Secret Service agents once went along.

The idea of studying about a man is to see his accomplishments as much as his mistakes. The best way to succeed in life is to look at the mistakes others have made and learn from them and also look at the achievements others have made and adapt them to your own life.

Reading about Ford should not be limited to mere inquisitiveness of places and dates, gossip and hearsay. It is about looking at him with the intent to understand yourself and your potential.

After all, we are all geniuses trying to make it in a world that others have already learned about and have already passed through. That is the important aspect of any biography, be it Carnegie, Rockefeller, Morgan, or even Mahatma Gandhi.

As we condense his life, it is important to understand where a man came from as much as it is to understand the reasons why he did what he did. It is also important to take as an example what he did and what he said and try to place these in the context of his vision. The best way is to look at things is as a student.

It is never beneficial for the student to look at things from a single point in time or space. Rather, it is important to look at the life of a man using the threads that link him to his past and the rails that connect him to the future.

A man's accomplishment is about many things, but most importantly it's about what he believes. Henry Ford believed in a world that was very different from the one he lived in. He believed in a world that was more efficient, and he was instrumental in bringing that about.

Take his production line. What is a moving assembly line if not a perfect picture of efficiency. That was the doing of Henry Ford. It is not as simple as one may think to come up with the results Ford did. It took vision to start, tenacity to overcome, patience to endure, and humility to learn. Ford was all these things and more. That was the essence of his actions.

But lest we misunderstand one simple and glaring truth, Ford was, like us, just human. He made his share of mistakes. He had his share of bias and prejudices and weaknesses. But that is what it means to be human. Everyone is similar in that regard. They do not know what they do, but the brief glimpse they do get and figure something out is when the rest of us need to look at it and learn from it for what it is. But if we make the mistake of judging the bad and forgetting the good, then we lose the opportunity to learn and become better.

Chapter 1 The Automobile

The last century and a half has been to automobiles what the Cambrian explosion had been to life on earth. From our grandparents' generation to ours today, the leap in technology, availability, prevalence, and diversity of automobiles has risen at an unfathomable rate and with unrelenting persistence. This has had a significant impact on the productivity and advancement of our lives but also has had some detrimental repercussions in terms of the environmental impact. Overall, however, the good has mostly outweighed the bad.

When humans first came out of Africa two million years ago and fanned across the globe, they did so on foot. They diffused across the globe organically like salt diffusing in unstirred water, eventually occupying almost every corner of the globe that was connected by land. That rate of diffusion was a function of a number of factors but was mostly limited to whether or not food was available or if predators were present, creating a hostile environment.

Humans were extremely adept bipeds, able to walk, jog, and sprint, which combined with our natural sense of curiosity was the core impetus to the spread of humanity across the planet.

We didn't just pick up and walk. We were even able to carry loads over long distances. What we were limited by was how much we could carry, which determined the supplies we needed and how far we could go. More food and water meant we could go longer before refills. It also determined how much shelter we could take with us, i.e., tents and tools.

Nonetheless, our ability to plan and carry what was needed on a trip combined with our curiosity to explore what was over the horizon gave us the impetus to explore. Exploration is in our genes.

It was a fairly unique ability in the animal kingdom—to be able to load ourselves with the burden and move long distances. Camels and horses, popular beasts of burden, didn't have the ability to load their backs and move great distances. Yet, they had the strength and structure to do it.

Left to their own devices, animals would just move, unencumbered, on their own, carrying their own weight. It wasn't until humans were able to domesticate them and load them with cargo that we were able to increase our cargo and extend our range. Walking had been our sole mode of mobility for two million years before we conscripted animals to do it for us. That evolution happened about six thousand years ago.

The point to note is acceleration. We walked for two million years; then we used beasts of burden for six thousand years; then we advanced to mechanized transportation. The time it took from one mode to the next went from two million years to just six thousand.

After six thousand years, we mechanized, and the first form of mechanized transportation was the locomotive. British engineer Richard Trevithick built the first steam locomotive in 1804, which revolutionized mass transportation of people along great distances.

That invention soon found its way to the New World, and in 1827, just twenty-three years later, the Baltimore-Ohio Railroad became the first railway line in the United States.

The transportation game can't be seen as one by itself. Just because you can build a bicycle or a tricycle is not going to have a significant impact on society in general. To be able to make a large enough difference, it has to be able to move a large number of people over great distances.

The train fulfilled that need, and although caravans of horse-drawn carriages transported frontiersman across the harsh unpopulated lands, it was the railroad that led to wide areas of the country being populated. Without trains, cities could not have been a reality.

That was the second land transportation revolution, with the taming of animals as beasts of burden being the first.

If the train gave the power of exodus to the masses, what came next was an even more powerful iteration in the transportation saga. It was the automobile and its ability to move individuals anywhere without the necessary infrastructure of rails that characterized rail travel. The difference was that this new form of transportation allowed individuals to travel where they wished in a direct manner.

The automobile had two aspects that needed to come together: (1) an engine to drive it and (2) a structure to be able to carry the payload and the power plant. The problem was not the carriage. Any horse carriage could be adopted for the purpose, or so they thought. The real problem was to create an engine that had enough torque to propel the carriage forward.

A few men were trying to perfect the formula. Two in particular were highly successful—Karl Friedrich Benz and Gottlieb Wilhelm Daimler. They were working independently just sixty miles apart and came up with the necessary elements for a working vehicle.

Benz not only managed to design an effective contraption that acted as a four-wheeled carriage, but he also invented a successful two-stroke engine to propel the carriage. Daimler, also an engineer, developed the liquid petroleum four-stroke engine and had a carriage built to accommodate it.

Benz and Daimler had different philosophies in mating car to the engine and so had fairly distinct outcomes.

Cars at that time were not envisioned to travel over asphalt but just on dirt roads. That meant there was no need for massive construction costs, such as was involved with railroads, which required sovereign bonds to be issued in the early nineteenth century.

Paved roads were good but not necessary. These cars that were at the genesis of the age of the personal automobile still did not represent a transportation revolution. These new cars were crude, expensive to build, not affordable by most people, and still pretty much a novelty.

The potential for such an invention, however, was not lost on the strategic thinkers of the era. Most could see that the power of mechanized personal transport would be revolutionary, especially since it didn't need to have rails, a specialist engineer to drive it, or an animal to pull it. Anyone could drive an automobile and take it anywhere.

For the automobile to be widely accepted, it had to be rapidly built, affordable, easily powered, and easily driven. At the time Benz and Daimler made the first gasoline vehicles, just the opposite was true. They were slow to build because each unit was handbuilt, taking more than a month to build just one vehicle. That made the whole process expensive, and what was worse was that the materials needed for them came from still burgeoning industries.

The internal combustion engine had not been perfected, generating only about half horsepower and topping out at about 750 rpm. Fuel sources were still uncertain, labor was mostly uneducated, and rubber for tires was not prevalent. The driving issue in all this was economies of scale. None of the sub-industries had it.

Another problem in the development of the automobile also slowed its advance. To be affordable to the masses, a number of technological advancements needed to be made. From metallurgy to engineering to even the choice of propellant, numerous areas had yet to come together to make the automobile viable.

Without sufficient development, the necessary technology was lacking, and the cost was expensive. With expensive cars, only a few could afford them, which meant there wasn't enough money to direct toward investment and development. It also meant insufficient volume to demand development of other areas, such as fuel, tires, and upholstery. The ripple effect upstream in the nonexistent industry was having a hard time taking hold.

The third transportation revolution was sputtering to life but was not quite there yet. To be considered a transportation revolution, it had to alter the landscape in a profound and widespread manner in the way trains did before it and domesticated animals. But it didn't stop there.

In the United States, another problem needed to be overcome. It was of a legal nature and one that stifled the nascent growth of automobile innovation. An American patent attorney by the name of George Baldwin Selden was quick to realize that Benz's and Daimler's inventions would be a major factor in the development of transportation around the world, and he wanted to profit from that in the United States.

He was what many called the original "patent troll." Patents were designed to protect real inventors and their intellectual property, but Selden decided to sketch out his ideas similar to the cars that Benz and Daimler had developed and filed that as his patent in the United States.

Since he was a patent attorney, he knew the tricks and strategies of U.S. patent law, and the loophole he exploited was how patents are granted in pending status.

The point of that patent strategy was to exploit the limited life of the patent from the day the patent is granted in full. Selden wanted to circumvent that because he didn't know when the automobile would become popular in the United States. He would update the patent every few months, which would return the patent to pending status. He finally filed the final patent in 1895, and that expired in 1912. It was U.S. Patent No. US549460A.

In it he deliberately mentioned that his idea to build this petroleum-powered vehicle was to increase the efficiency of a vehicle that would otherwise have to work on steam, which needs the vehicle to carry water to convert to steam and coal to heat water.

His business strategy worked. When the news of automobiles reached the United States, budding entrepreneurs and inventors leaped at the prospect of building the first American car.

The Electric Vehicle Co. decided in 1899 that they wanted to get into the gasoline-powered market and purchased the Selden patent for $5,000 and $5 per car in royalties. In today's dollars, that works out to be about a quarter of a million dollars plus royalties.

The Electric Vehicle Company, through their lawyers, started sending out cease and desist letters to manufacturers and warning them that they were infringing on the Selden patent. Many of the manufacturers completely disregarded the letter and went on with their business.

EVC eventually started filing suits against many of those carmakers. The manufacturer that was highest on their list to go after was the Winton Motor Carriage Company, owned by the Alexander Winton.

Winton was the fastest race car driver in America at the time, and his company had the largest share of the U.S. automobile market. It seemed best to sue him and claim back pay for all the cars he had sold up to that point. For Selden, this was always about the money.

Winton fought the Electric Vehicle Company for two years until 1902, when he began to think of a way to end the feud. Because of the problem between Winton and the Electric Vehicle Company, several other automobile manufacturers united to form the Manufacturer's Mutual Association or the MMA.

It was founded by Frederic L. Smith and Henry Bourne Joy—Henry Bourne Joy was of the Packard Motor Car Company, and Frederic L. Smith was of the Olds Motor Works—a cofounder in fact—which created the Curved Dash Oldsmobile, the car that is credited as being the first to have been mass produced but was still very expensive.

Together, Joy and Smith said they wanted the royalties to be decreased and also wanted to take control of the licensing. In the end, the MMA was able to get control of the patent and the licensing in 1903.

It was also in 1903 that the organization was rechristened the Association of Licensed Automobile Manufacturers or ALAM. From there it evolved. The Electric Vehicle Company in concert with ALAM charged anyone who wanted to manufacture automobiles an annual fee of $5,000 and $15 per car as royalty. The proceeds were shared by ALAM, Electric Vehicle Company, and Selden.

ALAM's expressly stated purpose was to prevent anyone who seemed that they didn't know what they were doing and fly-by-night operators from setting up an automobile plant.

There were significant consequences to this move. First, it created a monopoly on the system. In addition to the licensing fee, not everyone who wanted to jump into the market was allowed to. There was no free enterprise in the industry, and the innovation that is needed in new industries was stifled by this unnatural requirement.

Second was that their patent was entirely undeserving. In many cases, it was a patent that had been obtained by the amalgamation of other ideas and used an engine that was wholly unsuitable for the task. In later years, it was found that if an engineer were to build a vehicle according to the plans that were submitted to the U.S. Patent Office, the resulting vehicle would not work very well.

The automobile has been a key factor in the development and advancement of human civilizations and societies. It is unique in its ability to provide mass transportation at an individual level. That is the true genius of cars. They represent the last-mile solution to mobility for a large number of people. Planes get you across continents, trains get you across long distances, but cars, in addition to being able to drive across regions, can also take you to and from major hubs to individual areas without the restriction of schedules.

Automobiles are the best of both worlds. Compared with the locomotive that provided mass mobility with little freedom to the passengers, automobiles provide mass mobility to individuals and the freedom to experience that mobility in any way they want.

The original car manufacturers in the United States, in the wake of Benz's and Daimler's invention in Germany, were focused on expensive vehicles that were handmade, inefficient, and had heavy engines. concentrating on individuality rather than mass appeal.

Henry Ford did not invent the car. He did not invent the manufacturing process, and he did not build the engine. What he did was solve the last-mile problem of putting a car in every driveway by refining the production and design technology that allowed a car to be affordable for almost everyone.

It didn't matter if you built a car, for if you made it unaffordable, it would not solve the last-mile problem since most individuals would not be able to afford it. Ford was instrumental in doing that. He didn't ask for subsidies in making the car. He altered the design, the cost structure, and the manufacturing practices within the design and building elements. In other words, he built the car from the ground up, keeping in mind that it had to be cheap enough so that everyone could own one. That is what changed everything. His pioneering work was so effective that the typical one-car household became a two-car household within fifty years of Ford's Model T.

It wasn't just the automobile. It was the automobile for everyone, which meant that city planning could change. It was no longer necessary that homes be close to factories or offices. Communities could develop in the suburbs and alter the average way of life.

These effects and more were a direct consequence of Henry Ford.

Chapter 2 Coming to America

In 1832, Samuel and George Ford arrived in Michigan Territory to stake their claim on frontier land. They left their father, William, and mother, Rebecca, as well as their elder brother, John, on the land the family was living on in Ireland.

At that time, Ireland was in economic flux, transitioning from military and shipping activities in the wake of the Napoleonic Wars to agriculture and transatlantic shipping.

The family that Samuel and George left behind continued to farm in Ballinascarty, a small farming community approximately twenty miles southwest of Cork.

Farmers here were used to a simple life, which was organized under a simple structure. Landowners would rent out tracts of land to families, who would farm the land. As long as a family paid its rent, their livelihood was secure. Irish law back then prohibited landowners from evicting farmers as long as they paid the rent. It could even pass from one farmer to the next if he so assigned it, and the landowner would have to abide by the transition.

William Ford Sr. continued such a rental agreement with Jonas Starvell for twenty-three acres of farmland that their family had been on for some time. The house the Fords originally built remained for some time and passed to the farmers that took over after the Fords left.

Remnants of the stone cottage that William and Rebecca Jennings Ford (Henry Ford's great-grandparents) first built on Starvell's land still remain. The Irish countryside was peppered with other Ford family members renting land from other landowners. They are still there to this day.

Ireland's population was about eight million people at the turn of the century, and 40 percent of them depended exclusively on potatoes for sustenance. As such, farming in Ireland was focused primarily on potatoes. Dairy and berries were important as well but to a lesser degree.

Unlike today's dinner table with a variety of nutritional sources, from meats to salads and carbohydrates, Ireland in the 1800s was predominantly a one-staple economy. Meat was too expensive for most of the population and reserved for special occasions.

This potato-based menu was across the board. Whether you farmed the land or worked in a factory, almost everyone had one nutritional source for breakfast, lunch, and dinner. It was always potatoes. From potato soup to mashed potatoes to boxty, coddle, and colcannon, that's what was available.

The Ford family—brothers, sisters, cousins—were all diligent workers, which paid off in a stable farming life. They settled in one generation after the other on this farm.

Cork, the closest major city, survived because it was a port serving transatlantic trade. Of the three major cities of Dublin, Limerick, and Cork in this predominantly agricultural country, Cork was the smallest. That would eventually change when the Ford Motor Company set up a plant here in 1912.

John Ford, Henry Ford's grandfather, lived in the same stone cottage his father had on Starvell's property and continued the same farming practice his father did. An intervening event, however, caused John and his wife, Thomasina, to rethink their lives. In the Ford household was John, his wife, children, and his widowed mother. John's father, William, had passed some time earlier.

Potato Famine

The Potato Famine of 1849–1856 shook the lives of the Fords and almost every person in Ireland when a type of water mold spread across the potato farms in Ireland, causing an infection called the potato blithe. That event hit Ireland hard in many ways. Aside from affecting the potato crop thereby reducing the income of the farmer to zero, it directly altered the nutritional profile of part of the country, which had a knock-on effect across other agrarian and nonagrarian industries. The result was a widespread famine that created a financial catastrophe for the farmers who relied on the income from potatoes to pay the rent.

When the crops failed, the population subsequently descended into starvation and poor health. The five-year catastrophe caused more than one million deaths and spurred countless numbers of people to cross the Atlantic on less-than-safe contraptions that passed for ships.

The mortality rate on board these ships, called Coffin Ships, was extraordinarily high, as many people were ridden with typhus and infected with lice. The lice compounded the problem with the typhus, as it was the vector that transmitted the pathogen. Even a healthy person who boarded any of these Coffin Ships at Cork had a very high chance of falling ill out on the Atlantic, as the inexperienced crew took anywhere from three to six months to make the trip.

Out of the total farming population, more than five hundred thousand farmers were evicted over the five-year period. Out of that number, about 20 percent tried their luck by boarding these Coffin Ships. One hundred thousand Irishmen set sail, most of them already facing severe malnutrition and disease. The conditions on the ships exaggerated the malady, and one in five died on their way to British North America.

As for the Ford family, the loss of the crop due to the blithe epidemic that destroyed the potatoes caused them to lose their sole source of income. Without that income and without the prospect of being able to plant any more potatoes or buy seeds to plant other crops, they were not able to pay rent on the land. They were left with no choice and had to give up the land before they were evicted or jailed.

There was a grizzly aspect to this that affected the Fords and many in the same predicament. The agricultural industry around the mid-nineteenth century was dominated by landowners who were rather ruthless in their dealings with the farmers who rented their land. There were two kinds ·of these landowners in Ireland. One group would place the head of the delinquent household under arrest and kick the family out onto the streets without any prospect of shelter or food. That was the reality for many of the farmers.

The other option was that the farmers gave up the land and left whatever they built or had on the land, and the landowner would take possession of the land and rent it to someone else. The Fords were fortunate enough to have been able to do the latter.

With this little bit of luck in the midst of death and chaos around them, John Ford and Thomasina packed up what little else they had and walked the twenty miles to Cork in hope of better prospects. In tow were John's mother and his seven children, his brother Robert, and the Roberts family.

They stayed with relatives in a rented a house on Fair Lane in Cork and settled into the community along with little William (Henry Ford's father). They had little money but faced overwhelming hardships from food shortages and lack of resources. The poverty they faced was not individual. It was systemic.

Henry had heard stories from his father about the time the Fords were in Cork and where little William would go from house to house and sell eggs that he bought from one of the shops close by. Everyone in the neighborhood knew the Fords back then, as they were amiable and hospitable farmers who had been hit by the famine and came to the city. They made a living here as best they could, but with current conditions dire and future prospects dim, they had to make a hard decision on what to do next. A farmer without a farm is like a baker without an oven or a carpenter without tools. There would be no means to put food on the table and a roof overhead.

It is easy to discount the decision-making process in light of what we see around us in the U.S. today. There is a sense that the pull factor toward materialism, consumerism, quality, and standards of living are all excuses that a person might first face in their country of origin. Today, it may seem that immigration is fueled by something other than dire necessity (some are, but most aren't), but back then no one could deny that leaving the Old World and going to vast open spaces in the New World was a life or death decision that needed to be made. It's like being on the top floor of a burning skyscraper. Victims are even willing to take their chances when they jump out the window rather than be engulfed by the flames. The reasons for the Fords' inclination to travel were more about the push than about the pull.

Indeed, for the Fords and many others, going to America was a hard decision to make. It was not going to be a life spent on a bed of roses. No one who made their way to America in the mid-nineteenth century had delusions about that, but they did know that life in the unknown was better than the life facing certain death.

With a million people out of three million dead, the mortality rate gave potato-dependent Irishmen a 1-in-3 chance of survival. That may seem good odds when seen through the eyes of history, but when you have a family of nine—two parents and seven children—that means that three of your family members would not make it. Those are horrible odds, and those three are members of your own family. It's always harder when it's kin.

John and Thomasina thought long and hard while they made their living in a city that was on its downward swing. With the Napoleonic Wars over and the port business going through changes and relying on trade rather than military-related activities, everyone was going through adjustments.

Because it was a time when nutrition was minimal, it meant falling ill frequently—more so for the parents than for the children and more so for the mother than the father. Thomasina sacrificed much of what she had so that her children could have the first pick at the meager meals and her husband could have what he needed to expend on labor. In time, Thomasina was perpetually ill due to what must have been an extremely low immune system.

Not only did they have to stretch the food, but they also knew that they had to save as much as they could to be able to get passage on one of the many Coffin Ships that were sailing to the New World.

Conditions on the Coffin Ships were more than what most of us today can imagine. They were crowded with improper and unhygienic facilities. Families who were ill and destitute were making a last-ditch effort aboard poorly built vessels that were built to accommodate the masses trying to flee Ireland.

There were two points of destination that they could choose from. They could sail to either New York or Quebec, the latter being significantly cheaper than the former. As such, the usual choice was to head for Quebec and then make the trek down to the United States by land.

The Fords saved all they could, led simple lives, and decided to cast their lot to the winds across the Atlantic. They sold what little they had, packed up the family, and headed for Quebec. Along with John, Thomasina, and the children, his mother, and brother Robert (and his wife and children) tagged along. If it weren't for the famine, the Fords would not have left Ireland.

The trip was approximately three thousand miles from Cork Harbor to the St. Lawrence River in Quebec, which is almost the same distance as the crow flies from New York to San Francisco.

The journey would normally take five weeks on a normal ship but took longer on a Coffin Ship. The ships' owners were not expecting many of the passengers to survive the trip and were in it to make money without providing proper food, water, and berths. Many of those on these ships were buried at sea. The captain and crew were not well trained and barely satisfied the minimum to get the boat across the Atlantic. They ships were also well insured and worth more sunk than if they made the trip.

One in five of the one hundred thousand who set sail perished at sea or at the medical inspection station. Thomasina was one of those people who didn't make it. She was buried at sea.

William was in his early twenties at this time and took it very hard as did the rest of the family. As painful as it was, however, it was also fortunate that the loss the family faced was limited to just one person. After getting to North America and settling down, John never remarried.

As a family that had survived the famine intact and being almost home free, for Thomasina to pass away at the last turn had a chilling effect on them. Out of the eighty thousand Irish who did make it alive, half of them remained in Quebec and traveled inland. The other half crossed the border into the territories or into the northern part of the United States.

Upon arriving at the Saint Lawrence River, the Fords entered the medical inspection facility before being allowed to enter Canada legally. It is worth noting that Canada was under the British Empire at the time and thus did not have the same immigration issues of entry as those arriving at New York's Ellis Island.

Once they arrived in Quebec, the Ford family—John, his children, and John's mother made their trek across the U.S. border by foot. Robert Ford and his family remained in Canada.

John Ford

John Ford was Henry Ford's grandfather. He led the family from Ballinascarty to Cork and then across the Atlantic. In his care were three generations of Fords. They crossed the border from Quebec into the United States on their way to Michigan. They headed here because John's two brothers, Samuel and George, who had left Ireland almost a decade earlier, had settled in Wayne County, Michigan. Thomasine's family, the Smiths, was also in Wayne County at the time.

Once arriving in Dearborn, they lived with Samuel Ford's family and immediately thought about buying his farm. The idea of owning a farm was something that was revered and cherished. The Irish had lived for generations in a land tenancy structure where they farmed the land they did not own. The landowners were revered and respected no matter how brutal some of them could be. That same respect had created a desire in the hearts and minds of the Fords who came to Michigan.

John Ford wanted to become a landowner and work his own soil. Once they settled down on Samuel's farm and helped him with the chores, John and William set about to buy their own land.

They worked as much as they could to raise the money doing manual labor in the surrounding area and on the rail that was being constructed between there and Detroit, about seven miles away.

They eventually found a close Irish friend of theirs, Henry Maybury, living in Redmond Township near Detroit. He was willing to sell John eighty acres of virgin forest land in Redmond. The total price was $350, but John and William had only $200.

They paid that $200 to Maybury in 1848 and owed the rest. William, a skilled carpenter in Ireland, continued to put his carpentry to work on the railroad, and both John and William set out to pay off the remaining $150. One of the carpentry jobs he took on was for Patrick O'Hearn. Patrick had a large establishment, which was one of the larger employers in the neighborhood. Patrick and his wife didn't have children of their own and had adopted an orphan by the name of Mary Litogot.

By December 1850, William had helped his father settle the mortgage, and John finally became a landowner.

William Ford

William Ford was born in 1826 in the cottage where his father and mother lived. He trained as a carpenter while working on the farm in Cork and was handy in many ways.

He grew up to be a slender young man with the trademark Ford frame and high cheekbones.

To say he was a dyed-in-the-wool farmer would not be far from the truth, but to think he had much interest in farming would not be accurate. He saw farming as a necessity and carpentry as a means to advance. Either way, William was very strong willed and used to harsh conditions and was always willing to work hard.

He was also a very conventional and thoughtful young man. He was creative in his own way and very interested in advancing the farm in nontraditional ways, such as thinking how to mechanize operations on the farms where he worked with his father.

William was ambitious. He continuously sought ways to improve the farm, and his efforts paid off. The farm did well, and both John and William grew more prosperous as the years unfolded.

He still continued to build houses and made a name for himself as an able carpenter. His friendship with the O'Hearns after he helped build their house was also a positive factor in his life. Patrick O'Hearn was a powerful ally to have and a person who would easily recommend or assist William whenever needed.

William also remained friends with the Maybury family. The Marburys went on to become one of the most influential and wealthy Irish immigrants in the Detroit-Dearborn area.

At the time when William was helping the O'Hearns build their home, he met Mary Litogot, the adopted daughter of the family. Mary was born in Michigan and just eleven years old when William was working on the O'Hearn family home.

Her natural parents who had emigrated from Belgium passed away when Mary was still a young child and left her to be adopted by an Irish family when she was three years old. The O'Hearns were well-to-do and had enrolled Mary in private school. There she was raised with proper etiquette and science, which resulted in a young lady who was intelligent and witty. They also raised her with many Irish practices and culture.

William continued to do whatever jobs that came his way, especially since Detroit was starting to transition from being frontier land to something more established, especially along the waterfront.

In 1858, William had saved enough to buy forty acres of his father's farm for $600 and closed the transaction on September 15. John sold the southern half of the property to William and the northern half of the property to William's young brother, Samuel, for the same price.

As he was climbing the rungs of opportunity, William fell in love with Mary Litogot. They had been friends since meeting when he was working on the O'Hearn house, and then they dated for almost a decade.

They were married in April 1861, eleven years after first meeting. The wedding was held at the home of Thomas Maybury in Detroit. While this was happening in the relative peace of the Michigan landscape, the first shell had exploded in the air above Fort Sumter in South Carolina. It heralded the arrival of one of the deadliest times in American history, but all that seemed a world away to the newlyweds.

She conceived during the first year after the wedding and gave birth the following year, but the child died soon after birth. Mary, who was naturally kind and loving, was devastated. It was something that was common in those days of frontier living, but it was still a painful experience.

Once married, William left his father's farm in Redmond and moved into the cottage that he had originally helped Patrick O'Hearn build. When they moved in, William decided to design and build a much larger home so that the two families would have plenty of room, and they also knew that more children would soon be on the way.

He ended up building a seven-room mansion for both families to live in. William and Mary stayed here for the rest of their lives and eventually inherited the house William built and 90 acres of land that belonged to Patrick O'Hearn. They renamed the place Greenfield Village.

While the war may have been a long way off, it was still, nonetheless, a major part of everyone's life and concern in the little town of Dearborn, Michigan. The Dearborn Arsenal, built in 1830, was one of the few locations where the U.S. government stored weapons and ammunition. Soldiers on their way to battle would stop at this armory to purchase and pick up weapons. It was a pretty busy place during the Civil War.

Dearborn Arsenal was just about a mile west of Greenfield Village.

Since William remained a British subject in the United States after his arrival and until 1864, he was not conscripted or bound to join the military during the Civil War. This allowed him to focus on his business and build the two farms, while most other Michigan male residents were drafted to serve the war effort.

With his father's guidance and his wife's support, he soon developed their family farm to be one of the most successful in the area. His brother's farm in the north was also doing well. The other successful farm in the area belonged to his cousin, William Samuel Ford—the farm where they had lived when they first arrived in Michigan.

By the end of 1862, Mary was expecting again. The Fords had comfortably taken up residence at the O'Hearn's, and the new mansion was ready. Mary gave birth to their second child, Henry Ford, on July 30, 1863.

Earlier that same month the Civil War had turned the corner. What was certain doom for the Union just prior to July that year during the Battle of Gettysburg changed course in Lincoln's favor.

William Ford had always adopted a forward-thinking mannerism in everything he was involved in. Whether it was designing and building a mansion or the way he managed the farms he was in charge of or owned, he was always innovating. He soon became well respected in the Dearborn area and also became deacon of the church and was elected to the school board and justice of the peace.

Chapter 3 Henry Ford—An Overview

At the time of Ford's birth, gasoline-powered automobiles were nonexistent. Karl Benz, the man who invented the automobile and the engine that powered it, was just nineteen years old and still at the University of Karlsruhe on his way to becoming a mechanical engineer.

America, which was a house still divided by war, experienced divided rates of prosperity. The North did better than before the war, while the South did considerably worse since most of the battles took place in the South and, consequently, suffered more destruction.

That meant two things: (1) farmers in the North had more opportunities since they did not have to rebuild, and (2) farmers and the industrial infrastructure were already owner operated and not overly dependent on slave labor.

The South's infrastructure was destroyed, and it had to restrict and restructure the way it mobilized its labor force. This created a net flow of benefit from commerce to the North, which set up foundations for prosperity.

Farmers in the South, however, were entrenched in labor practices, even if they believed that all men were created equal.

What was actually a boon to farming became its bane in the wake of the Emancipation Proclamation of 1863. With that order, more than 3.5 million slaves, or absolutely every slave that was brought into the country or born here, was given freedom, which altered the course of businesses in the South and, more importantly, their cost structure. Putting aside the moral issues of slavery, whichever side of the debate one may be on, what happened in 1863, the year that Henry Ford was born, was significant in the way he redesigned the labor force and utilization of work to propel the Second Industrial Revolution.

At the same time, the United States was actively opening its doors to immigration. Between 30,000 and 450,000 immigrants were arriving annually from Europe and the rest of the world, and this created a very large supply of labor in the country. While Ford's River Rouge plant was being built, immigration had risen to between 600,000 and 1.2 million per year, creating an even greater supply of labor.

Putting aside his sympathies and advocacy of Nazi Germany and accusations of anti-Semitism, Ford was not a racist. In fact, it was impossible for him to see anything else besides a fellow human being when someone stood in front of him. He didn't see color, height, weight, or religion. He did, however, recognize intelligence.

The River Rouge plant was the largest integrated manufacturing facility the world had ever seen. It employed more than one hundred thousand people who were housed in more than ninety buildings. These contained everything from convenience stores to offices, steel mills to machine shops, assembly lines to stores, and even fire departments and hospitals.

To staff this facility, he relied on the abundant supply of labor, both local and immigrant. He even set up schools to teach immigrants English, and when they graduated, he would have ceremonies to welcome them into the Ford family and to the larger family as Americans.

Henry Ford was a very compassionate person, but he was biased and had his quirks, one being that he considered a person's intelligence and ability to learn as their most important trait.

He was generous in the way he paid his workers in the factories; in fact, he paid the highest rates for a day's labor at the Ford Motor Company factory. When the average annual salary in the United States was $450,

Ford started his factory workers off at $5 per day, or $25 per week, or $1,200 per year—significantly higher than the national average at the time.

These people were factory line workers who didn't need or have tertiary education or actually any education at all. Many of them didn't even speak English because they were new immigrants.

In return, he insisted that they display intelligence, integrity, and self-respect. He believed that if a person didn't have these characteristics, then he wouldn't want them working at the factory.

As part of the hiring and continued working process, Ford's human resource department would conduct surprise visits to the workers' homes. If they lived in squalor or below the standard that was set by the company, the inspector would give them a warning. If the next time the inspector went to the home and found little or no improvement, that person would be fired.

On the surface, that may seem harsh, but also consider that Ford wanted to make sure that the people who worked for him lived a righteous life. If the worker was living with a significant other, Ford insisted that they would have to be legally married. If they weren't, they were given an opportunity to rectify it. If they didn't, they would be terminated from employment.

That need for a righteous life was not just steeped in moral considerations. It was also about efficacy. On the one hand, Ford held himself and those around him to high moral standards. Like Rockefeller, he was a teetotaler. He was also righteous in his dating life, having only dated Clara Jane Bryant, then marrying her, and staying married until the day he died.

Aside from his stringent moral sense and need for efficacy, Ford had a singular mind-set—to apply the requisite focus from everyone involved in the production of his cars. He wanted to boost efficacy and excellence in all things that he undertook. Ford was singularly focused on this goal.

Unlike his good friend Luther Burbank, the botanist, who was the total opposite of Henry in terms of spreading his focus across many different tasks, Henry would rise almost to the level of an obsession when he needed to solve a challenge.

That characteristic turned out to be the reason for his success, but it was also a stumbling block during the early part of his career. Even though he had a fairly easy beginning and a rather privileged youth compared with that of his neighbors, Henry kept floundering, allowing success to slip through his fingers because he demanded perfection from everything.

Perfection in daily life is elusive, and to demand perfection from pedestrian activities is a fool's errand, but Henry never understood that. It wasn't until he was neck-deep in designing the assembly process that his strict codes of conduct surfaced and paid off.

This same mentality caused him to reject formal schooling. Being in school seemed to be a waste of time for him—not because he would rather be out playing— but more because he would rather be investigating or learning something more substantive.

What was Henry's problem?

Aside from his meticulous and almost obsessive behavior, he was a perfectionist. That was one problem. On the other hand, he wanted to accomplish so much. Even at a young age, he wanted to get involved in so many things (all related to mechanization) and also wanted to dig deep into everything.

You may be a jack of all trades but a master of none. It is not really possible to be the master of all trades. Yet, that is exactly what Ford aspired to be. That dichotomy created immense demons within him.

Not only did he want to solve problems that existed, but he also wanted to find solutions for problems that most people did not even know existed. Imagine what it must have felt like to see a challenge and then try to find solutions that didn't exist.

It's similar to when one realizes the number of pesticides that are being used in the production of food and know this is a big problem. With this problem, they go about finding a solution, which is to switch to organic foods. Problem solved . . . and they move on. But what if there was no solution? What if there was no organic food? How do you match a solution to a problem when there is no existing solution? How many people would go about structuring the solution to that problem? Yet, that is exactly what Ford did with the automobile industry. He may have started out with a simple goal of making affordable cars, but what he wound up doing was creating a method of production that squeezed every ounce of efficiency from materials, labor, process, and design. It was revolutionary.

To be clear, Ford's life was not just about cars. He had a family that stood behind him, and he had concerns just as any father and husband have. He also had personal concerns and weaknesses that plagued him. His only confidante on these matters was Clara. She knew him best.

Even though he was a genius on the outside, he could not decipher and detect the problems inside him. He could not solve the demons within him. He was too much of a perfectionist that it troubled him to let go of something that was not yet perfected. It was this characteristic that led him to designing and building the River Rouge plant. One could not do something so detailed and exacting without being obsessive in nature.

That obsession allowed him to dig deeper at every stage of the inquiry be it design or his vision—whether it was taking apart the pocket watch his father presented him when he was twelve or building a better four-stroke engine and understanding the problem of gasoline and air mixture. Once he put his mind to it, he couldn't and wouldn't let go until it was resolved.

We all agree that Ford was smart, but most people seem to miss that his intelligence was not just some abstract and ephemeral quality that existed in the recesses of his brain. It was a practical and well thought out plan that he could visualize. He could hold detailed images of what he wanted in his mind while he built the steps needed to get to what he could visualize.

Take, for instance, the pocket watch his father gave him when he was twelve. Most people at that age have a hard enough time focusing on reading a chapter in a book. Ford, however, was able to observe the mechanisms in the watch and not only remember the parts but also where they went. More importantly, Ford could see which came first and which came later. That is three-dimensional thinking. It was the same skill he used when he built the River Rouge plant thirty years later.

It was this intense cerebral process and observation ability that resulted in his designing and patenting the first carburetor. It was this invention that increased the power output of the internal combustion engine. Today, it is not easily found in automobile engines since it has been replaced by electronic fuel injection. In Ford's time, however, it was a revolutionary addition to the engine.

Even though he designed his cars and thought of good innovative ideas for the improvement of the car, the invention of the car itself is not his to claim. Not even the invention of the carburetor could suggest that he had anything to do with the car or the engine that Karl Benz or Gottlieb Daimler had invented.

We hear more about Ford than Benz and Daimler because Ford had a larger impact on the automotive world, the social structure of the last generation, and the well-being of the generations that followed. And that was just the knock-on effect that came from production of his inexpensive cars. But there is more. Ford's assembly line is now used in manufacturing everything from iPhones to tractors.

In fact, the entire academic world is designed based on the needs of the modern manufacturing system. There is a pyramid-shaped organizational chart that has the largest number of workers on the factory floor who are controlled by a smaller number of supervisors, who are controlled by an even smaller number of managers and so on as it goes all the way up to the CEO of the company. In the same way, high schools and technical institutes pump out more graduates than colleges that pump out more graduates than regular graduate schools and they, in turn, pump out more than Ivy League business schools. Those two pyramids intersect.

Harvard Business School (and the other top business schools) grads are the most likely to sit on top of that pyramid, which was created by Henry Ford when he perfected the manufacturing system. A country's success is determined by how well those pyramids are shaped.

That is how deep Henry Ford's influence has extended to society today. It was all based on the manufacturing assembly line model.

The problem he focused on and solved was more than just industrial engineering. It was also in economics. The improvements in such factors as the assembly line, human resources, Just in Time inventory management, and cost management were all part of what came out of Ford's endeavor to create the most cost-effective product.

He realized what the top business schools teach today as part their curriculum. He realized that a product seen from the customer's perspective is different from a product as seen from the manufacturer's point of view.

The customer sees a product as a solution to a problem. The manufacturer, while cognizant of the problem and the method to solve that problem, sees the solution (the product) as an integrated string of tangible and intangible steps. Ford saw the solution to mass independent mobility as a catch-22. He clearly saw when no one else did that to produce at such a low process they need to sell a large volume. To be successful, they needed large facilities that were fully integrated. It was all connected like the gears in the pocket watch his father had given him all those years ago.

Ford is remembered today because he solved that equation. He did all this without any tertiary education during the interregnum period straddling the two industrial revolutions.

The Industrial Revolution that preceded the mid-nineteenth century set up the environment in which the North was able to mechanize more than the South. It was all built on Ford's plant design and philosophy. His method created better efficiency for industry.

The First Industrial Revolution also affected social structure. There was a move from cottage industries to factories, which resulted in rural/urban migration. It was the start of the move toward the building of large cities.

Before Ford's arrival on the scene, the entire world was primarily agrarian. It wasn't much different from John Ford's farm in Ireland. Everyone worked the farm with their hands, hand tools, and beasts of burden.

The social dispersion of societies was flung far and wide over farms. It's much like driving through the rural farms of Maine or the ranches in Nevada. They were dispersed.

Then came the First Industrial Revolution that changed society. Since factories that were powered by steam and coal were centralized, the working population had to live in the cities for work. Cities back then were dirty and smoggy. So came the first urban migration.

Then came a gap in the revolution of industry. The mid-nineteenth century saw a brief respite in innovation, but the next revolution saw even more innovation. This is where Henry Ford's contribution is important.

The First Industrial Revolution had solved issues in two areas: (1) infrastructure expansion, with iron and coal being the core of mechanization and power and (2) solving individual and specific problems. Steam was the new energy resource, and to make steam, one needed coal to fire up the water.

As for the second aspect of the First Industrial Revolution, they were innovations in mechanization. Take, for instance, the spinning jenny. It was a multispindle spinning machine that increased the speed of the job that would be done by one person. That meant that one machine didn't replace one person. It increased the output of that person. That increased output would translate to better dispersion of overhead costs and better consumer adoption.

The Second Industrial Revolution was a totally different set of innovations. It also had two aspects to it; for the first, think of such men as Rockefeller in oil,

Carnegie in steel, and Edison in electricity. Their innovations completely altered the landscape of business and opportunity. It was now the Gilded Age and unprecedented prosperity in America.

The Second Industrial Revolution straddled the use of softer factors, and while it did have some forms of increased mechanizations the Second Industrial Revolution. Not only were machines, factories, and contraptions making mass production easier, but new innovations were also coming online faster than at any time in the past. With the U.S. patent law taking effect in 1790, innovators and inventors had come out in full force.

People like Edison set up offices and businesses to innovate and commercialize products. The United States and to a large extent the rest of the industrial world had created machines to take on industries of the past, but other industries were to come.

Take car manufacturing, for instance, which was something that would evolve in the next half-century and not be geared toward being produced by other machines. This was the basis of the Second Industrial Revolution.

Henry Ford's good fortune as a young child gave him the time and ease to think about things that were not always a pressing matter for most other people. He had loving parents and a father who was not prone to any of the bad habits that many were at the time.

By the time he was born, the hard living conditions that the Fords before him had faced were in the past. Henry's father was well to do and respected. Whatever hardships that Henry Ford would come to know about would be from the stories his father told him through the years.

Those stories did not remain distant imagery and fodder for a rainy afternoon. They seemed to have stuck in his mind with intensity that is usually not characteristic of a child. As he grew older, the stories became more serious, and he later learned that his paternal grandmother had passed away on board a ship. It was the first instance for him coming face to face with death and the loss of a loved one.

Henry also had a deep sense of belonging. He took his name seriously and knew that it was his name that bestowed value to the life he would contribute to those around him.

The shift from a wartime economy to a postwar economy also had a significant effect on Americans. Industrialization had increased, and mechanization was beginning to form the basis of higher technologies.

In Pennsylvania, Carnegie was developing better ways to make steel. In Ohio, Rockefeller was bringing refineries and technology online, and in New York, J.P. Morgan was revolutionizing the financial world.

No doubt there was a generational gap between Carnegie, Morgan, Rockefeller, and Henry Ford, but all these served as the foundation for the Second Industrial Revolution.

Henry Ford's development of the Model T and the subsequent rise in the number of households that owned vehicles was significant in how John D. Rockefeller increased his wealth. Wealth may have been a driving factor for Rockefeller, but it was never just about the wealth when it came to Ford. In fact, just before he was able to get the idea for his vehicle produced, he was down and out on his luck.

Ford had taken loans and investments that were not yet panning out, which was stressful. It was Clara who held it together for him and got him to focus on what he needed to do.

Family

Clara had always been the force that held the family together for Henry. He was used to having a strong family support structure, even if he did lose his mother early in life. He had his siblings, his grandparents, and his father not to mention a whole host of cousins and their respective families.

When he was growing up, he had close relationships with his immediate family. He was set in his ways and not comfortable around strangers. Henry grew up in a full house. His father showered him with attention, and his mother was immensely close to him and taught him to read and did a good job of homeschooling him long before he went to a private school. His maternal grandfather would also take him around the farm and introduced him to the animals that roamed around and showed him flowers.

Between his mother and his maternal grandmother, he had a solid introduction to the power of nature and the beauty of farming. His father, uncles, and grandfathers were his role models and had a solid history of farming, and his introduction to nature was not just about the technical aspects of the earth but also about the almost spiritual aspects of being one with the creation and regenerative forces of the land.

This spiritual background and the fact that William was a deacon gave Henry a solid foundation in life. Although he would later not have much interest in organized religion and instead embraced more Eastern philosophies, the core of his spirit was always about doing the right thing. He was more about the spirit than about the commandment, more about being righteous than about being rich, and certainly more about being a husband than about being a successful businessman.

Aside from his guidance on nature and spirituality, William expertly guided young Henry for a life on the farm by forcing him to work in different areas, which was something Henry deplored. It wasn't clear if his idea to mechanize farm operations was for the love of machinery or because he hated manual labor. There was a sense of pride in the Ford and O'Hearn families of their heritage and farming in general. To be independent and respected, one had to put in the requisite toil and harvest the bounty of the earth, and the only way you could do that was by farming.

Henry, however, did not want to do that at all and actually disliked farmwork. He preferred dealing with machines but was not able to tend to his passion due to his duties on the farm. William was also a bit of a gearhead. Henry's eye on future technologies and mechanization was not developed in a void. It had a direct link and connection to the way William thought. Still, William did make Henry get his hands dirty and put him to work on the farm as soon as it was time to do so.

Ford enjoyed tinkering with machinery when he was young. His mother noticed this from a very young age said that he was "born a mechanic," as he wrote. His perspective, however, was that he wanted to find a better way to do farmwork, which made him enter the world of machines. Ford had a simple shed in which all his "tools" were kept, which were not really tools but just pieces of metal that he used as tools. Ford wrote in his autobiography, "In those days we did not have the toys of today; what we had were home-made. My toys were all tools—they still are! And every fragment of machinery was a treasure."

This writing shows how much he absolutely loved machinery. For most children, marbles and wooden toys were their favorite things to play with. For Ford, he had fun tinkering.

When Ford was twelve years old, he used to see the steam-powered engine that would pass near his home while he and his family were going to the town. He would be so fascinated by it that when his father was driving the carriage, he would jump down to see the engine. He and the man who ran the engine would discuss the train, and the person who ran the train was more than happy to explain to young Ford how it and each part worked.

It was also during Ford's twelfth year that his father gave him a pocket watch. He very quickly became adept at dismantling and putting watches back together and soon became known as someone who could repair watches. Ford was in school until only his eighth year. Consequently, he did not know much about facts, dates, whos, whats, and wheres, but he did have a knack for knowing about machinery. He learned about machines by working with them and experimenting with them. His knowledge came from doing, not reading.

Ford wrote in his autobiography, *My Life and Work*, that one cannot really learn everything out of books. He said that one would learn better by doing—not just by researching. His opinion was that doing an action yielded more and was better than just reading. He was right. Doing is good; reading is good; both work even better.

From a very early age, Ford thought that farming could be improved. He would later succeed in building a lightweight tractor for farmers, making their jobs much easier. The cars he would later manufacture, such as the Model T, would also be of great help to farmers.

Ford's mother passed away in 1876. It was a hard blow for young Ford, and now there was no longer any reason for him to continue to stay at the farm. He would later write, "I never had any particular love for the farm—it was the mother on the farm I loved."

Chapter 4 Detroit

In 1879, Ford had just turned sixteen, and he wanted to advance his skills as a machinist and his knowledge of tools and metallurgy. He left the family farm in Dearborn and walked nine miles to the city of Detroit.

Once there he tried to get a job, but there weren't many for boys who grew up on the farm. He was specifically trying to find a job in factories or machine shops. If he were looking for a job as a factory assistant or something similar, it would not have been too much of a problem, but he was looking for a job that was typically done by a specialist. In today's terms, he was looking for an engineering job without an engineering degree.

Remember that Ford didn't have much formal education, and even though he was sharp, he had no paper qualifications. He spent some time looking for a job, but it wasn't easy. His father also tried on his behalf, contacting acquaintances in Detroit, but nothing seemed to work.

He finally found a job working for James Flower and Bros. Co. and later went on to have the same position at the Dry Dock Engine Works as a trainee. Ford would learn from this experience how to use engines. This knowledge later helped him develop engines for his Quadracycle. He found that making automobiles powered by steam engines would not work, as the power-to-weight ratio of the heavy steam engine would not be enough to adequately power a chassis loaded with goods and passengers.

Ford left Detroit in 1882 and returned to the Ford family farm in Dearborn. He worked on the farm for his father and adapted the farm engine made by the Westinghouse Company. He was so good that he taught the company representative how to work the machine better.

It was during Ford's time in Dearborn that he met his wife, Clara Jane Bryant. It was 1885, and they both attended a dance celebrating the New Year. He and Clara liked each other considerably from the very first time they saw each other.

Henry became distracted. It was the first time since he had turned sixteen that he had his thoughts on something other than his car or something mechanical.

For her part, Clara liked Ford for his knowledge of machinery as well as his tenacity and uncommon cerebral powers. Several years later and many years after their marriage when Ford was an influential figure in the United States, he said to the press, "The greatest day of my life was when I married Mrs. Ford."

The courtship between Ford and Clara was very wholesome indeed. They enjoyed boat rides, dancing, and corn husking. The two were engaged to marry by 1886, but Clara's mother thought that her daughter was still too young to get married and convinced them to wait until 1888. After all, she was three years younger than Ford and was only twenty years old by the time of her engagement.

Finally, on April 22, 1888, Clara's birthday, Henry Ford and Clara Jane Bryant became husband and wife. For the next five years, the couple tried for a child. Clara eventually became pregnant with Edsel Ford, their only son. Edsel was born in Detroit on November 6, 1893.

Ford loved his family deeply. He was very close to his wife, and when he was suffering from senility and partial dementia as well as several strokes in his later years, he would always want her in his sight, relying on her for safety, familiarity, and comfort. Initially, he was also very close to his son, but this seemed to change when Edsel grew up. Edsel's untimely death in 1943 was a stinging blow to Ford's emotional state and stability.

Chapter 5 The Ford Quadracycle

Over the next few years after the wedding, Ford would experiment and try to build a lightweight vehicle. After several years of experimentation, he built his first car in 1895. It was the Ford Quadracycle. He named it the "Quadracycle" because its *four* wheels were bicycle wheels. It was a simple car with a side plate at the front and a tiller to direct the car. There were just two speeds that the Quadracycle could travel at, and it was incapable of reversing. At the time, Ford's first car seemed like a bother. It held up traffic, frightened the horses, and was noisy.

Ford was about the only person driving a vehicle in Detroit at that time, and everyone was greatly interested in it, although it was a problem for the townsfolk. Ford said that when he was not by its side, people would come, get inside, and try to start it. They weren't doing it to steal the vehicle, but their curiosity pushed them to try to start it. Ford had to chain the vehicle to a lamppost whenever he stopped driving and left the car for a moment or two.

Ford drove his Quadracycle a thousand miles from 1895 to 1896 and then sold it to Charles Ainsley for $200. Ford was actually not planning to sell the Quadracycle in the beginning, but it turned out to be beneficial. Ford wanted to begin building a second car, and he needed funds for it.

When his new car was completed, it did not look any different from his first Quadracycle—but it did weigh less. At the time, Ford was using the belt drive in his cars, which worked well when the weather wasn't hot. It was this problem that later made Ford switch over and start using gears. When it was hot, the belts would expand and misalign with the drive and axle gears. This caused it to derail.

The year that Ford built his second Quadracycle a new model Benz automobile was on display in New York. Ford went to see it to get some ideas for his own invention, but he found nothing he could take from it and also found that it was considerably heavier than his own car. He wrote, "I was working for lightness; the foreign makers have never seemed to appreciate what lightweight means."

A couple of years after Ford sold his Quadracycle to Charles Ainsley, he bought it back for $100 from someone who had bought the car from Ainsley.

Ford liked machinery and gizmos so much that he had a room in his Dearborn house that was filled with what he called his "mechanical treasures." One of these was a dynamo that had been previously used at the Edison Illuminating Company.

He had some history with this particular dynamo. Ford had purchased the dynamo from another place that had purchased that dynamo from the Edison Illuminating Company. He had the dynamo upgraded and then installed it at the Canadian electrical plant that Edison's company was building. When the company was going to build another plant, Ford took the dynamo and placed it in his room of "mechanical treasures."

In the late 1890s, the Edison Illuminating Company, the company where he was working as Chief Engineer, offered him the position of General Superintendent, but it came with a condition. If Ford wanted to hold that position, he needed to drop all of his automotive activities and dedicate himself to the Edison Illuminating Company.

Ford was at a crossroads, the first of many in his life. He could choose to drop his vision and hold a prestigious position at one of the largest companies in the nation or he could risk it and strive to make his dream a reality.

Ford chose the latter. On August 15, 1899, he said goodbye to the Edison Illuminating Company and plunged headlong into the automotive business.

Quitting his job at the Edison Illuminating Company was risky. He did not have any money of his own. Despite the tight situation, however, Clara supported her husband in his decision. How many of us today would do something like that?

It was during this time that Ford was part of the Detroit Automobile Company, founded in 1899. He was the engineer and in charge of the production of cars. The owners and other controllers of the company were not focused on making a car for the masses or creating a cheap, affordable car. They were more interested in creating expensive cars that the rich and wealthy could easily afford—they were focused on making money—that was their sole purpose. Ford, however, was not interested in that. He soon realized what the company was doing. He wrote, "And being without authority other than my engineering position gave me, I found that the new company was not a vehicle for realizing my ideas but merely a money-making concern—that did not make much money."

Ford spent his time experimenting and trying to make a car that would be affordable and available to the people. Meanwhile, the owners and investors of the company became upset, and to placate them, Ford assigned work to his thirteen workers to make parts for cars that he had no intention whatsoever of building.

Finally, when the investors felt that Ford was lagging too far behind, they dropped him, and Ford was left out in the cold. He resigned from the company on March 2, 1902. During his time with the company, it had been renamed the Henry Ford Motor Company, a purely honorary thing. After Ford left the company in 1902, the Lelands came to the company, and it became the Cadillac Motor Company.

Ford was then extremely upset with investors—he absolutely despised them. He never wanted to deal with them again, but he would in establishing the Ford Motor Company—but he would later force them out. After leaving the Henry Ford Motor Company, he rented a workplace at 81 Park Place and began experimenting.

At the time, people were interested in the automobile for racing purposes. They only cared to look at one that was fast. Ford was not building cars for that purpose, but he would soon have to change.

Chapter 6 ALAM & A Rising Star

On his own, to build his cars, Ford approached the Association of Licensed Automobile Manufacturers with his design of the car and was seeking their permission to manufacture and sell his cars. ALAM had the rights to the Selden Patent and the authority to say who sold cars and who didn't.

So, companies that wanted to make and sell their own cars needed to come to ALAM and ask for their permission. Ford was later rejected. He did not care, though, as he didn't need some monopoly's permission to do something. Despite ALAM's not allowing him to sell his cars, he went ahead and did it.

Before that, however, he needed to gain popularity to attract a market. So, he called for a race with Alexander Winton, who accepted the challenge, and the two raced at the track at Grosse Point in Detroit in October of 1901.

Ford built a special car for the race, the Ford Sweepstakes. It had a two-cylinder engine built very tight and rated high in compactness. Ford's

Sweepstakes was incredibly fast, and it was then that he challenged Alexander Winton to a race.

Throughout the entire race, Ford was always lagging behind, and only on the sixth lap was he able to pass Winton, which happened because Winton's engine began to smoke, and it slowed Winton's vehicle, allowing Ford to pass. Ford's victory over the fastest race car driver in America made him a celebrity and famous. Everyone then knew his name—Henry Ford—the new fastest man in the United States.

Although Ford could not pass Winton for the first six laps, the fact that Winton's engine began to smoke and Ford's did not showed that Ford's car, a car that he built, was stronger and more durable that Winton's, proving that his car was better. Ford's victory gave him the idea of building a four-cylinder engine.

As people were only interested in a car that was fast, Ford had proved that his car was what they were looking for. People began to pay attention to him, and he was even able to attract some investors even though he didn't like them. Two notable investors were the Dodge brothers, John Francis and Horace. Then, in 1903, the Ford Motor Company was established.

During the first few months, they made the first Model A, which would be produced from 1903 until 1904. Thus, it was from here, that Ford's career began.

Chapter 7 The Ford Motor Company

After establishing the Ford Motor Company, Ford began selling his cars to the masses, and it did not go unnoticed by ALAM. The organization filed lawsuits against Ford for copyright infringement. The lawsuit was filed in 1903, but the case would only be heard in court in 1909.

Unfortunately, Judge Hough, the judge who was conducting the case, ruled against Ford on September 15, 1909. Ford's fellow automobile manufacturers—his competitors—took advantage of the defeat at once. The rumor had spread that if Ford had a lawsuit filed against him, then all those who owned a Ford car would be liable for damages.

Ford released an advertisement which said, "In conclusion we beg to state if there are any prospective automobile buyers who are at all intimidated by the claim made by our adversaries that we will give them, in addition to the protection of the Ford Motor Company with its some $6,000,000.00 of assets, an individual bond backed by a Company of more than

$6,000,000.00 more of assets, so that each and every individual owner of a Ford car will be protected until at least $12,000,000.00 of assets have been wiped out by those who desire to control and monopolize this wonderful industry."

Ford had thought that potential customers of the Ford Motor Co. needed to be reassured, but he was mistaken. Potential customers and buyers were completely satisfied with purchasing from the Ford Motor Co., and the firm actually did better, selling eighteen thousand cars that year, which was more than they had sold the preceding year.

Ford said that the case against the ALAM monopoly was actually the best sort of advertising the company had received. People trusted and had confidence in the Ford Motor Co., and the affair led to the loss of power and authority that ALAM held. Ford wrote that he had complete confidence that they would come out victorious. That notion was justifiable—the Ford car was popular, cheap, and available for anyone who was earning money—everyone loved Ford and thus supported him.

As it turned out, ALAM did not really own the patent, and Ford won the case.

Henry was not someone who backed down from what he believed to be right, which is shown by this episode involving ALAM.

Chapter 8 Henry Ford and Thomas Alva Edison

A deep, penetrating history binds these two giants of history. Henry Ford used to work for Edison Illuminating Company, and he decided to work there because Edison, an avid inventor, was one of Ford's greatest heroes.

Edison, who was born in 1847, was sixteen years Ford's senior. He had invented the vote recorder in 1868. It was his first invention that was patented. Edison was twenty-two, and Ford was a toddler.

Since Ford was interested in all things new and all things mechanical, he avidly read innovative journals and articles, where he found a direct line of information to the world of gizmos and inventions. The one that struck him the most was Edison's. By the time he was reading all the journals, he was about nine years old and had seen the invention of the vote recording device that Edison had invented and patented.

Edison soon became Ford's hero, and Ford began to think in the same way as Edison. For Ford, Edison was larger than life. Ford also learned that Edison did not have any formal education and thought that formal education dulled the mind more than liberated it.

As Ford kept track of his idol's development, Edison kept churning out his inventions from his Menlo Park facility. There was still no electricity as yet, and the light bulb hadn't been invented. It was merely from Edison's lesser inventions (if one could label them as such) that Ford had already determined that Edison was brilliant.

Edison continued entertaining Ford's interest by coming out with the stock ticker the following year and other phonographic recording devices, all of which he patented.

By 1874, when Ford was just eleven, Edison had developed the quadruplex telegraph, which could transmit several messages simultaneously. It was patented and the rights sold to Western Union. Ford was watching intently. He was absolutely amazed that the patent was sold for $10,000. He did the math and realized that the amount of money his father had paid for forty acres of land ($600) was a fraction of the price of the rights of Edison's invention. This thrilled him— not because he saw the monetary value or gain—but he saw the price very differently from how most people did.

Ford had a particular view of money that he also shared with Edison. They didn't see money as a means to purchase happiness or fun; they saw monetary value as a valuation of their contribution. While both men were not interested in the commercial value of money (i.e., the ability to buy more things), what they were truly interested in was the validation they received from the valuation.

In this same vein, Ford watched carefully as Edison went from the sale of one patent to the next and was constantly producing inventions in his Menlo Park office.

Ford was also impressed by how Edison had gone about institutionalizing his invention process. Ford had seen how farming was done all around Dearborn, and it was a very tedious process of one person doing many tasks day in and day out. That was one of the things that he didn't like about farming. It was slow and mind-numbing, but many people were more than happy to do just one thing and do it repeatedly. He kept that at the back of his mind and would eventually use it in his assembly practice.

As for Ford, he watched how Edison created his inventions in an atmosphere where Edison would spark the idea, draughtsman would draw it up, machinists would make it, and then they would see how well it worked. Through the process of iteration, they would either make it work or abandon it because there was no way to make it cost effectively. He would shelve these ideas, knowing they would be able to make use of them sometime in the future.

By 1877, the phonograph had been invented, which was one of the inventions that made Edison famous. By this point, Ford was a busy teenager, and he was highly impressed with the phonograph, which he had not yet actually seen or experienced, but the descriptions of it were enough to peak his enthusiasm.

It would be sufficient to say that Ford was an ardent fan of Edison. Then came the invention that changed everything, including Ford's life and thought process. If the other inventions had been great, they were only the beginning, and nothing could really compare with the invention of the light bulb and the electricity generation and transmission that came about in 1880 (it was actually in 1879, but by the time Ford had heard about it was the next year).

He had read that Edison had taken an existing idea of a contraption that could illuminate an entire room without the need for kerosene, which is what they had been using at Greenfield. What was more interesting was that Edison had also invented the way to commercially make electricity in large quantities so that an entire township could be illuminated at the flick of a switch.

Ford was very impressed. Within two years, Edison had built the first commercial power generation plant in New York to supply homes in the city. That was the one that sent electricity to J.P. Morgan's house in New York—the first house to have power from the grid (Morgan had financed Edison).

This was a significant development in a number of ways. It taught Ford three things that influenced him in the future.

He realized that if you are going to do anything it has to be for the wider public, and it has to be in a way that changs their lives. Mechanization didn't just apply to factories but also to the general public. You see that today in a way that Ford saw it—you see it through YouTube in giving someone the ability to broadcast information. You also see it through the Web, and you are now even seeing satellite launches where there are nanosatellites that individuals can launch so that they have their own means of global communication. It all started with Edison, but it was Ford who institutionalized it.

Ford also learned that it was not so much the light bulb but the infrastructure behind it that made all the difference. It would not have been that important if Edison had gone ahead and perfected the light bulb and then just let it be. He had to create a robust infrastructure behind it, from the power generation plant to the copper wires that transmitted the power to the fuses, switches, and safety features that made it possible for the consumer to just flick a switch and have a bulb illuminate a room (without the smell of kerosene).

Edison also opened Ford's eyes, though he didn't very much like this part, to the inclusion of the moneyman in the equation. In Edison's case, he had used J.P. Morgan to finance some of his ideas. Morgan had seen the genius in Edison and realized that he could invest in Menlo Park and take a profit when products were commercialized.

Thus, Edison didn't need to worry about finances and was free to invent. Ford saw the genius in that, and he approached the Marburys when the time was right. The Marburys were the first to invest in Ford's ideas and were actually the ones who also financed the development of the carburetor. But the idea of bringing investors on board soon lost its appeal for Ford after he dealt with them firsthand.

These lessons were at the core of Ford's thinking. He realized that Edison was indeed a wizard and had a brilliant mind and kept close tabs on his progress.

By the time the Edison Illuminating Company came to Detroit, Ford was twenty-five years old and had been working in Detroit for almost ten years. He had left his family farm when he was sixteen and worked at various machine shops in Detroit. It was during this time that he became a certified machinist.

When there was a vacancy in Edison's company, he couldn't help himself and decided to seek employment from the company of his idol. Its director, James Hood Wright, interviewed him and offered Ford a job as an engineer. Clara, his new bride, supported him, as she did with everything Henry undertook in their long life together.

Within three years of getting the job, he had done so well and had proven himself to such a degree that he was promoted to Chief Engineer in 1893.

As Chief Engineer, his job was less hectic and less predictable. He was no longer working for a fixed number of hours during the day but instead was on call twenty-four hours a day. He was making more than $125 and had a comfortable life.

He would then stay at home and work on other things that interested him. If a problem arose, he would be dispatched to monitor, fix, or solve it. He would then promptly return home to wait for the next call.

This gave him a lot of time to pursue his own interests, which is when he started building the Quadracycle. In the meantime, many other branches of the Edison Illuminating Company were being established across the country. Each would have a different board of directors and different management policies. They all formed an association, and each year a convention would be held in New York. Edison always attended.

As Chief Engineer of one of the companies, Ford was given the opportunity to attend the 1896 convention held at the Oriental Hotel in Brooklyn, New York. As excited as he was, he remembered to take two things with him—a camera to capture his childhood idol and his Quadracycle.

At the meeting, he managed to capture a few photographs of Edison, which are now in the historical record, but more important was that he actually managed to meet Edison one evening at one of the banquets for the attendees. At this meeting, they had a short but pleasant conversation, and Ford was able to show Edison his Quadracycle.

That brief encounter did three things: (1) it served as the spark to a lifelong friendship, (2) it solidified his endeavor in automobiles, and (3) it made flesh what was once mythical. It was an absolutely joyous occasion for Ford.

Edison was impressed with Ford's creation. A number of other people at this time were also trying to make cars and commercialize them. It seemed that everyone was trying to build a car and make some money out of it. In fact, that was one of the reasons AMAL had stepped in to enforce their patents. They effectively blocked many people from trying to build cars.

Creating a car was an uphill battle. What went on in Ford's mind will always be unknown because he never discussed or wrote about it in his autobiography. What we have are his actions and concerns during each decision-making process as he developed a production model.

One thing, however, is clear: he was entering a field that was competitive, and he was not sure at each juncture which path to take. In fact, his efforts to build a viable and working model failed completely and spectacularly twice in his life, but the number of daunting decisions he had to make was significant.

That encounter with Edison made all the difference. Being impressed with the Quadracycle and that Ford had a patent on the carburetor, Edison told Ford that he should keep up with it. He said Ford needed to keep working at it, which was the only way to eliminate the bugs.

Edison also told him that he should make the car electric. He expounded on the benefits of electricity (pollution was not one of them), saying that it was the energy source of the future. Ford took him seriously and tried to make the car electric, and he even built an engine that would use electricity, but the technology of electrical batteries was not very advanced, and Ford was forced to choose the kerosene engine because that was what was available and needed to get the car to market as quickly as possible.

In fact, Ford even built an engine that worked on ethanol, but because of Prohibition and subsequent law ethanol was cost prohibitive as a possible fuel source.

After the convention, Ford returned to Detroit. He would later send letters and telegrams to convey wishes and update Edison on how his endeavors were going.

For his part, Edison was glad to make a friend in Ford and would write back to the young engineer as often as Ford would write to him. Their friendship grew over the years, and Edison had kept track of Ford's progress.

Their friendship by mail lasted sixteen years. While each man continued to develop his own life, they only kept in touch through telegrams and letters. When they finally met again, it was 1912, and they decided to take a vacation together.

Their destination was the Everglades, where they would be surrounded by nature. This was the first of more than fifteen trips the two men would take and be accompanied by others, including Harvey Firestone, the tire magnate; John Burroughs, the naturalist; and even President Harding.

The first trip involved Ford, Edison, and Burroughs. It was a classic trip, and they would ride in Ford automobiles on long-distance trips with Edison usually in the lead car and guiding the way.

They would spend the evening by a crackling fire while they discussed philosophy, Shakespeare, and Mozart. Burroughs would spice up the conversation with talks of nature and the bird calls he would teach Ford.

Edison would discuss advances in the science, and Ford would fix the cars when they broke down during any of the trips. One such trip saw the fan break off and rupture the radiator. By this point, Ford was already a well-known industrialist, and Edison was one of the most famous men in America. Still, it was Ford who got out, got his hands dirty, and fixed his car.

As the years rolled on, the annual trips, with various other luminaires, grew the number of Ford cars in the caravan that would drive off the beaten path. At its height, what started off as a quiet holiday for two men (or three) became a caravan of fifty cars. One was even outfitted with a portable refrigerator. The trips also started to include reporters and fully dressed waiters and chauffeurs.

After sixteen years, they slowed down and instead decided to just go somewhere on vacation. Ford decided to buy a house right next to Edison in Fort Myers. The two spent the winter months there with their families.

As Edison grew older and was eventually confined to a wheelchair, Ford bought one, too, and would accompany him, although Ford didn't need it. They would even race their wheelchairs and bump into each other for fun. They were as close as two friends could be. Their friendship was widely known, and even

Edison's children and family knew how close they were.

When Edison passed, his eldest son found a test tube in his father's office. He thought of Ford and sealed the tube with paraffin wax and gave it to Ford. It was filled with air that Edison had breathed. It sits today in the Henry Ford museum.

Chapter 9 Ford and Edsel

Edsel Ford, the son of the great automobile manufacturer, was born November 6, 1893. He was the only child of Henry and Clara, and in his early life he made his father proud. From an early age, he began fiddling with cars and would follow his father to work and was generally enthusiastic about his father's business.

Edsel grew up to be a very nice and friendly person. Ford, however, was looking for his son to be a more serious, firm, and commanding figure. This was the main cause of Ford's later disappointment with his son.

Edsel was the kind of person who liked style and fashion. He partied with rich people, who Ford thought of as people who were good for nothing. Much to his father's dismay and anger, Edsel drank alcohol. Ford never drank liquor and did not allow it in his house. Ford wanted people he dealt with to have the same attitude, and he didn't want his son to drink alcohol. Edsel's habit drove Henry up the wall.

When Ford and his wife had built their home in Fair Lane, they constructed a bowling alley and a swimming pool inside the house. This was meant for

Edsel, but, again, he was out having fun with other rich kids.

Henry Ford retired from Ford Motor Company in 1919 and made his twenty-five-year-old son president of the company. Ford wanted to kick investors out of the game. Two of them, the Dodge brothers, had caused some trouble for Ford, and he wanted them out.

Edsel's sudden rise to the presidency of the Ford Motor Company worried Ford's investors. The ploy was meant to scare them and make them want to back out of the company by selling their interests. Ford, now publicly out of the company, said that he was going to start another car manufacturing company and was going to hire several hundred thousand workers and sell cars for $300 or less. This price was less than the price of a Model T. This worried investors, and they soon sold their interests in the company, which was then in full control of the Ford family. Outside stockholders would only be a part of the Ford Motor Company after Edsel's son, Henry Ford II, took the president's chair following Henry Ford's death.

One great difference between Edsel and Ford was that Edsel was more about style, and Ford was more about practicality. The Ford Motor Company was producing Model T after Model T, with no change in system or appearance—which was what Ford liked. Edsel, however, wanted cars to look nicer. The automobiles manufactured by other companies were flashy and stylish—much to Edsel's taste.

Edsel always tried to convince his father to build a new model with a nicer appearance, but every time he proposed the idea his father always refused. It was only when Chevrolet began manufacturing stylish cars that were both good and functioned well that Ford would yield to building a new model. What happened was that the market by the late 1920s was not limited to buying just practical cars, such as the Model T. People now had enough money to buy more expensive cars that also looked better and were stylish.

Edsel pressured his father to make a new model, and Ford finally decided to do so. Edsel took charge of the chassis. He designed the body. If you pull up an image of the Model A, which was produced from 1927 or 1928 to 1931, it looked very stylish—much more than the Model T.

Unfortunately for Edsel, however, his father showered in the spotlight of the Model A, while he stood in the shadows watching his design be attributed to his father.

Over the years, great tension built up between Edsel and his father. Ford was upset that his son was mixing with the useless rich. He was upset that his son drank alcohol. He was disappointed with his son for his lack of firmness, authority, and fire. Instead, Edsel was a nice guy—not at all like the commanding figure Ford was.

Although Ford may have been hard and harsh on his son, he doted heavily on his grandchildren. In fact, it may be said that Edsel's children got more pampering than Edsel did when he was a child.

Due to Edsel's activities, Ford had Bennett spy on him to keep tabs on what he was doing.

For a great part of Edsel's later life, his relationship with his father badly deteriorated, which perhaps made Edsel unhappy.

During the last few months that he was alive, Edsel had not been feeling right and was somewhat ill. In the end, it was found that he had end-stage stomach cancer. He underwent surgery as doctors tried to remove the tumor, but they were unsuccessful, and Edsel died prematurely. He had not told anyone of his condition, not even his father. The only person who knew about it except for his doctor(s) was his wife, Eleanor.

As Edsel lost more and more strength over time, Ford was upset, thinking that if his son stopped drinking so much and spent less time with those rich kids he would get better. Ford did not know what his son was going through.

Ford even sent someone to tell Edsel that he needed to fix a long list of things in his life, but upon hearing this, Edsel began to cry.

The stress Edsel was put under by his father was much too difficult for him to bear. One day, while at the office, Edsel fell to the ground. From that point on, he could not work and remained at home. When Eleanor told Henry what was actually going on and that Edsel was actually going to pass soon, Henry was in denial. Edsel passed away May 26, 1943, at only forty-nine years of age.

Edsel's death had a very devastating effect on Henry. The relationship between the two had been very uncomfortable for the last several years, and press videos in which they were both present showed the discomfort between them.

Edsel's untimely passing may have been the catalyst for Ford's senility. He died just four years later in 1947, and his last few years were not at all pretty. He became president of the Ford Motor Company once again but was not at all the same person he had been several years earlier when he handed over the company to his son.

After Ford died, the company produced a series of cars called the Edsel. They were supposed to be flashy and stylish, but they were not very popular and did not last long.

Chapter 10 The Mind of a Genius

Ford had only a few years of formal schooling and the apprenticeships in Detroit that enabled him to be certified as a machinist. That was the extent of his formal and semiformal learning. Everything else he learned on his own by the power and volition of his own intellect and vision.

We all have a certain level of genius within us. It is unfortunate that many still see the description of being a genius as an exclusive trait. It is seen as something that only a few people have, but that is not true. There is a genius in everyone.

In the words of Ford himself when he was designing the moving assembly line, he noted that most people were intelligent, but they chose to not be. He defined people in two categories: (1) those who were intelligent and smart and had the tenacity and mettle to do what was necessary and (2) those who were smart and intelligent but had no intention of putting in the work that was necessary. Henry labeled the former as a genius and the latter as lazy.

Ford did not care if a person was formally educated or went to school. He hadn't been and neither had his best friend, Edison. So when he interviewed factory workers who came to work for him, he would not ask for their qualifications or their certificates but would pose questions of intelligence to them where they would have to use their minds and think. There was not any real answer to the questions, but it would show a person's process of thinking.

In time, those who had no idea what the question meant were annoyed and wondered what the question had to do with turning a wrench, but that is the way Ford saw things. His intelligence was the same way.

Just like his father before him, Ford was a silent man in the presence of people other than his family. At work, he listened more than he spoke and thought more than he listened. Ford was the quintessential thinking man, which is what characterized his genius.

The problem with deep thinking is that it sometimes cuts out the forces of reality. It is sometimes hard to come out of one's own thoughts and apply them to the world outside. It is also hard for others around the thinker to realize what he is doing. Ford faced the same issue. For that, he had a solution: Clara.

Clara formed the bridge between him and the world around them. Without Clara, Ford would not be able to understand the world as he saw it and wouldn't be able to interpret his thoughts and apply them to the world around him.

Clare was also the bridge between Ford and Edsel. Ford wanted Edsel to have so much more than he did. He also wanted Edsel to advance the skill set and knowledge that Henry had fought to acquire. For this reason, he pushed Edsel in many ways. He loved Edsel but thought he was weak.

Because he knew he had to be tough to manage the Ford Motor Company, he wanted Edsel to be sharp and intelligent, which Edsel was but not in the way that Ford had envisioned. That was the core of the friction between the two men. Henry for his part, however, loved Edsel deeply. He just never got around to showing it in a way that Edsel understood.

The situation worsened after Ford hired Harry Bennett, a famous boxing champion and former Navy sailor, as head of security. Bennett was responsible for running a tight ship at the River Rouge plant. Ford become close to Bennett over the years and saw a strong man in charge of things who couldn't be pushed around. It was the same kind of perspective he had hoped for Edsel, but Edsel was nothing like that.

The closer Henry got to Bennett, the more he felt disappointed by Edsel's approach to things. Edsel was more refined and thoughtful. Bennett was rough and direct. Bennett was the embodiment of what Henry wanted Edsel to be.

Because of this gap, it fell on Clara to be the bridge yet again between Henry and their son. Whether this helped or was more detrimental is hard to determine, but Clara always tried to bring the two men together.

The mind of a genius, especially in Ford's life, was both a boon and a curse. He could decipher the problem that others didn't even know existed and then fashion a solution to it inside his head. What didn't come to him naturally was the business aspect of it. That was just in the beginning. As time passed, he grew more adept with management style, and his ability to foresee the business angle of things allowed him to be one step ahead of the game.

Ford had ideas far beyond what most men could see— even his investors. The investors who financed Ford in his business were not willing to spend as much as he wanted, which led to friction on both sides.

When Ford first brought on investors, he didn't know how the investment and private equity world functioned. Financiers ended up dictating what Ford could and could not do, and he soon realized that his vision differed greatly from theirs. They were all about the bottom line with a short-term horizon; he was all about customer growth and satisfaction and a long-term horizon.

These were basic differences. When they first got together, no one really understood or appreciated how shrewd Ford really was. Once he had learned how the financing world worked, he did not like the way he was being pinned down to do things he didn't like, so he played a ruse on them.

He started off by making Edsel chairman of the company. That alone caused everyone to feel a little uncomfortable. Then he told them that he was getting ready to start his own car production company, which caused all his investors to find a buyer for their stock, and Ford scooped them up at a low price.

The genius of Henry Ford is evidenced in two ways. For a boy from the farmlands of Michigan who never had formal schooling, he certainly understood how high corporate finance worked.

He also knew human nature very well and knew what the investors would do when he behaved a certain way. In this instance, he and Rockefeller had the same way of thinking.

To draw a comparison between Rockefeller and Ford, just consider a similar episode that took place in Rockefeller's business life.

In January 1865, when oil was struck in Pithole, Rockefeller asked Clark to sign for another loan. Clark was incensed and didn't keep quiet. He said to Rockefeller, "We have been asking too many loans in order to extend this oil business." Rockefeller replied by saying, "We should borrow whenever we can safely extend the business by doing so."

To check Rockefeller, the three Clark brothers tried to intimidate him by saying they would break up the relationship between the partners by ending it. To do this, all partners needed to agree, which would mean the end of the business. This was not the first time or the last that they tried to intimidate him by threatening dissolution, but Rockefeller had wised up to the trick and decided to use it to his benefit.

Rockefeller wanted to end his relationship with the Clark brothers and was finished with working in his current business of selling and buying on behalf of others. Rockefeller was successful in getting Andrews to join him in his venture and break off from the Clark brothers.

He said to Andrews, "Sam, we are prospering. We have a future before us, a big future. But I don't like Jim Clark and his habits. He is an immoral man in more ways than one. He gambles in oil. I don't want this business to be associated with a gambler. Suppose I take them up the next time they threaten a dissolution. Suppose I succeed in buying them out. Will you come in with me?"

Andrews agreed to join Rockefeller since he, too, could plainly see that his fortunes would fare better by staying with Rockefeller than the crazy Clark brothers. Several weeks later the trigger for Rockefeller to enact his plan took place. He had an argument with his first Clark partner, who said he would break up the partnership of the produce firm. "If that's the way you want to do business we'd better dissolve, and let you run your own affairs to suit yourself."

On February 1, 1865, Rockefeller prepared for the final blow. He called his partners to his home and talked about how they could expand their business in a way he knew the Clark brothers would absolutely dislike. Jim Clark tried to intimidate Rockefeller into backing off by saying, as before, "We'd better split up." Rockefeller then asked everyone to say whether or not they supported the breaking up of the partnership. They all did, but they were merely using it to threaten him and when they left his house that night, they thought nothing of it and were confident they had gotten the better of him.

After the Clarks left his home, Rockefeller quickly rushed over to the *Cleveland Leader* newspaper office and demanded that an announcement be printed in the papers that the partnership was breaking up. The newspaper ran the notice in the next morning's edition, and before even getting to the office, the brothers saw it.

When the Clark brothers saw this announcement, they were stunned. Rockefeller's first partner, Maurice B. Clark, asked Rockefeller, "Do you really mean it? You really want to break it up?" Rockefeller replied by saying, "I really want to break it up."

In the end, it was decided that the oil refinery division of Clark and Rockefeller would be auctioned off. It turned out that the bidders for the auction were Clark and Rockefeller themselves. Essentially, the buyout would mean that the company would go to either the Clark brothers or Rockefeller.

By this point, Rockefeller was a man who could handle the most difficult situations with ease. His character was also such that when the people around him became more upset he became even more poised.

When the Clark brothers went to the auction, they had a lawyer with them who was the auctioneer himself. Rockefeller, however, did not bring a lawyer of his own. He thought he could handle it himself.

The bidding began at $500. It then increased to several thousand dollars. Then it reached $50,000, $60,000, and $70,000. By this point, Rockefeller was afraid that he would not be able to make the purchase. Then, the Clarks put up $72,000. Rockefeller quickly bid $72,500. Clark let go at that point, and Rockefeller asked, "Shall I give you a check for it now?" Clark denied it and said Rockefeller could pay when he was ready. It was a gentlemanly gesture, and he was shocked that Rockefeller had amassed that much money to make the purchase.

It turned out that Rockefeller's strategy of being prudent and being bankable worked to his favor. When the time came, he had lined up a line of credit from the banks that supported his takeover of the company. It was with their backing that he had the strength and tenacity to bid the price up to that level.

The price of $72,500 in 1865 would be about $1.2 million today. Although the price was high for the time, it was an important purchase. Rockefeller was just twenty-five years old and owner of the largest oil refinery in Cleveland, which was refining five hundred barrels of oil every day. Approximately two weeks after the Clarks met with Rockefeller in his home, the *Cleveland Leader* announced that Rockefeller had purchased the firm of Andrews, Clark, and Company. It went on to say that Rockefeller had purchased all the materials of the company, and that work would continue under the firm of Rockefeller and Andrews.

Both Rockefeller and Ford had learned how to take on those who had leverage over them. They managed to get out of the binding agreement in a way that was smart and clean. In Rockefeller's case, it was the Clark brothers; in Ford's, it was the Dodge brothers.

In the case of Henry Ford, there was a significant difference in doing business that is not widely practiced today. Both despised unions. Although in Rockefeller's time there were no unions, there was the burgeoning pressure on trusts, and the government was interested in breaking up trusts. In Ford's time, the government was trying to instill labor laws, and with that came labor unions.

Ford did not believe in labor unions any more than Rockefeller believed in antitrust laws. Both of them stood fast against the government overreach. Ford, being the genius that he was, saw how the people in his factories needed to do their work. He was not interested in keeping them as slaves, but he was strict that their hands were his when they were on the clock.

Bennett helped him in this regard. Bennett hired thugs and gangsters whom no one else would employ because of their criminal record. Bennett would make the rounds around the River Rouge plant, and he would not allow people to take breaks or chit-chat during working hours.

Ford treated his workers with respect and paid them well. He did not discriminate in hiring policies. He would just as soon hire nonwhites as whites, and he would just as soon hire those with physical disabilities as someone in perfect health. His concern was whether or not the person had the intelligence to work and the honesty to put in a good day's worth of work.

In this way, he did not encourage extended breaks and chatter during the assembly line process. How could he? The profitability of the company was based on how many cars could come off the assembly line. At one point, the Ford Motor Company was producing over a thousand cars per day.

Most people were in awe with the number of cars that were produced in a fully integrated plant such as the one in River Rouge, but they failed to see that to be successful Henry had to be strict with the policies of how the workers did their job. If they were busy chatting and not doing the work, one of two things would happen: (1) the line would slow down, which would result in fewer cars per day and increase the cost per unit or (2) the quality of the assembly, whether they were making finished cars or assembling magnetos, the quality of the product would suffer if employees were distracted by chatter. This is why Ford was strict about talking on the job.

Unions had a problem with this policy. Unions wanted the workers to be given the freedom to do certain things, and the collective bargaining they had was a disruption to work in Ford's eyes.

In that way, Ford and Carnegie were not different.

Carnegie had quelled a strike, popularly known as the Homestead Strike. During that time, Carnegie's head of security brought in mercenaries, or paid security professionals, to break up the strike. It was no different from what Ford did decades later at his plant.

At the River Rouge plant, Bennett's goons had beaten men who were urging the workers to unionize. The men were beaten up badly and then forced out of the factory. In the end, they managed to prevent the start of a union at the plant. That didn't last long, however, and Clara later convinced Ford to let the unions come into the factories.

The mind of a genius sees things in only one way—in this case, Ford wanted to put a car in every garage, and to do that he had to make it affordable. To make each unit affordable, he had to push the assembly through the plant at the best rate possible. He couldn't achieve the best rates when the men were chatting and taking time off.

That was why he was paying above-market rates, which provided two benefits: (1) it gave him a steady stream of workers so that he could boot out anyone who was not working well without worrying if he could replace that man and (2) he could tell them to do what he wanted without cause for revolt. But the unions would alter that equation. Even though he paid them well, the unions would ask for things that would slow down the production levels of the assembly line.

What he didn't see, however, which is what others saw, was that to the outside it looked as though he was driving a slave factory. How else would it look when you had guards walking around the plant and beating up anyone who was not working and then not allowing them to unionize?

Conclusion

Different men need to be looked at differently if you want to understand them on a deeper level. As much as we all share common traits, each of us is made unique by virtue of our experiences, our environment, our heritage, and our perception. We are further made different by the times we live in and our friends.

In the case of Henry Ford, many things affected him. Most important were his parents. He was extremely close to his father, but he was significantly closer to his mother. Her sudden passing was a blow that turned him inward. That event drew him closer to his father. The loss of his mother at a young age drew parallels in his mind between the circumstances he experienced and those his father had endured on board the Coffin Ship.

Besides his parents, Henry Ford was significantly influenced by Thomas Edison. The first layer of that influence came from his admiration as a young boy. The next layer resulted from the talks and correspondence he had with Edison. It was something that shaped his mind and moved his heart.

The challenges he faced in building his car and dealing with the patent infringement lawsuit with ALAM would have been enough to cause any man to give up and move on, especially since he was easily employable after his stint at Edison Illuminating Company. But it was Edison's words when they first met to "keep at it," referring to the Quadracycle, that made him relentless in his pursuit of the automobile.

For Ford, his relationship with his son was his greatest disappointment—not that Edsel was bad or behind at anything. Edsel was compassionate and smart in his own right. He had the pulse of the new generation, and his contributions were significant for the company's prosperity, but Henry's disappointment was about the way he treated his son. Henry, to the pain of any father, outlived his son, which gave Henry plenty of time to ponder and regret his actions.

To be clear, Henry did not neglect his son or love him any less. In fact, Edsel was the light of his life, and when he built the house in New York, he had specifically built up the grounds and included a tennis court so that Edsel could play his favorite sport. Henry wanted to raise a son who was independent and sharp—the way Henry was. What Henry missed was that Edsel had strengths in other areas. During the course of trying to raise his son in a way that Henry saw fit, he crossed his son in many ways that made Edsel feel unwanted and incompetent. But Henry had no such judgment against his son. Nonetheless, Edsel felt heartache before he died, and his father was heartbroken after Edsel died.

The sharpest pain for Henry came after Edsel died from cancer, and he started to realize the differences they had and was told by a close confidant that Edsel faced many difficult moments under his father. To this revelation, Henry asked this confidant if he had been cruel to Edsel. The man said he hadn't been cruel but was unfair.

That stayed with Henry for a long time and was something that he could never forgive himself for or forget.

The greatest influence in his life and the star that shone brightly for him was his wife. Clara was there through all the toils and challenges a young man could ever face all the way to the point when Henry lost control of his mind. The several strokes and the pain of losing his son had stretched his mind to the point of fracture, and it was Clara who held it together for him in the end—the same way she had always held him together and encouraged him.

The end was no different from the beginning. He and Clara were so in love with each other and had become so much a part of each other that even when Henry Ford had lost his mind he could not forget her.

During the last eleven years of his life, Ford suffered strokes. The first occurred in 1938, which was after the River Rouge plant had been completed. Production and operations were running fast, and the company had grown to a size that he was not sure Edsel could handle, but even though he was significantly slower than before, he continued. By this point, Edsel was also not in the best of health, but he still showed up for work every day, something that Henry did not fully understand. From that point, Henry had several other strokes, and each stroke left him weaker than the one before.

The strokes started to increase in frequency, and he was in precarious health after the passing of Edsel Ford in 1943. By this point, Bennett had taken charge of much of the operations, and Ford trusted him. Clara, on the other hand, didn't and thought Henry was being unkind to Edsel. She did not like the way Henry treated Bennett any better than Edsel, and she made it known as strongly as she could. However, it was hard to argue with Henry while he was stubborn and not always lucid after the first stroke.

After Edsel's passing, Clara eased up and decided to just focus on Henry. She was still strong and robust compared with him. By April 1947, Henry was weak and relied on Clara more than ever before. Not only was his body frail and he was unable to walk long distances or sit up straight for very long, but his mind was also not always clear, lucid, and coherent. He would often ramble in conversation.

It reached the point that he would follow Clara everywhere, and he was never fully aware of his surroundings. His last stroke took every last measure of his cognitive and physical ability. He was placed on his bed, and Clara had the housemaid call the doctors who were a few hours away. The conversation he was having before he died was about Edsel. After the stroke and while he was in bed, he didn't say anything. It was most likely that he had finally lost all ability to converse. He was restless, and Clara propped him up with more pillows. He recognized her, though, and sought refuge and safety in her arms. That seemed to comfort him, and he was at ease for the moment.

After some time had passed, he wanted the lights extinguished in the room, as they bothered him. The maid turned the lights out and opened the door so that the light from the other room would provide some illumination to an otherwise pitch-dark room.

As he sat up, more pillows were added for his comfort, but instead he chose to lean and rest his head on

Clara's chest. The two of them had been inseparable for almost sixty years since they married. It was April 7, 1947, just four days short of their fifty-ninth wedding anniversary.

As his breathing began to struggle once again, Clara soothed him by stroking his hands and patting his forehead, all while wondering how long it would take for the doctor to arrive.

As she kept him company and whispered in his ear, Henry became more peaceful. His breathing stabilized, and he appeared to be at peace. Being on Clara's chest was the only place he wanted to be.

By 11:30 that night, all had fallen silent, and Clara realized that the doctors wouldn't be there anytime soon and this was going to be the end. She remained strong for her Henry just as she had been through all his struggles and through all his medical conditions, and she had even been there for him while he grieved deeply for the loss of his only son.

As she sat beside him holding the frail body of the giant of the automobile industry, she could feel the changes in his breathing until it finally stopped. She held onto him for a little while longer and then gently placed him on his back. The genius who was responsible for mass production of the automobile and personal freedom, the man who pioneered and perfected inventory management and assembly line effectiveness died at 11:40 p.m. on April 7, 1948. He had lived a full life, a fullness defined by the contributions he had made.

The *San Francisco Chronicle* wrote that "Henry Ford was comparable only to Christopher Columbus in his impact on civilization in the west."

No truer words have ever been spoken.

Cornelius Vanderbilt

The Commodore

Cornelius Vanderbilt

The Commodore

Insight and Analysis Into the Life and
Success of America's First Tycoon

J.R. MacGregor

Introduction

Not many people would like the life that Cornelius Vanderbilt I lived. To many, his ways may seem uncouth and his methods beyond the pale. Before judging, however, it is best to remember that this was the Wild West of the 1800s. Placing twenty-first century ideals on nineteenth century life is not exactly being fair.

The Commodore himself probably wouldn't care about how one felt about him. Many people insulted him to his face, but it never bothered him at all. He was too busy to be offended.

What one should know about America in general and New York in particular, where he grew up, is that they were very different places then compared with where we are now. The differences in lifestyle, thinking, the environment, law, and politics were different in absolute terms. The only thing that remains similar is that the composition of New York then and now has always been ethnically, culturally, and religiously diverse.

What worked then to make it big still works today. If you look closely and choose to look beyond the crass words and tawdry actions, what you end up seeing is a boy who grew up with a very specific focus in life. He could not see anything else. All he wanted to do was take advantage of every possible situation and fight hard to stake his claim.

Thousands of immigrants were coming here and heading out to the territories to stake their claim in a new land, but Vanderbilt staked his claim right where he was born. He had elevated the game without a shred of education much less an education in some fancy academic setting.

By climbing and altering the way businesses were run, he set up the infrastructure for the next generation of industrialists to build on top of it. When the United States was in its early stages, Vanderbilt saw the importance of sea travel. He saw the importance of having a canal run through the isthmus in Central America long before it became a national security imperative to dredge the Panama Canal. It was Vanderbilt who spoke to the leaders of Nicaragua and obtained a lease for the land that extended from the Pacific to the Atlantic, a distance of 150 miles.

It was his idea to consolidate the fragmented railroads that came into New York, and it was his idea to build Grand Central Station, which still stands in New York City today. All this and more Vanderbilt did in a way that was focused and without distraction on the niceties of everyday living. He did whatever he wanted without caring for anyone's impressions or comments.

His character is worthy of study for those who wish to take the world stage by storm. The first lesson you will learn is that he never took anyone seriously—not in a hilarious and joking sort of way—but he never allowed anyone's ideas to influence his own mind and thinking. No one except perhaps his mother could influence him once he made up his mind.

It may be easy to fall into the trap of thinking that would be the best way to never learn, but in Vanderbilt's case, it didn't turn out that way. He actually listened intently but never told anyone that he actually did. He was in search of ideas and thoughts, but it had to be something that he thought of—the point being that he was too strong to blindly follow another's ideas, thoughts, and advice.

He was also not the kind of person to give his money to charity. The only person he gave his wealth to was his favorite son. Everyone else didn't get much by comparison. He didn't believe in philanthropy or inheritance. What he believed in was vision and hard work. As clichéd as that sounds, Vanderbilt embodied it.

Of all the robber barons and titans who lived, Vanderbilt was probably the crassest. Some biographers have called him vulgar, and others have pointed to his lechery, but this book will not critique a man who who died almost 150 years ago. That is not the purpose of this book, and neither should it be for any biography. Biographies are intended to instruct us from beyond the grave as to a path that should be considered. It is not up to us to label a man or pass judgment on him based on our own moral and ethical constructs.

One specific and interesting aspect of Vanderbilt is that he had no interest in being someone that he says he is not. In other words, he didn't pretend to be one thing and then act differently. What you saw is what you got. That takes strength.

Take philanthropy, for instance. He never gave a cent to any cause. In fact, the bulk of his will passed to only one of his sons. He didn't give for the sake of giving or to alter public opinion. In Rockefeller's case, it was different. He went to great lengths to polish his legacy by recording videos and giving to charity amidst fanfare and publicity. He was a pioneer in modern-day public relations.

For Vanderbilt, there was no such thing as a public relations campaign. He was who he was. He had no intention of being portrayed as anything or anyone else. He didn't need to be someone he wasn't, and he didn't need his own persona to be advertised. He was not a hypocrite or a charlatan.

On his commercial side, he was a cutthroat competitor. He was a visionary but also an imbecile. He couldn't read well and wrote phonetically. He had no use for grammar, punctuation, or an extensive vocabulary. On his private side, he was lascivious. He didn't have a sliver of magnaminity in his body, but most of all he never tried to convince anyone that he wasn't any of these things. He stood proud of himself, and if you want to learn from him, you have to take him as you find him.

Vanderbilt knew that his fortunes did not come from whether he was virtuous or upstanding. It didn't come from how much philanthropy he engaged in or how well he treated his wife. It came from how much he could carry, how reliable his delivery was, and how much it cost. As long as he handled that aspect of it, it didn't matter what he did or didn't do in his private life.

He was pragmatic and found tremendous freedom in that. Even his ability to fight was not wasted on bar fights and brawls. He fought hard when he needed to, but as soon as the fight was over, he'd move on without any malice other than a note to remember the person he had just brawled with. It was his cargo and his customers that he wanted to satisfy. They didn't need to know anything about him except that they could trust that he was reliable and would deliver their goods safely.

What was particularly distinctive about Vanderbilt as he built his reputation in and around the harbor and then up and down the Hudson River, and then all the way down the coast, was that he always delivered what he promised. The peace of mind that he gave his customers was worth every penny they paid him. His reputation preceded him in that way. People sought him out and tried to get the best bargain, but when they only got the bargain that he dictated, they knew that was exactly what they would get.

Vanderbilt was the consummate opportunist. He didn't tie himself down to a rigid business plan or fix his schedule and activity. Other boat captains would just sail their periaugers, sloops, or schooners, specializing in one thing or another. If a boatman specialized in ferrying passengers from Port Richmond to Manhattan, then that is what he did day in, day out, almost all his life, but Vanderbilt was an opportunist who took on any load at any time as long as he was paid, and then he promptly and consistently delivered.

This tied in with his desire to keep his vessels and later in life his trains full.

In his lifetime, he was one of very few people who were involved in a landmark Supreme Court case. The case would turn out to be the bedrock principle that dictated that the power to regulate interstate commerce was reserved to the federal government, and that states could no make law or enforce laws that were counter to federal law.

He built a solid base of steamships that grew from one to the next. He started sailing a 25-ton boat and finally built a 500-ton vessel that sailed down to Central America. The time that most men spend pondering and worrying about things that didn't matter Vanderbilt spent building his business.

Chapter 1 America at the end of the 18th Century (politics, economics, and social)

America had just declared its independence, but the battles Washington waged with Britain still raged on. We were formally declared as a country, but there still wasn't any leadership at the federal level. Washington was still leading armies in dozens of battles, from the Battle of Long Island in August 1776 to the Siege of Yorktown in October 1781.

From the time the dust settled after Yorktown, it took another six odd years for the Constitution to be written and another ten months for the states to ratify it. Until that point, the American government was given force by the Articles of Confederation.

Drafting of the Articles of Confederation started as soon as the Declaration of Independence was announced. It was submitted in a dozen days after the Declaration, but it took the Continental Congress more than a year to debate it and rewrite parts of it. At the heart of the problem that caused the delay was the issue of the powers that would be held by the national government.

Even before the Constitution was drafted, debated, and ratified, there was already a deep divide in the philosophy and principles of governing that preferred distributed governing rather than a centralized government. Based on their experience with Britain, no one wanted to cede their freedom to a concentrated center of power.

Once the Articles of Confederation had finally been ratified, it had departed somewhat from the original version drafted by John Dickerson. A compromise to leave some powers with the states and elevate some powers to the central government was reached. In its final format, the Articles of Confederation defined what the central government would be responsible for and that the rest would fall on the states to govern.

You can see that from the very beginning there was a split in the overall plan. Even with America born, the key issue was over who controlled what. Those who saw the value of collaborative unity saw the prosperity that could be achieved. Those who opposed a central power were still reeling from the effects of colonization and the power of London and the Crown over their lives. Both had a valid point to make.

Furthermore, under the Articles, the central government consisted of only a unicameral house (as opposed to the bicameral legislature we have now). There were no senators, just members of the House of Representatives who were chosen by the state's legislature. Regardless of land size or population, each state had only one vote in the House to ensure that the smaller states would not be ridden roughshod by the larger states. There was no provision for a president or an executive branch in any form, and there was no Supreme Court.

What's important to remember here is that there were two camps with a differing opinion. One wanted sovereignty over their own state, while the other wanted a centralized government so that they could bring about collective strength. That debate continues more than 250 years later in much of what we do and enact today.

The Constitution as we know it today didn't come about until 1787. It was in this Constitution that the Legislative, Executive, and Judicial branches of government were set up in Articles 1, 2, and 3 respectively. At the time of drafting the Constitution, there was yet another difference in opinion between those who saw the importance of unifying and those who were afraid of creating a new tyranny.

It wasn't until 1788 that General George Washington and sixty-five members of the House were elected. The Senate hadn't been set up yet and were originally chosen by the state legislatures unlike today's popular election in each state. It was only after the individual states had ratified the Constitution that two of each state's senators were chosen by their state's legislators and took their seat.

Once Congress was seated in April 1789, they passed the Judiciary Act pursuant to the requirement of Article 3 of the Constitution. This gave rise to the Supreme Court, which consisted of six justices at that time.

During the first few years following the Declaration of Independence, there weren't any political parties—no Republican or Democratic parties, no conservative or liberal groups—just newly minted Americans. The Founding Fathers were not inclined to adopt a party structure that had evolved elsewhere.

Early statesmen, such as Alexander Hamilton, Thomas Jefferson, and many others, did not initially believe in the need for political parties because they felt that they eroded the democratic process, put people and policies in silos, and brought unnecessary friction to a system that would work better when operated without friction.

Political parties only arose later because they were seen as the only tool available to organize the two sides of the divide. It is one of the reasons why the U.S. political system has been a two-party system. Before the parties got sidetracked by moral issues of liberalism and conservatism, they were arguing about where the power rested—with the states or the federal government.

The first party was formed in 1786 before the first election in 1788. The candidates, however, did not run on a specific party platform. When the party was finally organized, it was called the Federalist Party. As the name suggests, it believed in strong central governance and the need for the federal government to regulate, promote, control, and protect the states. They were primarily supported by bankers, businessmen, and the elite.

As soon as the Federalists came about to advocate the power of the federal government, the anti-Federalists were born to counter them. They were called the Democratic-Republicans, who were founded by Thomas Jefferson and James Madison. The debate over the adoption of the Constitution was vigorous. It was a time when the masses were consumed by politics and such people as Thomas Paine, who advocated the power of a strong federal government, wrote his pamphlet, *Common Sense*. It sold more than 150,000 copies, and James Madison wrote articles in the local newspaper that came to be known as the Federalist Papers.

In the end, the Constitution as it stood then could not be agreed upon between the Federalists and the anti-Federalists. The solution was to add ten additional amendments, which came to be known as the Bill of Rights. With that, the Constitution was ratified, elections were held, and the federal government started to take shape.

The adoption of the Constitution was a unique event and served, among other things, as the root of industrialization of the United States through the nineteenth century. That, in turn, formed the foundation for the success that the country enjoys today as the undisputed hegemony in today's geopolitical climate.

Before the Constitution was ratified and the subsequent industrialization, America was exclusively an agrarian society. Historians have zeroed in on the decade that saw the genesis of industrialization in America. Regardless of when other countries, namely Britain and France, underwent their industrial revolution, America's is deemed to have begun in 1790.

The 1790s, which can be seen as the decade in which a Constitutional America began, coincided with the introduction of industrial opportunities in addition to agrarian that had been the basis of the economy to this point. This went on until the 1860s when Abraham Lincoln was elected, the Confederate states seceded, and the Civil War ensued.

That period from 1790 to 1860 was critical in the development and foundation of America. On one side, immigrants were pouring in through numerous ports of entry, specifically New York. On the other side, resources from American agrarian efforts were being exported to the Old World. More than other ports in the North and South, New York bore the brunt of the heavy traffic. It also became the center for banking because farmers would receive and deposit money for their products and keep it in their banks in New York.

This made New York and the surrounding boroughs focused on banking, government (for a short period), shipping, insurance, and travel. As the city's population increased, the neighboring burroughs experienced an increase in sea ferrying. There was no bridge yet to speak of—construction of the first major bridge, the New York Brooklyn Bridge (we know it today as the iconic Brooklyn Bridge), only started in 1869.

The only way goods and people traversed the waterways between the islands of the New York City area was by small ferries. The surrounding area of New York City, not just Manhattan but also the waterways between the various land masses, was one of the busiest places in the country at the time. It was crowded with all sizes of boats coming and going and little ferries shuttling between them.

The issue of federalism versus states' rights was a battle from the first time the idea of forming a union emerged. In today's context, this battle can sometimes be lost because we have now been one nation seemingly forever, but it was not always so. Even the Declaration of Independence was a marriage of convenience to place a united front against the British. It was partially thought of as a means to an end, but then the Federalist argument gained traction because there was so much more to gain. State versus federal control still remains a wide-ranging issue. One such issue involved commerce within the states. The Supreme Court battle that settled interstate commerce involved shipping, and by extension, Vanderbilt himself.

At the end of the eighteenth century, America was getting ready for the likes of the robber barons that were about to alter the way the world worked and civilizations operated. Andrew Carnegie, John D. Rockefeller, Henry Ford, and JP Morgan were men of extreme accomplishment that were yet to arrive on the scene and make a big difference in the way the story of America unfolded. Before them, however, was another man—Cornelius Vanderbilt I.

Chapter 2 New York Trade and Industry

Even though the U.S. capital had been moved to its new location, New York continued to prosper as the heart at the center of life. There were shipping agents, hotels, trading houses, and other activity that supported its core business of commerce and finance.

New York City is a city like no other. It is not a city that is all in one place or bisected by a river that runs through it. In New York, various boroughs exist on different land masses. The Bronx and Manhattan occupy one island, Queens and Brooklyn sit on another, and Staten Island, to the south, exists on its own. Across the bay was New Jersey, and none of this was connected by any tunnel or bridge that would transport people and cargo between the islands.

At the start of the nineteenth century, three businesses dominated the New York landscape. The first and most important was the cotton industry, which featured cotton farmers who sent their cotton to New York to be loaded on ships bound for Britain. They were paid by buyers by way of New York banks.

Another product that was brought to New York was tobacco, which was then shipped to Europe. Tobacco farmers also deposited their proceeds from these activities with New York banks.

Besides these products were textiles, feed, corn and grain, and others.

Immigration was also increasing and considered a great resource for the country. It was also the inflow of new money and capital as well as new customers for everything from hotels to travel.

New York grew exponentially in the early part of the nineteenth century. As for Vanderbilt's success, aside from his own actions, his environment must be considered. It was a booming time for America in general and especially so for the development of New York Harbor and the city itself.

New York's dominance in the world of finance is entirely the result of the events that happened there at that time—from trading and shipping to banking and the railroad industry that flourished here to support the farmers who came from the inland states to export their produce as well as the imports that came from Europe—all converged on this small area.

From the day of his great-great-grandfather's arrival to the day he first piloted his own vessel in these waters,

Vanderbilt's life is the story of New York itself. Vanderbilt was tough as nails, which was the only way to survive at the time.

As he grew, so did New York, and as New York flourished, so did he.

Chapter 3 The Vanderbilts Before the 19th Century

Holland was a powerful country in the seventeenth century. It controlled large amounts of trade and shipping routes in tropical South America and Asia. Holland was also the first to make a claim for land in New York, which was named New Amsterdam before the British renamed it New York in 1664.

When Jan Aertsen Van der Bilt left the Dutch town of Bilt, which was just a few miles from Utrecht, he did so as an indentured servant. In the seventeenth century, between half and two-thirds of the immigrants who came to work in North American colonies were indentured servants.

The typical agreement that existed in the 1600s between an indentured servant and his master is that in return for his work and expatriation to a new land he would receive full travel, board, and lodging and would remain the servant of the master for a set number of years—anywhere between three and five years or more. At the end of that period, he was paid a certain consideration in the form of land, livestock, clothes, money, or some combination of that.

When Jan arrived in New Amsterdam, there were no immigration issues, and it was still part of his country. It was 1650, and he was twenty-three years old. He traveled to New Amsterdam and remained indentured for three years. He then received land, clothes, some money, and livestock. Jan settled in Bergen, New Jersey, and farmed the land he received. He then sold that farm and moved to the outskirts of today's Flatbush. The farm he purchased is located within today's Prospect Park.

He married Annaken Hendericks, who was also a Dutch immigrant from Doesburg, Holland. They were married in 1650 while Jan was still indentured. Annaken was born in 1620, while Jan was born in 1627, making her seven years older. They had four children together: Gerritje Janse, Aris Janse, Marittje Janse, and Aert Janse. Sometime after the fourth child was born, Annaken passed away. Jan then married his second wife, Dieber Cornelis, and had one child with her—Jacob Janse Vanderbilt. She brought along two children from her previous marriage. After she passed away, Jan married Magdalena Hanse and had one more son with her, Aris Janse Vanderbilt.

Our story today branches at Jan's third marriage and to the child from that marriage, Jan Janse Vanderbilt.

By the time Jan was married, he had already officially changed his name from van Der Bilt, meaning from the Village of Bilt, to Vanderbilt, a single family name. This he passed on to his progeny, including Aris Janse who was born in 1653 on the farm in Flatbush.

Aris and his stepbrother Jacob worked hard on their father's land, and they bought more land for investment with the help of loans, mortgages, and by working hard to pay off those loans. They succeeded in buying more land in the Flatbush area. Eventually, the two brothers accumulated close to one hundred acres of land in Flatbush and more land across the Hudson in New Jersey.

It was the same year that the Dutch built a fortification in the lower part of the city that ran from the Hudson River to the East River. The landscape of lower Manhattan today looks nothing like the landscape that originally mapped the island. What is today's Greenwich Street in the west was where land met the Hudson River. On the east side, where today's Pearl Street is located, is where the East River used to border.

The Dutch built a wall at the edge of that, which ran between the two rivers that defined the east and west shorelines and was called The Belt. It was called *Het Cingle* by the Dutch.

When the British conquered the city and Governor Peter Stuyvesant surrendered New Amsterdam to the British, it happened without any fight by the Dutch, and the Dutch colonists were allowed to stay peacefully. These included Jans and the rest of the Vanderbilts. Their citizenry was transferred from being that of Dutch to being English subjects.

Once the area was occupied by the British, the wall along *Her Cingle* was demolished, which had come to be known as Wall Street. The land below it, including areas of Battery Park today, was then reclaimed from the sea and built upon. Reclamation was also conducted on the East River embankment and on the Hudson as well. After years of reclamation and reshaping the island, the southern part of Manhattan that we know today finally came to be the shape it is as you see now.

Aris spent some time learning to speak and cultivate the land, and then joined his father, elder brothers, and stepbrother working the farm and helping the family put food on the table. The family was not as poor as some were in those days, but they lived hand to mouth and spent all their money on buying more landed property.

Aris eventually married Hillitje and continued working on the farm. Together, they had eleven children, including Jacobus Vanderbilt (named after Aris' brother), which is the line that leads to the topic of this book. Jacobus was born January 24, 1692. As the Flatbush area offered no more land for purchase, Aris turned his sights to other islands around the New York harbor. He found vacant land on an island that had been named after the Dutch Parliament, *Staaten Eylaandt*, by Henry Hudson. Hudson, although English by birth, was sailing under the Dutch flag when he came to the New World.

Aris purchased about eighty acres of land on the southern side *Staaten Eylaandt*, now known as New Dorp. It was a magnificent spread of land with clear views of the bay to the east and mainland New Jersey and Sandy Hook Bay to the south. Most of the acreage he purchased was densely forested. It is now part of the landscape that holds the remains of the Vanderbilt family, including Commodore Vanderbilt.

Jacobus, or Jacob for short, married Neltje Denyse and made a deal with his father to buy sixty-eight acres of the New Dorp land for a relatively low price of three hundred pounds. He had no cash to pay for it, so he struck a mortgage on the property, which his father held. As for his other properties, Aris divided them among his children. He died soon afterward, releasing Jacob's liabilities.

The land that Jacob bought was densely wooded. he cut down the timber to clear his land and used some of it to build a home for himself and Neltje. Here the Vanderbilts of the seventeenth century lived a sparse life of minimalism and frugality. The home they built was merely a shelter from the elements, the children shared beds and clothes, and the family ate what they harvested and slaughtered.

Jacob was unable to work all of the land, and they saved much of their meager earnings to buy a slave.

By 1720, Jacob had a few more slaves on his farm, but he was not a typical slave master. He worked with them and treated them relatively well. As he increased his enterprise, he was able to buy more land next to the original sixty-eight acres he had purchased from Aris— fifty acres that bordered his own land. By this point, he had twelve children, and everyone worked the land.

Among the twelve was Jacob Vanderbilt II, who would become Commodore Vanderbilt's grandfather.

It was around this time that the once Protestant Van der Bilt converted to Moravian teachings. The long line of Dutch Vanderbilts had been broken by Jacob II when he was the first of his family to have a wife who was not Dutch. Jacob II married Mary Sprague whose father was from New England and of British stock.

Jacob II had two children with Mary: Eleanor Johnson and Cornelius Vanderbilt (Sr). Cornelius was born August 28, 1764, in Rahway, New Jersey.

By this point, the British had already imposed the Sugar Act on the colonies. It was the beginning of taxation without representation in the colonies, and the thirteen existing colonies at this time were starting to rumble beneath the surface with revolt.

At the time of his birth, Cornelius Vanderbilt, Sr. was part of a well-known family. The Vanderbilts were upstanding members of the Staten Island community. They were bilingual, spoke Dutch and English, and were all senior members of the Moravian church. They had been involved in the building of *Irene*, the ship that sailed between New York and Holland to rescue Moravians persecuted for religious beliefs.

The population of the New York city area around 1700 when Jacob I was born was about six thousand. By the time Cornelius Sr. was born, it had doubled to twelve thousand. The American Revolution was around the corner, and Cornelius Senior was about two years old when Jacob II passed away. Much of the land that had been in the family in the New Dorp area was slowly whittled away and given to other children and relatives. The prosperity that was to be enjoyed at birth was slowly dwindling, and two years later Mary Vanderbilt passed away, leaving Cornelius Sr. an orphan just four years old.

Those who had stayed near Jacob II during his lifetime and managed to scrape a living off of him were now running in the other direction not wanting to take Senior and raise him. He was finally taken in by an uncle who owned the Rose and Crown Tavern, which served British soldiers who had come to occupy the area. King George's son, Prince William Henry, frequently stayed here on his deployment to the colonies. Sir William Howe, the British general, also camped here for most of the war.

Senior worked the tables, took out the trash, and mopped the floors from the time he was five. He wasn't sent to school and was illiterate all his life. The experience of being put to work in such harsh conditions at such a tender age altered his trajectory and made him bitter with a rough demeanor. He grew up to be a man who had no patience for anyone else and was always negative in his outlook. He passed a lot of this on to his son later in life.

By the time he was an adult, Senior did not get any part of his father's vast acreage in New Dorp. It had all been given to relatives and later sold. He left New Dorp when he was sixteen and old enough to strike out on his own, but he only got as far away as Port Richmond on the north side of the island, just across from today's Bayonne.

Here, Senior got a job as a sailor. He was to sail periaugers, a thirty-foot, two-masted flatboat that carried produce up to Upper New York Harbor around lower Manhattan and Jersey City. This area was busy in the 1700s and early 1800s with exports increasing and immigrants arriving. By the time Senior started plying these routes, the British Navy dominated the scene.

He was a hard worker. He kept his head down, not wanting to get into trouble for anything and just kept doing his job. He saved every penny, not wasting any of it on drink or anything fancy. In time, he saved enough to get his own periauger and was able to now ply the same route for all the profit. When he turned twenty-three in 1787, Senior met and wed Phoebe Hand. The two were polar opposites, but Senior was a handsome man, and Phoebe fell in love with him on sight.

She was also of British ancestry just like Senior's mother, and she, too, had been orphaned at a very young age. In her case, however, she was educated and had been surrounded by educated people. This union had tremendous benefit for Senior, as she guided him on what to do and how to expand his business.

Phoebe was raised by the family of a Protestant minister in Rahway, New Jersey, and she brought that culture and piety to the home of Cornelius Vanderbilt, Sr.

Chapter 4 Cornelius

Senior had worked hard before the marriage and worked harder afterward but this time with more direction and purpose. When he was young, he did not drink or gamble, but as he grew older and after getting married, he took to drinking rum. Phoebe, however, had a hand in keeping all that to a minimum and being frugal with the family's finances.

Once married, they rented a small farm and house that overlooked the water in Port Richmond, and with her great stewardship and his hard work, they saved enough to buy that farm. It wasn't just Senior's earnings that went toward buying it but also a lot of her inheritance.

Senior tilled the farm, and they had four children while he was still running the periauger service up and down the harbor. The produce from the farm was enough to feed the small family of six. Life was not easy but certainly a lot better than what Senior had faced after his mother's passing.

They named their children Mary, after Senior's mother; Jacob after his father; Charlotte after Phoebe's sister, and Cornelius Vanderbilt I, who was born May 27, 1794. The war was now over and the

British mostly gone—at least the soldiers were—and General George Washington was now President George Washington. More Vanderbilt children were to come, but that would happen in the next house the family moved to.

In late 1795 once Cornelius Junior was a year old, Senior decided that it was time to move to a larger home. The Vanderbilts sold their waterfront farm and moved to a house overlooking the Narrows and Brooklyn on the east side of the island. Here they had five more children. Not all of them survived, but in sequence, they were Phoebe, named after Senior's wife; Jane; Eleanor; Jacob; and Phoebe. The last two were born and named for two other Vanderbilt children who had died young.

Even though the house was more expensive than the last and stretched the family's expenses to the brink, it was not a bad investment in any way. Due to Phoebe's expert hand and constant frugal ways, she raised all her children and her husband with the guidance and love of a saint. The kindness of a preacher's daughter was something that saw the family through all the ups and downs that raising a big family entailed.

In retrospect, this home was worth the extra sweat and toil because of its great influence on Junior. The house sat a mere two hundred feet from the beach and offered a first-class view of the various ships that sailed up the Narrows into New York Harbor.

As young Cornelius sat by the window and looked out, the view was never the same two days in a row. He could see sails of navy frigates and European freighters as well as schooners and brigantines. By the time he was four, he knew what all the ships were and where they were coming from. He had a head for the colors and sails.

Junior knew that his father sailed up and down the harbor. He couldn't wait to do the same. It created a desire in his heart and sharpened his will to do more than just sit around watching the boats sail by. Records indicate that Senior was only able to launch and offer his services by using a few periaugers that he bought and hired other sailors to operate. That is how they made their money and paid the bills. Rumors suggest that Senior had a ferry service and passed that down to Junior, but this cannot be confirmed. It seems more likely that Senior hauled produce and did not ferry passengers.

Nonetheless, the business of hauling goods and produce went well, and the Vanderbilts did not have significant problems while Junior was growing up. The beach offered more than just a view of magnificent boats. It also offered many activities during the summer months. As the weather became hotter, children would find their way to the shores and play. Young Vanderbilt loved riding horses and would do so without a saddle even at a young age.

He was able to tame wild horses by the time he was seven and ride along the eastern shore of Tompkinsville.

He was naturally athletic, which made him a natural at running, horse riding, and even boxing in his later years. The outdoors and everything athletic came to define Junior's preteen years and even his young adulthood to a lesser degree. He also had a sharp mind and soon wanted to make money in any way that he could.

The young Vanderbilt was rough and tumble. Although he was handsome and charming, he did not have any problem with getting in the dirt to beat up someone. There was nothing refined or gentlemanly about him, which he freely admitted.

By the age of eleven when his elder brother died, Junior was now the eldest boy in the family, and it fell on him to help his father with ferrying. He did this gladly since it called upon two of his dearest attributes—to make money and sail. He started off taking one of his father's periaugers and going up to the Battery (south of Manhattan) and charging customers of opportunity that came along. He made a few pennies every day, and was doing what he loved. He was significantly much more daring than his father and would make many trips each day if the wind and tide allowed.

As he became more familiar with sailing and the bay area, Senior hired another boy, and the two of them would take the vessel out on more runs, and he would get paid a decent wage by his father. He made more money now than before, and the work was more consistent.

But it wasn't as good as what he learned to do next.

South of Staten Island between Raritan Bay and Sandy Hook the ground rises up just under the surf. Most of the pilots who came up the lower bay knew a sandy shoal is here and avoided it. Sometimes, however, cargo ships had inexperienced pilots and ran aground. When this happened, the law indicated that salvage operations could be conducted, and the salvage operator had all rights to the salvaged goods.

Junior and his father would constantly keep their eye on Sandy Hook and rush down to a disabled ship and unload goods and then sell what they salvaged. In many cases, Junior made more money through salvage work than with his daily operations.

Chapter 5 Enterprise and Negotiation

Junior had two things going for him at this point in his life: (1) he had an innate desire to do something with ships. He absolutely loved anything that moved on the water, and (2) he wanted to make money in any way that he could. Considerable evidence indicates his desire to make money for both the sake of living an opulent life—a life that money and wealth can buy in terms of material accumulation—as well as the power that entails.

The United States at that time had no railroads or steamships, and the Industrial Revolution had not yet occurred.

The Industrial Revolution had just altered the way America went about its business. Until just after the American Revolution, productivity had increased, and textiles were now a major export as was cotton. The period in New York after the war saw a rapid increase in population. The increase in activity in and around the harbor bode well for the Vanderbilts, and their on-demand ferrying business did well. The only limiting factor in all this was Senior. He did just enough to get by and would not work harder than was absolutely necessary.

Junior saw the world differently. He wasn't blinded by the pain of a rough childhood. He had his mother and father and to a certain extent his brothers and sisters who were always there in a safe and secure environment. His mother had given him the start he needed, and he was clear in his thinking and ambitions. He didn't know how he was going to do it. He just knew he would be successful.

As any young man thinks, Junior wanted to do what he knew best, and this was the Upper and Lower Bay—where he knew how to maneuver his little craft and get goods and people to the many different shores that lined the harbor.

As he was still a minor, he was unable to leave home and make it on his own. So he came up with a plan to advance himself. He was after all sixteen years old and ready to hit the world just as his father had done when he left the tavern. In this case, however, it was also his mother who couldn't bear to see her eldest boy flung far away from her care. Junior recognized the leverage he had. He wanted more but only had his youth and strength to trade at this stage of his life. It was the first evidence of his ability to want something, work at it, and then execute the plan needed to be successful.

He was quite the negotiator and told his parents that he wanted to earn a living on one of the boats that were sailing out, and that he was old enough to be able to do it. He seemed to try to convince them that letting him go on one of these ships would enable him to make the money he wanted.

His mother strenuously objected but could see that he was determined. His father, who didn't think it was such a bad idea, didn't acquiesce mainly because he wanted his son close to him to help with work and because he knew Phoebe would be upset. What they both didn't know is that they were being played.

Junior then told his parents that if they didn't want to let him go at least they should loan him $100 (this was circa 1812, so that value is approximately $2,000 today) to buy his own periauger. Compared to permitting him to board a transatlantic cargo ship, the periauger idea was significantly more palatable. Both parents agreed.

They did, however, attach some conditions to the loan. The first was that they shared his profits for the rest of the year in addition to paying back the $100. The second was that he had to clear an acre of land that the family owned.

Junior agreed. His plan had gone off without a hitch. He got to work on the land and within a month had it cleared out. Then he bought his own periauger. It is said that the day he got into his own vessel he could feel the exhilaration. He fancied himself a captain of one of those ships he saw sailing up the Narrows. It was what he had wanted to do from as far back as he could recall.

This experience set the path for the rest of his life. It began to occur to Junior that he could get anything he wanted if he just desired it and then set his own brand of negotiations.

He had displayed a significant ability to negotiate, but it was not the kind of negotiation we think of in our daily life. Junior had the innate ability to foresee the path to getting what he wanted, and he would lay the strategy so that his counterparts would follow like lambs to the slaughter. In time, as he matured, so did his ability to negotiate until it took on a competitive shade, even being unscrupulous at times. As time passed, he only got better at it, and all he wanted to do was to get the next goal and the next pot of gold.

Then came his next challenge. At this point, he was in debt for $100. As much as the loan was from parent to child, he saw it as a ball chained to his foot. His first job was to pay off this debt and give the profits to his parents for the following year.

He paid off the $100 within six weeks and then in the course of the year netted his benefactors a shade over a thousand dollars in profit. This was the path to his second lesson in life. With the burden of debt on his shoulders, he had to make every fare and fill every last square inch of space on his periauger every day that he was sailing.

He learned about capacity utilization at sixteen in the same way that MBAs learn it in Ivy League B-schools except he learned it on the job. He would sail in the foulest of weather and on the calmest of days when it was enticing to just lay back on the beach and enjoy the sun on one's face or go to the local tavern. Junior would have none of that. When conditions were bad, he would sail; when the weather was good, he would double his efforts. His philosophy was to keep his asset working at all times to generate the most amount of income. Keeping his transportation full was more important than the price that was levied on the customer. In later years, he would have the same strategy when dealing with Rockefeller's oil coming out of Titusville. He would give a 30 percent discount to the average price so that Rockefeller would fill his trains rather than letting them run at partial capacity.

At sixteen, Junior proved himself to be a tough teenager. The shores of Staten Island were a nice place to relax, especially in summer, but the ferry business was not something that was filled with niceties and fun. It was a cutthroat business. Many of the fights that Junior had were fights with other competitors who didn't like that he was always making money while they weren't. Some of the strategies they did not like were that young Cornelius would undercut the prices he charged someone just so that he could keep his hull full.

They also didn't like that he would charge above-market rates when it was raining or the surf was choppy. He took risks that others wouldn't and charged more for it. Junior had the innate ability to understand pricing and charging mechanisms. He understood the equations of supply and demand and realized that a full hull at a cheaper price was better than a partially empty hull at a more expensive price. This strategy was something he also applied later in life when he ran ships down to Nicaragua.

He became involved in his Southern shipping business when he wanted to take advantage of the Gold Rush. When East Coast residents were paying almost a thousand dollars to cross the plains, Junior devised a way to sail them down to Nicaragua, where he could find a relatively narrow part of the isthmus, and then load his customers on a land journey to the Pacific coast. He would then ship them on another boat up to California. It saved each passenger time and hundreds of dollars. He had undercut all the stagecoach businesses that were going from both coasts and the other ships that were rounding the Cape in South America to make the trip.

Operators who were losing big money decided to pay him $50,000 per month just to get him to stop his service. How many businesspeople can one name who would be paid to stop doing what they were doing? That is how efficient he was at doing what he did.

He then developed his next skill in the harbor area. After spending the first year running the ferry service and paying off his parents' capital and profits, he zeroed in on his second boat. He borrowed the money necessary, but this time he only borrowed a quarter of the amount he needed instead of the full amount. He had already saved all the rest. His second boat was piloted by two other sailors whom he hired. He was notoriously vicious with the schedule. He never left it up to the sailors as to when they would sail. He decided. They sailed whenever he told them to, and he would fill up two vessels every day regardless of the weather. If the sailors were not doing a good job or hesitated, he would fire them. If a fight broke out between him and the sailors, he would take them on, and he never lost a fistfight with one of these rough and tough men.

He paid off the debt owed on the second boat within two weeks, and then it dawned on him that there was enough capacity in the harbor to warrant even more boats. By the time he turned eighteen, he had four periaugers, all of them were paid for in full, and they were working across the water on a daily basis. His loads were always at capacity. At this point, he started to calculate that it was time for a larger boat. Junior realized that periaugers weren't the best craft for New York harbor. In the fall and early winter, it was windy, and the periauger, which does not have a keel, was not the best vessel to maneuver the waters. When a vessel has no keel, it can't control the tendency of the boat to slip sideways in the direction of the prevailing wind. It was hard to maneuver, and there was an overreliance on wind and tide conditions. That was one of the main reasons why strong currents dictated that periaugers would only sail in when the basin filled with the incoming tide and sailed out when the basin drained at low tide.

He decided that a sloop would work best for him. He zeroed in on one that was sixty-five feet in length. With its keel, single headsail, and fore and aft rig, he concluded that it would be a better craft to use on even the harshest days. He was already out on the water more often than most periauger sailors on the bay, and now with the sloop, he would do even better. He commissioned the ship in 1813 and set sail that summer when he was nineteen years old.

What made it even better was that the deep centerboard hull allowed him to make many more trips between Manhattan and Staten Island because he was no longer at the mercy of the tide and wind.

He christened the sloop *Swiftsure* after the British warship. Since he was a young boy, he had fancied himself as a British navy captain, and this was his first opportunity to live that fantasy.

For all his desire to captain a boat in the British navy, he was not in any way loyal to the navy, the British, the Americans, or the Dutch. He was in it for himself. He didn't care whom he worked with or what flag flew high above him. He was more interested in the tangible effects of the world around him than the abstract matters of state and loyalty.

Chapter 6 1812

Napoleon took power in France in the wake of the French Revolution. He quickly moved to become emperor by 1804. Within four years, he had waged numerous battles against other European countries and conquered a sizeable portion of Europe.

More importantly, Bonaparte had the hearts and minds of the French. The British were on the run in many places, and Napoleon defeated the British in several sea battles.

The British constantly needed to replenish their ranks with sailors and started to look to America. In the Treaty of Paris, which was signed after the American Revolution, Britain had agreed to hand over the forts they had occupied. Almost two dozen years had passed since the signing of the treaty, but the forts had still not been returned. The British were using those forts to blockade the French from trading with the United States. The French were allies of the newly independent colony since it was because of the French that Washington was able to defeat Lord Cornwallis.

The British army was also capturing, or "impressing," local sailors and putting them in the British navy to fight Napoleon. Both of these actions were an act of war.

It all came to a boil on the eve of 1812, and the busy trade all along the waters of New York's harbor dwindled to almost nothing. Between the blockade at sea that halted trade and the indiscriminate capture of sailors, New York activity had come to a halt.

The government had decided that they would not stand for it, and along with the battle that ensued between America and Britain, the army started to build batteries and walls with canons along the harbor.

The Army Corps of Engineers was called in to build the necessary walls, embankments, and other defensive structures to protect the harbor and New York City. While all the other periauger boat sailors and captains of the other ferries had slowed down during the blockade, Junior was one of the few who started offering contracts to the U.S. Army to ferry men, equipment, and supplies to various areas of construction in the bay.

What had been a downfall for most of the sailors and ferry operators was actually a tremendous opportunity for the industrious Vanderbilt. During the war, it has been said that Junior was the only one who was willing to exchange passage for payment regardless of the weather. He continuously kept his boats full during the lean years of the War of 1812.

Even though few sailors were active in the harbor, and all who did worked for Vanderbilt in one way or another, their lean years became his first golden opportunity. When others went out of business, he bought their boats and expanded his fleet with the contracts he received from the army.

With more boats, a secure contract, and few competitors, Junior started to see what it was like to have a meaningful amount of money. He started to spend it on loose women who were present in areas with sailors. It was at this time that he started to behave this way himself. He was not a drunkard, as he didn't want to lose his senses or his money, so he wasn't interested in drink or gambling. It was always about women, especially those who were cheap. This activity excited him, and it didn't stop even after he married or could afford significantly better.

He had become a businessman by this time and was far more astute than his father. The Dutch Van Der Bilt genes he shared with his grandfather, his uncles, and great grandfather who had worked hard and developed the lands in Flatbush and New Dorp, between which he sailed his growing fleet, had a lot in common. He was indeed a businessman by instinct, and he knew how to apply muscle and brain to the same problem. That ability to think about, take advantage of, and work hard at anything and everything he did brought success to him in every undertaking in which he became involved.

By this point, Junior had developed into a strong man with a purpose. He found that making money was significantly easier for him than his father. He also started to realize that making money was a state of mind that absorbed him. He no longer had anything or anyone more important to him than the concept of making money.

This subconscious and superconscious (at the same time) state of existence turns every endeavor into materialistic pursuit. There was nothing bad about this. In fact, it made him supereffective and superefficient in all activities.

He had upgraded from the periauger to the sloop. It was not that he was a trained seaman. He learned on his own and observed. His state of mind was that he was always looking to improve himself. In the case of the upgrades, he realized that the boat that he wanted would do better than the boat he had, and that would translate to more money. For as long as his father was ferrying people across the bay, he never once taught of trading up. He was happy where he was and did just enough to get by. Junior was significantly different. His ability to trade up was inherent and persistent.

Also important at this time were his relationships with the opposite sex. He was a transactional person. It didn't matter if he was trading with sailors or brothel workers, it was always just a transaction—nothing more and nothing less.

This transactional attitude with all things that he undertook and his ability to always trade up meant that Junior was always a person in search of a better deal in return for something that he didn't want. His later dealings with Rockefeller also exemplified this trait.

Of all the people he dealt with, from his father down to his children and all the ruffians and sailors on the shore, he showed only some form of deference to his mother and would listen to her if she lectured him. The same could not be said for his father or the woman he would soon marry. From the time before he proposed and married her all the way to the point when they lived in different houses later in life, he was never faithful to her. Their relationship was no more transactional than the fleeting relationships he had with his most favored lady of the brothel.

As 1812 drew to a close and the war still raged on, Junior was working hard at his business and playing hard at the seafront brothels of Manhattan. From all accounts, it didn't matter how much he played. He always appeared at work bright and early and ready to put in a sixteen-hour day. One activity never took away from the other.

Chapter 7 Converging Heritage

The Vanderbilt family lived all across Staten Island and Queens. Junior's grandfather, Jacob II, had a large holding of land in the New Dorp area. Aside from Cornelius Sr., grandpa Vanderbilt also had a daughter, Eleanor Vanderbilt, who was Senior's sister. She married a man by the name of Nathaniel Johnson. The couple had a son, Nathaniel Johnson II. which made Nathanial Johnson II and Junior cousins. Nathanial Johnson II married a lady named Elizabeth Hand. Phoebe's maiden name was also Hand. (Phoebe and Elizabeth were cousins.)

Nathanial Johnson II and Elizabeth Hand had a few children, one of whom was born in 1795 and named Sophia Johnson. That makes Sophia related to Junior twice over. Through his father, they are second cousins (Junior's aunt's granddaughter). Then again through his mother, they are second cousins.

This proximity in the family tree was enough for Junior's mother to reject the union. It was one of the few times that Junior refused to take his mother's council, and he persisted. She had a sultry and mesmerizing look with a hit of Phoebe's features that attracted him. As for Sophia, she was attracted to Junior's height, muscle tone, and charming good looks.

Even though Junior was enjoying the waterfront brothels, he still needed a transaction to get his family and a stable of sons lined up. Getting married to the prettiest girl on the northern shore in Port Richmond was also a feather in his cap.

It turned out that his mother was right. The bloodlines were too close to escape the effects of a consanguineous relationship. One of their children would later be born with epilepsy, which Junior could not tolerate.

After a relentless campaign to obtain his parents' approval, he eventually received it, and the happy couple were married December 19, 1813. The War of 1812 was still being fought, and the construction and military activities that still continued in the harbor caused Junior to continue working 16-hour days. He was back at work the day after the wedding.

From this point, it would serve us well to refer to Junior as Vanderbilt.

The couple got busy with building a family. They moved into a rented house not far from Senior and

Phoebe. That move was intentional because it allowed Phoebe to look in on them and also to keep her new daughter-in-law company.

A string of children soon followed, as was the tradition of the time. In all, there were thirteen children, almost born annually. In sequence, the children were Phoebe Jane in the middle of 1814, Ethelinda in 1817, William Henry in 1821, Emily Elmira in 1823, Sophia Johnson in 1825, Maria Louisa in 1827, Frances Lavinia in 1828, Cornelius Jeremiah in 1830, Maria Alicia in 1834, Catherine Juliet in 1836, and George Washington in 1839.

From all accounts, Vanderbilt and Sophia had a strained relationship. His transactional nature only saw her as the mother of his children. He never consulted her on his business or his plans. That he left to his mother and sometimes his father. His parents had continued to be his partners in the business starting from the first boat for which they loaned him the $100. All the subsequent boats also had their names on it even though his money paid for them.

Sophia's name was not on any of them.

She would look after the children while he was out working and strolling the waterfront. He would also not bring money home. He had her on a very tight budget to feed the increasing number of children, while he spent most of the money in expanding the business.

In part, this was done with Phoebe's approval. By the time the War of 1812 was over, Vanderbilt had added three more ships to his fleet. Two were schooners, and one was a larger sloop. These were launched in the summer of 1814 just after the Treaty of Ghent was signed officially ending the War of 1812. The timing could not be more perfect, as the harbor came back to life with more trade coming in, and the first pick of the business went to the man with the larger boats. Vanderbilt had swooped in at the right time and anticipated the upswing in trade in New York.

While he was putting money away for the expansion of his fleet, Sophia was managing the budget at home and making sure he always had a warm meal when he came home.

Even though money was always tight, they moved into a larger house a few years after the War ended and continued to have more children. Sophia continued to try to earn her husband's confidence but to no avail. She didn't give up hope, though, and continued to respect Phoebe and Senior, who came around as often as they could to see the grandchildren and make sure that Sophia was taking care of things.

With a number of the original periaugers still in operation and a couple of schooners and sloops plying the shores of upper and lower New York Harbor, Vanderbilt started to set his sights on routes farther up and down the Eastern seaboard.

He would still get into fights with other sailors and boat operators and always win. His reputation all along the shoreline was that of a tough character who needed to be respected. For lack of a better term, he beat his competitors into submission.

As the revenues went up, so did Vanderbilt's propensity to expand. He had no intention of staying stagnant, and now he was seriously considering a new venture. He would expand his routes beyond the bay area and started sending his ships up the Hudson River carrying grain to the mills and flour on the return trip. Now he wanted to venture to the south, but since he was not experienced in this area, he decided to take on his brother-in-law as a partner.

Charlotte Vanderbilt had married Captain John DeForest. He was a seasoned sailor and captain who had years of experience sailing up and down the Eastern coastline from Boston to New York and down to Charleston and Savannah.

Vanderbilt and DeForest partnered on a large schooner they named after Charlotte. The *Charlotte* was designed specifically to ply the open waters and navigate the rougher seas of the Atlantic. It was the largest vessel that Vanderbilt had ever owned. Captain DeForest and Vanderbilt made the maiden voyage down to Savannah in the fall of 1815, where he taught Vanderbilt all the theory and practice of open sea sailing. It was an eye-opening event for Vanderbilt and something he realized that he had wanted to do ever since the days of sitting in his parents' house across the Narrows as a toddler.

He was now on the open ocean, and the feeling was exhilarating, but he was there to make money, and he never forgot that. They reached Savannah and dropped off their maiden cargo and started their voyage back up north. Vanderbilt was able to learn and was quick at grasping the skills he needed to pilot his new boat.

On the way, they moored in Chesapeake Bay and filled the empty cargo bays with oysters. When they returned to New York, they sold the cargo for $1,500. This was in addition to the money they made from the maiden cargo they dropped off in Savannah.

In another example of profit at all costs and under all conditions, Vanderbilt displayed his ability to extract opportunity out of all situations. A typical captain would have just quickly sailed back to port to get back to his family or visit one of the taverns onshore. For Vanderbilt, it was always about business first.

When there weren't goods to ferry or passengers to put up with (he despised carrying passengers but did so only to maximize his haul), he turned to fishing. He would dispatch all his vessels up the Hudson across Long Island Sound and into the bay to catch shad. He would have the *Charlotte* go into deeper waters for a better catch. He would get other boatmen to convoy together and lay nets off the New Jersey coast and catch whatever they could. They could then come back to the docks and sell their catch to the wholesalers. He was never idle. If he didn't work sixteen hours a day, he would become grumpy, and Sophia would hear about it when he came home.

After returning to port, he assigned Captain DeForest to the southern routes on the *Charlotte* and sold all but one of the periaugers—the first one he bought. He also kept the other sloops and schooners. In all, he now had five vessels and four sailors and himself working them. They all worked twelve- to sixteen-hour days, and every penny that was brought in went to paying wages and saving for future expansion, while Sophia sat at home dutifully looking after Vanderbilt and raising their children.

Not once in all the time they were married did he ever update her on the business or ask for her opinion even though she was more educated than he was. He was almost illiterate and only able to read a little and write even less. He knew his numbers and how to calculate the shipping number he needed and the cost of money and the interest that was levied on his borrowings, but that was it.

Sophia had the patience of a saint. She waited for the time he would give her more attention and trust her advice, but she knew it was not her place to speak. She paid dutiful reverence to her in-laws and continued to serve in the best maternal role she could for her children. The more he excluded her from decision-making and sought Phoebe's counsel, the more she longed, but the moment she hoped for never came.

The only thing she had from the marriage was the thirteen children whom she loved dearly. She was a dutiful wife that he had married because she looked like his mother, but he never gave her the attention she deserved. In her last days, she remained in the mansion he built for her on Staten Island and died while he lived in the townhouse in Manhattan. She had chosen not to move to Manhattan.

Chapter 8 Opportunist

When you consider almost every wealthy entrepreneur, you will find that they have no loyalty to a single idea. Look at every robber baron or titan of the gilded age and you will find that to be true. Wall Street traders call it "not falling in love with a stock." In other words, you do not find one product and stay with it until you die. Bill Gates started with DOS and went to Windows. Steve Jobs started with the iMac and went to the iPhone. Carnegie started with iron bridges and went to steel, and just to make the point, Rockefeller started with produce and went into refining petroleum.

What all of them had in common was that they were opportunists. An opportunist in this sense is not about fleecing others when the opportunity comes up but to take opportunities of an enterprise when it arises in front of them. A blind man and an unfocused man will not see it and be inclined to pass on it.

In Vanderbilt's case, he saw vessels and ships pass in front of him every day, morning and night, and had ever since he could remember, and he dreamed of becoming wealthy, but then the time came to give it all up for an opportunity that was much greater than his seafaring vessels, and he gave it up after just a moment's thought. He sold his entire fleet to take advantage of the new form of transportation in America—trains.

His unemotional move from the boats he added one at a time and sailed each one had no bearing on this emotion or his nostalgia. He was not loyal to boating; he didn't fall in love with it. When the time came to trade them for something more, he did.

An opportunist needs certain characteristics to be able to make use of the opportunities that come his way. He must be pulled to them, not pushed away. Carnegie, Rockefeller, and Vanderbilt did not push their initial businesses away because it was hard to do. They didn't hesitate even for a moment because what they were doing was hard or causing them grief or even because they were failing at it. They didn't get pushed from what they were doing in search of an easier alternative. No matter how hard it was to sail the periaugers on the unpredictable waters of New York's harbor or how difficult it was for Carnegie to build his bridges and do so on time or how hard it was for Rockefeller to increase sales of his produce, they never left the business they had in hand because it was hard. They left it because they had something more that interested them.

Opportunists also do not fall in love with what they are doing and let an opportunity for advancement sail past them. If you see an opportunity that is better than what you are doing, then it's time to take what you have from this one and apply it to the next.

Opportunists do not confuse knowledge and skill for academics. Vanderbilt did not read many books in his life. In fact, it wouldn't be too much of a stretch to conclude that he did not read a single book in his life. He knew how to read a little, and Sophia taught him a little, and so did his mother. If there were things he didn't know, he relied on them to read it to him and even explain it as needed. His role model, Senior, was also fairly illiterate, and he, too, relied on his wife to relate the contents of mortgages or documents that needed his mark. What he lacked in academic schooling and formal education, however, he made up for in intellect.

The same can be said of Carnegie who only went to school until the age of thirteen, similar to Rockefeller, who only grazed past schooling for a short time as well—just enough to read. What all these men did know, however, was how to manage numbers in their heads. That was important in understanding what was important in their business.

Academics levy an opportunistic cost on the student. They get to learn all the theory they can possibly spread themselves offer in return they get to learn none of it in real life. They lose the ability to adapt their mind to realities and instead rely on formulas and rules. Vanderbilt relied on neither. You could say that he was a realist.

Opportunists are also humble. It is ironic to include Vanderbilt in any list that is derived from humility. The picture that his life paints does not seem to project that quality, but in fact he was humble. He did not see any job to be beneath him, and he did not see any fare to be beyond his effort. In other words, he would do the job as long as he had the time to do it and if he promised it.

When he wanted the seed capital to purchase his first periauger and managed to convince his parents, he had to clear a plot of land to make it ready to farm. The land had brush and trees, rocks and debris, and it took considerable work to clear it. He did not have the money to pay additional workers. When he set out to do the job, he did not see how much work was in front of him but only that there was a benefit at the end of the job—and it wasn't a hundred dollars. His benefit was the freedom to have his own enterprise. That made the effort at hand a small price to pay.

Vanderbilt's opportunistic ink was prevalent. He was colored by it in all aspects of his undertaking. It was also part of the reason he seemed transactional in all that he undertook. From his dalliances with waterfront women to his seemingly cold relationship with his wife and even his casual relationship with the people who came to work for him, he was evidently transactional. It was always about the transaction—this for that. He had no love for anything in his life—not his wife or his children. His only one true love may have been his mother, but even that may have been tinged with the ink of transaction. He trusted his mother's counsel and relied on her acumen for the business decisions he made. Even that, though, was a transaction.

There was no opportunity on the harbor that he did not try—from moving goods up and down the river, harbor, and eastern shoreline to fishing in the off days and even using his smaller vessels to sail up to ships and act as a delivery service for whatever they wanted from shore to be delivered to them, and even applied if what they wanted were services from the nearby brothels.

He certainly had a powerful imagination with what he could do with his vessels. That was how he was able to return the investment to his parents in six weeks and then give them a thousand dollars in profit within one year.

By 1820, the war had become a distant memory, and trade had started to expand rapidly. The growth before the war was admirable, but after the war it was even greater. The effects of the Industrial Revolution and the demand for goods that were coming out of America, between its natural resources, from fur to timber, for finished goods from textiles to ships, and in agriculture from corn to cotton, made New York Harbor alive with activity.

With the increasing business of the banks in New York, it was certain that ships that came from Southern ports would stop in New York so that bankers' agents could sight the cargo that was being exported. That meant that regardless of where the product was coming from or going to, it was more likely now that it had to stop in New York for banking and insurance purposes.

There would even be ship-to-shore transfers of goods coming from the South aboard vessels that were suited to ply the coast but not suited to sail the waters of the deep Atlantic. These ships would unload their cargo at the port and then sail back down the coast, while larger ships would load those items and then set sail for Europe.

Vanderbilt would often provide his services for all these activities, including the transfer of cargo from the ships that had no place to berth. They would anchor at sea and transfer the goods aboard their smaller ships to be unloaded at the port.

From transporting all kinds of goods across all the ports up and down the coast to contractual services and impromptu services, nothing was too good or too difficult for Vanderbilt. Within a few short years of taking ownership of the *Charlotte*, Vanderbilt was known in every port from New England to Georgia.

This was the height of his business as he knew it. Then came the next phase of his life—something that only an opportunist could see. Through the 1700s and the early part of the 1800s, most of the traffic that dotted New York Harbor was powered by the wind, tide, and oars. The power of the vessel was determined by how many masts it supported and how large a sail those masts flew.

Vanderbilt grew up seeing those sails and colors that stretched from the topsail to the jib in the fore to the mainsail and the aft jib. Now, a man by the name of Livingston had developed a new beast—the steam engine—with its boilers that burned pine wood to heat large amounts of water and use that steam to turn wheels that functioned as perpetual paddles.

When they first started appearing in the Narrows, Vanderbilt didn't think much of them. He pejoratively referred to them as "boilers."

Chapter 9 Steamers and Boilers

The New York shore was indeed dotted with an increasing number of sails that propelled most of the vessels that navigated the waters of New York Bay. Then an inventor in Britain by the name of James Watt improved the steam engine, which could be used to power textile mills that eventually altered the textile and cotton industries. The steam train was an offshoot of Watt's steam engine. That extended the global distribution of populations and remapped and refaced the world to what we see it today.

It wasn't the first time that steam had been used to create mechanical motion of a repetitive nature. The original inventor of the steam engine had accomplished the feat a few decades earlier. Coincidently, it was the year that James Watt That steam engine was indeed the start of the Industrial Revolution—a revolution that shook the known world and caused a seismic shift in how civilizations were organized. It was the same revolution that brought mechanization to mills, factories, and transportation.

Once Watts had refined and improved the steam engine, it was adapted in many other ways. By 1783, the steam engine had been adapted to boats. It was first done by two Frenchmen new Lyon. By 1787, the idea of a boat powered by steam had made its way to New York, and the New York Legislature passed a law (Law of 1787) that gave the inventor of steamboats monopoly over steamboats in New York. John Fitch was awarded the monopoly for fourteen years to operate steamboats anywhere in New York. Ten years later, Robert Livingston licensed that monopoly and entered into a contract to build the steamboat in a foundry in New Jersey.

Livingston was the first man to put a steam vessel into the waters of New York Harbor and sail it up the Hudson to Albany. Livingston was sent to France as the ambassador for President Thomas Jefferson. In France, Livingstone met Robert Fulton, and the two of them entered into a contract in 1802 to build passenger steamboats to shuttle between Albany and New York by way of the Hudson River. The following year the first steamboat on the Seine River in France successfully navigated a portion of the river that runs through Paris. Then Fulton steamed to New York, and Livingston received an extension for this monopoly. In 1807, the *Clermont* steamed up the Hudson to Albany and returned to Manhattan in a total of four days. That successful trip prompted the New York Legislature to pass a law giving monopoly to Livingston and Fulton for a five-year period and an additional five years for each steam-propelled boat they deployed on the river, for a maximum of thirty years.

This monopoly was a stranglehold on the industry, as the state government also added a new law that impounded any steamship that was caught infringing on the monopoly during the time the case made its way through the courts. That grew extremely expensive for those who were tempted to infringe on the rights of Livingston and Fulton. It was 1811.

By 1817, Vanderbilt was being stretched thin and even considered retiring. Captain DeForest was no longer there to help him keep an eye on things. Managing all his vessels and the men in his employ was becoming difficult. The pilferage alone, by his workers, on the fleet that stretched from Albany inland to New England in the North and as far south as Savannah was becoming unmanageable. In all, historians calculate that he had saved up about $9,000 in cash and about $9,000 in assets. If he liquidated his position, he would hold $18,000, which is about $300,000 today. Vanderbilt was twenthy-three years old.

This event showcases another layer of Vanderbilt. He had worked himself so hard and acquired a sizeable sum, but he did not have anyone he could trust to manage it. He wasn't sure how to take the next step or what that step would even be. He had competition from the steamers that were becoming more common along the shore, and he was not able to keep tabs on his operations.

His first encounter with a steamer was when he intentionally purchased a ticket for a round-trip from Manhattan to Albany and back. He sat observing the new steamer and how it worked. It was obviously one of the Livingston-Fulton steamers. Even he had to agree that it was a much better ride than the periaugers he first started out with and even as good as one of his schooners.

His second encounter with a steamer was not under such congenial conditions. A Nor'easter—a strong storm that is endemic to New York and, in particular, the harbor area—had caught one of the steamers and sent her out of control heading down the Narrows. The steamer had also flooded, and the passengers were in grave danger. There weren't many boats in the water that day except for Vanderbilt who was sailing his schooner, *Dread*. A storm was not that important to him, but he saw that the steamer was in distress, and so he sailed up to her in the crosscurrents and windy bay and pulled off twelve shaken passengers and brought them to shore.

That event got his name in the papers the next morning as a hero. His fame spread even more than it already had. Then, a week later, his name appeared in the newspapers once again. This time the *Neptune* coming up from the southern coast carrying almost half a million dollars in currency and coin had run aground near Sandy Hook in a storm. The only boat that was in the area was the *Dread*, piloted once again by Vanderbilt. This time he went abeam the *Neptune*, boarded her, and rescued the crew and the boxes containing the cash. He then piloted the crew and money safely to shore.

Two rescues in one week in stormy conditions was unheard off and certainly something that attracted attention. One person who was interested was Thomas Gibbons.

Gibbons summoned Vanderbilt to his estate in Elizabeth, New Jersey, and Vanderbilt agreed. Gibbons was one of the wealthiest men in the country at the time, and Vanderbilt had heard of him. If he wanted to meet, one shouldn't decline.

When Vanderbilt met Gibbons, an instant bond formed in Vanderbilt's otherwise cold heart. Gibbons was all that Vanderbilt was except Gibbons was wealthy beyond what Vanderbilt had thought he himself could ever be. Meeting Gibbons at his estate redefined Vanderbilt's measure of wealth, and it cast a new light on the path that lay ahead for this young schooner pilot.

Until this point, Vanderbilt had been moving ahead on raw ambition, and his meeting with Gibbons now served to fine-tune his mind and give him direction. Gibbons offered him a job as captain of one of the steamers, the *Mouse*, for a tiny consideration. Most people would have declined, but Vanderbilt could see the future down this path, and so he took it. He would make just $60 a month.

He liquidated his schooners and sloops and all but one of the periaugers for an amount slightly less than what they were valued at. He got $7,000 (instead of $9,000) for them and went to work for Union Line.

Chapter 10 Steamboat Captain

Vanderbilt's decision to liquidate his proprietorship and take on employment may seem a setback in most eyes, but when you want to progress forward it is never an unrelenting march but rather a waltz that goes two steps forward, one step back, and then two forward again.

In the spirit of catching a breath and rubbing shoulders with one of the wealthiest men in the country, Vanderbilt's instinct to take this opportunity paid off, but he still had to put some muscle into it and work hard at what he was doing. This time Sophia helped.

Part of the deal between Gibbons and Vanderbilt was that he would move from Staten Island and live in a run-down tavern that he owned in Elizabeth, New Jersey. This establishment had been shuttered for some time and was in utter disrepair.

This was Sophia's new project. She was to polish it up and get it ready for business and then manage it. Gibbons would not charge them any rent but instead take 20 percent of the profits.

Vanderbilt had not paid attention to Sophia and left her on the sidelines to look after the Vanderbilt home and increase the famly's head count, but finally, she was in the game, and for some time she was actually doing better than Vanderbilt himself.

She managed to clean up the tavern, the kitchen, and the living quarters and then open it for business. She dealt with the cooking, the cleaning, and tended to the children all while she was pregnant in alternating years. In the third month since they moved in, Sophia had opened the doors to customers who were arriving by stagecoach in Elizabeth and waiting to take the ferry the next morning. The stagecoach was also one of Gibbons' operations, and the tavern was designed to be a waypoint where travelers could spend the night and get a warm meal. Within a month of opening the doors, Sophia was sending a pleasantly surprised Gibbons the 20 percent that was promised. The tavern did very well while Sophia looked after the business. She even kept the accounts and even better than Vanderbilt himself could keep with his vessels.

While she managed the tavern and took it from nothing to prosperity, Vanderbilt was out chasing his dreams. He was put to work on a tiny steamboat, an old ship that was much smaller than the other steamers in the harbor, but it was a start. Captain

Vanderbilt had an opportunity to learn his way around sailing a larger boat. He had much to understand about balancing the hull and getting a feel for the steam output and speed that he could get from the boat.

The passengers soon started to complain, however, because of the dilapidated conditions of the boat. To compensate for that, Vanderbilt convinced Gibbons to reduce the fare, which he did, but that didn't last very long. Soon, the revenues started to drop, and Vanderbilt decided to put a case for a new boat to the owner.

He was successful, and Gibbons decided to commission a new steamer that displaced 140 tons, which was about five times the size of the old ship, and they decided to make something that was top of the line.

They sent the old boat in for repairs, and while the new boat and engine were being built, Vanderbilt had to monitor and make decisions on how the boat was to be designed. During this process, he made many alliances, from shipbuilders to steam engine fabricators, all of which would come in handy in the near future.

While the ship was being built, Vanderbilt still went back to his periauger and took on work for those who needed to ferry supplies around the bay. Between monitoring the construction of the new boat and sailing his tiny vessel, he was working sixteen to twenty hours a day, while Sophia managed the tavern and the children.

If nothing else, the Vanderbilts were a hardworking couple.

In due course, the new steamer was completed and put to water. The old steamer had also been repaired and refurbished, and now another captain was hired for it, and both ships sailed up and down the harbor. All was going well until the owners of the monopoly granted to Livingston and Fulton started to object.

A man by the name of Ogden decided to sue Gibbons for violating the monopoly granted by the State of New York to Livingston and then licensed to him. Gibbons knew what he was doing. Gibbons was a Federalist and a lawyer by training. He understood that the federal government had jurisdiction over this matter, and he was looking forward to filing his case in state court knowing that the judge would rule against him. He was right. The moment the court ruled he filed a petition with the New York Court of Errors (the older version of the state appeals court). Here, too, his case was found for the defendant but not without a little drama thrown in.

The states that were part of the union had only been so for the last forty years. Most of the arguments of states' rights versus federal rights were still being fought. Certain things were obviously states' rights, and the way the Constitution was worded was that all federal matters were explicitly stated therein. Anything that was not stated would be in the jurisdiction of the state.

The Court of Appeals judge, the plaintiff, and the defendant, as well as all the legal minds in New York who were following the case, including Gibbon's friend, the Attorney General of the United States, knew very well that the Supreme Court would decide to hear the case, and they also knew with fair certainty that the Supreme Court would rule in Gibbons' favor. For this reason, the Court of Appeals pulled off a delay strategy. They didn't rule on the case for three years. If there was no ruling, there would be no appeal.

In light of this underhanded tactic by Ogden and the court system, Gibbons, who also had a few friends in the New Jersey Legislature, got the state to enact legislation that would spite the New York crowd. He had already done this before when he got them to pass legislation that said that any law enforcement officer who incarcerated a New Jersey resident for piloting a boat would be arrested. It was intended to challenge the state of New York not to impound or incarcerate

Gibbons' property or a person. This time they enacted legislation that would demand damages paid to New Jersey residents.

He also managed to get the New Jersey Legislature to disallow New York steamboats to ply the New Jersey shore and rivers. This effectively blocked the Livingston boats from navigating the waters down to Elizabeth and the other towns by the Raritan River

In the meantime, the shenanigans between New York steamship operators, the state legislators, and the mayor, who happened to be part of the Livingston clan, continued incessantly. They were all finding ways to stop Vanderbilt and impound Gibbons' steamship. Vanderbilt was smart enough never to let the boat that was in his charge be taken from him. If in the event he were captured, Gibbons would be present in short order to get him out of jail. This went on for the entire time Gibbons vs. Ogden remained undecided in the Court of Errors.

What's interesting about this is that Vanderbilt had played his cards well. He had framed the whole affair as a case of privilege over the working class. He framed it to appear that the entire state of New York was trying to place Vanderbilt under its heel. In time, Vanderbilt became a folk hero. His reputation was already solid in the bay area, but now he was a hero and a captain. He started to earn the name the Commodore.

In the end, the New York Court of Appeals ruled against Gibbons. At this point, he filed for an appeal in the U.S. Supreme Court. On his side was the Attorney General of the United States as well as a lawyer for Gibbons. They argued that Gibbons had the necessary licenses and permission to conduct business from New Jersey and into New York under the interstate commerce provision of the Constitution, and that he could not be barred by the state court.

Finally, after three years of delaying tactics by the Court of Errors, in 1823 the Supreme Court agreed with Gibbons, and the state's lower court judgment was overturned. Gibbons was able to keep sailing his steamships in and out of New York and New Jersey without any more obstruction.

Not only did Gibbons crack open the New York waterways but the decision handed down by the Supreme Court also shattered all the monopolies that Livingston had tied up in other waterways in the United States.

Chapter 11 Being One's Own Man

With the issue with the Supreme Court concluded and with Ogden out of business, Vanderbilt and Gibbons were free and clear to reap the benefits of an integrated line of transportation from Philadelphia to New York. Gibbons provided the carriages on land, and Vanderbilt navigated the rivers and the bay. Up in the morning and back in the afternoon.

The tavern Bellona Hall, which Sophia managed, was doing so well that she convinced Gibbons to invest another $3,000 to upgrade and extend the facilities. The tavern had been profitable ever since she took over, and Gibbons didn't hesitate for even a moment.

Vanderbilt's salary was raised to $300 per month from the initial $60. He still kept 20 percent of the bar's profits on all the steamboats, which at this point numbered three—the *Belona*, which was the 140-ton steamboat; the original smaller steamer that Vanderbilt initially stewarded, *Mouse*; and the latest and largest that was brought online, the *Thistle*. Two other captains had been employed to navigate the

Belona and the *Mouse,* while Vanderbilt took on the significantly more luxurious and larger *Thistle.*

It was still a bargain for Gibbons, and there was a tacit understanding that when the time came Vanderbilt would be given a good deal on buying up the steamship business. There was nothing in writing and no handshake to seal the deal. In fact, it was one of Vanderbilt's only serious errors that he learned from and never committed again.

Just a few days before they took delivery of the largest steamship to sail between New York and New Brunswick—a behemoth of three levels and displacing two hundred tons—Gibbons passed away. In his last will and testament, he left the lion's share of his estate to his son. There was nothing in it for Vanderbilt, not even a severance package.

While Vanderbilt was not expecting anything, he did expect that when the time came William, Gibbons' son who inherited everything, including Union Line. Union Line was the company that employed Vanderbilt and owned the steamboats and Bellona Hall that Sophia managed.

The new steamboat they took delivery of was christened the *Emerald*. It came at a cost of $75,000.

Vanderbilt took command of this behemoth and hired a new captain for the *Thistle*.

Before the *Emerald* came online, Union Line started attracting competitors for its New Brunswick/New York run. The new company had purchased Ogden's boats inexpensively but highly leveraged and hoped to beat Vanderbilt on the same route. There were distinct differences between the two companies. The first was that all but the *Emerald* were fully paid for. As for the new competitor, they had heavy interest and capital repayment schedules. As for speed, they were both equally matched. At first, Vanderbilt would take the morning line, and the competitor took the afternoon schedule, and there was not much conflict, but then they decided to go head-to-head in the schedule. In response, Vanderbilt sought and received permission to cut prices. He was back to his old tricks, and when all else failed, Vanderbilt always relied on price wars. It used to cost $5 to travel from Philadelphia to Manhattan. Vanderbilt dropped it to $2. For travel from New Brunswick to Manhattan, the trip used to cost seventy-five cents. He dropped it to thirteen cents.

At first, it seemed to work, but then the competitors dropped their price as well. Not to be outdone, Vanderbilt switched boats and put up the Bellona, which was fully paid for to compete and dropped the morning fare to zero. He also threw in free food.

After some resistance, the competitors were not sure what they could do since they couldn't go any lower on price, so they started to advertise faster trips. Vanderbilt continued to offer free trips and knew that his competitors were finding it hard to keep up. When they switched to competing on speed, Vanderbilt didn't bite. They started pressurizing their boilers artificially, meaning that they disabled the safety valve and made the steam build up to a higher point so that the paddles would be able to revolve faster. That was not a good idea, and the boilers exploded and killed a number of people on board.

Ticket sales dropped, as no one wanted to travel with them, and in just a few months they went out of business. Gibbons was impressed, and the rest of New York knew not to compete with the Commodore.

Vanderbilt and his wife put their heart and soul into the business, and they made money for everyone involved. Gibbons' son, who inherited everything, was not aware of any of this, as he was looking after the assets in his father's plantation in the South.

When Gibbons passed, the gratitude and relationship he had built with Vanderbilt did not translate to his son. William had no sense of camaraderie or admiration or even gratitude for that matter. It is not something the father would have discussed with his son.

Vanderbilt went on managing the business in the North, while William continued in the South. With everything going well, it came as a surprise when Vanderbilt heard in New York that Union Line had been put up for sale. William had not let Vanderbilt know beforehand.

To make matters worse, he had placed it on the open market and had set the price at $400,000 in cash. By this point, Vanderbilt only had 10 percent of that saved up.

What was working in his favor, though, was that everyone in the North knew that it was Vanderbilt who made that business work, and if he wasn't part of the deal, no one wanted to take the business off young William's hands. After keeping the sale alive for a few months, William took the Union Line off the market.

The precariousness of the situation was not lost on both Sophia and the Commodore. He had bought some time while he determined what to do, but William had shown his intentions. For whatever reason, he wanted to dispose of the business—most likely because he was not familiar with the operations or had too much going on in the South to bother with the smaller business in the North.

Whatever his reason, Vanderbilt had to prepare to set out on his own. It was at this point in his life that he swore to Sophia that he would never work for anyone else ever again. This time when he set out he would do it as his own man.

Chapter 12 What Goes Around

As wonderful a life as they had been living for ten years, Bellona Hall was not their home. It was the business that Sophia was managing and doing a good job, but that period was a critical stage in the lives of the Vanderbilt children, now numbering eight. They had made friends at school and had played in the river that was just behind the tavern. They had room to play, laugh, and grow up as children do.

Now they had to leave. It was the middle of December 1828. Vanderbilt was thirty-four years old and had decided to leave Union Line. He had saved $30,000 and by all measure was doing better than most men his age, but his miserly streak was becoming more prominent.

As soon as Vanderbilt had submitted his thirty days' notice to leave, William Gibbons went into a full-scale panic. He put all his steamboats up for sale at a fraction of the $400,000 he had so arrogantly priced the assets just a few months before. Vanderbilt arranged for the financing and bought two of the vessels—the *Bellona* and the *Emerald*. He was also able to raise enough financing to commission a new steamboat, which was one of the largest at that time. It was displacing 240 tons and was luxurious and well outfitted. It was personally designed by Vanderbilt, and he made it in such a way that the hull was designed to slice through the water in the front. It was hydrodynamically sound and one of the fastest in its class.

When they moved to Manhattan, they moved to a part of town that was more like the slums than it was the well-heeled side of New York. Vanderbilt's actions here should be heeded by any entrepreneur. Even though he had what was equivalent to three quarters of a million dollars in today's money, when he left Bellona Hall, he was not willing to spend $300 a year on rental, which would have put his family in a nice neighborhood, one suitable for the children and a family environment. Instead, they took a three-bedroom apartment in a building that was tenanted by dock workers and laborers with as many as twenty people to an apartment. Conditions were horrible, but Sophia, who was still reeling from losing the one thing that had brought her joy and accomplishment, made do. There is no indication that she had any idea that her husband had that much money saved. She had some savings as well from the money she had been making at the tavern.

Vanderbilt chose that location for two important reasons: (1) his ships were docked nearby on the Hudson and (2) and more important was that he was stepping into the unknown. He obviously had plans, but there was no sense in spending money when it could be used to expand and develop a business. The problem was that he still didn't have a good fix on what the business would be.

He knew it would involve steamboats, but he also had to think about other things. He needed to consider the route and the operations, and with all that still in the air, it was better to be frugal than to live it up in the city and not have any idea of what the future would hold.

It took him less than a few months to get things in order, and this is when he bought the four ships. He had decided to sail the same route he had been while under the employ of Gibbons. He was familiar with the landscape as well as the businesses that lined the river and the clientele that he would engage. The problem was that he didn't buy all of the Union Line boats. He only bought two. The others were sold to a businessman from Philadelphia who had known the Gibbons family well. He took on the rest of the boats and became a direct competitor to Vanderbilt.

As before, a price war erupted. This time Vanderbilt was outmatched and outfinanced. In a classic case of karma, what goes around had come back around, but Vanderbilt didn't believe in karma. He believed in winning. Vanderbilt was facing the same issues with price cutting, but he had a different plan and a different strategy. He continued to cut his price. In the last instance, the strategy was to beggar the competition, but this time it was different. He knew the competitor well enough to instinctively know that if given enough trouble that person would buy him out. In one year, that is exactly what happened. He bought two of Vanderbilt's boats for cash and royalties made from the New Brunswick/Manhattan line.

It was the first time that someone had literally paid Vanderbilt to stop working, and it wouldn't be the last.

He took the money he made from the sale of these two boats and bought two more. He was back to four boats, but this time he decided it was time to take on a new route. He decided to go up the Hudson, but he faced another hurdle.

The Supreme Court had ruled in Ogden vs. Gibbons that federal law trumps state law in interstate commerce—the steamboats that traveled between New Jersey and New York. The Constitution could not regulate commerce within the state, however, which meant that the unholy alliance of Livingston and

Fulton that caused the monopoly to be in place was unaffected by the Supreme Court ruling.

Supreme Court ruling notwithstanding, the monopoly that was created by the New York Legislature was not popular, and it hinted of unfavorable practice by one of New York's wealthy and influential families. By 1827, the winds of change had swept the Livingston-Fulton monopoly to the rocks, and the waterways were once again back to competitive forces.

It was at this point that Vanderbilt took his four ships and set them to travel on the Hudson from Albany to Manhattan. He now faced a new competitor, and he fought back.

He named his venture "The People's Line" to sway public sentiment against this monopoly that was operated by some powerful and wealthy backers. The plan worked. Vanderbilt was able to stir the hornet's nest of class warfare.

He won again and continued expanding his line, commissioning more steamboats to travel between Albany and Manhattan. The Erie Canal had been completed, and the effect increased the growth rate of New York and the transportation business between the two cities.

It was all going well when he had to go to Philadelphia on business. He decided to take the train to see what all the excitement was about with this new mode of transportation. It is rumored that he shared the trip with President Quincy Adams, who was in the coach just ahead of him.

The train was speeding along its tracks at almost twenty-five miles per hour. Compared to a stagecoach, it was floating on a cushion of air, and there was plenty of room to sit comfortably. As the train approached a ravine and began its transition to a wooden bridge, something serious happened.

The iron tracks on the unstable wooden platform started to come loose after the heavy locomotive and the first car had passed. The second and third car were not so fortunate. The couplings came loose as the second car came off the tracks and plunged down a thirty-foot ravine. Most people in the second and third cars died. Vanderbilt was not one of them, but he did break a few ribs and was severely injured.

He was transported back to New York, where he spent his time recuperating for the better part of the following year. It was too much for Sophia to handle on her own, so she had her cousin live with them in their small apartment to help with the chores while she nursed the Commodore back to health.

A doctor was chosen for him, a young man who would eventually become one of Vanderbilt's closest friends. The doctor would visit almost daily at first to tend to the wounds and monitor his progress. As Vanderbilt regained his strength, the doctor visited less often.

He had hired another captain to take his place as captain on the *Bellona*, and he continued to run the other vessels as well. He was now thinking of expanding his route eastward into Long Island Sound to be able to move up to Connecticut and possibly even Boston, which was also a busy harbor, and the route that hugged the New England coast was fairly lucrative.

Just before the accident, he had bought the southern routes between Elizabeth, New Brunswick, and Philadelphia. Those routes added to the opportunistic trading he did for cargo on short hauls and products from the fishermen along the shore and helped his business thrive. His reputation also allowed him to have a ready line of credit, which was useful anytime he wanted to buy a used steamboat or commission a new one.

Each time he entered a new market the same formula applied. He or the current dominant service in that market would initiate a price war. It had become

Vanderbilt's legacy to wage these wars, and he hardly ever lost one.

He had understood early on that the key to long-term gain was to have a dominant market share as quickly as possible. Regardless of the cost on the front end, which could translate as a loss for some period of time, the end result was worth the initial hardship.

He had learned with Gibbons' boats the value of fully paid assets and the way to trounce any competitor who was highly leveraged. It turns out that most of the boat owners at the time had financed their boats and were under the heel of interest payments.

That was partially the reason why he was always very frugal with how he spent money. His cash reserves were actually worth more than the value of the cash. It was worth the making or breaking of the route that he ventured on. In case of competition, the person who could outlast a war would be the one to reap the benefits. The person who could last the longest was the person who had the least financial obligations and depended on the cash flow from the business to sustain.

For most people, it was one of two things. It was either a bank loan they had to sustain or a family they had to support. It was also that many of the boat owners focused too much on one particular route.

Focusing on just a single route placed one's entire asset base in competition with the other person, and it was like a duel at noon. One person either lost everything or gained everything. In those days, losing everything was not a good option, especially in New York, where there were such things as debtors prisons. Ogden had faced a similar fate when he went up against Gibbons and lost. He had invested heavily and then borrowed more to compete and fight the lengthy court battle, and when he lost to Gibbons, in the end, he had no way of paying off his debtors and went to prison for it.

Vanderbilt was acutely aware of all this. Aside from the fear of taking on a loan he couldn't pay, he was aware of the loss that he would face in the event of stiff competition. He was setting himself up to lose the entire business if he borrowed too much or got used to spending too much. Vanderbilt knew that cash was king.

For his strategy, the more reserves he had, the less he borrowed, and the leaner his operations were, the longer he could wage a war that may have included free travel and free food for as long as he needed to drive away the competitor.

The trick was to also spread his ships around different markets. He had already conquered the Philadelphia/Delaware market. He had definitely conquered the New Brunswick/Manhattan market, and he was already set up to conquer the Hudson/Albany market, and now it was up to New England.

By the time he had spread his proverbial sail to the four corners of the Northeast, other operators had learned from him and were vicious in their war on price. What went around had come around. He had to deal with the same strategies that he had grown to adopt.

The difference between Vanderbilt and every other single steamship operator was that Vanderbilt had one thing going for him—his mind-set. He never cared about living the good life. He only cared to save his money. This gave him little reliance on how much he had to make from the fare. He would just as easily make the fare zero, while his other competitors could not. To do this, he had learned to become one of the best cash managers in the business.

Chapter 13 The Advent of Rail

The advent of rail in America was the driving force behind the development of the interior of the country. Before this time, there were two population dispersion patterns. The first reflected people living along coastlines. With a series of canals, such as the Erie canal that connects Manhattan to Albany and proceeds on to the Great Lakes, it allowed more people to move inland, but vast areas were still unpopulated. There were occasional outposts and frontier settlements, but those areas would remain sparsely settled until the arrival of the train. As railway lines started to make tracks inland, the population also increased.

The same could be said for the major rivers and waterways all along the eastern portion of the United States. Vanderbilt had a front-row seat to the development of the rail industry in the United States. Instead of being the death of steamships, railroads actually enhanced the industry. Rails could not reach certain parts of the country, and other areas were inaccessible for steamships. Both had their strengths and weaknesses, and this complementary relationship increased the freedom of travel and access for the masses.

The much older Vanderbilt now planned his boats around the trains and stagecoaches. When the Boston-Providence Railroad went into service, Vanderbilt had commissioned new boats that were larger, more luxurious, and faster to travel the two hundred miles from New York to Providence. This allowed him to provide almost seamless travel from Philadelphia all the way to Boston under a single fare. Passengers would travel from Philadelphia to New Brunswick and then from there to Manhattan. From Manhattan, they would board the new steamer that would travel at top speeds of twenty miles per hour up to Indian Point in Providence. Then they would board the train that went straight to Boston. Vanderbilt had brought the far-flung cities just a little closer. In the center of it all was New York—his stomping ground.

New York's growth in the 1800s was spurred by three factors, one of which was Vanderbilt's doing.

(1) New York served as the port of influx of immigrants and products and also the point for export of all raw materials and finished goods.

(2) The Erie Canal allowed travel up to the Great Lakes and then down again to western Pennsylvania. In the days before rail travel, this was the least treacherous route even if it did take more than a week to make the journey.

(3) Vanderbilt's organization of steamboats and their coinciding schedules to meet with stagecoaches was also important. The comparative ease of travel from one major town to the next, with stops in all the smaller towns, altered the way people conducted business and forced the different states to come together as one nation.

It was not any form of altruism that caused Vanderbilt to take on these routes or to have this kind of impact. He didn't wake up one morning and have the epiphany that he wanted to build in a nation instead of a fragmented set of states. He didn't have the nationalistic streak in him to do that, and he also didn't have the academic background to consider that. He saw the world as one big series of transactions, and he just wanted to do what was best for him.

Central to his plan of making the trips almost seamless was his ability to have no problems at Indian Point in Providence. The station and the wharf were right next to each other, and the transition was as good as could be. People would disembark at the wharf and then take a short walk to the platform to catch their train. It was perfect except for one small glitch. Once again the powers that be, in this case the Providence legislative circles, were not interested in having Vanderbilt frequent their town and compete with the business their group and cabals had planned. They caused him as much trouble as they could. Vanderbilt did not care much about what they were doing, though, and he would do what he had to as he had when Livingstone and New York were giving him and Gibbons trouble. In Providence, he just started doing what he wanted to do.

At the same time, another rag-to-riches kind of person by the name of Grinnell had set up another ferry service that stretched from Boston to Providence. There was some traffic that frequented the Grennel steamboat, but it wasn't as profitable as it could be. Most travelers preferred the train for the same price. Besides, Grennell's boat just went to Providence and didn't go on to New York. They would still have to change carriers.

With all the trouble that Providence was giving Vanderbilt, he decided to try something new. Instead of engaging in a price war—there was no one to wage war with because his competitors were not the ones causing the problem—he came up with a new scheme. Instead of predatory pricing, he engaged in collusion.

He approached Grennell and made a deal with him to charge customers the same price from Boston to New York, but instead of stopping at Providence, he would stop at Stonington. Vanderbilt would then sail up to

Stonington, and the passengers would transfer from one boat to another and go all the way down to New York. Together, they would charge a dollar less than the train/ferry combination that customers would have to take.

The plan was a success, and passengers were more than happy to pay a dollar less for the same trip. This plan pulled customers away from the Boston/Providence rail line, and it also precipitously reduced the number of passengers that came into Providence. That had a more serious impact. With lower passenger traffic in Providence, the city was worried that it would attract less revenue for the city.

Vanderbilt had learned a long time before that the value of a line was not just in the price of the ticket that a person paid. In fact, it was even acceptable to accept a loss for the price of the ticket because the bar and café on board, especially on a twelve-hour trip, made substantial revenue to cover part of the cost of the pinewood needed to fire the boilers.

This was the same logic that the Providence town managers had in mind. The revenue they generated from the mere traffic of passengers arriving and spending money at the wharf was considered good income for the city. With Vanderbilt's new plan, Providence would be affected by fewer passenger arrivals, but it didn't matter that Vanderbilt's passenger traffic was at an all-time high.

A few years later he sold the steamship that would make the New York-Stonington run to Grennel himself, and he replaced it with a 500-ton steamer. That same year after the sale the ship burst into flames while anchored in Long Island Sound. Out of the two hundred passengers and crew on board, only four survived.

Even though he had redirected his business to circumvent the rail, Vanderbilt still fully realized the power of the railroad and the even greater power of the combination of the railroad and steamship. For now, however, he focused on steamboats.

By 1840, his wealth had grown. He now made more almost $40,000 a year in profit and was worth almost $1.5 million, which would be about $40 million today. While the lion's share of his wealth came from the income from the steamships, he had also invested in land up and down the New Jersey coast as well as in Manhattan. From the people who boarded his steamships to the children playing in the wharf, everyone knew him as the Commodore. He was only forty-six years old and more successful than any of the Vanderbilts before him.

Nothing controlled him, and nothing could compete against him. As the years passed, the only thing that would dictate the routes he took were the railroads and the timing of the trains. He didn't need them, but when he worked in concert with them, he realized that the passenger traffic was high, and that appealed to him. In his mind, it didn't matter if he was not making any money right then. It was more important to fill his ships. Capacity utilization, as any MBA student will tell you, is the key to long-term profitability and value even when the short term looked bleak. Those who tried to mimic him did not always succeed. Vanderbilt knew how to keep his vessels full and make money in the long term. He knew when to hold and when to let go, and when the time came to let go, he did it without any hesitation or remorse.

By 1845, the Long Island Railroad had been completed all the way from Brooklyn to the farthest tip in the east—at Greenpoint. The point of the railroad was not to serve any of the Long Island towns. There weren't as many when the line was first built as there are today. Once the line was built, it was mainly meant for traffic to go all the way to the farthest reach of the island and then transfer the passengers to a steamship so that they could then sail up to Boston. At this point, Vanderbilt's fortunes changed He was invited to sit on the board of directors of the Long Island Railroad (LIRR).

This move was beneficial for the LIRR and for Vanderbilt. For the LIRR, it meant they would have a steady passenger load from Brooklyn to Greenpoint, where they would then be transferred to the Commodore's steamboats and sent northbound. That was the plan, but it got better. Instead, Vanderbilt sold two of his steamers to the LIRR. They used these to carry passengers from the edge of Long Island up to Norwich, where they would then board the Boston Norwich line and head straight to Boston.

Thereafter at Vanderbilt's behest, the LIRR partnered with the owners of the Boston Norwich line and offered a packaged deal that would go from Brooklyn all the way to Boston for just $4. All they had to do was get to Greenpoint, take the short ferry ride across Long Island Sound, and then board the train in Norwich. From there it was a straight shot to Boston. No one could compete with that, and it became the preferred route for all Boston-New York passengers. His interest had begun to shift from steamships to the railroad. It wouldn't be long before he would immerse himself in the railroad industry, and he would do it by way of something called the stock market.

Chapter 14 Better Quarters

Ever since the day when the entire family of ten—eight children and two adults—left the comfort and safety of Bellona Hall, Sophia had been gently, albeit persistently, lobbying for better quarters. The home they lived in on Madison Avenue (as hard as it is to believe now) was a putrid place. It didn't just look run-down. It was one of the worst tenements on the island. It housed some of the hardest roughnecks the city had come to accommodate, and it was packed well beyond what it was designed to hold. The stench of the facilities on one floor would stretch across several floors and spread like a green mist. It was not what the Vanderbilt children who had grown up amidst the clean air of the river and densely wooded forest of Elizabeth, New Jersey, could get used to.

But Vanderbilt was on a mission. It was more important to him that they had a home than to live on the street, which is what they would end up doing if they were not careful with their resources and didn't use what they had to invest in future businesses. Besides, Sophia really had no idea how much he had saved.

Finally, in 1839, just before becoming a director of the LIRR, she had whittled away any form of resistance that he had been putting up. He was also motivated because he was doing better, and his business, while competitive, had sucked the energy out of him, and he felt better about his future prospects.

They moved back to Staten Island, where he built a mansion of such palatial proportions that Sophia could not fathom how he did it, and it was the first time she began to understand just how wealthy they had become. He commissioned the construction of a mansion on the shore at the northeastern corner of Staten Island near the same spot that his mother and father had first bought their home when they moved to the island so long before. The house was magnificently designed, no doubt fueled by the imagination that sparked from his visit to Gibbons' estate when he was still skimming the harbor in his schooners and periauger. The house was built at cost of just under $30,000 and had ornate furnishings, stained glass windows, tall Greek columns to support the large roof, Egyptian marble in the floors and mantle, grand staircases that were intricately designed by masons with banisters carved by expensive craftsmen, French drapes hanging from vaulted ceilings, and a skylight in the ceiling to illuminate the cavernous home. There were four floors and a basement, each with twelve-foot ceilings that welcomed light from the skylight and breeze from the tall open windows that overlooked the Narrows on one side and the bay on the other. It was the view he had admired when he was three years old, looking at the colorful sails that went past his window every day. The view had changed. Now it was rows of steamers puffing smoke from burning coal and steam rising from boilers.

The house was the monolithic depiction of this simple man—the Commodore. It was visibly strong, tall, and substantial. Visitors were in awe, but Sophia wasn't. Little did she know that she would eventually die in this house all alone.

Sophia didn't say anything about the house, and Vanderbilt really didn'tcare one way or the other. She had other things on her mind. Her health had not been in the best condition for some time, and she was exhausted. Between the dilapidated conditions of the tenement, giving birth to a large number of children, nursing, and then looking after them while Vanderbilt himself was out building his business and spending some of his time in the company of transactional women, she was getting sicker by the day.

She was diagnosed with syphilis in 1840. She was already aware that her husband was cavorting with a wide array of women on the wharf, but she didn't realize that it would come to this. It was not just her physical state that was deteriorating but also her mental state. Between her menopausal years that would come quickly and the complications from syphilis, she had become an altogether different woman.

In reaction to her deterioration, Vanderbilt first threatened and then carried out the act of committing her to an asylum. Both business and family carried on for the next decade with more of the same. Billy had grown up and had disappointed his father. It took a lot to satisfy Vanderbilt with anything his children did, but that is not to be misunderstood. As a man who had made his own way from the time he was eleven years old, he was always hard on his children so that they would be able to show a fraction of his tenacity in making their own way. He may have been stingy to an extent, but that doesn't seem to be the reason why he cut off most of his children. It was more because he was of the frame of mind that that was the best way to teach them how to survive in a tough world. Vanderbilt himself, if he had to be described with one word, would bring to mind "tough." He indeed was tough not just in fistfights but in the mental sense of the word as well. Nothing was able to knock him off his saddle, but if by chance something did, he was back up on it again in short order.

One example of this is when one of his children who behaved in a way that was slow Vanderbilt would not stand for it. He got the boy a job at a Wall Street firm, and as a favor to Vanderbilt, the firm employed him at a small salary that was fully subsidized by Vanderbilt. He did it to get the boy to feel confident of his own ability. That confidence, however, was misplaced, as his son thought he should be able to get married. He found a wife and decided to marry her without his father's approval. He had no idea that his salary was being subsidized by Vanderbilt himself.

Once they were married, Vanderbilt decided his son could not live on a small salary with a wife, and so he bought the farmland that was near his grandfather's in New Dorp. It was almost eighty-nine acres. Vanderbilt presented it to his son and daughter-in-law and told him to never ask for money again. He was to work the land and support his wife and family. The two never spoke after that.

The point is that it is not easy to get into the heart of a man and understand what drives him to do certain things. He may not have seemed to love his family, but it is not for us to say that he did or didn't. We also do not know if he was really capable of loving.

What we do know, though, is that despite his proclivities he was a man who worked hard and provided for his family. For those who say that he left Sophia to raise the children, you have to balance that by considering he was building a business and working 16-hour days. Not many people can work that number of hours in the cold and rain on many days, wet from the waters of the bay, and then come home and have the strength to display magnanimity or patience.

Conclusion

Prospectors found gold in the Sierra Nevada Mountains in 1849. This resulted in the Gold Rush that year, as entire families with gold in their eyes rushed to the West Coast to find their fortune. The trek west was hard. There weren't many waterways and only a few outposts along the way that served the crowds that made their way across dense forests, hot deserts, and some of the most picturesque mountains in North America.

Vanderbilt saw it another way. He didn't see gold as the holy grail. He saw the money he could make by transporting people who were going after the gold. His logic was simple. By providing those prospectors with a service, he was assured of his payment. By digging for the gold himself, it was a long shot. So he decided to be the man who would transport the prospectors heading west. There was one problem: no waterway was available.

Instead, he looked at how the U.S. government was having mail transported to the West Coast. They were doing it by sea. Since the way to the West Coast by sea would take the ship all the way down to Cape Horn in South America and then back up, it was considered too long to make the trip. It would take about six months to a year for a ship of fifty people to make it.

The mail ships had a better way of doing it. They would sail down to the slimmest part of the isthmus in Panama, and then passengers would go overland until they reached the Pacific shore. Then they would take another boat up to California. The overland phase of the trip would be through forests, and they managed it with a train of mules. It was only fifty miles, and they could do it in about a week.

This idea appealed to the pragmatic Commodore. Instead of using the Panama route, however, he went to Nicaragua and negotiated a twelve-year contract with them where he would build a canal in the 80-mile crossing from east to west, and then he would own the rights to that passageway. The deal was struck. He would pay Nicaragua $10,000 in cash and $10,000 every year and $20,000 in company stock. It would take twelve years to build the canal. Once built, Nicaragua would then take 20 percent of the profits, and the rights would extend for eighty-five years. Vanderbilt also included a clause that stipulated that in the event the canal could not be built he would be able to build some other route of transportation, such as a railway track to cross the isthmus.

In 1850, he set sail from New York to Nicaragua for a test run. The plan was to reach the west coast of Nicaragua and then sail up the San Juan River to Lake Nicaragua, which was close to the western coast. When they reached the river, Vanderbilt himself navigated the vessel at full speed with the boiler valve locked in place. No boilers blew on that trip. Instead, all the power was transported to the paddles, and the vessel made record time over the rapids and to the lake 199 miles inland. Vanderbilt was the first man to take a steamship up the San Juan River. On board with him were the engineers who were to study the route and decide where to blast and make the river deeper or smoothen the rapids.

When they returned to New York, he was deemed a hero. From here on, he would charge customers who wanted to sail to San Francisco from New York for $399 compared with $600 charged by those who were using Panama. He also made it to California faster than they did. He had brought his New York price war to Central America. The price eventually dropped to $145 for deck customers and $45 for steerage.

In time, he saw that it was more profitable even in the midst of an all-out price war to focus on the Nicaragua passage, which he called the Southern Route. He slowly and quietly started divesting his other New York ships. He still maintained his railroad interests and investments.

What started in the 1840s as a side interest was now gaining traction for Vanderbilt. While the southern route continued and prospered, he started working on the railroads in New York. He began buying railroad stocks and organized them to make it more efficient, and to do that he designed and built Grand Central Station.

In the end, he was confined to the upstairs bedroom in his midtown townhouse. It was the fall of 1876, and syphilis had caught up with him. He was in end-stage syphilis just like Sophia, who had died in 1868. By Christmas, he was bedridden and sometimes incoherent. He died January 7, 1877. At all schools, government offices, and buildings—anywhere where a flag flew—the flag was flown at half-staff.

If you enjoyed learning about the men who built America, I would be forever grateful if you could leave a review on Amazon. Reviews are the best way for readers to give feedback to newer authors like myself. Thanks in advance!

And make sure to check out my other biographies, too!